Flash MX 2004 Games

Thanks to Pam

Flash MX 2004 Games
Art to ActionScript

Nik Lever

ELSEVIER

AMSTERDAM • BOSTON • HEIDELBERG • LONDON • NEW YORK • OXFORD
PARIS • SAN DIEGO • SAN FRANCISCO • SINGAPORE • SYDNEY • TOKYO

Focal Press is an imprint of Elsevier

Focal
Press

Focal Press
An imprint of Elsevier
Linacre House, Jordan Hill, Oxford OX2 8DP
200 Wheeler Road, Burlington, MA 01803

First published 2004

British Library Cataloguing in Publication Data
A catalogue record for this book is available from the British Library

Library of Congress Cataloguing in Publication Data
A catalogue record for this book is available from the Library of Congress

ISBN 0 240 51963 9

For information on all Focal Press publications visit our website at:
www.focalpress.com

Typeset by Newgen Imaging Systems (P) Ltd., Chennai, India

Printed and bound in Great Britain

Contents at a glance

Contents in summary

Section 2: Action   81

Having developed the animation we now look at how to add interactivity to this art using ActionScript.

Chapter 7: So what is a variable?   83

After the first blistering introduction to ActionScript in Chapter 1, we now take a leisurely tour through the basics of programming starting with variable types.

Chapter 8: In tip-top condition   101

In this chapter we look at using conditional code using the marvellous 'if' statement. We also look at how we can extend the flexibility of the condition using Boolean logic.

Chapter 9: Using loops   118

No programming language would be complete without the ability to repeat sections of code. Games regularly need to run a section of code several times. In this chapter we will look at creating sections of code that repeat.

Chapter 10: Keep it modular   136

Programming can be made very hard or very easy. Good structure makes it so much easier. In this chapter we examine the options.

Chapter 11: Debugging   152

Nobody is perfect and in this chapter we look at what to do when your code doesn't work.

Chapter 12: Using external files   168

The game you create can be made to operate differently on different servers. Using ASP pages we can load variable data from a database. We look at linking to static files or generating dynamic data on the fly using server-based ASP pages.

Section 3: Putting it into practice   183

You know your stuff, so how about using this knowledge to make some games?

Chapter 13: Small games to keep them loading   185

If your game is over a meg then you will have lost your audience before they even see it. In this chapter we look at creating 20 K or less games to keep their interest while the remainder of the game loads.

Chapter 14: Quizzes   205

An interactive quiz where the questions are pulled in from a database forms the basis of this chapter. This develops the presentation of using external data first covered in Chapter 12.

Chapter 15: Mazes 226

Mazes can be generated dynamically or statically. The graphic view can be overhead, isometric or first person. In this chapter we look at the options and how to show the user when they are doing well or badly.

Chapter 16: Board games 244

A board game involves a legal move generator and a mini-max search routine for a good computer move. In this chapter we look at the strategies involved in presenting some classic board games in Flash form.

Chapter 17: Platformers 260

Creating a platform-based game is quite a challenge, but by this stage in the book the reader has all the skills necessary. In this chapter we look at the problems of game world and screen space calculations.

Chapter 18: Sports simulations 282

One effective way of getting input is to use the keyboard. In this chapter we look at creating games where the user has to press keys at a fast rate in order to score highly in sports simulations.

Section 4: Flash for mobiles 307

The mobile games market is growing exponentially. With Flash MX 2004 developers have a new target platform, Flash Lite. This new section shows the limitations and possibilities of the new platform.

Chapter 19: Flash Lite – how does it affect game developers? 309

Using the many new templates available in Flash MX 2004 Professional we can target lots of mobile devices. Flash Lite is a compromise between Flash 4 and 5; this chapter introduces you to how developing Flash Lite games differs from Flash games for desktop PCs.

Chapter 20: Using Flash on a PocketPC 318

The PocketPC is as near to a desktop as mobile devices get; as such, the content you can successfully handle includes most games you can develop for a desktop. We look at porting existing content to the PocketPC.

Section 5: Flash for boffins 327

Sometimes you will need to extend what you can do in Flash using external methods. This last section introduces you to things you should be thinking about.

Chapter 21: High score tables 329

High score tables encourage users to stay online in order to see their name appear in the high score list. The tables are usually stored in a database and then loaded into Flash when a call to a high score table is required. This chapter explores the options.

Introduction: Learn to write ActionScript and have fun doing it!

Flash MX 2004 provides the perfect platform to create fun games for Internet distribution. This book takes the reader through the entire process from creating the art and animation for these games, through to programming them ready for users across the world to enjoy the results. The book is split into five sections. The first section introduces the new user to the drawing tools in Flash and explains how to create the animation frames that you will need for your games while keeping the files bandwidth friendly. Section 2 takes the reader on a guided tour of using ActionScript. The emphasis is on explaining computer programming to readers from a design background; no previous computer programming is assumed. In Section 3 lots of practical examples are offered of specific games; all the source code is provided in Flash MX 2004 format on the included CD. The mobiles games market is growing exponentially. With Flash MX 2004 developers have a new target platform: Flash Lite. Section 4 shows the limitations and possibilities on the new platform. Finally in Section 5 and the Appendices advanced topics are included about using sockets, databases and Flash Communication Server; there is even a section on embedding Flash into VB, C# and PocketPC programs.

Using the CD

You can browse the folders on the CD. Each chapter and appendix has a unique folder in the 'Examples' folder. All the projects and source can be found here. To use a project file, open the file directly from the CD in Flash and then save it to your local hard drive if you intend to make changes. The 'Utilities' folder contains a small exe file for Windows machines that can create a MIME encoded query string from a text file.

Who is the author?

It all started with a ZX81, a hobbyist computer released in Britain in 1981, which was soon replaced by the Sinclair Spectrum, an amazing computer produced by the same company. The Sinclair Spectrum boasted an amazing 48 K of memory, and an eight-colour display. From those early days the author was smitten, writing code became something of an obsession. Having graduated as a graphic designer in 1980 he had already started work as a professional animator when the interest in computers surfaced. All too soon, his computer hobby merged with professional life, the first example being a computer-controlled rostrum stand, a camera for filming 2D animation. Much more recently he has been producing CD-ROMs and web-based multimedia productions for clients including Kellogg's, Coca-Cola, BBC, Cartoon Network and HIT Entertainment. The first interactive web-based work used Java, but the latest work all tends to be Flash or Shockwave 3D based. With compression and streaming abilities that are so web-friendly, Flash is set to be a standard for some time to come.

Check out www.catalystpics.co.uk to see the author's handiwork or www.niklever.net/flash for the web page associated with this book.

Who is this book for?

Designers

If you are a designer who has worked with Flash and wants to go further, you will find lots to interest you here. You will learn about applying your creative skills to the many stages of game production. If you have never played with Flash then fear not, you will be guided through the art, animation and programming involved in creating sophisticated games.

Animators

Perhaps you have created the sprites for other people's games and always meant to look into how to create your own; in this book you will learn how. You will see how to use motion tweening in Flash to create smooth animation and then how to add interactive functionality to your game using ActionScript. Even if you have never written a line of code before then you will find the tutorial style easy to follow.

Web developers

If you haven't started writing Flash code then shame on you, start today. Flash offers a sophisticated development environment with good tools for the production of both artwork and code. In this book you will learn how to use Flash to the best by creating animation and then adding interactivity, producing exciting and dynamic Internet content.

Students

The Internet is rapidly turning into a rich source of employment for visually literate students. If your skills also include adding the code then you will be in demand. In this book you will learn all the skills necessary to create highly dynamic web content.

So what are you waiting for?

Boot up your computer, go straight to Flash MX 2004 and turn the page, where you are about to create your first game in a Flash!

1 Your first game

Rather alarmingly it is now over 20 years since I wrote my first bit of code using a Sinclair Spectrum computer and Sinclair Basic.

In 1980 in the UK, Clive Sinclair, an entrepreneurial inventor, advertised for sale a very simple computer. The ZX80 connected to the TV set and enjoyed 1 K of RAM. Each machine came with a simple programming language, BASIC (Beginners All-purpose Symbolic Instruction Code). This early machine started a revolution of young bedroom and garage programmers. Some of these early starters went on to become very successful in the games industry. Sinclair's inexpensive computers, including the Spectrum, are one of the main reasons why the UK has an internationally respected games industry.

Animation had for several years been my main motivation. I still get a buzz from making things move. Although initially unconnected, programming shares many similarities with animation. It is a creative pursuit. If you come to programming from an art background then you may find this doubtful. Surely *creative* implies the visual, written or musical arts. But programming is not a case of just one solution to a problem; there are many solutions and it is the path you take to the solution where the 'art' comes in. I got such a buzz from seeing my first programs work that I now spend rather more of my time writing code than creating animation artwork. In this chapter we are going to rush headlong into creating a game. Not a massive multi-player 3D first-person extravaganza, we may have to wait until day two for that! No, the game we will produce will be familiar to anyone who has ever played a computer game. It is a very simple version of 'Pong'. Along the way we will discover the Flash interface. You will learn how to create simple artwork with Flash, where to find all those panels and what they do. You will add a little code, test your work and do some simple debugging. So without further hesitation, let's get going. I strongly advise reading this chapter while using your computer. You will get much more from it if you enter the code and follow the tutorial throughout rather than just dissecting the final program.

Creating simple artwork using Flash

Figure 1.1 shows the basic Flash interface. The biggest area is used for the stage. This is where we put the imagery that the user will see. Above this in the figure is a grid; this is used as a timeline. In Flash a scene is broken down using time segments and layers. A single column in the upper section represents one time segment and a row represents a layer of graphics. So how long is a time segment? By default a time segment is one twelfth of a second. The user can alter the duration

1

Figure 1.1 *The Flash MX 2004 interface*

of a time segment by clicking in an empty area of the stage and selecting the properties window. The window should look like that shown in Figure 1.2.

Figure 1.2 *Altering movie properties*

The first thing to do when following this tutorial is to open the file 'Examples/Chapter01/ Pingpong01.fla' from the CD. You must save the project to your local machine if you intend to edit and keep a project. You should be looking at something similar to the view shown in Figure 1.1. Here in addition to the timeline and main stage area you will see a panel on the left containing the important tools you will use when creating graphics with Flash. The graphics produced using Flash are vector based. That is, you define lines, curves and fills and Flash paints the screen using this information. So let's look at creating our first graphic element. To help you, the example already includes the background for the game. The background shows an overhead view of a sports hall. We are going to create a ball and two bats, then add some code to allow the user to move the bats, and finally add some code so that the ball bounces off the bats and walls.

Creating new layers

The first stage of this tutorial chapter is creating the ball. When creating a game in Flash we can sometimes create everything in the same layer, but usually we will use extra layers for different elements. Look at Figure 1.3; here you can see that three layers are involved. To add a layer, click on the icon shown in the lower left corner of the figure. To delete a layer click on the trash can. Try adding a layer and deleting it now. When you have the feel for this add a layer and click on the layer name; it may be 'Layer 2' or another number. When you click the name it goes into renaming mode; now you can give the layer a useful name, for this tutorial call it 'Bats and Ball'. When there are only a few layers and you are just creating a game you may be tempted to take the default name. Fight this! Get into the habit of naming everything; if the project gets bigger then you will be glad you did. Also you may come back to a project months after it was completed and you will find it much easier to find your way around if everything has a useful name. If you are working in a team then you will enjoy working on someone else's project if the project is well organized with easily identified names; if everything is poorly structured then the project becomes a nightmare to maintain.

Take a look at the top left corner of Figure 1.3; here you will see that it says 'Scene 1'. In addition to breaking a project down into time segments and layers, Flash also allows you to divide it up using Scenes. When producing a game or any other computer program, structure can make a huge difference to how difficult the project is to produce and maintain. Flash allows the developer to use a very good structure, but equally you can also use a very poor structure. Another aim of this book is to help you understand how to create well-structured projects and to learn how to attack a complex problem so that the task becomes manageable.

Figure 1.3 *Adding and naming layers*

Now that we have created a layer to store the ball artwork, make sure that this layer is highlighted before we move on to the next section.

Creating the ball

Take a look at Figure 1.4; here the ring highlights the tool that you should select. Before we do any drawing in Flash let's briefly look at each of the tools in the Tools palette. Starting in the top left is the selection arrow, which allows you to select and edit a part of the artwork. The white arrow lets you edit a curve using the control handles that tell Flash how to draw the curve. The next row down has the Line tool for drawing lines and the Lasso tool for more complex selection. Moving down you will find the Pen and Text tools, the Oval and Rectangle tools, the Pencil and Brush tools,

Figure 1.4 *Using the Oval tool*

Figure 1.5 *Selecting the colour*

the Resize and Edit Fill tools, the Ink and Fill tools and finally the Eyedropper for picking up colours and the Eraser for deleting part of the artwork. If you have a tablet for drawing then you will find that some of the tools use the pressure sensitivity of the tablet to adjust line width. Recall that Flash is a vector-based drawing package; it distinguishes between lines and fills. A line has a consistent width that is set using the Properties panel for the Oval tool. When you have selected the Oval tool, take a look at the Colors palette (Figure 1.5). Notice that there are two colours, a colour for the lines you draw, which is to the immediate right of the pencil icon and a colour for the filled areas, to the right of the paint bucket icon. When you create a circle or oval it can include an outline, a fill or both. Click on the colour square and this brings up a further dialog box. In this box you can select from a pre-defined palette or you can use the mixer panel, 'Window/Design Panels/Color Mixer', to create a new colour. For the ball we are now going to create we will select both an outline colour and a fill colour; in the example we use black for the outline and a mid blue for the fill colour. Before we draw our first element we need to select one further setting, the stroke width. With the Properties panel for the Oval tool visible set the stroke width to '1'. The type of stroke will be 'Solid'. Now we are ready to draw.

Figure 1.6 *Setting the width of a line*

Figure 1.7 illustrates the four stages in drawing the ball. Stage 1 – on the stage area click to define the top left extent of the ball, then drag to the bottom right. This sets the size of the ball and creates the ball we see on the left of Figure 1.7. We are going to enhance this simple drawing by adding a shadow to the bottom left. To do this we will use the Line tool.

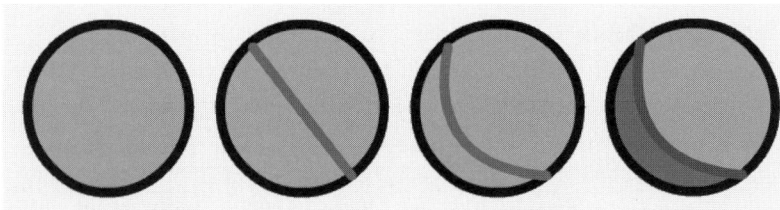

Figure 1.7 *Stages in drawing the ball*

Using the Line tool

Select the Line tool by clicking on the icon highlighted with a ring in Figure 1.8.

A line is initialized using a click. Click on the ball to define the start of the line and drag to the end. If the line is not quite in the right place, then select the arrow 'Selection tool' icon and click on the line. The line is highlighted; now press the delete key to remove this line.

By now you should have a ball with a line drawn through it. You can also use the arrow selector as an important editing tool. Move the mouse so that it is near one end of the line. Notice that the mouse cursor includes a corner at the bottom right. Now move the mouse so it is near the middle of the line, and you will see that the corner changes to a curve. Unlike most vector editing packages, Flash does not show editing handles on a line, unless you use the white 'Subselection' arrow. As a user you can determine what will happen when you edit a line based on the mouse cursor image. If you click and drag when the mouse cursor has a corner showing then you are moving one end of a line segment, whereas if the mouse cursor has a curve then you can stretch the curve without moving the endpoints by dragging the mouse. Try clicking and dragging near the middle of the line and you will see the curve bend. You may find that it is difficult to see any detail on the ball because it is too small. If so then try zooming in; remember that Flash is a vector package and as such you can zoom in without any loss of quality. Use the magnifying glass to select the zoom option, or select the level of zoom from the combo box in the top right corner of the application. When the Zoom tool is selected you can drag a box around your artwork and Flash will resize and centre your view of the artwork to this box.

At this stage your ball should look like the third ball from the left in Figure 1.7. To give the illusion of depth to the ball we will add a shadow of a darker colour to the bottom left of the ball. This area has a bounding shape defined by the circle and the line we have just drawn, so you can use the Fill tool shown highlighted in Figure 1.11. Use the mixer panel to create a darker blue for the bottom left and then click in this area to apply the colour.

At this stage you could choose to remove the outlines. Figure 1.12 shows the completed ball with all the lines and fills selected. The dots over the artwork indicate a selection. If you click on

Figure 1.8 *Using the Line tool*

Figure 1.9 *Using the Selection tool*

Figure 1.10 *Zooming in*

a frame layer in the timeline then everything in that frame layer will be highlighted. To select just a section of the image click away from the artwork to deselect, then click on the part you wish to select. To remove the outlines you would click on any outline in the ball, then double-click to select all the outlines of the same colour and stroke connected to the first selection. Try using firstly the timeline to select and then the arrow selection tool, and try selecting individual and connected parts. It is important when developing artwork in Flash that you are familiar with the selection tools. Finally highlight the completed ball; the easiest way to do this is by using the timeline selection method. Your selection should look like Figure 1.12.

Figure 1.11 *Using the Fill tool*

Using symbols

Flash lets you turn pieces of artwork into symbols. With the whole of the ball selected choose 'Modify/Convert to Symbol...' or press F8. This brings up the dialog box you can see in Figure 1.13.

When creating a symbol you have three choices. The symbol can be a 'Movie Clip' in which case you will have control over it using ActionScript. It can be a 'Button' so

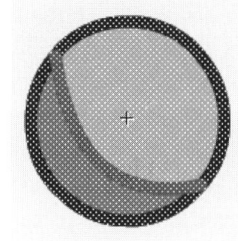

Figure 1.12 *The ball selected*

that it will respond to the position of the mouse or it can be a 'Graphic'. For now we will choose 'Movie Clip' and give it the name Ball. Having clicked 'OK', the highlighting will change from that shown in Figure 1.12 to a rectangular bounding box drawn around the symbol. Although you can still move and resize the symbol you cannot edit it using the drawing tools. To get at the actual artwork you will need to edit the symbol itself. You can get at the symbol by any one of three ways: either open the 'Library' window using 'Window/Library' or right-click on the symbol and then choose the option to 'Edit in Place'. This will change the timeline so that you are now editing 'Scene1/Ball' rather than 'Scene 1'. The final option for choosing to edit a symbol is to use the 'Edit Symbols' button at the top right of the stage window, as in Figure 1.14.

Figure 1.13 *Creating a symbol*

Adding the bats

At this stage you have an option; you can try yourself to create the bat as shown in Figure 1.15 or you can take the easy way out and open the project on the CD 'Examples/Chapter01/Pingpong03.fla'. Each bat uses the same symbol, with the left bat flipped horizontally by using 'Modify/Transform/Flip Horizontal' to create the right bat.

Figure 1.14 *Selecting Edit Symbols*   **Figure 1.15** *The bat*

Adding a little code

Now is the time to start to enter a little ActionScript. Click on the right-hand bat to select it, and then open the Actions panel either by selecting 'Window/Development Panels/Actions', or by pressing F9, or by clicking on the blue arrow icon at the right of the Properties panel. You should see something similar to Figure 1.16 on page 8.

Fear not if the sight of all this gibberish fills you with dread, we will examine this code a bit at a time. Firstly, the opening line:

```
onClipEvent(enterFrame){
```

What does this mean? Remember that we created a symbol, and we chose to make this symbol a 'Movie Clip'. Movie clips can have code attached to them and one of the ways you can add this code is by clicking on the symbol, selecting actions then adding an 'onClipEvent'. The curly brackets { and } contain a section of code, in this case they contain all the code that occurs for the 'onClipEvent'. An 'onClipEvent' can be passed a little information in the form of a *parameter*. The syntax for Flash is very similar to the syntax for JavaScript, which is often used by pages that you will view in an Internet browser. A parameter is contained within regular brackets, (and). In this example the parameter passed is 'enterFrame'; this occurs as the timer flips on to the next time segment. If you set the movie frame rate to 20, then this section of code will run 20 times a second. If this sounds a lot, bear in mind that many commercial games aim for frame rates of 50 times a second or above. The higher the frame rate the smoother an animation will appear; however, the computer hardware must be able to sustain this level of computation. For now we will leave the frame rate at 20 and hope for the best. If Flash cannot sustain the intended frame rate then it just tries to maintain the highest frame rate it can. As you progress through the book you will learn of different parameters you can pass to the 'onClipEvent', but for now we will limit it to just 'enterFrame'.

```
onClipEvent(enterFrame){
    //Bat moves up when K(75) is pressed
    //and moves down when M(77) is pressed
    //Speed of the move is governed by moveY
    //moveY is set to zero when neither move
    //key is pressed. If there is a change in
    //direction then moveY is initialised to 1
    //for down or -1 for up. moveY is incremented
    //by multiplying by 1.2 for each frame until
    //the bat reaches maximum speed.

    keypressed = false;

    if (Key.isDown(75) && _y>50){
        //trace("LeftBat onClipEvent: A pressed");
        if (moveY>=0){
            moveY = -1;
        }else if (moveY>-15){
            moveY *= 1.2;
        }
```

RightBat

Line 37 of 37, Col 2

Figure 1.16 *Entering ActionScript*

Following on from the first line are several lines each beginning with '//'. The use of // at the beginning of a line indicates that everything following this on the line is a comment. It does not affect the code; its use is as a convenience for the programmer. You are strongly encouraged to comment your code liberally. It has no effect on the performance, yet makes your code easier for yourself or others to understand. A section of code that seems obvious as you write it can often seem like hieroglyphics when you return to it weeks or months later.

The next line we will consider is:

```
keypressed = false;
```

All computer programming uses variables. A variable is a slot where you can store information and return to it later. You may want to store a number, a word, a sentence or just whether something is true or not. Flash lets you store all this information. A variable takes a name, which can be any name that you find useful. In this instance I chose the name 'keypressed' and I have set this to false. So at this stage in this section of code the variable 'keypressed' is false.

Then we move on to use a most important tool in the programmer's armoury, the 'if' statement. The syntax of an 'if' statement is

```
if (test){
    //Do this if test is true
}else{
    //Do this if test is false
}
```

The standard brackets contain the test. What could we use here? It can be anything that evaluates to *true* or *false*. In Chapter 8 we will look in detail at how to use the 'if' statement but for now just remember *true* or *false*. If something is *true* then do whatever is in the first set of curly brackets. If it is *false* then do whatever is in curly brackets following the optional 'else' statement.

We are using the clip event to move the bat up or down. It will move up if the 'K' key is pressed and down if the 'M' key is pressed. In Flash we can test whether a key is pressed using

```
Key.isDown(75)
```

The number in the brackets selects the key; you will learn how to find out a key's number later in the section on debugging. If the key is down then the result is *true*, if the key is not down then the result is *false*. In the 'if' statement test we look for two things, one is the whether a key is down and the other is the value of '_y'. This value is stores the position up and down the screen of the movie clip itself. To avoid it going too high we want to make sure that this value is always greater than 50. We can combine these two tests by using the operator '&&'. Now both the tests must be true for the combination of the tests to evaluate to true. This is called logical 'And'. Again later we will look into combining logical operations, for now just accept that the test decides whether the K key is pressed and whether the movie clip is not too high up the screen. If all this is true then we move on to the code within the curly brackets.

```
if (moveY>=0){
    moveY = -1;
}else if (moveY>-15){
    moveY *= 1.2;
}
keypressed = true;
_y += moveY;
```

What, another 'if' statement? Yes, programming often involves the use of many conditions. Here we know that the user is pressing the K key and that the bat is not yet in the top position.

But we want the bat to speed up as it moves. So we use another variable, this time we have called the variable 'moveY'. It could have been called 'threeBlindMice' but 'moveY' describes what the variable is used for and this is very useful when examining your own and other developers' code. So what are we testing? If 'moveY' is greater than or equal to 0 then we do the bit in the first curly brackets. The symbol '>' means greater than and obviously the symbol '=' means equals. So '>=' means greater than or equal to. If 'moveY' was equal to 0 then the bat was previously stationary, if 'moveY' was greater than 0 then previously the bat was moving down the screen. In either case we need to set the movement of the clip so that it is going to start moving up, which we will do by setting 'moveY' to −1.

> A movie clip's location is set using the attributes _x and _y. If _x = 100 and _y = 100, then moving the clip to (25, 80) would involve setting _x to 25 and _y to 80. This would have the effect of moving the clip to the left (by reducing the _x value) and moving the clip up (by reducing the _y value). Similarly if the clip were moved right and down then the _x and _y values would both increase.

If 'moveY' is already less than 0, then it must already be moving up so we want to speed up its motion as long as it is not already going too fast. In this instance we test the speed by using, yes, you guessed it, an 'if' statement. If 'moveY' is greater than −15 then we can speed up the motion by multiplying the existing motion by 1.2. If the speed was initially −1, then the speed after multiplying by 1.2 will be −1.2. Don't worry, the maths doesn't get much harder than that!! After we've done all that we can set 'keypressed' to true, because we know that the K key is pressed and we can move the bat by adding the moveY value onto the '_y' attribute for this clip. When you are adding, subtracting, multiplying or dividing in Flash, you can use one of two methods.

```
x = x+3; or x+ = 3;
```

If x were initially 6, for example, then after either of the above x would be set to 9. I prefer the second option, simply because if x does equal 6 then it patently doesn't equal 9, so the use of the equals symbol can be confusing; what it means is assign the new value of x to be the old value plus 3. The symbol '+=' does not have a simple arithmetic alternative and so there is no confusion. If you prefer the first method then by all means use it; code is like that − you will get into ways of doing things that you will feel comfortable with and if it works for you and the method works then use it. But do remember to comment any code; I cannot stress this too firmly.

The next section of the code repeats all the same tests with the 'M' key. This time we test for a limit of movement down the screen by ensuring that '_y' is less than 270. When setting 'moveY' we initially set it to 1 rather than −1, because we are moving the bat down the screen and '_y' increases in value down. After testing for the 'M' key we finally check whether the variable 'keypressed', which was initially set to false, has been set to true. The '!' symbol in front of a true or false variable reverses the value of the variable. In English

```
if (!keypressed) moveY = 0;
```

would translate to 'if keypressed is not true then set moveY equal to 0'. So if neither the K nor the M key is pressed then 'moveY' is set to 0. That's all that is needed to move the bats up and down without them going off screen. Here is all the code for the right bat.

```
onClipEvent(enterFrame){
    //Bat moves up when K(75) is pressed
    //and moves down when M(77) is pressed
    //Speed of the move is governed by moveY
    //moveY is set to zero when neither move
    //key is pressed. If there is a change in
    //direction then moveY is initialised to 1
    //for down or -1 for up. moveY is incremented
    //by multiplying by 1.2 for each frame until
    //the bat reaches maximum speed.

    keypressed = false;

    if (Key.isDown(75) && _y>50){
       if (moveY>=0){
          moveY = -1;
       }else if (moveY>-15){
          moveY *= 1.2;
       }
       keypressed = true;
       _y += moveY;
    }

    if (Key.isDown(77) && _y<270){
       if (moveY<=0){
          moveY = 1;
       }else if (moveY<15){
          moveY *= 1.2;
       }
       keypressed = true;
       _y += moveY;
    }

    if (!keypressed) moveY = 0;
}
```

Now try running the program. You can do this by pressing 'Ctrl+Enter'; Flash then enters run-time mode, showing you how the user would see your game. At this stage the only thing happening is the movement of the right bat using the 'K' and 'M' keys.

Testing and debugging

If you have 'Examples/Chapter01/pingpong03.fla' open then you will see that there is a fourth layer, labelled 'Debug'. No developer ever gets it all right first time and when something doesn't work discovering where the errors are can be something of an art. One useful method is to send information to a text box that you can see on screen. You can create a text box by choosing the Text tool (the A icon) and then placing your mouse on the stage and typing in some text. You can set the text box to operate as a Dynamic Text box using the Properties panel for the Text tool.

Figure 1.17 *Setting up a Dynamic Text box*

In this example the settings are for a Multiline box that tracks the variable 'debug'. Now if you set the variable 'debug' to 'Hello' using ActionScript then that would appear in the box as the program runs. We can use this tool to test lots of useful information about our program. We will look into debugging in detail in Chapter 11.

The movement of the ball is a little more complicated than the movement of the bats. Open 'Examples/Chapter01/pingpong04.fla' and press 'Ctrl + Enter' to test it. Now the ball bounces off the walls and the bats. Stop playing the game and try clicking the ball and selecting Actions. Take a look at the code and see if you can work out what is going on. Don't worry if you can't, this chapter is just a quick introduction and although the code in the ball isn't too hard, it is much more complicated than the script for the bats. By the time you have worked through the later chapters of this book it will all be second nature.

Adding a scoreboard

One thing that we can do to improve the game is to add a score. Those strange boxes that both have 123 in them will be where we put the score. The LeftBat scores every time the ball goes out of screen right and the RightBat scores every time the ball goes out of screen left. So how do we accomplish this?

Take a look at the section of code in the ball clip event that follows the comment '//Ball moving right'. See how useful the comment is. Now you know that the ball is moving right in this section. If it is moving right then the RightBat should hit it, if it doesn't then the LeftBat scores a point.

```
...
//Ball moving right
if (_x > 370){
```

```
    _x = startX;
    _y = startY;
    moveX = 0;
    _root.LeftScore++;
    ...
```

If the ball's '_x' value is greater than 370 then it is off-screen at the right so we can add one to the LeftBat's score. This is achieved by the curious code

```
    _root.LeftScore++;
```

The '++' symbol simply means add one to the variable that comes before it. But the variable isn't just called 'LeftScore', it is called '_root.LeftScore'. Why? Variables have something called scope. If we are in the clip 'Bat' and want to access a variable that is in a different clip then we can use one of two methods: either relative addressing or direct addressing. Let's look at an example; in the current example we have the hierarchy:

```
_root
   |____ Ball
   |____ LeftBat
   |____ RightBat
```

All Flash movies have as the highest level of the hierarchy, '_root'. The value of 'moveX' in 'Left-Bat' can be accessed from the 'Ball' by using '_root.LeftBat.moveX', each layer in the hierarchy being separated by the '.' operator. This method is direct addressing. The alternative approach uses relative addressing, '_parent.LeftBat.moveX'; in this method we move up a layer from the current position, before looking in the movie clip 'LeftBat'. Although they seem similar they are actually quite different. A more complex hierarchy can often require several '_parent's before the appropriate clip can be accessed, such as '_parent._parent._parent.LeftPlayer.RightArm.Bat.moveX'. If the clip called 'LeftPlayer' was at the root of the movie then the same variable can be accessed using '_root.LeftBat.RightArm.Bat.moveX'. In the current example the score variables are at the '_root' and so when we are in the 'Ball' clip we need to append '_root' to the name of the variable in order to access them. Variable scope can be a confusing issue and is covered in much more depth in Chapter 7.

Having inserted in the code to add the score for the 'LeftBat' we repeat by adding the score for the 'RightBat'.

```
    ...
    //Ball moving left
    if (_x < 30){
        _x = startX;
        _y = startY;
```

```
        moveX = 0;
        _root.RightScore++;
    ...
```

The final stage of the game is saved as 'Examples\Chapter01\Pingpong05.fla'.

How to improve it

To finish the game there needs to be a beginning and an end. The beginning would give instructions for key presses and the end would show the final score. In this simple example we will exclude these details but you are encouraged to develop the game further to include these aspects as your skills progress.

Playing against the computer

It would be nice if the player could compete with the computer. To achieve this one of the bats could be under computer control, so the clip event for the bat would judge where the ball would hit the bat and move the bat accordingly. Although this is a little complicated it should be within your capabilities after completing Section 3 of this book. When the computer is in control it may be impossible for the player to win. It is your job as a developer to set the skill level so a player is not frustrated but is challenged. Setting the game play level so that a player is progressively challenged as their skill level develops is one of the hardest aspects of game play development but one of the most important.

Summary

This was a quick look at creating a Flash game; hopefully it gave you an overview. If you found the code confusing then don't worry, we will be going at a much slower pace in the later chapters when looking at ActionScript. In principle, I want you to take away from this chapter an initial awareness of the Flash interface, how to use some of the drawing tools, the use of symbols and where to enter bits of ActionScript. As you progress through the book you will be encouraged to enter your own code and develop the examples that you will find in later chapters. Nothing improves your skill more than trying it out yourself. Practice really does make, if not perfect, then at least much better.

Section 1

Animation

The first section looks at creating the artwork and animation that will feature in the games we create.

2 Drawing with Flash

Flash provides you with all the tools you will need to create great games. In this chapter we look at the basics of using the package to create artwork. Most games will require animated artwork and later in the chapter we will look at the principles of animation.

The Flash toolbox

Flash includes all the drawing tools you need to create character animation; indeed some professional studios are now using Flash to produce TV animation. Unlike some drawing applications there are not many tools to learn. Before we start to do any drawing let's look at all the tools and what we can use them for.

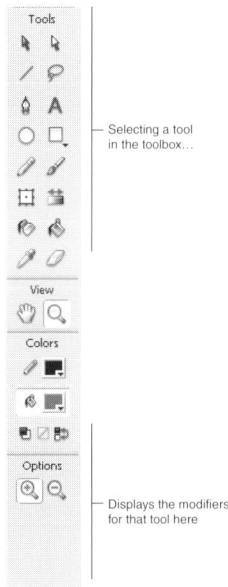

Figure 2.1 *The Flash toolbox in outline*   **Figure 2.2** *All the tools named*

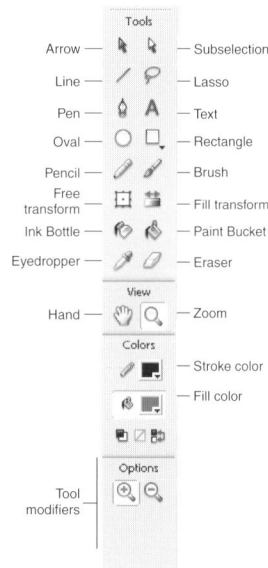

The tools in the toolbox let you draw, paint, select and modify artwork, and change the view of the Stage. The toolbox is divided into four sections:

- The Tools section contains drawing, painting and selection tools.
- The View section contains tools for zooming and panning in the application window.
- The Colors section contains modifiers for stroke and fill colours.
- The Options section displays modifiers for the selected tool, which affect the tool's painting or editing operations.

We will look first at using the drawing and painting tools.

17

Using the drawing tools

The Line tool

Click and drag to draw a straight line in the currently selected colour and stroke. To select a different colour, choose 'Window/Design Panels/Color Mixer' to open the colour mixer panel. You can select a colour by clicking in the colour spectrum box, use the bar to the right to set the brightness; you can also set the level of opacity using the 'Alpha' setting. The number underneath the box displaying the current colour is the hexadecimal equivalent. Internet browsers use this number to set the colour of backgrounds and fonts.

Figure 2.3 *Selecting the Line tool*   **Figure 2.4** *Selecting a colour in Flash MX 2004*

To adjust the stroke, that is the line width and style (solid, dotted etc.), use the arrow 'Selection' tool to select the line. You will find that the Properties window, which is context sensitive, will be similar to that shown in Figure 2.5.

Figure 2.5 *Adjust the stroke characteristics*

You can adjust the stroke width using the arrow next to the box displaying a '1' in Figure 2.5. You can also choose whether the line is solid or not using the combo box to the right of the stroke width selector.

Having selected a colour and stroke, try drawing a few lines. If the magnet 'Snap to Objects' button is selected then the lines will jump to horizontal or vertical if they are close to those angles. If 'View/Snapping/Snap to Grid' is selected then the ends of the lines will jump to an invisible grid. You can edit the grid using 'View/Grid/Edit Grid' and you can display the grid using 'View/Grid/Show Grid'.

If you want the line to be curved, then select the black arrow 'Selection' icon in the Tools panel. Move your mouse close to the ends of the line. Notice that the cursor shows a corner icon, whereas away from the ends the cursor shows a curve icon. If the mouse displays a corner then clicking and dragging the mouse will move the corner of a curve. If the mouse cursor image shows a curve then clicking and dragging will bend the curve. If you double-click on the line then you will select the entire line. The mouse cursor will show the 'Move Object' image. Clicking and dragging will move the whole line.

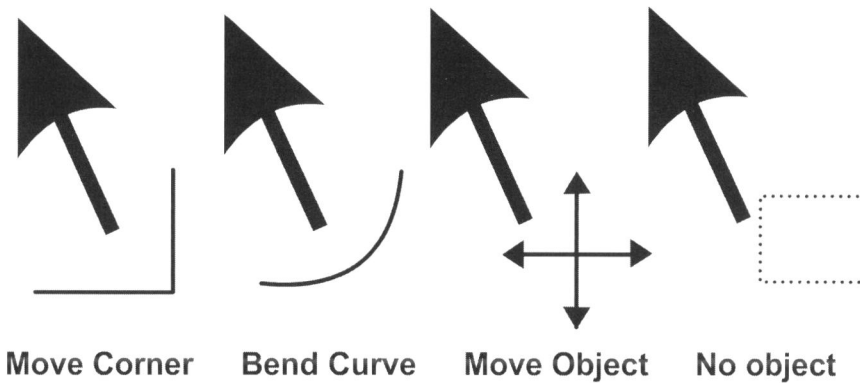

Move Corner   Bend Curve   Move Object   No object

Figure 2.6 *Arrow tool cursor images*

If you want to get a curve that doubles back on itself then you will need to cut through the line.

1   First draw a simple line by clicking and dragging.
2   Bend the line using the black arrow 'Selection' tool.
3   Draw a line across the first line. Bend one side differently from the other.
4   Delete the short line by clicking on the line segment and pressing the 'Delete' key.
    With magnet on, move the middle of the line until the circle is displayed.
5   If you select the 'Subselection' (white arrow) tool then you will see that the curve now has three handles.

The Subselection tool can be useful when you want to see how Flash is actually drawing the curves that you create. It highlights the 'handle' in the curve whereas the black arrow Selection tool lets you do the same editing without showing the underlying structure.

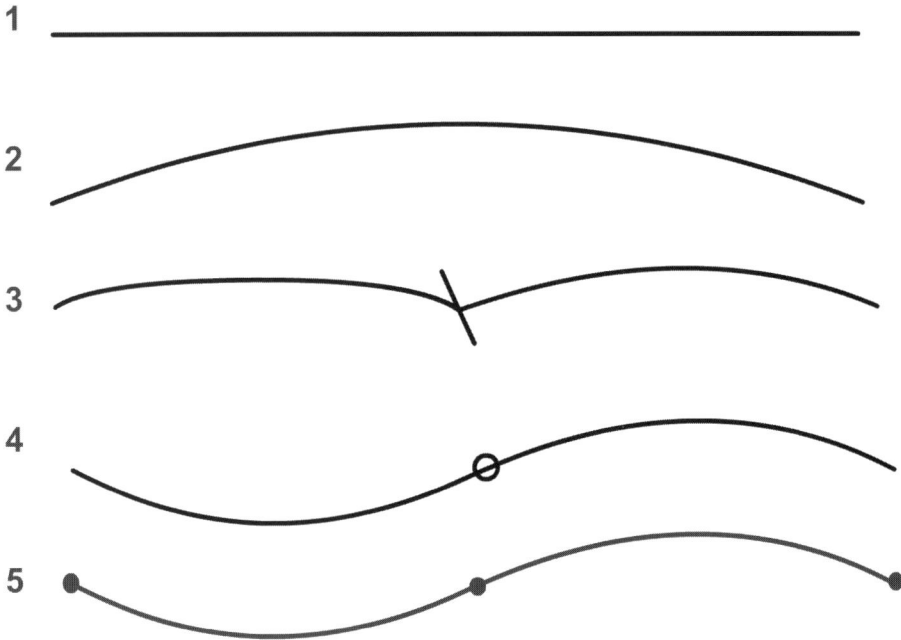

Figure 2.7 *Stages in drawing a multiple curve line*

The Pen tool

The Pen tool is used for creating precise curved lines. Start by clicking with the mouse to define the start of the line, now click for each connected line segment. The upper curve in Figure 2.9 shows the first stage in creating a curved line with the Pen tool. Having placed the basic straight edge curve, select the Subselection (white arrow) tool and click on a handle, a blue circle or square. By moving the handle, or adjusting the tangents (the short sticks that protrude from a handle), you have total control over the flow of a complex curve. Try doing it now to familiarize yourself with the method.

Figure 2.8 *Selecting the Pen tool*

The Oval and Rectangle tools

The Oval and Rectangle tools can use both the stroke and the fill colours. If a stroke is selected then this will form the outline for the oval or rectangle. If a fill colour is selected then this will be the colour for the interior fill. The tools are used simply by clicking and dragging to reshape. Once you have created an oval or rectangle it can be adjusted with the arrow Selection or Subselection tools. Any vector artwork that you place on the stage is made from lines and fills so an oval or rectangle is just a set of lines and fills.

Figure 2.9 *Using the Pen and Subselection tools*

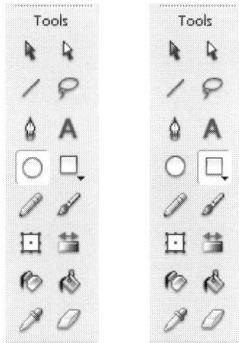

Figure 2.10 *The Oval and Rectangle tools*

Figure 2.11 *Options for the Selection tool*

Figure 2.11 shows the options for the black arrow Selection tool. The first option is the magnet icon 'Snap to Objects'; using this causes dragged artwork to snap to objects. The next two buttons allow you to smooth or straighten the edges of a selection. You can easily bend the edges of a rectangle or adjust the curve of an oval using the arrow tool.

The Pencil tool

The Pencil tool uses the current stroke settings. To use the tool, select it in the toolbox, then select the options you want.

Figure 2.12 *Selecting the Pencil tool*

Figure 2.13 *Options for the Pencil tool*

'Straighten' causes the lines that you draw to be drawn as straight connected line segments. 'Smooth' creates smooth lines if they are within the boundaries set for your current preferences. You adjust your preferences using 'Edit/Preferences...'. If you are not happy with the way the line is smoothed then check the setting 'Smooth curves:' under the 'Editing' tab.

Figure 2.14 *Adjusting drawing settings using Edit/Preferences...*

The final option for the Pencil tool is to set it to ink mode. In this mode the freehand drawing that you produce is not affected by Flash and you see exactly what you draw.

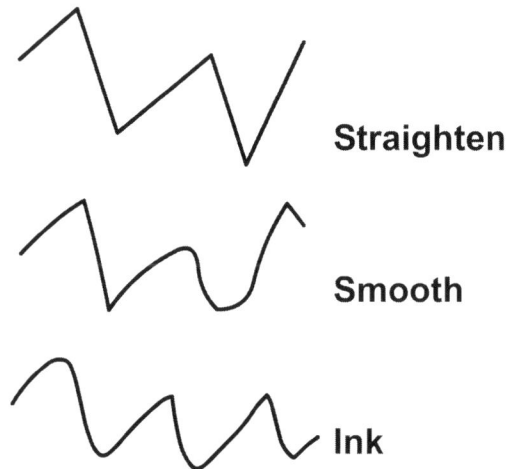

Straighten

Smooth

Ink

Figure 2.15 *The effect of the different options for the Pencil tool*

The Brush tool

The Brush tool, unlike the Pencil tool, does not take the current stroke settings. A Brush uses the fill settings, because you are creating a fill rather than a line when using the Brush tool.

The options for the Brush include how the Brush is applied – whether pressure sensitivity should be used. If you have a pressure-sensitive tablet then the pressure you apply to the pen when you use this option affects the width of the Brush. A drop-down box allows you to select the Brush size and a second drop-down allows you to select the Brush shape. Finally you can lock the fill that you are drawing to another fill area.

Figure 2.16 *Selecting the Brush tool*

Figure 2.17 *The options for the Brush tool*

Figure 2.18 *The Brush mode option for the Brush tool*

When you use the Brush it can be applied normally, within fills only, behind fills, within a selection area or inside an object. Figure 2.19 shows the effect of the different modes.

Figure 2.19 *Using the different Brush modes*

The first image shows the original artwork. The second shows the effect of using 'Paint Normal' where everything on the current layer is overwritten by the application of the Brush. Image three shows the effect of 'Paint Fills', where only fills are overpainted, not lines. Image four uses 'Paint Behind'; now any fill or line on the layer is protected and only blank areas are used. To use 'Paint Selection' you obviously need a selection. Finally 'Paint Inside' applies the Brush to the fill that is under the mouse cursor when the mouse is first pressed.

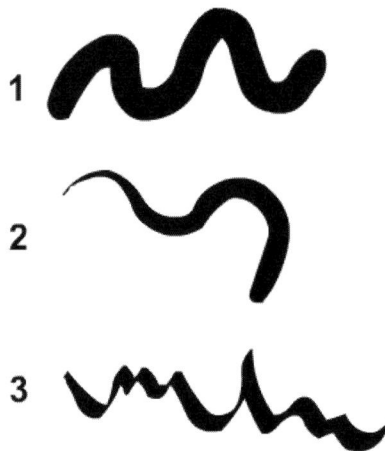

Figure 2.20 *The effect of using pressure and different Brush shapes*

The Free Transform tool

The Free Transform tool allows you to rotate, scale or distort a selection. The tool has four options, shown in Figure 2.22.

Figure 2.21 *The Free Transform tool*

Figure 2.22 *Options for the Free Transform tool*

Option 1, Rotate and Skew, allows you to rotate the current selection. When rotating, placing the mouse cursor over a corner handle changes the mouse cursor into a circular arrow. In this mode a click and drag allows you to rotate the selection.

If the mouse cursor is over the handles at the middle of the edge lines then a click and drag will skew the selection.

Figure 2.23 *Rotating a selection*

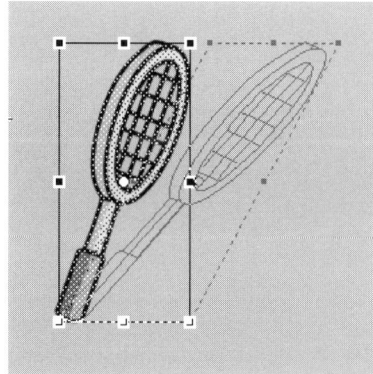

Figure 2.24 *Skewing a selection*

The second option is to scale the selection. When using the Scale option, clicking and dragging in the corners scales the selection up or down, while clicking and dragging the middle handles allow you to stretch a selection in one axis only.

Option three, Distort, allows you to pick up the corners of the selection and distort it; it is useful for adding perspective into a drawing.

The final option, Envelope, allows you to distort a selection in a very complex way introducing curves where lines were previously straight.

The next button on the Tools toolbar is the Fill Transform tool, which we will look at a little later.

Figure 2.25 *Scaling a selection*

Figure 2.26 *Distorting and applying an envelope to a selection*

The Ink Bottle tool

As you know, Flash distinguishes between lines and fills. If you want to change the characteristics of a line then select the 'Ink Bottle'. By changing the current stroke colour and current stroke width and style you can, by clicking on a line, fill that line with a new line style and colour.

Figure 2.27 *Selecting the Ink Bottle tool*

Figure 2.28 *Selecting the Paint Bucket tool*

Figure 2.29 *Options for the Paint Bucket tool*

The Paint Bucket tool

If you want to affect the colour of a fill area then use the Paint Bucket tool. The options panel for the Paint Bucket allows you to select how to fill an area that is not fully surrounded. A small gap may exist but Flash can still fill the area if you select 'Close Small Gaps' from the 'Gap Size' menu. If this still doesn't work then you can choose either 'Close Medium Gaps' or 'Close Large Gaps'. The right-hand button on the options panel is 'Lock'.

Filled areas can be filled with a colour, a gradient or a bitmap fill.

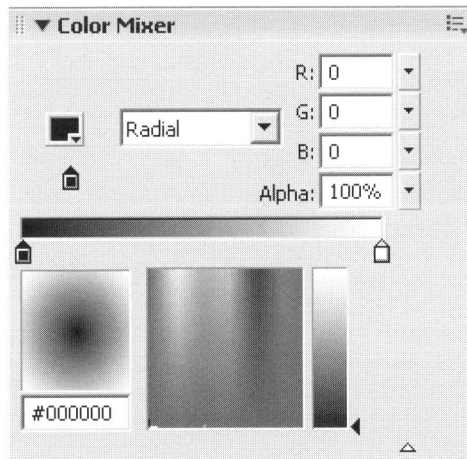

Figure 2.30 *Selecting a gradient using the Fill panel*

To use a gradient select a linear, radial or bitmap fill in the colour mixer panel. You can add as many colour segments as you need to the gradient bar to make the gradient. Now click inside a bounded area, making sure that 'Lock Fill' is unselected. The area is filled with the gradient. If the positioning of the gradient is not to your liking then you can choose the Fill Transform tool button and click on the gradient. You will get something like the image shown in Figure 2.31, if you have chosen a radial gradient. You can move the centre of the gradient using the central circle handle. The square handle stretches the scale of the gradient. The circle on the outer edge between the two other handles sizes the gradient and the lower circle rotates the gradient. If you selected a 'Linear Gradient' then the handles for adjusting the gradient will be rectangular. The square one is for stretching and the circular one for rotating. Clicking and dragging the central circular handle adjusts the position of the fill.

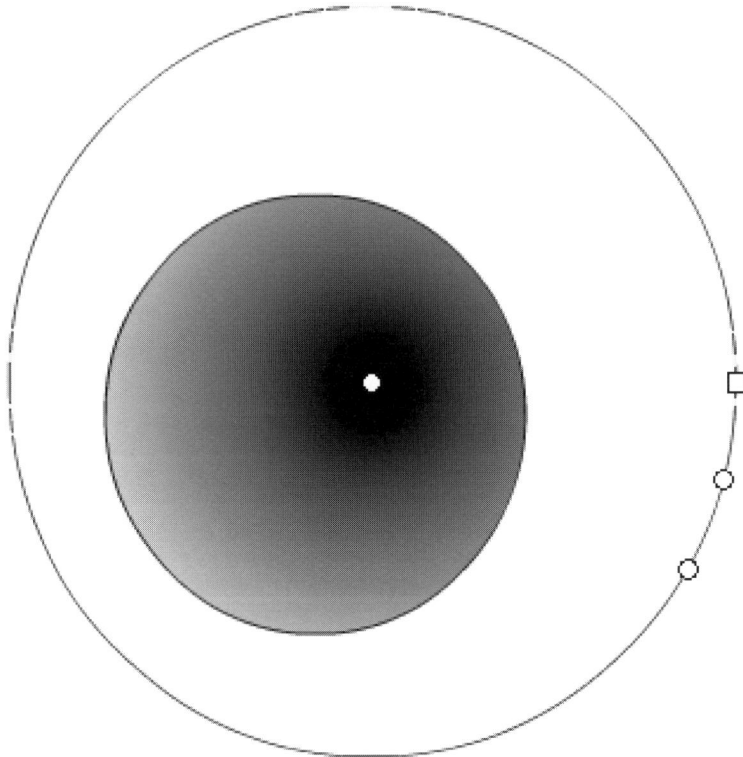

Figure 2.31 *Moving a gradient using the Transform Fill option*

If you want to fill an area with a bitmap then import a bitmap into Flash using 'File/Import. . .'. Select the bitmap by clicking on it and choose the menu option 'Modify/Break Apart'. The bitmap selection changes from a surrounding rectangle to a patterned area. If you use the Eyedropper tool, then you can pick up the image as a fill. Now click on an area to apply the image. If the area is bigger than the image then the image will be repeated in both the width and height.

Figure 2.32 *Using a bitmap as a fill*

The basics of animation

Now that you know the basic drawing tools we are ready to start work on a little animation. Animation on TV uses around 12 drawings to the second, and because these still drawings are changed so quickly we perceive them as showing a moving image. In Flash the pace with which the images are changed is set using the 'Modify/Document...' dialog box or by clicking in a blank area of the stage – the context-sensitive Properties panel will now show dialog controls that allow you to alter the movie's frame rate. The default Movie frame rate is set to the TV favourite of 12 frames per second. Just to get started let's bounce a ball. Open 'Examples/Chapter02/Ball.fla'. In this project there are three scenes. Take a look at scene one. Choose 'Control/Loop Playback' then press 'Enter' to see the ball move. The ball does move but it is not very 'bouncy'. To stop the animation press 'Enter' again.

Figure 2.33 *Using motion tweening in Flash*

The animation has been done using motion tweening. First the 'ball' was drawn and then this was turned into a graphic symbol by pressing F8, or selecting 'Modify/Convert to Symbol...' from the menu. A position was set at frame one, six and twelve by pressing F6 to insert a keyframe then moving the ball symbol. Finally frames one to six were selected and using the 'Frame' panel,

29

tweening was selected for these frames. The motion produced using this technique is illustrated in Figure 2.34.

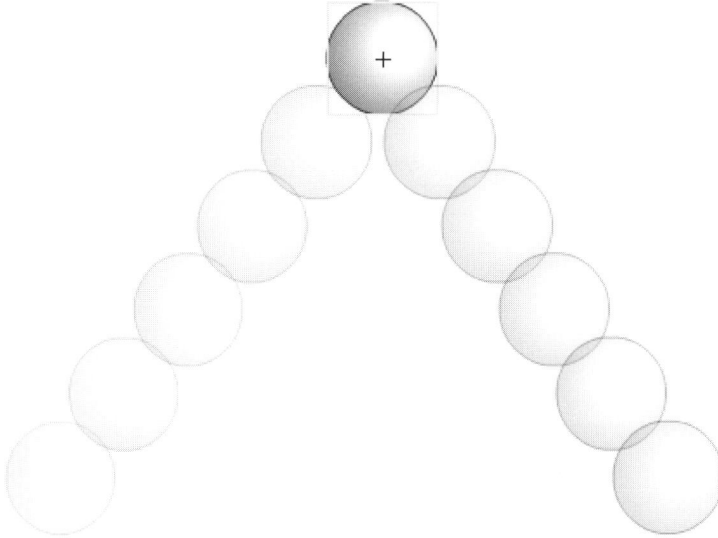

Figure 2.34 *First step to a bouncing ball*

Figure 2.35 *Selecting onion skinning*

The motion produced by Flash, by default, using tweening is a linear interpolation from one key position to the next. That is, the gaps between the positions will be the same for each step. To see how the motion will behave turn on 'onion skinning' using the button second from the left at the bottom of the timeline area. Having selected onion skinning, you can choose how many frames are displayed using the grey areas to the left and right of the current frame rectangle in the timeline.

To improve the movement we want the action to slow down up to the maximum height then speed up as the ball falls under gravity. We do this in the Properties panel by setting the 'Easing' for frame 1 to 50 and the 'Easing' for frame 6 to −50. This gives a somewhat more realistic action but the motion is still not a curve. There are two ways to achieve this. Either we can put keyframes in throughout the animation and not use motion tweening at all or we can use a curve to control the motion. The latter option is the best to use for simple actions while keyframes throughout works best for complex actions.

To control an animation with a curve, first put the start and end frames for the ball, then right click the layer and choose 'Add Motion Guide'. This adds a new layer above the current layer. Draw a curve in this layer and then with the 'Magnet' on snap the ball to the start of the curve on the first frame and the end of the curve on the last frame. The ball will now be centred on the curve.

Figure 2.36 *Using a curve to control a motion*

Scene 2 from 'Examples/Chapter02/ball.fla' shows how this motion can be set up. The 'Easing' has been set by adding an extra keyframe at frame six. The 'Easing' for frame 1 is set to 50 and at frame 6 the 'Easing' is set to −50.

Designing a character

Personally I don't think you can beat a real pencil for getting the feel for a character design, but some colleagues prefer to use a tablet and draw directly in Flash. Whichever method you choose you will need to be prepared to revisit your design many times before a really good character design develops.

Character design is greatly affected by the fashion of the moment. Nevertheless there are a few golden rules.

- Make sure the character is distinctive.
- Be prepared to exaggerate features.

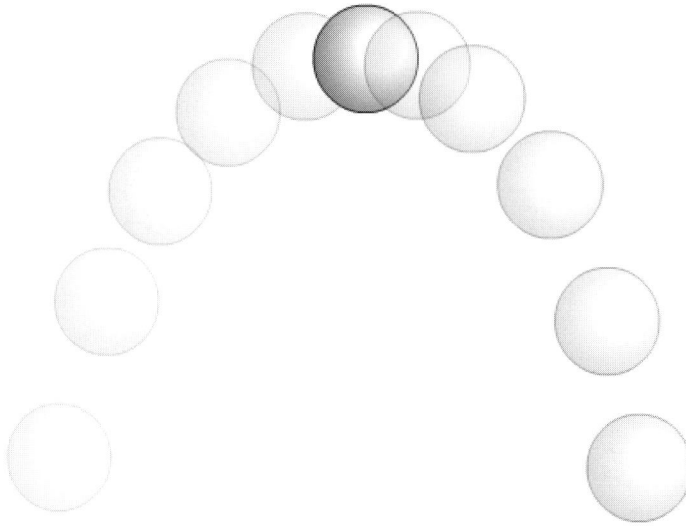

Figure 2.37 *Using keyframes throughout*

Figure 2.38 *First scribbles for a character*

- Keep the design simple.
- Think in colour, not black and white.

Dramatic performance in most games is usually very limited. Your character will rarely be called on to be a great actor, but an expressive face is usually going to be an asset to a design; it is better that your character can convey a range of emotions even if they may never be called on to prove it.

Figure 2.39 *The final design*

Summary

Flash is a great tool for experimenting with animation. In this chapter we looked at the principal drawing tools and studied some methods for producing simple animation. In the next chapter we will look at creating effective character animation with the minimum of artwork.

3 Simple cut-out animation

Flash is often used to display animation within a web browser. In many parts of the world most web users still access the web using a modem. Their connection speed is around 4 K per second. That means that a 40 K file will take 10 seconds to download, while a 400 K file will take around 100 seconds. As a developer you need to be aware that the patience of your viewers is limited. File size is likely to be a huge issue for Internet developers for the next several years. In this chapter we will look at how you can create animations that look fluid while using a minimum of artwork. This has a dual benefit: it is quicker to produce and it results in smaller file sizes.

Segmenting a character

Eyes

Body

RArm

LArm

RLeg

LLeg

Figure 3.1 *The segments in the simple walk*

Cut-out animation is produced by splitting a character into small segments and then animating the segments simply by moving and rotating. If you intend to use motion tweening, a very fast method for moving and rotating symbols in Flash, then you will need to place each segment on a separate layer. In this chapter we will take a very simple cat character and create several walks of increasing sophistication. The character was drawn directly in Flash using the drawing tools discussed in the previous chapter. Then the character was divided into sections by using the Lasso tool. To select the Lasso tool you need to click the Tools button indicated in Figure 3.2.

To use the Lasso tool draw around the character by clicking and holding the left mouse button. The selected area will show an overlaid dot pattern. To convert a selected area into a symbol press F8 or choose 'Modify/Convert to Symbol. . .' from the menu. In the dialog box choose 'Graphic' as the symbol type and enter a descriptive name. The selection will change from the dot pattern to a bounding box. The name that you give the symbol will be the name displayed in the Library. You can view the Library at any time by pressing F11 or selecting 'Window/Library' from the main menu. When the segment is a symbol you can use it as many times as you like either by dragging it out of the Library or by copying an instance of it on the stage and then pasting the instance into a new frame or new layer of the current frame. You can even paste a duplicate of the symbol in the current layer but remember that this will not work with motion tweening. The next step is to ensure that the rotation centre is correct.

Figure 3.2 *Selecting the Lasso tool*

No selection   Selected Area

Figure 3.3 *Selected area*

If you intend to use motion tweening then it is important to choose carefully the point about which the segment will rotate.

To adjust a symbol's pivot point select the Free Transform tool from the Tools palette and move the white circle. The white circle defines the point about which the symbol will rotate. To get an accurate placement it is usually best to use the Zoom tool. Using the Zoom tool you can move in and out by selecting either the '+' option or the '−' option and clicking, or you can drag a rectangle round the area you wish to zoom in on and then Flash will resize to suit this rectangle. The amount the artwork moves when using the arrow keys is dependent on the scale

Rotation Centre

Figure 3.4 *Selecting the rotation centre*

of your view of the artwork, because the pixel movement refers to screen size, not the original size of the artwork. Move the white circle until the rotation centre is in the most appropriate place. It is important that you understand the difference between the positioning of the artwork inside a symbol in relation to its rotation centre and the positioning of a symbol on the stage. This difference is very important. You can move the rotation centre so that it is a long way from the artwork inside a symbol, but the problem is that when you start to rotate the symbol it will stray away from where you intend it to be, consequently you will need to add multiple keys to get it back in place. These multiple keys negate the advantage of using motion tweening. If you find you have to use a great number of keyframes because of problems occurring when you rotate a symbol, then the first thing to check is the location of the pivot centre using the Free Transform tool.

A first walk with this character

Now is a good time to open the project 'Examples/Chapter03/FatCat.fla'. Take a look at Scene 1. Recall that you can select the current scene using the 'Edit Scene' button at the top right of the timeline or by using the 'Window/Design Panels/Scene' panel.

Take a look at Figure 3.1 and you can see that the segmenting of this character is very simple. Each segment appears on a new layer inside a new symbol called 'Walk1'. On the root timeline there are keys for the symbol 'Walk1' at 1, 7, 9, 15 and 17. These ensure that the cat goes up and down as he walks. Because all the limbs are inside the symbol 'Walk1' these will go up

Figure 3.5 *The principal keys in the simple walk*

Figure 3.6 *Selecting the current scene*

and down with the body so the arms and legs will not become separated from the body as it goes up and down. Nesting symbols inside other symbols in this way can make your animations easier to prepare. But before we put in the keys for the main 'Walk1' symbol we need to prepare the main key positions.

Figure 3.5 shows the extreme positions for the cat. The left leg is fully back at frames 1 and 17, while the right leg is back at frame 9. The arms are opposite to the legs when the right leg is fully forward the right arm is fully back. Always refer to your segments in relation to the character. The right arm should always be the character's right arm. If the character is facing you then it is tempting to call their right arm the left arm, because it is on the left in the screen view. But at some stage the character will be side on or from the rear; at what point do you swap? At least if the segments always refer to the character's right side then you can work it out and it becomes less confusing. Make the key positions that you have entered into 'Motion' either by selecting the frame in the timeline and choosing 'Create Motion Tween' from the context menu or by selecting 'Motion' from the 'Tween' combo box in the context-sensitive Properties panel for a frame. The character is now animated. Make sure that 'Control/Loop Playback' is checked in the menu and play the animation using the 'Play' button, 'Control/Play' from the menu or by pressing the 'Enter' key. Because you are inside the symbol, the cat's legs and arms swing but the body does not go up and down. Go back to the root timeline either by double-clicking in an empty space or clicking on 'Scene 1' at the upper left corner of the timeline. To complete this animation, adjust the height of the 'Walk1' symbol at frames 1, 7,

Figure 3.7 *Using motion tweening for this animation*

9, 15 and 17 so that the feet stay on the floor. Make frames 1, 7, 9 and 15 'Motion' type frames and play the animation. It's very stiff but at least it has started to move in a very basic way. You have a walk this way in very little time and if you do a 'Control/Test Scene' you will see that the file size for this scene is only 6 K, not bad for an animation.

Improving the walk

To improve the walk the arms and legs will need further segmenting. At this stage the benefits of nesting clips inside clips start to be outweighed by the difficulties of actually editing the animation. The segments we are going to use are shown in Figure 3.8. Each of the named segments is a symbol in the library. The layers used have been reduced somewhat because we are not going to use any motion tweening; we are going to add all the keys individually. Take a look now at Scene 2.

Because all the positions are going to be individually animated this animation will take a little longer to do. First set up the extremes: the stretched leg positions at frames 1 and 9; frame 17 is simply frame 1 repeated because we want the animation to loop. Second, put in the passing positions at frames 5 and 13. The body will be higher at the passing position.

Then add the down positions at frames 3 and 11 and the up positions at frames 7 and 15.

Finally do all the in-between positions by using the onion-skinning technique. To use onion skinning, click on the onion-skinning button in the lower left of the timeline. Select the range of the onion skinning by moving the circle handles in the onion-skinning range indicators. Onion skinning allows you to see the frames that precede the current frame and those that follow it. The fewer preceding and following frames that you view the easier it is to work out what is happening. For these final in-betweens you only need to view one preceding and one following frame. To do the in-betweens start by just moving the body, feet and hands. If you have difficulty moving a segment because it is behind another, lock the offending layer using the lock button in the timeline options.

Before you move the thighs, calves, biceps or forearms, switch off onion skinning. You will have a much better view of the artwork by then and the position of the body, feet and arms will dictate where the other segments need to go. Scenes 2 to 5 show various stages of creating this walk. I hope you agree that it is much looser than the first walk. This is a standard walk but a

REyebrow

REye

Body

RBicep

RFArm

RHand

RThigh

RCalf

RFoot

LEyebrow

LEye

LBicep

LFArm

LHand

LThigh

LCalf

LFoot

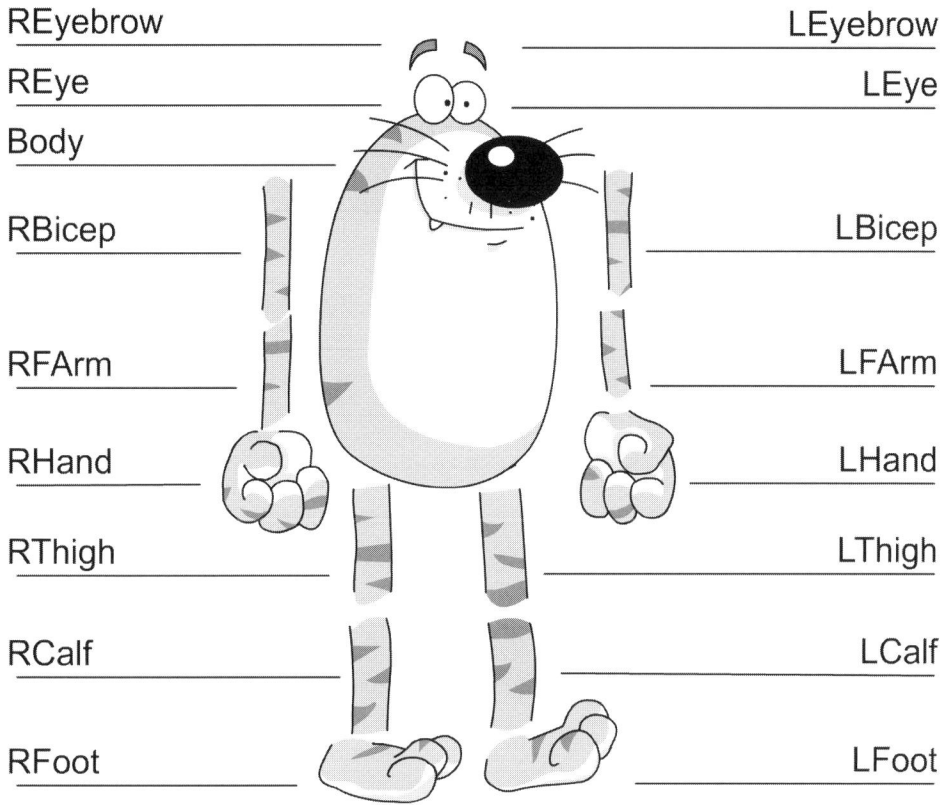

Figure 3.8 *Extra segments in the developed walk*

Figure 3.9 *Layers used for the animation*

Figure 3.10 *The extremes and the passing positions*

Figure 3.11 *Adding the up and down positions*

standard is made to be broken. Scene 6 shows how the walk can look by making the passing position a low position. The effect is to create a walk with a double bounce, which is a popular technique for many cartoon characters. Try to adjust the walk to get as much life and vitality as you can.

We have made progress but the character is still rather glazed. We need to add a blink.

Figure 3.12 *Selecting onion skinning*

Combining cut-out animation and cell animation

The blink is added to the eye symbol. But the eyes are inside the body symbol, so how do we get them to show the correct frame? Now is the time we really need to discover the difference between a 'graphic' and a 'movie clip'. A movie clip is independent of the main timeline. At design time it will only show frame 1; however, at run-time it will show a looping animation unless told differently. Because we are creating animation and do not intend to control the eyes from ActionScript we set the 'Eyes' to be a graphic. The 'Body' is also a graphic. Graphics try to keep in step with the timeline. If we place a graphic on the timeline at frame 11 and the graphic contains six frames, then at frame 16 the graphic will be displaying frame 6. If we go on to show frame 17 then by default the graphic will loop back and show frame 1. This behaviour can be easily adjusted, however; a graphic can be set to 'Loop' in which case a six-frame graphic will loop four times as the timeline moves on 24 frames. The graphic can be set to 'Play Once' in which case the six-frame graphic will play once then stop on frame 6 as the timeline moves on 24 frames. The third and final alternative for a graphic is to display a single frame, in which case a six-frame graphic will display a static frame as the timeline moves on 24 frames. To create the blink we will add two frames to the 'Body' symbol, simply by clicking in 'Body' layer on frame three and

Figure 3.13 *Animating a blink*

pressing F5. The timeline shows a grey bar stretching from frame one to frame three. Now we edit the eyes to include frames 2 and 3, which are edited as shown in Figure 3.13.

Figure 3.14 *Setting the appropriate frame*

In the 'Body' clip set frames 2 and 3 to show frames 2 and 3 of the 'Eyes' clip. To do this, click on an eye. In the Properties panel you will see that the 'Behavior' is set to 'Graphic', the method to 'Single Frame' and the 'First' option is set to the frame that you wish to display. Alternatively you could set the first frame to 'Play Once' in which case the eyes would stay in sync with the timeline for their parent. You should find that displaying frame 2 of the 'Body' symbol shows half-closed eyes and frame 3 shows closed eyes. Now switch back to the main timeline. To get the blink to display you will need to set which frame to display for the 'Body' clip. If you look in Scene 7 and click on the 'Body' layer frame 4, you will see that the frame to display is set to 2, for frame 5 it is set to 3 and for frame 6 it is set to frame 2. Finally frame 7 goes back to the default behaviour of displaying frame 1. Controlling the displayed frame by using 'graphics' and the three display options gives you total control over the behaviour of nested animations and is the preferred method for animation that does not require user intervention. Later in the book we will look in detail at how user input can be used to control the behaviour of 'movie clips'. Movie clips are much more flexible when dealing with interactive behaviour but because they only display frame 1 at design time they are not very suited to creating animations. You can easily embed graphics inside a movie clip to get the best of both worlds.

Creating a usable sprite

We will finish this chapter by showing how the animations you have created can be combined to create a sprite character and place this under simple user control. What we are going to need

Figure 3.15 *Creating a new pose for the turnaround*

is a standing animation, a start walk animation, a stop walk animation and a turn. Then we will need all the animations facing the opposite direction. Scene 8 shows all these actions. Each action must link to another for the animation to flow smoothly. We can move between actions using labels.

Figure 3.16 *The timeline for the cat sprite*

You can see from Figure 3.16 that the labels in the sprite animation are:

AmbientRight
StopRight
StartRight
WalkRight
AmbientLeft
StopLeft
StartLeft

43

WalkLeft
TurnLeft
TurnRight

Notice that the labels are all added to a separate layer. Although this is not strictly necessary it is the recommended method. The same layer is used for any code we are going to add. At the end of the 'AmbientLeft' and 'AmbientRight' actions we force the playback head to move back to 'AmbientLeft' or 'AmbientRight' respectively using the following 'ActionScript' statement.

```
gotoAndPlay("AmbientLeft");
```

or

```
gotoAndPlay("AmbientRight");
```

To add ActionScript, click on the frame where it is going to go, making sure that you have a keyframe in this position. If no keyframe exists then press F7 to create a blank keyframe. Then select 'Actions' from the context menu or select 'Window/Development Panels/Actions'. This opens the Actions panel. Type the command shown above.

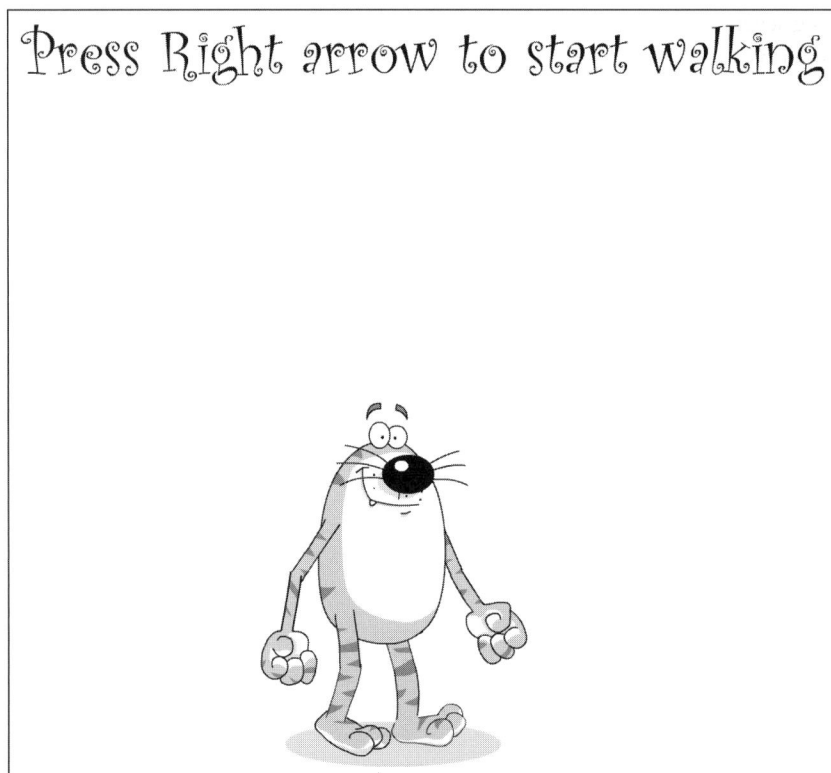

Figure 3.17 *Moving the character using the keyboard*

Most of the script simply tells the playback head to move to another label. The only code that is a little more complicated is for the loop back for the walks; in this code the keyboard is tested and if the arrow keys are not down then the playback jumps to the 'StopLeft' or 'StopRight' dependent on the current direction. Now that the animation is all prepared we need to place this inside a symbol. Open the project 'Examples/Chapter03.FatCatSprite.fla'. In this project the animations from the earlier project have all been pasted into a symbol called 'Cat'. To paste the frames, simply select them all in the timeline and choose 'Copy Frames' from the context menu. Then move to the new location and choose 'Paste Frames' from the context menu.

By pressing the left or right arrow keys the cat will now walk either left or right, turning at the edges of the screen. See if you can work out how the code works; it is very simple and after you have completed Section 3 of this book you will definitely understand exactly how it is done. But that is for a later chapter.

Summary

In this chapter we looked at how to create interesting and dynamic animation that is both quick to produce and small in file size. We looked at creating this using motion tweening and using keyframes. We looked at how to enhance a cut-out animation using additional drawn frames and how setting the properties for a 'graphic' can control the playback of these. Finally we looked at connecting several animation loops together so we can put a character under user control. In the next chapter we will look into how we can create animations using computer animation packages and import these into Flash.

4 Using CGI programs to create animation

Although Flash is a great tool for creating and editing drawn animation, another method for creating animations for Flash games is to use a computer animation program. Teaching the techniques required to use all the many computer animation programs is way beyond the scope of this book, but the principles common to all programs are briefly covered in this chapter. Having created your animation images you then need to get them into Flash. To do this you can use certain import methods such as swf generators like Vecta3D, Swift3D and Flicker, or you can use bitmap images directly from within Flash. We will consider the options, which you can then judge from both a design perspective and the impact on file size. A further option that will lead to the most highly optimized files is to hand trace the images that are created by the computer graphic (CG) programs, we will look at how, by tracing the images, you can achieve file sizes one sixth that of using trace bitmap. Along the way we will create a couple of test animations to highlight the differences between the methods in terms of both design and file size.

Character animation using a computer animation program

Since 1985 I have been the managing director of an animation company in Manchester, UK, called Catalyst Pictures. At Catalyst we have been using Lightwave for character animation since 1998. The reason is totally pragmatic; it is the cheapest program to offer all the facilities needed for TV quality character animation. Indeed I wrote a little character animation plug-in called 'Bendypoints'. As you no doubt gather I am something of a CG fan. Having spent the best part of 12 years doing drawn animation for clients who seem to like nothing better than changing things for no reason, CG is an absolute blessing. If the character changes colour or has to move faster or should be viewed from the left, right, top or bottom then the CG work has the blessing of being constantly editable. This is in marked contrast with drawn animation where almost all changes mean starting from scratch. The character that you see in this chapter was created from a clean sheet and animated in a morning by one person. There is no way that a drawn character could ever be done in that time. OK, let's look at the process.

Modelling with a computer generated imagery (CGI) program

Computer animation is a three-stage process. First, you create a virtual model of the character that you are going to animate, then you animate and finally you render. When modelling, most CGI programs show four views of the model, as you can see in Figure 4.1. These days interfaces

Figure 4.1 *Fatcat in Lightwave 7*

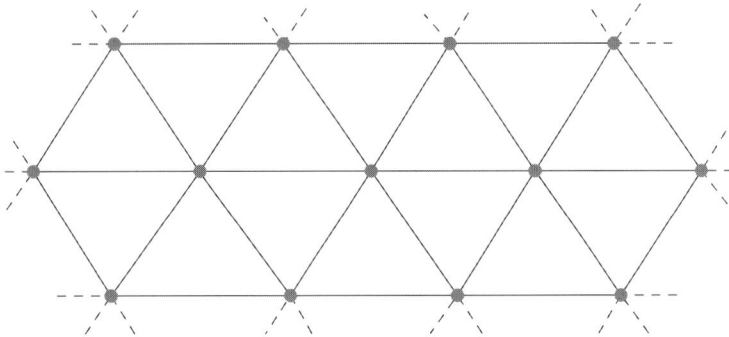

Figure 4.2 *A 'standard' triangular mesh*

are all so configurable that you can usually set up the display to show you whatever you like but the default is to show a top view of the character in the display to the top left, a front view in the bottom left, a 3D view in the top right and a side view in the bottom right. Different programs approach modelling in different ways. A few years ago there was a craze for NURBS (Non-Uniform Rational B-Splines) modellers. This craze has waned because NURBS modelling is extremely hard to do for arbitrary meshes. What is an arbitrary mesh? It is a mesh that has points that sometimes have six lines meeting and sometimes more or less. A totally standard mesh of triangles would have six lines meeting at every point.

The new craze is for polygon modellers that use subdivision surfaces. A polygon model is the simplest type of model that you can have in CG. Essentially to create a polygon model you join points in 3D space to create polygons, usually you will create either three or four sided polygons. Having created this mesh, the software uses the polygon mesh as a control cage; each polygon is converted into four polygons for each subdivision. With three or four divisions you have a smooth shape. Take a look at the first of the strip of images in Figure 4.3. Look at the point at the top of the cat's right shoulder. Notice that eight lines meet at this point, while the point immediately above it has just six lines meeting. This is possible for a polygon cage, indeed any number of lines can meet at a point, but a NURBS cage has to have the same number of lines meeting for every point.

Polygon Model   Subdivision 1   Subdivision 3

Figure 4.3 *Using subdivision*

To show you how the cat model was developed we will look at the Lightwave modeller. As a polygon modeller Lightwave is often considered the best there is and after using it you will quickly see why. The tools you use are very simple and easy to use. For the cat model we first start with a basic ball.

All polygon modellers offer a ball creator. In Lightwave you can specify how many segments around the ball there are and how many slices. Having created the ball, certain polygons are pulled around to create the inside of the mouth. If you look closely at the side view, you can see how what used to be the cap is now inside and facing in the opposite direction. As you create a polygon model you will constantly be adding and modifying the geometry. In Lightwave a useful tool is the knife, which allows you to cut through a model and so create more geometry. Another useful technique is to smooth shift a polygon. Notice in Figure 4.4 that the top right view shows two sticks pointing out of two polygons. By highlighting the polygons in this way and selecting the

Figure 4.4 *First step in creating the cat model*

Figure 4.5 *Adding the arms and legs*

Figure 4.6 *The arms and legs in place*

'Smooth Shift' tool we can add geometry. The polygon is moved in the direction of the lines and four new polygons are added to fill in the gap.

We can repeat this method several times to create the geometry that we will use for the arms and legs.

Having added the geometry we then resize the bits to fit the design we are creating. Next we need to create the hands and feet, which we do using Smooth Shift and the Knife tool to create more geometry. Again a little dragging of the points and we have a rather clumsy hand shape. One of the features of subdivision surfaces in Lightwave is that they tend to be slimmer than the control cage. So we often need to create a control cage that looks a little clumsy so that the subdivided result looks good.

Finally we can add teeth and other features.

When the geometry is complete it is time to set the colouring and surface details. For the cat we use a bitmap that is wrapped around the cat by the rendering software to create the stripes. This is called texture mapping. The texture map was created in Flash and then exported as a 'bmp' file.

When we have finished we have a model that is starting to look like a very strange cat character.

Now we need to set this up so that we can animate the character. Most computer animation programs that can animate a character use some kind of 'bone' system. Lightwave is no exception. You can create the bones using the modelling tools. The purpose of a bone is to modify the

Figure 4.7 *Creating a hand*

Figure 4.8 *The texture map that is used for the cat's body.*

Figure 4.9 *The main body for the cat model*

position of the points in a mesh. Lightwave can decide which points a bone modifies on the basis of location. A point will be controlled more by nearby bones than by distant bones. This method works for some meshes but can cause errors in character animation as limbs are so close together that the left thigh bone may influence the right thigh bone. Another technique is to create a definite relationship between a bone and certain points in the mesh. To set up a character to use bones in this way you create vertex maps; a vertex map is simply a list of vertices with each vertex getting a specified weight. A weight of 100 per cent means total control over the vertex while a weight of 50 per cent means partial control. In this way you can control exactly which bone adjusts which points and errors are eliminated.

Animating the character

Once the character is set up to use bones you have control over each part of the mesh. Another useful feature of most computer animation programs is the use of Inverse Kinematics (IK). This is just a fancy name that means that you can move the body but the feet will stay put. When animating a character, IK is a very useful feature and well worth setting up. You create a Null object (an object which is used for animating but contains no geometry so it is invisible to the camera) and this will become the target for the feet. Using IK, the feet will move to the target and can be made to rotate towards the target. The cat character uses IK on the feet, tail and eyes.

Figure 4.10 *Animating the cat character*

Figure 4.11 *The main keys in the cat's walk*

Once set up correctly you can move and rock the body and the feet stay anchored, while the eye target ensures that the eyes stay locked in a direction even as the body moves.

Animating the character uses the principles that have been outlined in the previous chapter. For a walk you put in the extremes, then the passing positions and finally the up and down positions.

53

As you get experienced using a CG program you will be able to create a short animation for a Flash game sprite very quickly.

Importing the animation into Flash

One method for creating animation that will be suitable to use in Flash is to use one of the specialist exporters. Vecta3D and Swift3D both work well with 3D Studio Max animations, while Flicker is a plugin for Lightwave. Unfortunately both these options involve you spending another US$200–US$500. If you use it regularly then no problem, but if you only use it rarely then here's a couple of techniques that you might like to consider that don't involve extra cost.

The first method is to use bitmaps in Flash. Although Flash is a vector package it does handle bitmaps fairly well. All computer animation programs have an option to save an animation as a sequence of frames. When saving the frames it is important to consider the on-screen size in pixels of the bitmaps. Unlike vector images bitmaps have a definite size, if you create the bitmaps too big then you can resize them in Flash, unfortunately this will incur a performance hit and a files size hit. Create them too small and the picture quality will be poor. If the little guy is going to be 200 pixels high then render the animation with the little guy 200 pixels high. Most computer animation packages will allow you to save off an alpha sequence, a silhouette of the animation. You need the alpha to cut out the bitmap so that an irregular-shaped bitmap can be placed over a background. An alternative approach is to render a png sequence that can contain an alpha.

When importing artwork into Flash you choose 'File/Import…'. Make sure you are on a clear layer and navigate to the folder where the colour images have been rendered. Select the first in the sequence. Flash prompts you with a dialog box.

Figure 4.12 *Multiple bitmaps dialog box*

Each consecutive file in the sequence of images is placed on a new frame of the current layer. Repeat this action on a new layer for the alpha sequence if your images use a separate alpha. If the alpha images are larger than the colour images then use scale to size them down using 'Window/Design Panels/Transform' or the context menu 'Panels/Transform'.

Make sure that 'Constrain' is checked and type in 50 per cent if the image was rendered at double the size. You will need to repeat this for each image in the sequence. Once the sequence is sized appropriately, make sure it is in exact alignment with the colour image. To do this, zoom in so that the bitmaps fill the stage area. Make the stage as big as possible by minimizing the Actions and Properties windows. Use the magnifying glass tool by dragging a rectangle around the bitmaps.

They will size so the dragged rectangle fills the stage area. If the alpha images need to be moved, use the 'Edit Multiple Frames' button in the lower left of the timeline.

Figure 4.13 *Resizing a selection*

Figure 4.14 *The Edit Multiple Frames button*

With the button selected, drag the frame range circles in the same way as using onion skinning. Finally select all the bitmaps using the arrow tool, by dragging a rectangle around them. Now move the bitmaps together so that they align with the colour bitmaps.

For each alpha bitmap use the 'Modify/Trace Bitmap…' menu option. This brings up the dialog box shown in Figure 4.15.

Figure 4.15 *The Trace Bitmap options*

The purpose of Trace Bitmap is to create a vector image from a bitmap. 'Color Threshold' defines the boundaries between colour areas; a low value means there will be lots of small areas of colour, and a high value means there will be fewer. The 'Minimum Area' option is the minimum distance between control points on a curve. 'Curve Fit' and 'Corner Threshold' set how curves will appear and when sharp corners will appear. Because we want to convert the alpha image into just black and white we can have a high colour threshold. In this example we set the minimum area to 5 pixels. By clicking OK the bitmap is turned into a vector image. Click in the white area and press the delete key to remove it. You should now be able to see the colour image on the layer below. Remove any remaining white bits and repeat for all the alpha images in the sequence.

Having completed the alpha, hide the alpha layer using the eye button for that layer. On the colour layer choose 'Modify/Break Apart' for each bitmap. The image is turned into a pixel set and can be edited in a limited fashion. Show the alpha sequence once again. For each image in the sequence, cut it out by pressing 'Ctrl + X' or selecting 'Edit/Cut', and then paste it into the colour layer using 'Ctrl + Shift + V' or 'Edit/Paste in Place'. At this point you should be up to stage three of Figure 4.16.

Figure 4.16 *Removing transparent areas from a bitmap*

Finally click on the black area and delete it. You should now have a bitmap with an irregular shape. You can achieve a similar result using the magic wand option of the Lasso tool, but in our experience you will get a better result using the alpha image option or a png sequence with an embedded alpha. When you have done this to each image in the animation sequence you can use the animation on any background. Take a look at 'Examples/Chapter04/FatCatCG.fla' to see how the animation looks. The file size for this 16-frame animation loop is 44 K.

Figure 4.17 *The final result from 'Examples/Chapter04/FatCatCG.fla'*

Using Trace Bitmap to get a cartoon effect

Figure 4.18 *Using Trace Bitmap*

Most computer animation software includes options to output the images as a non-photo realistic render. Usually this means a cartoon look. This can be a very effective way of getting animation graphics into Flash. First you set up the renderer to output using outline edges and flat colours. Then you bring this into Flash as a sequence of images. Finally by using 'Modify/Bitmap/Trace Bitmap…' on each image in the sequence they can be converted into vector images. The parameters to set for the Trace Bitmap dialog box will vary from one bitmap sequence to another, the most important being the use of 'Color Threshold': this needs to be set as high as possible while retaining the colours in the original image. You are aiming at avoiding the Trace Bitmap function retaining the anti-aliasing. Having converted the sequence of images it is usually a good idea to go through the sequence using 'Modify/Shape/Optimize…'. This brings up the dialog box in Figure 4.19.

Figure 4.19 *The Optimize Curves dialog box*

A higher setting will delete more curves. The curves are all checked and reduced based on a sophisticated algorithm. If the animation is usually shown at a small size then optimizing the frames will make a great difference to the size of the file and improve the performance. The final result is shown in Figure 4.20 and can be seen as 'Scene 2' of 'Examples/Chapter04/FatCatCG.fla'. The file size for this version is 188 K, huge by comparison to the bitmap version. Bitmaps traced in this way often result in large file sizes.

Figure 4.20 *Trace Bitmap animation sequence*

Hand tracing a computer animation

The slowest method for getting data out of a computer animation program is to import the bitmaps as before, then in a new layer hand trace the images one by one. This is a very slow process but results in by far the smallest files. Once the images have all been traced and coloured remember to delete the bitmap layer. A single image in the cat animation uses just 2634 bytes when hand traced and 12 274 when Trace Bitmap is used. If file size is the most important issue and production time is available then hand tracing cannot be bettered.

Figure 4.21 *Hand traced image from the cat animation loop*

Summary

In this chapter we looked at how an animator can use a computer animation program to create animation that can be imported into Flash. We saw that Flash does not always have to work with vector images but can use bitmap images very effectively. We saw how to best to publish and display the file so that bitmap images are seen to the best effect. What we are missing is some great background art to place these animations over. In the next chapter we will look at creating background art for our games.

5 Background art

All your games will require some kind of background artwork. Your animated characters will need to appear in some context. In this chapter we look at creating backgrounds to act as a setting for the action that takes place in your games. There are many options for creating the background artwork; most of these are aesthetic, but some are pragmatic. For example there is no point creating a fast scrolling game that will not scroll fast because of the complexity of the background artwork. Remember that Flash is essentially a vector-based package. It tries to create beautiful, anti-aliased artwork, but this image quality comes at the expense of speed, so it is your job to balance the two competing aspects of game design in Flash. Even if you have no intention of creating background art you will find the tips in this chapter useful.

The benefits of keeping the design simple

Design is such a subjective thing. One person may like something that another finds horrible. Design is connected with fashion, so the art and design of thirty years ago differs markedly from the art and design of today. But there is one thing that persistently holds true and that is that simplicity is attractive. Complex imagery can be fascinating but the understated usually wins out. Warner Brothers cartoons often had the barest of backgrounds but they were just enough to give context without detracting from the main focus of a scene. All the images in this chapter can be seen in the project file 'Examples\Chapter05\bgs.fla'. Many of the images look so much better in colour, therefore you are recommended to look at the artwork so that you are better able to judge the comments about each example. The first image we will consider is the simple tree shown in Figure 5.1. This design by Christian Holland is a perfect example of the attractive quality of simplicity: just simple flat colour and the barest suggestion of leaf structure says tree instantly, but with style and charm.

Figure 5.2 by Suzie Webb shows the surface of the moon in four colours and again just the hint of detail. The design has just enough form to evoke the place yet is understated enough so that the Flash engine is not overwhelmed by the detail.

Figure 5.3 shows another design by Suzie that again in just a few bold colours creates a terrifically sunny bedroom that has a modern yet retro fifties feel. That is another import-ant aspect of design – a clever designer can take influences from another time and place, and create artwork that has a feel of the original while being totally new and modern at the same time.

Creating games is a complex technical challenge but the user sees the design first before they are captivated by the game play. Most designers assimilate the influences around them. These can be painting and the traditional arts but it can just as well be a cooker or a chair that catches their attention. Comic book art, children's books, advertising, films, toys, newspapers, photography;

Figure 5.1 *A very simple tree*

Figure 5.2 *Moon and stars*

Figure 5.3 *A simple bedroom*

the inspiration is out there. If you are interested in design then arm yourself with a camera and capture images that inspire you. This helps you remember and may form the catalyst when faced with a new design project.

Using a keyline

Traditional comic book art uses a keyline, for reasons of convenience rather than design as the artwork has often been created with a team of people such as an artist, colourist and inker. The colourist could keep to a handful of simple colours and the inker pulled out the detail using a keyline. When creating artwork with Flash the use of a keyline adds to the work that Flash will have to do as each frame of a game is painted. Sometimes you can use a keyline to minimize the amount of colour changes; in such circumstances the use of a keyline reduces the work that Flash has to do. Figure 5.4 shows an image design by John Ashton. The bendy nature of the design is a classic cartoon signature.

Figure 5.5 takes the use of a keyline to perhaps the ultimate conclusion. This is a very complex graphic and would be totally unsuitable to form the background of a fast moving game. This particular example was used as the menu screen for a graphic adventure, so the speed of screen updates was not vital. Nevertheless as artwork becomes more and more complex it may be

Figure 5.4 *Incorporating line in the design*

Figure 5.5 *A complex background*

better to export the image as a bitmap from Flash and then import the bitmap as a replacement for the vector art. A bitmap can be as complex as you want and yet make no difference to the speed of updating. A bitmap is still slower than a *simple* vector graphic, but a bitmap is much faster than *complex* vector art. If the image is never scaled, then you will not suffer a big reduction in picture quality moving from vector to bitmap. If, however, you intend to use scaling in the game then you will get much better imagery using vector art. Commercial artists have always had to balance the problems of delivery and aesthetic and Flash artists have very similar problems.

When you create your background art make sure that it does not overshadow your characters; make sure that they have the space to move around and are not overconfined by the design. Also consider using several layers so that your characters can appear from behind a section of the background. Figure 5.6 shows a simple medieval room set; the design allows the central magician character to walk up the stairs, disappearing behind the wall as he climbs the spiral steps. The design incorporates the chimney for the magician's cauldron on a separate layer so that the character can go behind this element of the set, giving extra depth to the animation.

Figure 5.6 *Give your characters space*

Importing scanned artwork and artwork created in other paint programs

Remember that you are not limited to creating your artwork in Flash alone. Figure 5.7 shows a background that has been hand painted with watercolours. Not a computer in site! The final result was scanned and imported as a bitmap. This technique has the feel of a children's book illustration and gives a texture to the graphic that is sometimes missing in vector art. Of course there are numerous paint programs that allow you to create textured graphics directly on your PC if you prefer.

Figure 5.7 *Using a scanned painted background*

Using very simple designs when creating a scrolling background

If your game is going to use a scrolling background then you must be very sparing with the detail to maintain a high frame rate. Scrolling backgrounds need a frame rate of at least 30 fps to look smooth and 50 fps would be preferable. Getting the frame rate to be maintained at this level requires developers to use all their ingenuity to minimize screen redrawing. Flash will run faster if it is only drawing a small section of the screen as opposed to the whole stage. Sometimes the best technique for achieving a high frame rate is to have a background where most of the design remains static. Figure 5.8 shows an overhead view of a section of road. This background was used for a game with a man running along the pavement. In the black and white version shown here it may be difficult to see the image as a road and you are advised to look at the colour version on the CD, which is much easier to understand. The narrow double line forms the edge of the road; two yellow lines indicate a no-parking zone in the UK where this game was first used. The strip to the left is green grass. Reading from left to right, the stripes are grass, pavement, road markings and road. None of these elements would change if you were flying over the road in a helicopter, so to give the illusion of movement we need an item to move down the screen. In the game we used a fence between houses, fire hydrants and post boxes. These moved down as the player stayed in the middle of the screen, suggesting movement along the road. Because only a small area of the screen is changing the frame rate is maintained even on a slower computer.

Figure 5.8 *Keeping it simple to allow for scrolling*

Using abstract imagery

Another interesting technique for creating backgrounds is to use abstract imagery or imagery derived from type. Figure 5.9 shows the background of a game that featured the pop group 'Steps'. At first glance you may well have missed that the shapes at the top of screen form the word steps. A second look makes it easy to see the letters. The graphic that forms the word was used repeatedly with a fading effect to create the remainder of the background design.

Figure 5.9 *Using an abstract background design*

The advantage of using a single symbol is that the file size will be reduced and the overall design is strengthened by the lack of complexity. Using type symbolically you can very quickly create lots of background designs.

Building complex art using symbols

Symbols are very useful when creating a background. Figure 5.10 shows the inside of a student's fridge. Students are notorious for avoiding housework. In this illustration it is years since the fridge was given a healthy spring clean and as a result the fridge is beginning to have a life of its own. Mould and curry splatters are mixed with spilled bean cans and other monstrosities. Creating this disgusting scene required lots of research! The mould growing at the edges was created from a single symbol. By combining the symbol several times, stretching it and altering the alpha, an effect is created that looks impossible using just radial or linear gradients.

Figure 5.11 shows another clever use of symbols; this evocative background uses single cloud and pole graphics that are flipped, squashed and stretched to form the mysterious landscape. The background was used for a fun email game that features two Ninja Warriors facing each other in a deadly game. It is one of many great games to be found at mohsye.com.

Figure 5.10 *Using symbols to add texture*

Figure 5.11 *Keeping the file size small using symbols*

Using computer graphic packages to create the background art

Figure 5.12 *Using a computer graphic background*

Another very effective way to create background art for your games is to use a computer graphic package. The image in Figure 5.12 shows a simple set created in the Lightwave 3D package. The image is pre-rendered to the correct size for the game then imported as a bitmap file. 3D packages are great for putting together background designs or buttons. You can very quickly create detailed environments using just a few interesting textures and some simple meshes. If you are regularly creating artwork for games then you are advised to spend some time learning a 3D package. After meddling with a few different packages we settled on Lightwave, which provides the best combination of modelling tools, animation and rendering at a reasonable price.

Using tiled backgrounds

If your background uses repeating elements then consider creating the background as sections, importing each section as a 'png' bitmap. The advantage of the 'png' format is that it is lossless and can incorporate an alpha channel.

Bitmaps come in many different file formats. A Flash developer is likely to use jpeg, bmp, gif and png. The 'eps' format is not a bitmap, instead it is a vector format, but an eps image can contain a bitmap; this is not recommended because the bitmap image is resolution dependent while the eps is regarded as resolution independent. Remember that an eps is only truly resolution independent when it only contains vector elements. A list of advantages and disadvantages of the different formats is given in Table 5.1.

Table 5.1 *Advantages and disadvantages of different file formats used for importing and exporting image data*

Format	Advantages	Disadvantages	Flat colour	Half tone
Jpg	Small file size	The compression method loses detail from the image. Can have strange speckled artefacts	Likely to create strange artefacts	Best for photographic images
Bmp	Big files	Only the most basic of compression methods	Reasonable choice, bmp images can have 16, 256, or 16 m colours	Will result in a very big file
Png	Uses a clever compression that loses no information in the image. Can incorporate an alpha channel	Compression method will not create files as small as jpegs	Not the best choice	Good choice for images that need to be maintained at optimum quality
Gif	A relatively small file size can be achieved without losing information in the image	Cannot use 24 bit palette, the maximum number of different colours in a gif file is limited to 256	Best choice for flat colour images that need a high level of compression	Not suitable
Eps	Vector format ensures resolution independence. An eps can contain a bitmap; the bitmap will not be resolution independent	Not suitable for bitmaps	The best choice if the image is in vector format	Not suitable

The image in Figure 5.13 was created by first creating some brick tiles, the horns, the round window and the arch. Each element was imported as a png and combined in Flash. This results in a smaller file size and allows you as a developer to create different backgrounds using a limited number of tiles. Tiled backgrounds were very popular when computers had more limited facilities and are not used as often these days, but they do offer flexibility and small file sizes so they should be considered for some game formats.

Figure 5.13 *Using photo compositing to build the background*

Figure 5.14 *Using a photograph*

Using photography

Sometimes the simplest way to create a great background is to go outside and photograph the real world. For some games this can give a quick to produce and effective result.

Summary

There are many ways to add a background to your game. You can create the background entirely in Flash or entirely in another package and import it. In this chapter we looked at some of the options available and examined why certain approaches may not be effective for particular games. You are now armed with the graphic skills necessary to start creating your games. Now we will turn our attention to writing the code.

6 Creating artwork for mobile devices

At the time of writing, December 2003, mobile devices are finally reaching the processing and display capabilities that make a Flash player viable. Despite this, designers still need to be aware of huge limitations when creating artwork for these little computers. Things that you may take for granted on a desktop machine are simply not possible on most mobile devices. In this chapter we will look first at the types of devices that your animation may be seen on. We will look at the problems of different colour spaces to the familiar full colour space you are probably used to when developing content for a desktop. While we are looking at mobile devices we will also consider the user input options and how these vary from device to device. Mobile devices are definitely here to stay and it is going to be many years before they match the capabilities of today's desktop so it is important to know how to milk the best from them.

Flash enabled devices

Figure 6.1 *Flash enabled devices*

Flash is now available on PocketPCs, Sony CLIÉs, many mobile phones and set-top boxes. The list of devices that will run Flash grows almost daily. Macromedia keep updating the device area of their

Website and you are advised to check in regularly at www.macromedia.com/software/devices. Each device presents different challenges for the designer and programmer. Macromedia provides content development kits (CDKs) for the devices that the developer can target. Step one in creating any content is first to be aware of the target platform, then to download the appropriate CDK, if a template is not already available. Flash MX 2004 Professional comes with several templates already installed and ready to be used. To use an existing template simply use 'File/New…' then click the 'Templates' tab in the dialog box that opens. A list of the available templates is shown under the 'Mobile Devices' option in the list box. Figure 6.2 shows the dialog box being used to create a template for a DoCoMo device.

Figure 6.2 *Starting a new document using an existing device template*

There are huge differences between devices, for example the PocketPC has a minimum display resolution of 240×320 pixels and 16 bit colour. The processor available in these machines runs at a minimum of 206 MHz. The lowest spec devices will have a processor that is at best capable of 25 per cent of this performance. For this reason starting with the current release of Flash you can target the standard Flash player or a stripped-down version that is referred to as Flash Lite. For many of the lower spec machines only the 'Lite' version is available. This makes substantial differences to the ActionScript you may write but makes less of a dent in the development of the graphic content. Although Flash scales well when used on a desktop, it is invariably best to tailor the content to the target resolution. Figure 6.3 shows a highly detailed image. The image uses 4836 curves for the background and 452 curves for the helicopter and stunt man.

Figure 6.3 *Developing a PocketPC game*

The project was developed as a simple demonstration; you can open it as 'Examples/ Chapter06/detail01.fla'. Some simple ActionScript sends the helicopter across the screen and back. As it does this it updates the fps (frames per second) display every 10 screen updates. The movie should run at 20 fps. When transferred to a 200 MHz PocketPC it dropped to just 2 fps as the helicopter reached the middle of the screen. At this point Flash has to redraw all the anti-aliased lines for the background behind the helicopter and the helicopter itself. So what can we do to improve the frame rate? 'Examples/Chapter06/detail02.fla' shows exactly the same scene. This time both the background image and the helicopter are bitmap images. This time on the same machine the frame rate stayed up at 8 fps. If we also set the quality to medium, then the frame rate maintained 12 fps. On the small screen with a reduced colour depth there is little discernible difference between the two except for frame rate. Creating the bitmap images is very simple:

1   Create the content in Flash as you would normally.
2   Use 'File/Export/Export Image...'.

3   Choose 'png' as the file format and choose a folder and filename.

4   Set the 'Resolution' to 'Match Screen' by pressing the button.

5   For 'Include' choose 'Full Document Size'.

6   For 'Colors' if you want the image to have transparency then include the alpha channel. If not just use the 24 bit setting.

7   Then save the current project with a new name.

8   Import the 'png' image and replace the vector image with the bitmap one.

Figure 6.4 *Exporting an image*

Bitmap images do not resize well, so it is very important to create the images to the correct size. If you change your mind about the size then return to the vector version and resize this. In some projects we retain the vector image as a 'guide' layer. These do not export when you 'Publish' the movie, but you can edit the content of the layer. Using this method you can retain the flexibility to edit your images while keeping the speed of updates that is so important when creating games.

Although the PocketPC has the processing power to cope with animated games, other Flash enabled devices are more suited to games that do not require regular screen updates. When designing for mobile phones, for example, at the time of writing the games you develop should be of the board or card game style rather than dynamic.

12- and 16-bit colour

When you are developing content on a desktop computer the colour palette you use is designed for 24-bit colour. A bit is the minimum unit on a computer. A bit can be either on or off. With one bit you can specify just two values, 0 or 1. But if you join two bits together then you can specify four different values. As you add each subsequent bit you double the amount of data that can be specified.

Table 6.1 *Number of colours possible with different bit counts*

Bits	Colours
1	2
4	16
8	256
12	4096
16	65536
24	16777216

Figure 6.5 *Specifying a colour using hexadecimal*

Notice that a 24-bit device has over 16 million different possible colours while a 12-bit device has only just over 4000, rather than half of 16 million. But we are developing using a 24-bit environment, so how does this conversion occur? On a 24-bit machine there is 8-bit resolution for the red, green and blue colours. See Chapter 12 for more information on how colours are specified. Eight bits gives a total of 256 different values for each channel. On a 12-bit device there is only 4-bit resolution per channel or 16 different options. When doing the conversion the bottom four bits of each channel of the 24-bit image are effectively set to 0.

Take a look at Figure 6.5, which shows the Flash MX 2004 colour mixer dialog. In the bottom left there is an input field where a colour can be specified using numbers and letters. This combination of numbers and letters is a *hexadecimal* representation. Each number or letter corresponds to 4 bits of data. The six different letters or numbers specify the 24-bit image using the following code '#RRGGBB', starting from the left the first two are the red channel then the green and finally the blue. The numbers go in the following order 0,1,2,3,4,5,6,7,8,9,A,B,C,D,E,F with F being the maximum possible value for 4 bits, i.e. the same as decimal 15. To move from 24-bit colour space to a 12-bit colour space, every second value must be zero. As far as a 12-bit device is concerned, the colour #876543 is the same as #806040. Try entering some values in Flash and comparing the difference on a 24- or 32-bit monitor. There is a significant difference. But the main place where the conversion will be noticeable is when using gradients. All gradients will appear significantly banded on a 12-bit machine. Take a look at Figure 6.6; here you can see a Nokia 3650 displaying a banded gradient and a smooth gradient.

The smooth gradient was achieved by converting a 24-bit bitmap of the gradient to 12-bit using dithering. At this small size the dithering is not noticeable and is a suitable way of converting an image if a gradient is essential. You are advised, however, to avoid gradients where possible. You will also find that fades and transparency will affect the performance on the mobile device. Again it may be better to avoid alpha transparency and to reveal new content using wipes rather than fades.

User input on mobile devices

User input is handled very differently on mobile devices.

PocketPC

A PocketPC has a pointing device but no cursor. So for this reason the rollover event is meaningless when creating buttons, you only need to consider the default image and the image to use if the button is pressed. Just as with a desktop machine you can have Input text boxes and embedded fonts.

Mobile phones

Mobile phones have generally less screen space, no pointing device and no such thing as an Input text box. Flash Lite for i-mode, DoCoMo mobile phones, uses three keys for navigation: Up, Down and Select. The Left and Right keys are reserved for the i-mode browser. These three keys correspond to the Shift+Tab, Tab, and Enter keys on the desktop versions of the Flash Player. The keys 0,1,2,3,4,5,6,7,8,9,★, and # are also available. These correspond to the same keys on the desktop versions of the Flash Player.

Figure 6.6 *Gradients and mobile devices*

Ten top tips for migrating content from desktop to mobile

Not all content that you have created for a desktop will port to a mobile device but there are some golden rules to follow when creating artwork:

1. Use bitmaps for complex artwork.
2. Convert bitmaps to the correct colour depth for the device.
3. Don't use gradients.
4. Don't use alpha transparency.
5. Avoid full screen redraws, such as occur when fading up a scene or doing a full screen tween.
6. Set the quality to medium.
7. Use 'Modify/Shape/Optimize...' to reduce the number of curves in a scene to the minimum.
8. Don't have an outline around a fill unless absolutely necessary.
9. Simplify detail where possible.
10. Use a thick line instead of a fill if possible.

You should also limit the number of simultaneous tweens. Don't tween symbols that have alpha levels that are not fully opaque (less than 100 per cent). Avoid large masks, extensive motion, alpha blending, extensive gradients and complex vectors. Experiment with combinations of tweens, key frame animations and ActionScript-driven movement to produce the most efficient results. Test animations frequently on your target phones whenever possible and remember that 505i phones have a maximum swf file size limit of just 20 K.

Creating content for mobile devices

In 2003 the PocketPC market went over 10 million units and mobile phones were selling at the rate of over 400 million units per year. Although only a handful of the mobile phones are Flash enabled it is still a huge potential market waiting for the fun distraction of an enjoyable game. In Section 4 we will look in more detail at how to make games for these devices but in this chapter we are considering the artwork implications. 'Examples/Chapter06/Conker01.fla' is a short animation developed originally for the web. At only 56 K it is totally suited to the PocketPC but it uses gradients and was originally designed to be seen at a resolution of 550 × 400. On the PocketPC this is reduced to 240 × 268. A PocketPC has a full screen resolution of 240 × 320, in general. When title and status bars are included this reduces the screen space to 240 × 268. The first step in the optimization process was to resize the artwork, simply by turning the entire animation into a symbol and resizing the lot. Then any artwork that ran off the edge throughout the animation was deleted. The next step is to go through any complex artwork or symbols and reduce the number of curves to suit the new screen size. Choose 'Modify/Shape/Optimize...'. This opens the dialog box shown in Figure 6.7.

Figure 6.7 *Optimizing artwork*

Using this technique a saving in the complexity of the artwork of around 35 per cent is not unusual. This could mean a doubling of the frame rate. When doing the conversion it was also seen that the large bulk of leaves that falls around frame 370, remains static from frame 380, but the artist had copied the symbol on consecutive frames because some small leaves continued to drift down. By moving the static content onto a layer that was unchanging Flash only 'thinks' about the artwork that has a new keyframe on each move of the playback head. Don't make Flash do things it doesn't need to do. After all the changes the file size had reduced to just 22 K and the sustained frame rate had doubled. The overall optimization took around just 10 minutes and was well worth the effort.

Figure 6.8 *Optimizing the animation 'Examples/Chapter06/Conker01.fla'*

Summary

If Macromedia get their way then Flash enabled devices will be ubiquitous. In this chapter we introduced some of the issues involved in creating content for these devices. If this is a field that interests you then check out Section 4 where the topics related to mobile devices are fully developed.

Section 2

Action

Having developed the animation we now look at how to add interactivity to this art using ActionScript.

7 So what is a variable?

After the first blistering introduction to ActionScript in Chapter 1, we now take a more leisurely stroll through the basics of programming, starting with variables. The most fundamental aspect of programming is the ability to store and retrieve data. In essence all computer programming involves the manipulation of data. If your game uses a moving animated character running, jumping and shooting, you will need to store the position, size and action of the character as the game develops, as this information is not static; it varies as the user plays the game. In this chapter we will look at how a variable can be used to store lots of different types of information including the data you would need for your character. Some data will be numeric, while other bits of data will be text. We will look at how to set a variable's value and how to get the value stored in a variable. We will look at using chunks of variables in a structure called an *array*. Throughout we will include many small examples to get you into entering ActionScript.

What is ActionScript?

ActionScript is a list of instructions written as text, in a very specific way. Before the program runs this text is converted into a series of codes; when the Flash Player reads the codes, it performs the instruction in an unambiguous way. For example, if it found the instruction:

```
x = 23;
```

Flash would allocate a little piece of memory that it could refer to later and assign the value 23 to this location. You could retrieve the contents of the variable simply by referring to it, therefore

```
trace(x);
```

would result in the image shown in Figure 7.1.

The Output window opens automatically whenever a 'trace' statement is executed.

> It is possible to stop the trace action working by altering the 'Publish Settings'. Select 'File/Publish Settings...' and you will see the dialog box shown in Figure 7.2. Notice the check box for 'Omit Trace Actions'. If this is checked then you will not see any trace output in the Output window.

You will learn in Chapter 10 about where to place your code. Flash is very flexible, allowing you to enter ActionScript in many different places; in this chapter we will restrict all entries to

Figure 7.1 *Tracing variables using the Output window*

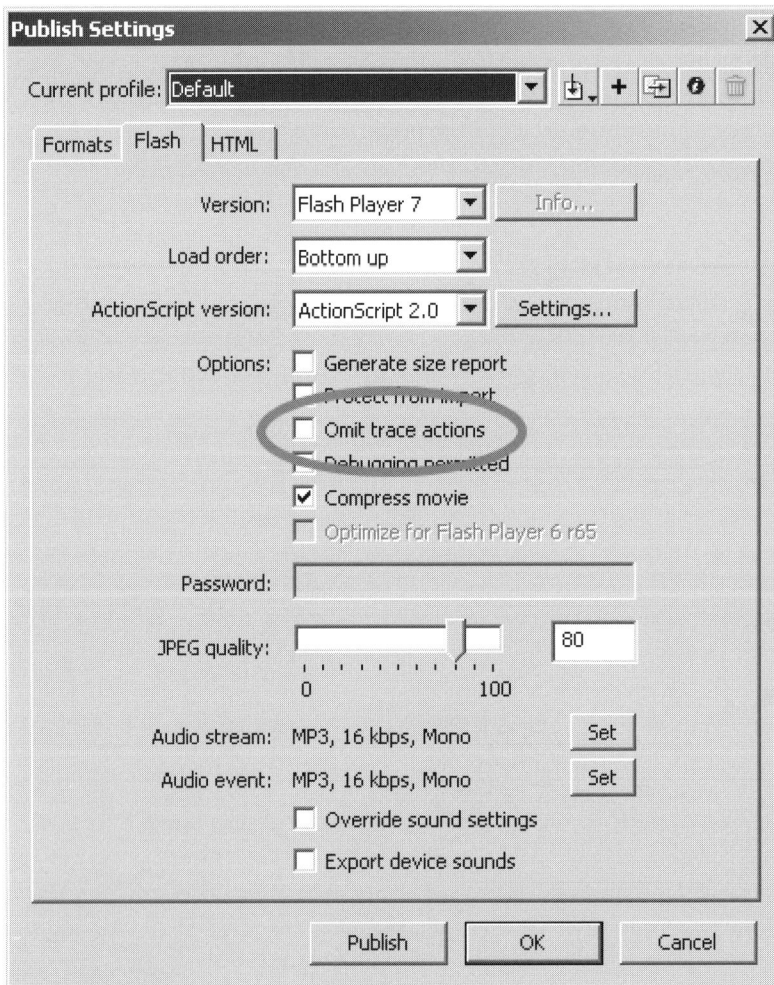

Figure 7.2 *Publish settings*

a frame action. As you experiment with code, you are encouraged to keep one layer of the timeline for frame actions; do not place frame actions in any other layer. To add a frame action, follow these simple steps:

1 Create the empty layer that you will use for frame actions. If the layer already exists then skip this step and go on to stage 2.
2 Click on the timeline in the frame action layer at the frame in which you want to add, or edit, the action. Open the Action panel using 'Window/Development Panels/Action', by pressing F9 or by selecting the arrow icon shown in Figure 7.3, which is found in the Properties panel.

Figure 7.3 *Icon used to open the Action panel*

3 The panel shown in Figure 7.4 opens. The pane in the top left shows the many objects and functions you can use. The pane in the bottom left gives an overview of your movie. For the purposes of this chapter and to keep things as simple as possible click the small left arrow on the divide between the left and right panes. This will close the left–hand panes.
4 Enter code simply by typing into the biggest pane. Remember every line of ActionScript finishes with a semi–colon.

Figure 7.4 *Entering ActionScript for a frame action*

Flash will often help by opening a popup list of options. For example if you enter 'Math.' then you will get the popup shown in Figure 7.5. This lists the various possibilities available by using the built-in Math object. More about objects later.

Figure 7.5 *The popup that appears when you type 'Math.'*

What is a variable?

There are lots of ways to visualize a variable if the concept seems strange. One suggestion is to think of a telephone book. If you have a friend called Jim and his telephone number is 01234 567890 then you would put the number 01234 567890 under the name Jim in your book. Whenever you want to know what Jim's telephone number is you look at the name Jim in the book and find out the number is 01234 567890. But suppose that Jim changes house and gets a new number. Perhaps the new number is now 09876 543210. You simply cross out the old number and put the new one in its place. Using the name Jim you can check the number, and this is how you use a variable in a computer program.

To create a variable in Flash you can simply use it for the first time:

```
bigfeet = 14;
```

This would create a variable called 'bigfeet' and set its current value to 14. Used in this way the variable 'bigfeet' would exist throughout the life of the movie. An alternative is to declare the variable:

```
var bigfeet = 14;
```

Used in this way as soon as the script exits the value of 'bigfeet' is deleted. Flash MX 2004 has introduced a new concept for ActionScript and one that you are encouraged to use, strict data typing. Strict data typing has many benefits; often a hard-to-find problem with a game can result in confusion over the type of a variable. If you think your variable is a number and Flash thinks it is text then testing to see if it is greater than a certain value will often fail. But if you use strict data typing then Flash will inform you if you use the variable in a way that it is not expecting.

```
1 var bigfeet:Number = 14;
2 //Try assigning a string to it
3 bigfeet = "Very big feet";
```
Listing 7.1

Listing 7.1 shows how to use strict data typing. The variable is declared in line 1 using the 'var' keyword then the variable name followed by a colon and then the data type, in this case a number. Now Flash knows that this variable is to be used as a number. The next line starts with '//' which Flash interprets to mean that the text that follows is ignored because it is a comment. In line 3 the variable assigned a section of text, which in programming is called a string. Flash knows that a string is not a number and when you run the movie it displays the error shown Figure 7.6 in the Output window.

Figure 7.6 *Error message displayed after using Listing 7.1*

Doing things with numbers

Now that you know how to create a variable, let's use that information to do some simple arithmetic. No, don't groan; images and animation will come soon, but for now let's concentrate on easy manipulation of simple variables.

```
1 var x:Number = 10;
2 var y:Number = 7;
3 trace( x + y);
```
Listing 7.2

The ActionScript in Listing 7.2 will give a result of 17 in the Output window. There are many operations that you can do using numbers,

Table 7.1 *Using symbolic operators with* $x = 10$ *and* $y = 7$

Operation	Description	Example
++	Increment	$x + +$ results in 11
$- -$	Decrement	$x - -$ results in 9
+	Addition	$x + y$ results in 17
$-$	Subtraction	$x - y$ results in 3
*	Multiplication	$x * y$ results in 70
/	Division	x / y results in 1.42857143
%	Modulo, remainder after division	$x \% y$ results in 3
|	Or	$x \| y$ results in 15
&	And	$x \& y$ results in 2
\	XOR	$x \backslash y$ results in 13
$\ll$	Shift left	$x \ll y$ results in 1280
$\gg$	Shift right	$x \gg y$ results in 0
$+ =$	Add and assign	$x+ = y$ sets x to 17
$- =$	Subtract and assign	$x- = y$ sets x to 3
$* =$	Multiply and assign	$x* = y$ sets x to 70
$/ =$	Divide and assign	$x/ = y$ sets x to 1.42857143
$\% =$	Modulo and assign	$x\% = y$ sets x to 3
$\| =$	Or and assign	$x\| = y$ sets x to 15
$\& =$	And and assign	$x\& = y$ sets x to 2
$\wedge =$	Xor and assign	$x\wedge = y$ sets x to 13
$\ll=$	Shift left and assign	$x\ll= y$ sets x to 1280
$\gg=$	Shift right and assign	$x\gg= y$ sets x to 0

Some operators are obvious whereas others need some explanation.

% (modulo) operator

This returns the remainder after division. In this example 10 divided by 7 gives 1 remainder 3 so the value returned will be 3.

Binary numbers

These numbers use only the symbols 1 and 0. The value of the first column (furthest to the right) is 1, the second column is 2, the third is 4. Each column is double the previous. Therefore the binary representation of 10 and 7 are

$$1010 \ (8 + 0 + 2 + 0)$$
$$0111 \ (0 + 4 + 2 + 1)$$

|(Or) operator

This combines the bits that make up the number. If either bit is set then the resulting bit is set.

1010 Or'ed with 0111 gives 1111 which is $8 + 4 + 2 + 1$ or 15.

&(And) operator

This combines the bits that make up the number. If both bits are set then the resulting bit is set.

1010 And'ed with 0111 gives 0010, which is $0 + 0 + 2 + 0$, or 2.

^(Xor) operator

This combines the bits that make up the number. If one bit is set but not both then the resulting bit is set.

1010 Xor'ed with 0111 gives 1101, which is $8 + 4 + 0 + 1$ or 13.

≪(left shift) operator

This moves the bits that make up the number.

1010 left shifted 7 places gives 10100000000 or $1024 + 0 + 256$ or 1280.

≫(right shift) operator

This moves the bits that make up the number.

1010 right shifted 7 places gives 0000, the bits are left to zero after shifting only 4 places so 7 still leaves the result as zero.

All the operators that include the equals sign simply do the same but assign the result to the variable on the left. 'Examples/Chapter07/Variables03.fla' shows all these operators in action. For most programs in the book we will just be using the simple arithmetic operators but it is useful to know how they all work.

A special kind of number

If you use

```
1 var ready:Boolean = false;
2 var x:Number = 10;
3 trace(ready);
4 ready = x>5;
5 trace(ready);
```

Listing 7.3

Here we use a special kind of number, a Boolean.

> Booleans are named after George Boole who was born in Lincoln, England, on 2 November 1815. In 1854, he published his greatest and most influential work, *An Investigation into the Laws of Thought, on Which are Founded the Mathematical Theories of Logic and Probabilities*, in which he brilliantly combined algebra with logic, the foundation of today's digital computers.

A Boolean can have only one of two values: it is either true or false. In the short Listing 7.3 we first set the Boolean variable 'ready' to false. Then we set a variable x to the value 10. In line 3 we trace the value of 'ready' to the Output window. At this stage the variable has the value 'false'. Then we assign to 'ready' the value $(x > 5)$. This reads as x is greater than 5. Clearly 10 is greater than 5 so the statement is true. When we again trace 'ready' in line 5 it now has the value true. Booleans are used extensively in game logic and we will meet them many times in this book.

Creating and using string variables

A third kind of variable is a string variable. A string is simply a sequence of characters. ActionScript contains lots of useful methods for combining and accessing the characters in a string. You can create a variable that describes someone's name:

```
var name:String = "Steve";
```

Or you can create a variable that can store a sentence:

```
var saying:String = "The early bird catches the worm";
```

'Example/Chapter07/Variables04.fla' shows how you can use several of the methods of the string object. Listing 7.4 shows the code:

```
1  var person:String = "Steve";
2  var desc:String = "The winner is ";
```

```
3   trace(desc + person);
4   trace("The length of desc is " + desc.length);
5   trace("The third letter of person is " + person.charAt(2));
6   trace("A sub string of desc is " + desc.substr(4, 6));
7   trace(desc.split(" "));
8   trace("The word winner is found in desc at " + desc.indexOf("winner"));
9   trace("The code for the first letter in person is " +
10      person.charCodeAt(0));
11  trace("The value of char code 65 is " + String.fromCharCode(65));
12  trace("Desc as all caps is " + desc.toUpperCase());
```
Listing 7.4

Combining strings

Lines 1 and 2 declare and initialize two string objects. Line 3 combines the two. A '+' operator when used with strings simply joins the two strings together. The output in this case would be:

```
The winner is Steve
```

The length of a string

Line 4 uses a property of a string, namely its length. If you count the characters in the string desc you'll find there are 14 of them so the trace from line 4 gives:

```
The length of desc is 14
```

```
▼ Output
  The winner is Steve
  The length of desc is 14
  The third letter of person is e
  A sub string of desc is winner
  The,winner,is,
  The word winner is found in desc at 4
  The code for the first letter in person is 83
  The value of char code 65 is A
  Desc as all caps is THE WINNER IS
```

Figure 7.7 *Output from 'Examples/Chapter07/Variables04.fla'*

Extracting a letter from a string

Line 5 uses the method 'charAt' to extract a single letter from the string, 'person'. The number in the brackets is a parameter passed to the method, the index of the letter to extract, starting with zero as the first letter from the left. The letter with index 2 in 'Steve' is the first 'e'.

Extracting a section from a string

Another useful method is 'substr'; this takes two parameters, first where to start extracting as an index and the second the number of characters to extract. Using the parameters 4 as the index and 6 as the length from the string, 'desc', gives the sub-string 'winner'.

Dividing up a string

The method 'split' can be used to divide a string into separate letters or words. It takes a single parameter, in this example we use ' ' (a single space). The return value is a list of all the words that we can display, separated by commas using the trace command as shown in line 7.

Finding a string inside another

Line 8 shows how to search through a string to find another. It returns either the index to the sub-string or –1 if the sub-string cannot be found.

Getting the code value of a character

Characters in a string are given code values based on the ASCII character codes. You can find a table of codes at http://www.asciitable.com/. Line 9 shows how this can be done.

Setting a character using the code value

Line 11 shows how you can use the method 'fromCharCode' which takes a single parameter, the ASCII code and returns a string. In this example using the ASCII value 65 returns a capital letter A.

Converting case

The string object contains methods to convert the entire string to either upper (toUpperCase) or lower (toLowerCase) case.

Although strings are usually used to store textual information, they can be useful to store more complex data in a very compact way. For example the string

W12U6T

could be used to represent walk forward 12 paces (W12), then up 6 steps (U6) and finally turn (T). A simple code reader could extract this information using the string methods. In this way you could create complex new actions using a simple code formula.

Placing variables into objects

Sometimes it is useful to keep a block of variables together, and one way is to create an Object.

```
1   var Clown:Object = new Object();
2   var RingMaster:Object = new Object();
3   var Elephant:Object = new Object();
4
5   Clown.feet = 14;
6   RingMaster.feet = 10;
7   Elephant.feet = 21;
8
9   trace(Clown.feet);
10  trace(RingMaster.feet);
11  trace(Elephant.feet);
```
Listing 7.5

Listing 7.5 shows how we can create an object. This can be a placeholder for any data that we choose. In this instance we create three objects and assign them to variables 'Clown', 'RingMaster' and 'Elephant'. Then we set the feet size and finally we display this size using a 'trace' statement.

You can access an object's variables by using the dot operator. You give the object's name, a dot and finally the variable name you wish to access.

Creating a new class

New with Flash MX 2004 is the ability to create new classes. Although these are easier to work with if you have the professional version you can work with them with the standard version. For the standard version you must work with a text editor to create the class files. In Flash MX 2004 Professional you can write them directly in the editor. The most important feature is to make sure the class name and the name of the file match and that it is in same directory as your current project file.

'Examples/Chapter07/Performer.as' is a class file. All class files have the extension 'as', short for ActionScript.

```
1   class Performer {
2       var feet:Number;
3       var job:String;
4
5   //Constructor function
6   function Performer (myJob:String, myFeet:Number){
7       job = myJob;
8       feet = myFeet;
9       if (job==undefined) job = "Jack of all trades";
10      if (feet==undefined) feet = 9;
```

```
11  }
12
13  //Method to return property values
14  function dump():String {
15      return("Hi, my job is " + job +
16              " and my feet are " + feet + " inches long.");
17  }
18 }
```
Listing 7.6

A class definition always starts with the keyword 'class', followed by the name you have chosen for the class. All remaining code is between curly brackets. Any variables the class contains are usually declared next along with their data type. A class usually will have what is called a 'constructor' function. A function is simply a block of code that is given a name; following the name will be ordinary brackets. Contained inside the brackets will be none or several parameters separated by commas. The code for the function is contained between curly brackets. A function can return a value; if so, it is a good idea to specify the type of value that is to be returned. If you don't actually create a constructor function for your class then Flash will create one for you. In this simple example we have the class 'Performer' that contains two variables, 'feet' and 'job'. It has one method 'dump', which returns a string description of the current instance of the class. It also has a constructor function; these must have the same name as the class. So having created the code that defines the class, how do we use it?

Using a user-defined class

```
1 var Clown:Performer = new Performer("Clown", 14);
2 var RingMaster:Performer = new Performer("Ringmaster", 10);
3 var Helper:Performer = new Performer();
4
5 trace(Clown.dump());
6 trace(RingMaster.dump());
7 trace(Helper.dump());
```
Listing 7.7

First it is vital that the syntax for the class definition is correct, second the class definition file must be in the same folder as the 'fla' and must have the same name as the class being defined with an 'as' extension. As long as these simple rules are kept to, the use of a class is simplicity itself. You use the 'var' keyword followed by the variable name and a colon. After the colon place your class name. Then use the equals sign, the keyword 'new' and then the name of the class, open brackets and then set the parameters. In this example we first give the 'job' name and then the feet size. Notice that at line 3 of Listing 7.7 we pass no parameters. This is OK and Flash will set the values to undefined. Lines 9 and 10 of Listing 7.6 set the values to a default value if undefined. In lines

5 to 7 we output the current value of each instance of the class using the class-defined method 'dump'. The final output is shown in Figure 7.8.

Figure 7.8 *Output from 'Example/Chapter07/Variables06.fla'*

Using user-defined classes is a very robust and worthwhile technique and it is for this reason that I have chosen to include it in this early chapter, we will find out more about using classes in later chapters, particularly Chapter 10.

How decimal values differ from integers

Numbers come in literally an infinite amount of values. Unfortunately computers, although fast and capable of storing very large and very small values, cannot store an infinite number of values. The way that developers have got around the limitations inherent in computer storage is to use two distinct types of number – *integers* and *floats*. The best thing about integers is that they are exact.

$$2 * 12 = 24$$

The '*' symbol is used to represent multiplication on a computer, not the × symbol. But the range of values that can be stored in an integer is limited; not very limited as you can use integers to store values into the millions, but not into the trillions. Similarly, integers are not very useful if your numbers all range between zero and one. For the very big and the very small you can use floats. There is a potential problem, however, as floats are not exact. They seem exact, but they are not. Suppose you multiply 0.01 by itself lots of times. The number will get smaller:

```
  0 = 0.0001
  1 = 0.00001 or 1e-6
  2 = 0.0000001 or 1e-8
  3 = 0.000000001 or 1e-10
  4 = 0.00000000001 or 1e-12
...
152 = 1e-308
```

```
153 = 9.99999999999998e-311
154 = 9.9999999998466e-313
155 = 9.99999999963881e-315
156 = 9.99999983659715e-317
157 = 9.99998748495601e-319
158 = 9.99988867182684e-321
159 = 9.88131291682494e-323
160 = 0
```

After the 160th iteration, the value becomes zero. This may seem unlikely, but a computer would whiz through the calculation in a blink of an eye. Once the value has diminished to zero the quantity has disappeared. If the intention was to use the result to multiply another variable then this too will become zero. Floating-point errors like this are another source of difficult-to-locate bugs in a program. Always remember that unless you are working with integers within a sensible range, all other values are approximate. You may test two floating-point values to see if they are the same, using

```
if (number1==number2){
    //Do something
}
```

Although this would work fine for integers, don't use it for floats. Instead use

```
if (((number1 - number2)*(number1 - number2))<0.0000001){
    //Do something
}
```

By subtracting the second number from the first you get the difference between two numbers. This could be positive or negative. By multiplying the difference by itself you guarantee it will be positive, as any number multiplied by itself is positive. Now you can test to see whether this is a small number. The choice of 0.0000001 is arbitrary and could be smaller if necessary, but the important thing is that you use a difference test and not an equality test. Another way to guarantee a positive value is to use

```
if (Math.abs(number1 - number2)){
    //Do something
}
```

Here the *Math* object is used with the operation *abs*, which is short for absolute value. You may prefer this method.

If you are totally new to programming then you will probably be in something of a daze at this time. This feeling is natural. We speak of programming *languages*. If you are new to programming then you will be feeling like a stranger in a strange land, where nothing is what it seems and nobody speaks your language. As you start to pick up a few words, you can at least order a coffee and buy a loaf of bread. In this chapter we are rather forced to introduce a few words, and a little punctuation. Please bear with us; as in the end you will no longer be a stranger.

Using arrays

Another very useful object is an array. You create an array using

```
var myList:Array = new Array();
var myList:Array = new Array(10);
var myList:Array = new Array("Steve", "Jim", "Nigel",
                            "Andy", "Mike", "Dave")
```

The first version creates an empty array, the second version creates an array with 10 empty entries, and the final version creates an array of six entries that are already set. To access one of the values in an array use

```
myList[3];
```

In this instance the value would be 'Andy', as an array's first index is zero. You can find how many entries an array has using

```
myList.length;
```

You can add to an array using

```
myList.push("Richard");
```

You can remove the top entry in an array using

```
myList.pop();
```

You can join all the elements in an array using

```
myList.join(" ");
```

The parameter in brackets is added between each item in the array; if you omit this then Flash uses a comma instead, in this instance the result would be:

```
Steve Jim Nigel Andy Mike Dave
```

You can reverse the order of an array using

```
myList.reverse();
```

If you join the list now the result will be:

```
Dave Mike Andy Nigel Jim Steve
```

You can join an array to another array using

```
anotherList = new Array("Sheila", "Anne", "Julie");
bigList = myList.concat(anotherList);
```

Now the bigList array will contain nine entries:

```
Steve Jim Nigel Andy Mike Dave Sheila Anne Julie
//bigList[0] contains "Steve"
//bigList[1] contains "Jim"
//bigList[2] contains "Nigel"
//bigList[3] contains "Andy"
//bigList[4] contains "Mike"
//bigList[5] contains "Dave"
//bigList[6] contains "Sheila"
//bigList[7] contains "Anne"
//bigList[8] contains "Julie"
//bigList.length equals 9
```

Arrays can be multi-dimensional.

```
1 var vegetable:Array = new Array("Potatoes", "Carrots", "Peas");
2 var fruit:Array = new Array("Apples", "Oranges", "Pears");
3 var meat:Array = new Array("Beef", "Lamb", "Pork");
4 var food:Array = new Array(vegetable, fruit, meat);
5
6 trace(food[1][1]);
```
Listing 7.8

Output from Listing 7.8 will give 'Oranges', because food[1] is 'fruit' and fruit[1] is 'Oranges'.

Building up a variable's name

Sometimes a variable's name will be stored in another variable. For example, if Arthur is an object, and this object contains a variable called feet, then you can access the value of feet using

```
charFeet = Arthur.feet;
```

But, what if you do not know the name of the object until the player clicks on a button? By clicking on the button the user can set the value of a variable you have created called `charName`, to 'Arthur'. Now 'Arthur' is a string that is stored in the variable `charName`. So how do you use the `charName` to access the value of `feet` in the object called `Arthur`? If you use

```
charName.feet;
```

this does not access the object; instead it accesses the string called `charName`. This does not have a `feet` setting so Flash would return zero or, with strict data typing, an error.

```
1 var Arthur:Object = new Object();
2 Arthur.feet = 12;
3 var charName:String = "Arthur";
4 trace(charName.feet);
```
Listing 7.9

The program shown in Listing 7.9 would result in the error message shown in Figure 7.9.

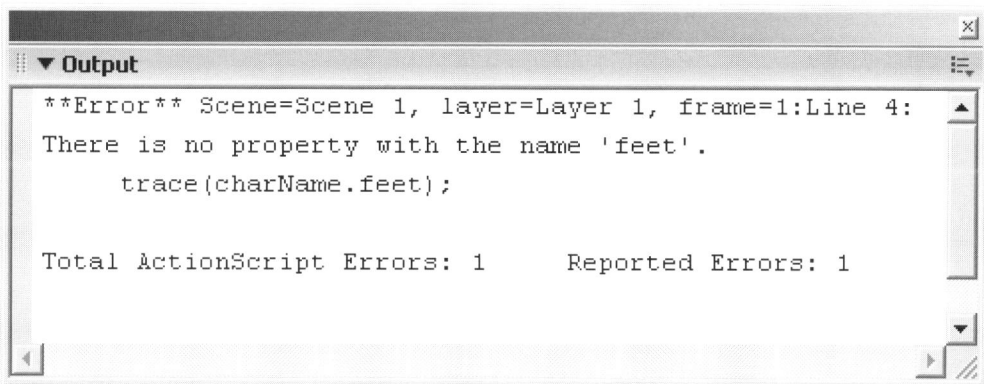

```
▼ Output                                                          ×
**Error** Scene=Scene 1, layer=Layer 1, frame=1:Line 4:
There is no property with the name 'feet'.
      trace(charName.feet);


Total ActionScript Errors: 1      Reported Errors: 1
```

Figure 7.9 *Output from Listing 7.9*

Instead you want to get at the object named 'Arthur'. This is achieved with the 'eval' keyword:

```
eval("charName").feet;
```

The function `eval` takes a string parameter and returns a variable or object with that name if it exists. The `eval` function can also be very useful for accessing movie clip instances when you have many copies of a movie clip all with names that include a number: Ball0, Ball1 ... Ball12. If you want to apply the same code to each instance then you would build up a name using a loop; we will look at using loops in Chapter 9. The format would be:

```
//Start loop with i=0, with each loop add 1 to the variable I
...
eval("Ball" + I)._x += 12;
...
```

You can even assign the value returned from the 'eval' function to another variable that then acts as a reference to the original. For example:

```
1   var Arthur:Object = new Object();
2   Arthur.feet = 12;
3   Arthur.name = "Arthur";
4   var James:Object = new Object();
5   James.feet = 6;
6   James.name = "James";
7
8   var objRef = eval("Arthur");
9   trace(objRef.name + " has " + objRef.feet + " size feet");
10  objRef = eval("James");
11  trace(objRef.name + " has " + objRef.feet + " size feet");
```
Listing 7.10

Listing 7.10 gives an output of

```
Arthur has 12 size feet
James has 6 size feet
```

Lines 1 to 6 simply define and initialize to objects, one using the variable 'Arthur', the other 'James'. Line 8 assigns a reference to the object called 'Arthur' to the variable called 'objRef' using the 'eval' function. This is then used for a trace action after which the value of 'objRef' is changed to be a reference to the object called 'James'. Again a trace action is used to generate some output.

Although this is a very simple example and you may wonder when you will use it, movie clip and object references are used extensively in game development.

Summary

We have covered a great deal in this chapter, from creating a basic variable to string slicing and even user-defined classes. You have learnt how to add ActionScript to a frame action and even to use code defined in a separate file. Along the way you have come across two of ActionScript's built-in objects: the string and the Math object. Now we want to move ahead by allowing our programs to make simple decisions, and in the next chapter we will learn how.

8 In tip-top condition

Should I go to Barcelona at Easter? If I have the money, there are flights available and I can get a hotel, then I'll go. Life is full of decisions: should I take that job? Should I join a gym? Should I make a cup of tea? Whenever you make a decision, you will consider a number of options and in the end you will either decide to do something or you will choose not to. As you embark on your programming career you may be thinking, if this doesn't get any easier then I'll stick to producing artwork. In this chapter we look at making decisions in your programs using the marvellous 'if' statement. An 'if' statement takes a logical argument that resolves to true or false; none of the difficult in-between concepts for a computer, it's either true or it's false and no half measures. Sometimes we need to combine several decisions before we come to our final conclusion. Multiple decisions are handled using Boolean logic, which is introduced in this chapter. We will illustrate some of these concepts using a keyboard-controlled walking bucket and some very attractive lights. So without further ado let us set sail on the sea of conditions.

The marvellous 'if' statement

Because it is almost impossible to write any program without making a decision, you have already seen the 'if' statement in action. The introductory chapter used the 'if' statement and so too did the last chapter. You probably had a good idea what was going on, but you were not properly introduced. The marvellous 'if' statement can be used in one of three different ways. The simplest way is like this:

```
if (condition){
 //Do something if condition is true
}
```

The line starts using 'if', and then in brackets we put a condition. This can be anything that evaluates to true or false. You can even put the keyword true in there and then the 'if' statement always evaluates to true, so the code in the curly brackets is always executed. Later in this chapter we will look at the different conditions you can use.

   The second variant of the 'if' statement takes this form:

```
if (condition){
 //Do something if condition is true
}else{
 //Do something if condition is false
}
```

This time we can not only execute code if the condition is true, we can also execute different code if the condition is false.

The third and final form of the 'if' statement takes the form:

```
if (condition1){
 //Do something if condition1 is true
}else if (condition2){
 //Do something if condition2 is true
}else{
 //Do something if neither condition1 nor condition2 is true
}
```

Here we have introduced 'else if'. We can have as many 'else if' conditions as necessary for the logic in the program. The final 'else' is optional and is only executed if all the previous 'if' and 'else if' statements in the block evaluate to false.

Tell me more about conditions

Flash has a form very similar to JavaScript. The logical operators it supports are:

Table 8.1 *Logical operators in Flash MX 2004*

Operator	Description	Possible usage
$a == b$	Evaluates to true if a equals b	$x == 23$
$a > b$	Evaluates to true if a is greater than b	$x > 12$
$a < b$	Evaluates to true if a is less than b	$x < -22.3$
$a >= b$	Evaluates to true if a is greater than or equal to b	$x >= y$
$a <= b$	Evaluates to true if a is less than or equal to b	$x <= -y$
$a! = b$	Evaluates to true if a is not equal to b	$x! = 1$

All of these operators take a left operand (in the table described as 'a') and a right operand (in the table, 'b'). Either operand can be a variable or a fixed numeric value. Suppose you want to know when a character on-screen is at a certain position (100, 200), that is 100 pixels to the right and 200 pixels down from the upper left corner. You can test for an actual position using the following code snippet:

```
if (_x == 100){
  //Movie Clip at _x equals 100
  if (_y == 200){
        //Movie Clip at (100, 200)
        //Do something
  }
}
```

All Movie Clips have a number of properties you can access: '_x' indicates the position across the screen, '_y' is the position down the screen. Notice how in this example we nest one 'if' statement inside another. You can do this as many times as you choose, but if nesting more than three then you are encouraged to find another way to execute the code, since nested 'if' statements are very prone to difficult-to-detect bugs, sometimes a condition is not met and the code goes screwy.

Testing for a specific position is not recommended; one reason for this is because positions in Flash are not integer values (whole numbers) and so the character may be at (100.1, 199.8), which is extremely close to the target position yet the condition would still fail. One way around this problem is to reduce the exercise to a distance away from the target.

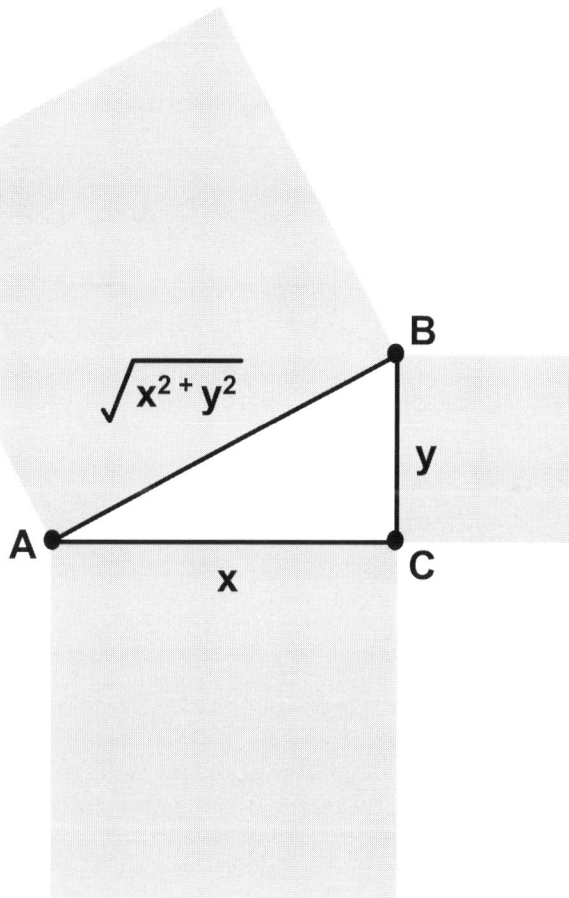

Figure 8.1 *That pesky Pythagoras*

Now, you may be thinking, how can Pythagoras help with this problem? The answer is that the relationship between the three sides of a right-angle triangle is one of the most useful devices you will find when creating graphical games. Let's start by reviewing the concept. If we have a triangle ABC where side AC has length x and side BC has length y then the length of side AB must equal the square root of the sum of the squares of the two other sides. Looking at Figure 8.1, this means that the area of the square attached to the side AC plus the area of the square attached to the side BC is equal to the area of the square attached to the side AB. Oh dear, this sounds like a maths lesson! Fear not, you are not going to have to do any proofs or solve any complex algebra; no, we are just going to use this very useful fact to get the distance between two points on our screen. Suppose we have point A and point B. Then we know from our good friend Pythagoras that the distance from A to B is found by squaring the distance from AB in the *x* direction and squaring the distance from AB in the *y* direction. If we add these two results and find the square root of the sum then we have the distance from A to B. In Flash code we can turn this into a useful little function.

```
function distanceBetween(x1:Number, y1:Number,
                         x2:Number, y2:Number):Number{
    var x:Number = x1 - x2;
    var y:Number = y1 - y2;
    return Math.sqrt(x * x + y * y);
}
```

If you understand the above then go to the top of the class; if it all seems a little hazy then let's take it a bit at a time. A function can be passed any number of parameters, which are the variables in the brackets, '( )'. If we have a point on the screen (100, 200) and another point (105, 210) then we can pass this information into this function by using

```
. . .
dist = distanceBetween(100, 200, 105, 210);
. . .
```

What happens when Flash sees this code is the Flash Player looks for a function, in the current scope, with the name 'distanceBetween'. If it does not find the function then Flash does not report an error, it simply sets the variable 'dist' to undefined. If it does find the function then it runs the code in the function, because of the values we have used in this example

```
//x1 = 100, y1 = 200, x2 = 105 and y2 = 210
```

The order in which they appear in the brackets dictates the value assigned to each of the parameter variables in the function. If we change the order then the variables will be assigned different values; for example:

```
. . .
dist = distanceBetween(200, 100, 210, 105);
. . .
//Assigns x1 = 200, y1 = 100, x2 = 210 and y2 = 105
```

Within the function we use these values to get the distance between the points along each axis, using

```
x = x1 - x2;
y = y1 - y2;
```

Now if you are being extra smart, you will realize that if *x*2 or *y*2 are greater than *x*1 and *y*1 respectively, both *x* and *y* could take negative values. How do we handle this case? The fact is that in the function we make use of the square of these values and a square can never be negative. If we multiply a positive or negative number by itself then we get a positive value. For example:

```
//-2 * -2 = 4 not -4
```

A function can return a value; to do this we use the keyword `return`. In this example we also use the square root function that is part of the Math object. The square root function takes a single parameter and returns the square root of this parameter. In this instance we are interested in the sum of the two squares.

Now we can make use of this function to test the distance between two points:

```
if (distanceBetween(100, 200, clip._x, clip_y)<2){
  //Do something
}
```

'Examples/Chapter08/Conditions01.fla' shows the function being used.

Because the function returns a value we can use it as one side of a logical operator. In this instance we 'do something' if the distance between the movie clip instance `clip` and the screen point (100, 200) is greater than 2. This test is much more robust and unlikely to do strange things. But a square root is quite a complex operation and in this instance not really necessary, as we can use the square of the distance between two points for the test. If we want the distance to be less than 2, then we want the squared distance to be less than 2 squared, or 4. We can change our function to

```
function squaredDistanceBetween(x1, y1, x2, y2){
 x = x1 - x2;
 y = y1 - y2;
 return (x * x + y * y);
}
```

And use the new test:

```
if (squaredDistanceBetween(100, 200, clip._x, clip_y)<4){
  //Do something
}
```

Computationally this uses much less processing power, for no loss of accuracy. Always look out for times when you can lower the hit on the processor because your games will play more smoothly.

It doesn't seem very logical to me!

We've looked at how we can use the 'if' statement to select which code to run. So far we have used a single condition. But we can combine conditions using either an 'And' operation or an 'Or' operation. Flash uses the symbol '&&' to represent And, and the symbol '||' to represent Or. So how do we use these to combine conditions? The 'And' option means that all the conditions must be true for the combined condition to evaluate to true. The 'Or' option just requires a single condition to evaluate to true for the combined result to evaluate to true. Truth tables are often used to show the results of combinations; Table 8.2 gives the truth tables for both 'And' and 'Or'.

Let's look at how we can use these options to improve our conditional statements. Suppose we want to run a section of code if our character is inside a rectangle on screen. We will define the rectangle using the upper left corner and the lower right corner. To be within the region the character's $\_x$ position must be greater than the value for left of the rectangle and also less than the value for right, in addition the character's $\_y$ position must be greater than the top line of the rectangle but less than the bottom line. So how do we put this into code? Let's consider the rectangle (100, 200, 300, 400). Here the left side is at 100, the top is at 200, the right is at 300 and the bottom is at 400. If we have a movie clip called `clip` then the code we would use would be:

Table 8.2 *And and Or truth tables*

And	true	false
true	true	false
false	false	false
Or	*true*	*false*
true	true	true
false	true	false

```
if (clip._x>100 && clip._y>200 && clip._x<300 && clip._y<400){
    //Do something
}
```

This reads as 'if the $\_x$ position of clip is greater than 100 and the $\_y$ position is greater than 200 and the $\_x$ position is less than 300 and the $\_y$ position is less than 400 then do something'.

But what if we want to 'do something' if the character is in one of two different rectangles? First let's put the test into a function.

```
function pointInRect(x:Number, y:Number, left:Number,
                     top:Number, right:Number, bottom:Number):Boolean {
  if (x>left && y>top && x<right && y<bottom){
    return true;
  }else{
```

```
        return false;
    }
}
```

This little function returns true if the point (*x*, *y*) is inside the rectangle (left, top, right, bottom). To use the function in the first example we would use:

```
if (pointInRect(clip._x, clip._y, 100, 200, 300, 400)){
    //Do something
}
```

'Examples/Chapter08/Conditions02.fla' shows this function in action.

But if we want to run the code if the character is inside the rectangle (100, 200, 300, 400) or the rectangle (400, 25, 500, 127) then we can combine two calls to the function using:

```
if (pointInRect(clip._x, clip._y, 100, 200, 300, 400) ||
        pointInRect(clip._x, clip._y, 400, 25, 500, 127)){
    //Do something
}
```

The symbol '||' is the logical Or, if one side or the other of the symbol is true then the combined result is true. Notice how Flash allows you to put a long line onto two or more lines; Flash ignores what is referred to as 'white space' which includes spaces and carriage returns, so you can fit the code into a narrower text box.

Let's try out a more colourful example

When you are learning about using any sort of programming language there is no substitute for hands-on experience. We are going to look at a practical example of the 'if' statement in action and you are firmly encouraged to run your copy of Flash and open 'Examples\Chapter08\Conditions03.fla'. Take a look at the _root level timeline. There are five layers; each layer has been named with a relevant name. Most of the code we are going to study is in the layer 'Control' on frame 1. When declaring new functions for a movie clip or _root level timeline, frame 1 is a good place to put the new function code. In this example we will be using a function that is placed on the first frame.

Figure 8.2 *The layers used in the Conditions03 project*

The purpose of the program is to detect when the mouse arrow overlaps with the box in the middle of screen. As well as detecting the overlap, we set the caption, which in Figure 8.3 displays 'No overlap', to indicate the current overlap and set the light to be red or green depending on whether an overlap is occurring.

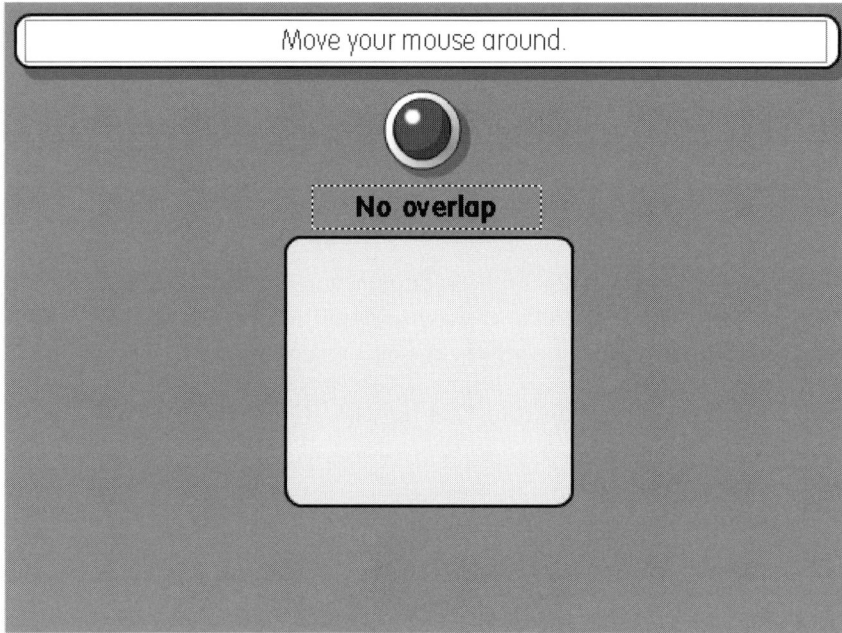

Figure 8.3 *The stage for the Conditions03 project*

For this project instead of placing all our code on frame one of the main timeline we are going to let one of the movie clips look after it. The top line displaying 'Move your mouse around' is a static text field. Click on it and look at the Properties window, 'Window/Properties' or press Ctrl + F3. You should see the panel shown in Figure 8.4. Using a static text field you can select your chosen font, and Flash will embed this into the compiled file, so you don't need to ensure that your users have the same font. A number of formatting details can be set such as alignment and font colour. You can even create a hyperlink to a web page.

Figure 8.4 *Properties window for a static text field*

Below the text field is a movie clip called 'Light'; click on the Light now and look at the Properties window. You should see a panel like that shown in Figure 8.5.

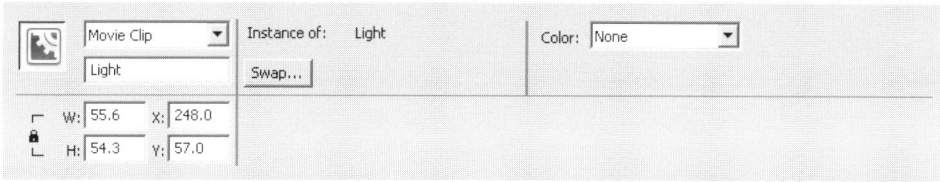

Figure 8.5 *Properties window for the movie clip 'Light'*

Notice that the box below the drop-down displaying the title 'Movie Clip' contains the word 'Light'. If you plan to access a movie clip in ActionScript then you must name it in this box. Below the Light is a dynamic text box displaying the text 'No overlap'. A dynamic text field is a text field that you can get and set with ActionScript. Figure 8.6 shows the Properties window for this.

Figure 8.6 *Properties window for dynamic text field*

The easiest way to manipulate the text is just to link it to a variable by setting the 'Var' property. Notice in the figure that this is highlighted and contains the word 'overlap'. If we set the variable `overlap` in code then we will see this displayed in this text field. If you want it look like you see it, then you must embed the fonts. Click the 'Character…' button and you'll see the dialog box displayed in Figure 8.7.

Because in this project we know that the dynamic text field will contain either 'No overlap' or 'Inside', just the letters that make up this type are embedded using the 'Include these characters:' edit box.

The final symbol that is on the stage is the box with the rounded corners. This has an instance name of 'Box'. It is this movie clip that contains all the functionality for the project. Listing 8.1 shows the code.

```
1  onClipEvent(enterFrame){
2      if (_xmouse>0 && _xmouse<_width &&
3          _ymouse>0 && _ymouse<_height){
4          _parent.overlap = "Inside";
5          _parent.Light.gotoAndStop(4);
6      }else{
7          _parent.overlap = "No overlap";
8          _parent.Light.gotoAndStop(1);
9      }
10 }
```
Listing 8.1

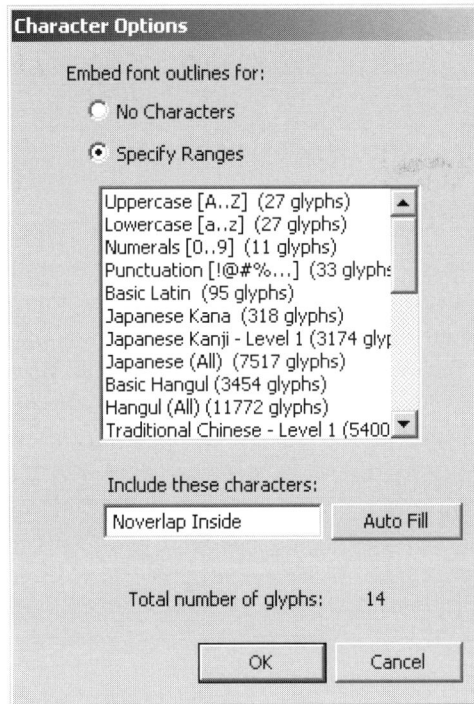

Figure 8.7 *Specifying which font outlines to embed*

But where do we put the code? Simply click on the movie clip then press F9 to open the Actions panel or alternatively you can click on the arrow icon highlighted in the Properties window for the 'Box' movie clip, shown circled in Figure 8.8.

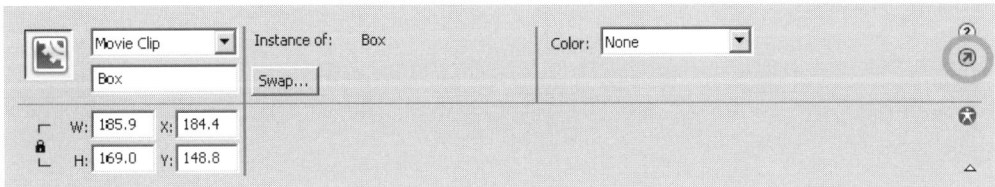

Figure 8.8 *Properties window for the 'Box' movie clip*

When you use movie clips you will often be placing code in an 'event'. Movie clips have several events; one that occurs many times a second is the 'enterFrame' event. This occurs as many times per second as the movie 'fps' setting. So if this is set to 20 fps, for example, this event will occur 20 times per second. All movie clip events have the same basic syntax: i.e. the call 'onClipEvent' followed by brackets containing a parameter. We will look at using other events as you progress through the book, but for now we will just look at this one. After the brackets we use the usual curly brackets to contain the code that will be executed when this event occurs. Finally we come to using a condition. Line 2 of Listing 8.1 shows how we test for the mouse location in relation to the box. One property of a movie clip is the mouse location; _xmouse, _ymouse, stores the mouse location in relation to the anchor point for a clip. For this clip the anchor is in the top left corner to make it easier to read the code. Another property of a movie clip is its size; _width and _height store the dimensions. In this instance if the x or y position of the mouse is greater than zero then it must be both to the right of the left edge and below the top line. If the mouse position is also less than the total width and the total height then it must be within the boundary of the box. We can combine all these tests into a single test using the logical And symbol &&. Every test needs to evaluate to true in order for the combined test to evaluate to true using this logical operator. If the test passes then the code in lines 4 and 5 executes; here we do two things. Line 4 sets the variable 'overlap' to 'Inside' and moves the frame position of the movie clip 'Light' to frame 4. Notice that each of these is prefixed with '_parent'. Because this code is inside the movie clip 'Box', we need to move up our _parent to get to the main timeline, where the variable 'overlap' and the movie clip 'Light' are placed. Later in the book we will look at the problems of moving between different levels of a movie. Sometimes this can be a complex exercise, but hopefully in this simple example you can see what is going on. If the overlap test failed then we run the code in Lines 7 and 8 that set the variable 'overlap' to 'No overlap' and the frame for the 'Light' movie clip to 1.

One movie clip over another

Another common problem is detecting the overlap of one movie clip over another. A very simple technique is to use the built-in method `hitTest`.

```
my_mc.hitTest(x, y, shapeFlag)
my_mc.hitTest(target)
```

Parameters

x	The x coordinate of the hit area on the Stage.
y	The y coordinate of the hit area on the Stage.
target	The target path of the hit area that may intersect or overlap with the instance specified by `my_mc`.
my_mc.	A movie clip instance.
shapeFlag	A Boolean value specifying whether to evaluate the entire shape of the specified instance (true), or just the bounding box (false).

Returns

A Boolean value of true if `my_mc` overlaps with the specified hit area, false otherwise.

Unfortunately `hitTest` doesn't give much detail, so we are going to develop our own hit test. Before we study the code let's try to understand the problem. The problem is to identify and classify the overlap of two movie clips. Figure 8.9 shows the possible locations of the two clips.

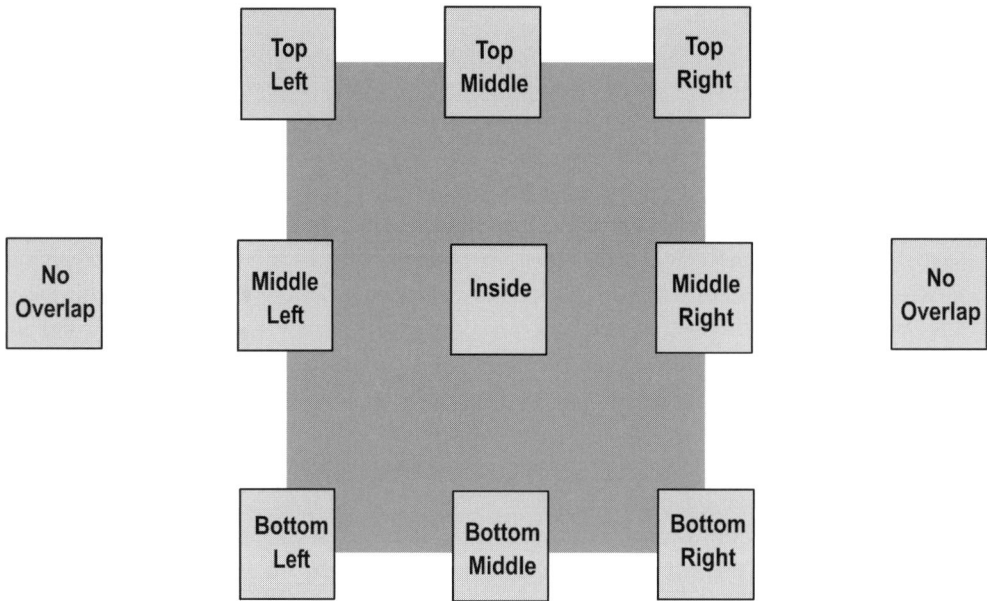

| Top Left | Top Middle | Top Right |

| No Overlap | Middle Left | Inside | Middle Right | No Overlap |

| Bottom Left | Bottom Middle | Bottom Right |

Figure 8.9 *How two movie clips can overlap*

The smaller movie clip A can be positioned in one of 10 possible places, in relation to the larger B.

1. No Overlap
2. Top Left
3. Middle Left
4. Bottom Left
5. Top Middle
6. Inside
7. Bottom Middle
8. Top Right
9. Middle Right
10. Bottom Right

If we were totally general and allowed the case where movie clip A can be bigger than movie clip B then there would be other cases, but for now we will only consider the case where both the width and height of clip A is less than clip B.

Table 8.3 gives the conditions that will identify the placement of the smaller movie clip in relation to the larger one; we use (left1, top1, right1, bottom1) to define the rectangle for A and (left2, top2, right2, bottom2) to define the rectangle for B.

Apart from the special case of 'No overlap' it takes four tests to determine the location; we need to test for the left, top, right and bottom of the first movie clip in relation to the second. The location determines which of these tests we need to do. If we first check the 'No overlap' case and find that this does not apply then we need to identify which of the nine other cases is the

Table 8.3 *The conditions necessary to locate movie clip A in relation to movie clip B*

Location	left1	right1	top1	bottom1
No Overlap	left1>right2	Or right1<left2	Or bottom1<top2	Or top1>bottom2
Top Left	left1<left2	And right1>left2	And top1<top2	And bottom1>top2
Middle Left	left1<left2	And right1>left2	And top1>top2	And bottom1<bottom2
Bottom Left	left1<left2	And right1>left2	And top1<bottom2	And bottom1>bottom2
Top Middle	left1>left2	And right1<right2	And top1<top2	And bottom1>top2
Inside	left1>left2	And right1<right2	And top1>top2	And bottom1<bottom2
Bottom Middle	left1>left2	And right1<right2	And top1<bottom2	And bottom1>bottom2
Top Right	left1<right1	And right1>right2	And top1<top2	And bottom1>top2
Middle Right	left1<right1	And right1>right2	And top1>top2	And bottom1<bottom2
Bottom Right	left1<right1	And right1>right2	And top1<bottom2	And bottom1>bottom2

current location. To do this we would test first for a column and then for a row in the column. For example a successful test for (left1<left2 and right1>left2) would place movie clip A in the left column of Figure 8.9.

'Examples/Chapter08/Conditions04.fla' shows a specific example. The stage is very similar to the previous example but in this instance a cartoon 'Bucket' has been added. Dragging controls the movement of the Bucket. Flash makes setting up a drag very easy. Inside the Bucket is a Button that triggers the dragging. Simply double-click the Bucket movie clip to move inside the clip. Every movie clip has its own timeline. This one is very simple, having just a single frame with two layers. The top layer is a button. Double-click again to go inside the button. A button is simply a special kind of movie clip that contains just four frames. Frame 1 displays the static button, frame 2 shows how the button appears when the mouse is over it, frame 3 is the look of the button when the mouse is pressed and frame 4 is the area used for hit testing. In this particular button only the hit area is defined. At runtime the button will be invisible; however, at design time Flash shows the button as a semi-transparent blue box.

The button was created as follows:

1 Select the Rectangle tool from the Tools palette.
2 Choose Black as the fill colour and No Color for the stroke colour.
3 Drag a small rectangle on the stage in a new layer inside the Bucket movie clip.
4 Use the Selection tool to click on the rectangle. You will find it goes dotted.

Figure 8.10 *Tools used when creating the button*

5 Press F8 and in the dialog box that appears, select 'Button' as the behaviour option and 'btnBlank' as the name. See Figure 8.11.

6 Double-click on the Black rectangle.

7 Inside the button timeline drag frame 1 to frame 4.

8 Click on the timeline title where it is labelled 'Bucket' to move back to the Bucket level.

9 Move the button over the Bucket and resize using the Free Transform tool.

Figure 8.11 *Converting the rectangle to a button*

Having created an invisible button you can now add a little ActionScript to make it functional.

```
1  on(press){
2      this._parent.dragging = true;
3      startDrag(this, false);
4  }
5
6  on(release){
7      stopDrag();
8      this._parent.dragging = false;
9  }
```
Listing 8.2

Just like movie clips, buttons are event based. The two events we are interested in are the 'press' event when the mouse is pressed over the hit area of a button and the 'release' event when the mouse button is released. You can add the code for both of these as shown in Listing 8.2. So that the main timeline knows that a drag is occurring we set a Boolean variable called `dragging` to true on 'press' and false on 'release'. A drag is started using `startDrag`. In this instance we pass two parameters; the first one is the movie clip to drag, which we set to 'this', referring to ourselves. The second parameter indicates whether the mouse position is set to the anchor point for the movie clip; we don't want this to happen so we pass false. When the mouse button is released we simply run the `stopDrag` function to tell Flash to stop the dragging.

Figure 8.12 *The anchor point for the 'Bucket' movie clip*

In this example we again place code in the `enterFrame` event for the 'Box'.

```
1 onClipEvent(enterFrame){
2     if (_parent.dragging){
3             _parent.Light.gotoAndStop(_parent.testOverlap());
4     }
5 }
```
Listing 8.3

Line 2 uses the 'if' statement to test the Boolean variable `dragging`. If it is set then we tell the Light to go to the frame returned from the function `testOverlap`. So the main complexity is in this function, Listing 8.4 shows the full function, which is considerably longer than any function we've examined so far but in fact is no more complicated.

```
1   function testOverlap(){
2     var a = Bucket.getBounds("_root");
3     var b = Box.getBounds("_root");
4
5     //These conditions indicate no overlap
6     if (a.xMin>b.xMax || a.xMax<b.xMin ||
7         a.yMin>b.yMax || a.yMax < b.yMin){
8         overlap = "No overlap";
9         return 1;
```

```
10    }else if (a.xMin<b.xMin && a.xMax>b.xMin){
11         //Overlap to clipB left
12         if (a.yMin < b.yMin){
13             //Overlap at top left corner
14             overlap = "Top left";
15             return 2;
16         }else if (a.yMax > b.yMax){
17             //Overlap at bottom left corner
18             overlap = "Bottom left";
19             return 2;
20         }else{
21             //Must be in middle on left
22             overlap = "Middle left";
23             return 3;
24         }
25    }else if (a.xMin<b.xMax && a.xMax>b.xMax){
26         //Overlap to clipB right
27         if (a.yMin < b.yMin){
28             //Overlap at top right corner
29             overlap = "Top right";
30             return 2;
31         }else if (a.yMax > b.yMax){
32             //Overlap at bottom right corner
33             overlap = "Bottom right";
34             return 2;
35         }else{
36             //Must be in middle on right
37             overlap = "Middle right";
38             return 3;
39         }
40    }else{
41         //Must be in middle column
42         if (a.yMin<b.yMin){
43             //Middle top of clipB overlap
44             overlap = "Top middle";
45             return 3;
46         }else if (a.yMax>b.yMax){
47             //Middle bottom of clipB overlap
48             overlap = "Bottom middle";
49             return 3;
50         }else{
51             //Must be completely inside clipB
52             overlap = "Inside";
```

```
53                    return 4;
54            }
55    }
56 }
```
Listing 8.4

Lines 2 and 3 get the Bounding boxes in _root level coordinates of the two movie clips that we are concerned with, namely 'Bucket' and 'Box'. The movie clip method `getBounds` takes a single parameter, which is the target coordinate space. Every movie clip has its own coordinate space just as it has its own timeline. A coordinate space is the position, scale and rotation of a clip. Since we want to compare these together we must get them into a shared space. We choose `"_root"`, which is the top-level coordinate space. The method returns the information as an object with the variables `xMin`, `xMax`, `yMin` and `yMax` all set. `xMin` is the same as left, `xMax` the same as right, `yMin` the same as top and `yMax` the same as bottom from the previous example. Lines 6 and 7 test for a 'No overlap' situation which occurs when either the left edge of the Bucket is greater than the right edge of the box or the right edge of the Bucket is less than the left edge of the Box, or the top of the Bucket is below the bottom of the Box or finally the bottom of the Bucket is above the top of the Box. If any of these conditions occur then there is no overlap, so we set the variable `overlap` to `"No overlap"` and return 1, forcing the Light to go to frame 1. The next test on line 10 tests whether the left edge of the Bucket is to the left of the left edge of the Box while at the same time the right edge of the Bucket is to the right of the left edge of the Box. If this is the case, the Bucket may be somewhere along the left edge of the box. We need to do a vertical test to be sure. Line 12 tests whether the top of the Bucket is above the top of the Box. We have already tested that the bottom of the Bucket is below the top of the Box so we can now be sure that the Bucket is in the top right corner of the Box and so we set the value of the variable `overlap` and return 2 as the appropriate frame to which to move the Light. The remainder of the code is just a series of further tests to detect the position of the Bucket clip in relation to the movie clip 'Box'. Each condition is handled using the ubiquitous 'if' statement.

Summary

The 'if' statement is one of the most useful key words you will find in any programming language and allows you as developer to select the code that will run based on current conditions. In this chapter we looked at using the 'if' statement in both simple and complex ways. The parameter of the 'if' statement must evaluate to either 'true' or 'false'. We looked at using simple conditions and also conditions that are built from several tests using the combining logic of 'And' and 'Or'. In the next chapter we look at how we can execute repetitive tasks easily.

9 Using loops

If there is one thing that computers are good at (but if yours has just crashed then you might be forgiven for thinking they are good at precious little) it is doing boring repetitive jobs. In this chapter we will look at how you can tell your program to repeat and repeat and repeat. No programming language would be complete without the ability to repeat sections of code several times. Games regularly need to run a section of code several times. In this chapter we will look at creating sections of code that repeat and show you how to control the program flow in these situations. We will learn how to jump out of the code if a certain condition is met. We will consider using repeats that run at least once and repeats that may never run at all. One of the most important aspects of using loops is the initializing of the data used in a loop. We will look at the potential pitfalls from initialization errors.

Creating sections of code that repeat

Flash has several options for repeating; the first option is used when you already know how many times you want to repeat a section of code. In this circumstance you use the 'for' statement:

```
sum = 0;
for(i=1; i<=100; i++){
    //Code that repeats 100 times with i=1, 2, 3.. 100
    sum += i;
}
```

The 'for' statement takes three lines of code as a parameter. Because they are lines of code, they are separated by semi-colons not commas. The first line is the starting condition. Most 'for' loops use a counting variable, in this instance i. The first line is usually where you will set the start value for the variable that you use as a counter. The second line dictates the condition that will cause the 'for' loop to be executed, and as soon as this condition fails the 'for' loop is exited. In the example above, the exit condition occurs when i is no longer less than 100. The final code line in the 'for' statement parameter is the repeat action, and this code snippet is executed each time the 'for' loop repeats. In the example above the English language equivalent would be 'Set $i=0$. Start the loop. If i is less than 100 then execute the code within the curly brackets. Having executed the code, increment (add one to) i. Now repeat from start of the loop.'

The 'for' statement is very flexible: the counter variable does not need to be called i and the repeat code need not involve simply adding one. Here is an alternative example using the variable n

and the repeat code takes 0.4 from its value for each loop. The loop continues while *n* is greater than zero.

```
count = 0
for(n=-100; n>0; n-=0.4){
     count++;
}
```

You don't need to use a loop variable at all; the following example is perfectly legal.

```
i = 1;
sum = 0;
for(;;){
 if (i>100) break;
 sum += i++;
}
```

Here we initialize two variables, *i* and *sum*, before entering the 'for' loop. Inside the loop we test to see if *i* is greater than 100, if it is then we use the 'break' statement. This causes the program to jump out of the 'for' loop immediately. If the 'break' condition is not met then the current value of *i* is added to the variable *sum* and then the variable *i* is incremented. The last line in the loop could have been changed to:

```
sum = sum + i;
i = i + 1;
```

Both code snippets do the same thing. Most people get into a way of writing code that they are happy with, and unless you work in a big team you will be able to write the code the way you choose. Personally, unless the case is very obvious, I would discourage using multiple code in a single line. I would prefer:

```
sum += i;
i++;
```

In the above example it is pretty clear what is happening but . . .

```
if ((code++)<(getCode(i++, n--) + 3) ||
        i++>(23 * getCode(i--, n++))){
        //Hmm is this going to happen or not
}
```

... is far from obvious. The code is in fact:

```
code++;
res = getCode(i, n) + 3;
i++;
n--;
testA = code<res;
res = 23 * getCode(i, n);
i--;
n++;
testB = i < res;
i++;
if (testA || testB){
    //Do something
}
```

Notice how the increments and decrements are only executed after the variable has been used within its current operation. By combining all the operations no speed increase is achieved, but the sense of the code is completely lost. The later example will be much easier to debug if there is a problem in the operation.

Jumping out of the code if a condition is met

With the 'for' loop there are two exit routes. The first is the repeat condition entered as the second line in the 'for' loop parameter; the second possibility is to use a 'break' statement. The 'break' statement can also be used inside the second type of repeat loop, the 'while' statement:

```
i = 1;
sum = 0;
while(i<=100){
    sum += i;
    i++;
}
```

This will give the same answer as the first of the repeat examples but offers a different construction. Used as above it is difficult to see why you would want to use this construction. But there is a reason to use the 'for' loop construction and the 'while' loop. Here is another simple problem much better suited to the 'while' loop construction:

```
i = 1;
sum = 0;
while(sum<5000){
    sum += i;
    i++;
}
```

Now instead of testing for the case where the loop variable *i* reaches a certain value, we look for when the sum gets to a certain value. The 'for' loop is best used with a loop variable that is incremented by a regular amount, usually one, and the test is for the loop variable reaching a certain value. The 'while' loop is best used when the knowledge of the loop condition is not so closely allied to the loop variable. It is possible with both constructions to create a loop that never terminates. In such circumstances your computer will briefly hang until Flash realizes that something untoward is going on and offers a dialog box enabling you to terminate the use of scripts in the existing program. Here are two obvious examples of loops that will never terminate:

```
//Example A
sum = 0;
for (i=0; i<100; n++){
    sum += i;
}

//Example B
i = 1;
sum = 0;
while(i<1){
    sum += i;
}
```

In example A, the repeat code increments the wrong variable; instead of incrementing the loop variable *i*, the variable *n* is used. This might seem an unlikely circumstance, but you will be surprised at the number of times you copy and paste a section of code then neglect to update all the variable references. In example B, the loop condition is always met because the loop variable *i* is not varied within the code block. This is the most common error when using 'while' loops. It is essential that the loop condition will ultimately fail. A common use of the 'while' loop uses the following construction:

```
i = 1;
sum = 0;
while(true){
    sum += i;
    i++;
    if (sum>1000) break;
}
```

Here the 'while' loop condition is always going to be true, since true equals true! But within the code block a terminating condition is included; if (sum>1000) then the code block is exited using the break statement.

Repeats that run at least once

The third and final repeat construction to use is one where we ensure that the loop code block is always executed at least once. You can have a 'for' loop where the format is:

```
a = 0;
for(i=min; i<100; i++){
    a++;
}
```

Here the initialization uses a variable *i* being assigned the value of the variable *min*. When *min* is greater than 100 this code loop will not execute at all. Similarly using the 'while' loop we may have:

```
a = 0;
i = min;
while(i<100){
    a++;
    i++;
}
```

Again, if *min* is greater or equal to 100, then the code block will be skipped. In most circumstances this is OK. But, you may use the loop to initialize another variable. Because it is skipped the variable is not set to the appropriate value. In the above example if you assume that *a* will have a value other than zero then this could lead to errors in your program. There is a simple solution to this dilemma; use a construction that ensures that the loop will execute at least once.

```
a = 0;
i = min;
do{
   a++;
   i++;
} while(i<100){
```

Using this construction the loop is guaranteed to run, so the minimum value that *a* can take is at least one, regardless of the value of the variable *min*.

Skipping part of the repeating block of code

There may be times in your repeating code block when you will want to speed on to the next loop, skipping the remaining code in the block. To do this you use the `continue` statement.

```
a = 0;
i = min;
```

```
do{
   a++;
   if (a==10) continue;
   //Do things as long as a does not equal 10
   ...
   i++;
} while(i<100){
```

The effect of the above code is to skip the case where *a* is equal to 10. You may have 10 movie clips that are being adjusted using the code loop, but Movie Clip 10 is the one under keyboard control and so should be bypassed.

Initializing the data used in a loop and ensuring the exit condition

When using code loops it is essential that you initialize the data for the loop before the loop is entered and that there will be a case when the loop will terminate. It is surprising how often these two important factors are overlooked. If you are using the 'for' loop construction in the standard way with a single variable that is incremented for each repeat of the code block, then the most common cause of problems is accidentally using the loop variable within the code block. Here is an example that is all too common:

```
for(i=0; i<10; i++){
    name = "Bucket" + i;
    eval(name)._x += 100 * i;
    if (i=9){
        eval(name)._y = 50;
    }
}
```

This section of code is supposed to repeat 10 times with *i* taking the value 0 through to 9. Instead it executes just once. Why? There is a classic error in the code block. Flash uses '==' to test for equality and '=' to assign a value to a variable. The line

```
if (i=9){
```

has the effect of making the variable *i* equal to 9, not testing whether *i* is equal to 9. Make sure you realize the difference; '=' changes the variable on the left, '==' tests whether both sides of the operation are equal. In this instance, having assigned nine to the variable *i*, the loop operation is executed. This operation adds one to the value of the variable *i* at which point the variable *i* is equal to 10. Since *i* is no longer less than 10, the next repeat of the code block is skipped. This is so easy to do and relatively difficult to spot. You may read through the code several times before you spot that you have used '=' when '==' is intended. This example is even more frustrating because it never exits:

```
for(i=0; i<10; i++){
    name = "Bucket" + i;
    eval(name)._x += 100 * i;
    if (i=1){
        eval(name)._y = 50;
    }
}
```

Because *i* is constantly set to one in the 'if' statement the value of *i* hovers between one and two. When Flash detects an infinite loop after a short time it realizes the problem and offers the developer the option to abort any further scripts, which returns control and the program can be gracefully exited.

Pitfalls caused by initialization errors

When using the 'while' loop construction you will find that the most common problem is due to inappropriate initialization. Take the following example:

```
while(i!=20){
    //Do something
    ...
    i+=2;
}
```

Here we enter the loop with no initialization, blindly assuming that *i* will default to zero. Never assume anything about initialization. You will find that almost all hard-to-locate errors will be the result of poor initialization. How do I know? Because I have done most of them! Don't be stupid like me; make sure that all variables that are used inside a code loop have a known and predictable value at the start and throughout the code loop. The example above also betrays another common problem with loops that use any kind of equality condition; in the above we allow the loop to continue until *i* is equal to 20. But what if *i* will never equal 20? Maybe it starts equal to 25. Therefore, as *i* increases for every iteration of the loop, it will never equal 20. You may find an instance where *i* starts the loop as an odd number. When two is added to an odd number the number stays odd, so it will never equal 20, as this is an even number. Always use greater than or less than as the exit condition, and you will eliminate at least half the problems you may encounter with loops by adopting this useful advice.

Two examples to help you understand

As usual, examples are the best way to learn. Boot up your machine and open 'Examples\
Chapter09\Loops01.fla'. Here is a very simple program that uses the Bucket from the previous
chapter to show how loops can work.

Figure 9.1 *The Loops01 project*

Figure 9.1 shows the 'Loops01' project in development. There are just five layers; any frame
actions are placed on the usual 'Control' layer. There is only one frame in this timeline, and the
action for frame one is just to set a global variable 'numBuckets' to the value 1, since we have just
one bucket on screen, then the second line is the ActionScript command 'stop( )'.

```
numBuckets = 1;
stop();
```

The code to move and update the Bucket is all inside the Bucket clip or as an 'onClipEvent'
action for the clip. If you are interested then click on the Bucket and view the Action panel by
pressing F9. The code we are interested in can be found by clicking the 'Duplicate' button and

selecting 'Action'. The value entered in the number box using the left and right arrow buttons can be between 2 and 10. When you click on the 'Duplicate' button the following code is run:

```
1   on(release){
2       if (numBuckets>1){
3            for (i=1; i<numBuckets; i++){
4                 removeMovieClip("Bucket" + i);
5            }
6       }
7       numBuckets = DuplicateValue.value;
8
9       var mc:MovieClip;
10
11      for (i=1; i<numBuckets; i++){
12           name = "Bucket" + i;
13           duplicateMovieClip("Bucket", name, i);
14           mc = eval(name);
15           mc._y = Math.random() * 250 + 100;
16           mc._x = Math.random() * 500 + 20;
17           if (Math.random()>0.5){
18                mc.gotoAndPlay("WalkRight");
19           }else{
20                mc.gotoAndPlay("WalkLeft");
21           }
22      }
23 }
```
Listing 9.1

The effect of this code is to duplicate the number of Buckets; we go from what we see in Figure 9.2 to the view shown in Figure 9.3.

Let's look at the code a section at a time. Firstly, this is an 'Action' for a button. Buttons have the following events:

1	press	Occurs when the mouse is pressed
2	release	When the mouse is released within the bounding box of the button
3	releaseOutside	When the mouse is released beyond the bounding box of the button
4	rollover	When the mouse enters the bounding box of the button
5	rollout	When the mouse exits the bounding box of the button
6	dragOver	When a dragged clip enters the bounding box of the button
7	dragOut	When a dragged clip exits the bounding box of the button
8	keyPress<xxx>	When the key 'xxx' is pressed.

Figure 9.2 *The Loops01 project at run-time*

Figure 9.3 *The LoopBucket project at run-time after the Duplicate button is pressed*

Most events are initiated by a mouse action. The event we trap is the 'release' event. This happens whenever the button is pressed and then the mouse is released within the area defined for the button, either by using the 'Hit' frame 4 of a button instance or by using the graphics defined in frames 1 to 3. The first part of the function, Line 2 of Listing 9.1, checks the current value for 'numBuckets', which is initialized using the frame action on frame one of the main timeline. If the value is one then the only Bucket on the screen is the one that was placed there at design time. To retain the functionality of the program this Bucket cannot be removed. If the value for 'numBuckets' is greater than one then there has already been a duplication so we remove the duplicated Buckets using a 'for' loop. In the 'for' loop, we initially set a loop variable i to 1 and test to see if the value is less than the total for the 'numBuckets'. If it is less then we must remove a Bucket. First we build the name of the Bucket, as all duplicated instances on the stage must have a name. To create the name we simply use the code

```
"Bucket" + i
```

This creates the names 'Bucket1', 'Bucket2', etc. as 'i' takes the values 1, 2, etc. up to one less than 'numBuckets'. The movie clip with this name is removed from the stage using the command 'removeMovieClip' with this name passed as a parameter. After this first loop has run through we set the new value for the number of Buckets, using the value that is controlled inside the 'DuplicateValue' clip. This value is set using the left and right arrow buttons inside the clip. We can extract the value in the Dynamic text box using the code:

```
numBuckets = DuplicateValue.value;
```

Finally we enter a loop where the new duplication value is used to create new randomly placed Buckets. A 'for' loop is again used; this runs through as a single integer moves up in value between two known quantities. The first value is 1 and the top value is one less than 'numBuckets' because there is always one Bucket on the screen. To duplicate a movie clip we use the command 'duplicateMovieClip' with three parameters. The first parameter is the instance name for the existing movie clip, the one we are about to duplicate. The second parameter is the name to use for the new movie clip and the final parameter is the level to create this on. This must be different from the duplicate's value and must be different from any other duplicated clip. In the example we simply use the value of the loop variable i.

Having duplicated the original clip we then get a reference to it in Line 14 and set up some initial conditions. The value for the movie clip's $\_x$ and $\_y$ values is set to a random value using Math Objects 'random' command. 'Math.random( )' returns a number between zero and 1. The $\_y$ value is set between 100 and 349 using this code on Line 15, since 100 is added to the value returned from the call to 'Math.random( ) * 250'. $\_x$ is set similarly. In addition to setting the $\_x$ and $\_y$ values we also set the current direction, and again the choice is dictated by the value returned from a 'random' call. The effect of the code is to remove all duplicated instances of the initial Bucket, then to duplicate a new or equivalent number of Buckets that are randomly placed, walking either left or right. See how much functionality we get from such a small amount of code.

Creating simple components

Although *you* are taking the time to learn how to write code, not everyone likes to get his or her hands dirty. Now you know about variables, condition statements and repeat loops, you are well on your way to becoming a Flash expert. But suppose you want to let others share your code. They would want to use your code in the simplest way possible, ideally just by dragging a movie clip out of the library and placing it on the stage. The drag and drop option would not give them any control over the behaviour of the movie clip, however. They would prefer to set up initial conditions using the minimum of fuss. Take a look at 'Examples\Chapter09\Fireworks.fla'.

Figure 9.4 *Developing the Fireworks project*

If you right-click on the star and select the Parameters tab in the Component Properties panel, you should see the window in Figure 9.4. This window lets the developer set the initial value for variables in the Component. In this example the variables are 'gravity', 'starTotal', 'subStarTotal', 'explodeDur' and 'recreateTime'. We will look at how the code works later, but for now try altering the values for 'starTotal' and 'subStarTotal' and then running the code using Ctrl + Enter. As you vary the values, the movie runs differently. The movie itself shows a simulation of a firework, with the number of stars in the firework being set using the 'starTotal' clip parameter.

As the stars pass the maximum height they explode, with the number of stars in the explosion defined using the 'subStarTotal' parameter.

Figure 9.5 *Defining Component Parameters*

To define the parameters that appear in the Components Parameters panel, right-click on the movie clip in the Library panel and select 'Component Definition'. You will see a dialog box like the one in Figure 9.5. Here you can set the name of the variable, what its default value will be, the value it takes just by a drag and drop without the user setting any specific values, and the type of variable. The new architecture of v2 components allows you to hide the complexity completely using separate class files and compiled components, so that the contents cannot be altered. In this example we use a simpler technique that is still very effective. By changing the variable values, the code inside the movie clip that uses these values is affected. The 'starTotal' and 'subStarTotal' parameters are used by repeat loops inside the clip. Here is an example:

```
for (i=0; i<starTotal; i++){
    name = "Star" + i;
    eval(name).gotoAndPlay("Fire");
}
```

Creating physical simulations

The firework project uses code in a physical simulation. If you are interested in this sort of thing then read on. If not then by all means skip to the next chapter, because the main purpose of this chapter, to introduce repeat loops, is now complete.

All physical simulation that you will meet when playing with other people's Flash code will be based on Newtonian mechanics. This complex sounding topic is really quite simple to use. The Fireworks example uses the simplest example – projectile motion under gravity with no friction. The classic formula for this is:

$$x = v_0 t \cos \theta$$
$$y = v_0 t \sin \theta - \tfrac{1}{2} g t^2$$

Here v_0 is the initial velocity of the particle, t is the current time in seconds, θ is the start angle measured from the horizontal and g is the acceleration due to gravity, measured in metres per second squared. The operations 'sin' and 'cos' are frequently used in both 2D and 3D games. They relate the lengths of the sides of a right-angle triangle to an angle in the triangle.

Take a look at Figure 9.6. The sides and angles are related using the following formulae:

$$\sin \theta = {}^{\text{opp}}/_{\text{hyp}}$$
$$\cos \theta = {}^{\text{adj}}/_{\text{hyp}}$$
$$\tan \theta = {}^{\text{adj}}/_{\text{opp}}$$

If we know an angle then we can convert this into a length using a sin or cos operation.

A projectile motion is based on the starting angle and the starting velocity measured in metres per second. The final aspect of the equations that govern the motion of the projectile is the use of gravity. The y value for the projectile is calculated using two components; a component based on the initial condition and one based on gravity. The initial condition is multiplied by the current time in seconds and the gravity component is multiplied by the current time squared. As time increases the gravity component will grow more quickly because it is multiplied by the value of time squared. Below one second the square will be smaller than the original value, and above one second it is greater.

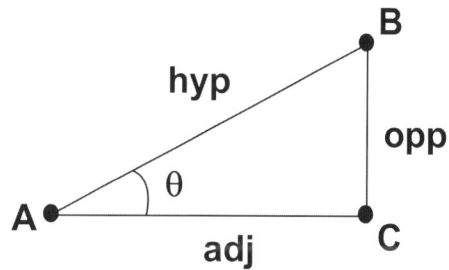

Figure 9.6 *A right-angle triangle*

Table 9.1 *How squared values grow*

Time	Time * time
0.5	0.25
1	1
2	4
5	25
10	100

Because of the use of a squared value in the gravity component, at some stage the gravity value will overtake the value based on the starting condition. At this time the projectile will be descending.

So how do we use all this theory? First we need a starting value for the velocity in the x and y directions. The developer needs to be able to relate this easily to the current scene. For this purpose we include a shape in the clip called 'Area' that gives a guide to the shape that the firework will have as it is moving. In the code for frame 1 of the movie clip 'Fireworks' we take the '_width' and '_height' of this clip and use it to set the width and height values we will use. Then we duplicate the movie clip 'Star0', 'starTotal' times using a 'for' loop. For each of the 'Stars' we set a value for 'spread' and 'speed'. 'spread' will control the '_x' values and 'speed' will control the '_y' values. The value set for 'spread' and 'speed' uses a 'random' value. Finally in the frame action for frame 1 of the 'Fireworks' movie clip we set the value for the origin and for the point we will use as a centre. The 'Area' movie clip is used simply to set the spread and height of the firework. After it has been used for this purpose we set the '_alpha' value to zero to ensure that it is not displayed. Having done all the initializing the movie clip playback is sent to the label 'Fire'.

```
1   //Create moving stars
2   width = Area._width * 0.5;
3   height = Area._height * 0.7;
4   heightrange = height/4.0;
5   averageheight = height - heightrange;
6
7   var mc:MovieClip;
8
9   for (i=0; i<starTotal; i++){
10      name = "Star" + i;
11      if (i>0) duplicateMovieClip("Star0", name, i);
12      mc = eval(name);
13      mc.spread = (Math.random() * width - width/2.0)/2.0;
14      mc.speed = (Math.random() * heightrange + averageheight)/2.0;
15  }
16  orgX = _x;
17  orgY = _y;
18  centreX = Area._x;
19  centreY = Area._y;
20  Area._alpha = 0;
21  gotoAndPlay("Fire");
```

Listing 9.2 *Frame 1 frame action of the Firework Component*

So what happens when the 'Firework' is launched? The playback position for all the duplicated movie clips is also set to 'Fire'. Because these are all movie clips inside the current movie clip, the 'Fire' referred to is the 'Fire' inside the subclips, not the 'Fire' inside the current movie clip. Further initialization is done which is specific to the current launch of the fireworks. The 'Firework' movie clip launches itself repeatedly using the 'Fire' frame action, and each time the launch is different; the initialization variables specific to the current launch are the ones that are set in the action, the initialization values of variables that hold their values throughout the life of the clip are set in the action for frame one. Because the calculation for the flight of the 'Firework' is dependent on time we set a 'startTime' variable that will be used while the 'Firework' is in flight to determine the time since launch.

```
1   //Initialise firing
2   for (i=0; i<starTotal; i++){
3       name = "Star" + i;
4       eval(name).gotoAndPlay("Fire");
5   }
6
7   _x = orgX + random(100) - 50;;
8   _y = orgY;
9   angle = random(80) - 40;
10  if (angle<0) angle += 360;
11  _rotation = angle;
12
13  startTime = getTimer();
14  gotoAndPlay("Flying");
```

Listing 9.3 *Frame 6 frame action of the Firework Component*

As the 'Firework' flies through the air the frame action labelled 'Flying' is called repeatedly. Again we use a 'for' loop and iterate through the different 'Star' clips. For each clip we set the _x position based on the 'centreX' value, which is simply the launch location, and the value of time in seconds. The value for time is set using the 'getTimer' function. This function returns an elapsed time value in milliseconds. To get the time since launch, first subtract the value for 'startTime' then divide by 1000, to convert milliseconds into seconds. Since we need to know when the 'Firework' is completely burnt out we set an initial value for the variable 'exploded'. If 'exploded' ends the loop being equal to the variable 'starTotal' then every 'Star' in the 'Firework' has burnt out and so the life of the 'Firework' is over.

To calculate the _y location we use a combination of a value that is specific to the current 'Star' and a value for the effect of gravity. Since the gravity component is the same for all the 'Stars' we can set this value outside the loop to avoid calculating it repeatedly. We use the simple product of time squared and the value set for 'gravity'. To decide whether or not to explode the 'Star' we use a condition statement:

```
if if (curY>mc._y && !mc.exploding && Math.random()>0.8){
```

Let's see how you are doing. What does the above condition statement mean? Can you remember what '&&' means? It means 'And'; when used in a condition statement it can be read in English as 'if condition 1 And condition 2' then do something. Here we have three conditions. The first condition checks the calculated value for the new _y position, 'curY'. If 'curY' is greater than the current value of the Movie Clip's _y value then the 'Star' must be moving down the screen (_y values increase down the screen). Next we test to see if the 'Star' is already exploding, in which case, the movie clip's variable 'exploding' will evaluate to 'true'. Finally the condition statement uses a 'random' test, otherwise every 'Star' would explode at its peak height. By using a random value we can make some 'Stars' explode at the peak height and others on the descent. So here is the code for the frame action labelled 'Flying'.

```
1   curtime = (getTimer() - startTime)/1000.0;
2   down = gravity * curtime * curtime;
3   exploded = 0;
4
5   var mc:MovieClip;
6
7   for (i=0; i<starTotal; i++){
8       mc = eval("Star" + i);
9       mc._x = centreX + curtime * mc.spread;
10      up = curtime * mc.speed;
11      curY = centreY - up + down;
12      if (curY>mc._y && !mc.exploding && Math.random()>0.8){
13          mc.gotoAndPlay("Explode");
14      }
15      if (mc.explodeComplete) exploded++;
16      mc._y = curY;
17  }
18
19  if (exploded==starTotal){
20      startTime = getTimer();
21      gotoAndPlay("Wait");
22  }else{
23      prevFrame();
24  }
```

Listing 9.4 *Frame 13 frame action of the Firework Component*

In the 'Flying' frame action there is a jump to 'Wait' when all the 'Fireworks' have erupted. The frame action at the frame labelled 'Wait' is just a simple delay. First we get the current time based on a call to 'getTimer' and then we test this value against the Clip Parameter 'recreateTime'. As soon as the wait delay exceeds this value the play switches to the 'Fire' label.

```
1 curtime = (getTimer() - startTime)/1000.0;
2
3 if (curtime>recreateTime){
4      gotoAndPlay("Fire");
5 }else{
6      prevFrame();
7 }
```

Listing 9.5 *Frame 20 frame action of the Firework Component*

Although this embedded clip contains code that is a little more complex than most of the code we have considered so far, there is very little that you haven't already looked at. That is because at the heart of almost all programming we have the same components – variables, condition statements and loops.

Summary

In this chapter we looked at the third vital component of all programming languages, loops. With this third important component you are nearly ready to get on and start writing your own code. You might think, great I'm ready, or you might think, how do I move from a game idea to a finished game? Planning and structure are the answer. Forward planning and good structure will make all the difference to the development of your next masterpiece. So before setting you loose I recommend spending some time reviewing the tips in the next chapter. There we look at how you can structure your programs to make your games easier to write, debug and maintain and you will see how you can use bits from one game in another.

10 Keep it modular

First, congratulations on your tenacity. If you have worked through the book and got as far as this chapter then you are well on your way to being a fully-fledged Flash developer. In this chapter we are going to introduce the skills you will need to really develop your own games rather than just copying someone else's code. This is an entire chapter with advice on how to structure your code from an idea to a game.

Flash can provide you with the programming tools to make your code well structured. Unfortunately, this flexibility can also be used to create very poorly structured code. Game development can be made very hard or very easy. Careful planning and good structure makes development so much easier. In this chapter we look at how to take an idea for a game, turn it into a well-planned project and then develop the code. We will look at using custom functions to make sure that you only have to change your code in one place to have a global effect. We look at using classes, a feature that lets more than one developer work on a project at the same time. We look at the difference between local and global variables. But most importantly we will look at how to embed complexity into your classes and movie clips so that they can look after themselves, and better still you will have code that you can reuse.

From an idea to a plan

The starting point for all games is an idea. Your idea is the basis for all subsequent development. Because we are concerned with games let us consider a game that everyone will be familiar with – 'Tetris'. In Tetris we have a board layout that is based on square cells. Each cell can either have a tile in it or not. At its simplest that is the game. But the game play is another matter. The game revolves around a block of four tiles either in a line, a square block, an L shape or a T shape dropping at a consistent rate from the top. When any one of the four tiles that make up the block hits the base of the play area the movement of that block of tiles stops and the block remains on the screen. At this point we need to create a new block of tiles and start this dropping. This new block of tiles and all subsequent ones stop when any one of the tiles either reaches the base or hits a parked tile. Over the course of the game the speed at which the tiles drop increases. Parked tiles can be removed if the current dropping block of tiles lands and creates a complete row of tiles. Removing tiles increases the score and if the user simultaneously creates more than one row then they get a higher score than a pro-rata multiple of the value of a single row. The maximum number of rows that can be removed in a single removal is four, which results in the maximum additional score.

Does that sound like a full description of Tetris? If it does then it only indicates how easy it is to overlook a very important feature. As described above the user does absolutely nothing! Such a game is unlikely to become a world-beater. The input from the user to control the horizontal position and orientation of the descending tile block has been overlooked in the summary. When you are writing your plan you need to work extremely hard to ensure that you have considered all the options. But the single most important consideration when writing the spec for a game is to decide *what the user actually does* when playing your game. If all they do is admire your lovely graphics then go back to the drawing board.

From a plan to a structure

Now we have a plan, but how do you intend to turn this into a working game? A very popular concept in computer science is to use the top-down approach. Start by presenting an overview of the game, and then break the game down into manageable chunks that can be developed in isolation. This methodology is a very effective technique when computer programming – creating chunks of an application that can be developed in isolation, and debugged separately.

Returning to our Tetris example, let's try to break down the overview into small chunks of functionality.

Table 10.1 *Overview of the methods required for game*

Initialization	When the movie clips that form the game board are created by duplication.
New Game	When all the game variables are initialized and the game board is cleared.
User Input	We are going to need a keyboard reader that moves the playing piece if such a movement is possible.
Next Piece Generator	We will need to be able to create the next piece that is going to be used in the game that randomly determines the next piece to fall. The game is over when a new tile cannot be added, so if this function returns false then this indicates the end of the game.
Legal Move Confirmation	We will need to be able to confirm whether the descending tile can move to a certain game board position.
Complete Row Checker	We will need to be able to confirm when a completed row has occurred.
Complete Row Removal	This is where the game board will be adjusted to remove a completed row.
Update Game Board	The game board is controlled using a multi-dimensional array.
Game Over	This could be a complex animation or a simple text box.
Timer update	If the score is going to use elapsed time as well as removed rows then we will need to show a timer.
Score update	The score should be continuously updated based on the rows removed and the elapsed time.

We are also going to need several variables to track the game's progress:

`Score:`	The current player's score.
`curTile:`	This is a 4×4 multi-dimensional array that describes the current tile, the possible values for which are illustrated in Table 10.2.
`curTileX:`	The x-position within the board where the descending tile is located. This is where the left column of the descending tile maps.
`curTileY:`	The y-position within the board where the descending tile is located. This is where the top row of the descending tile maps.
`gameBoard:`	This is a multi-dimensional array that stores the current board position. A value of '1' in a cell of the array indicates a tile is present and a value of '0' means it is empty.
`fixedBoard:`	Same as the 'board' array, without the current descending tile.
`startTime:`	Useful for generating the time elapsed since the start of the game.

Table 10.2 *Values stored in multi-dimensional arrays to store the current tile*

1	0	0	0		1	1	1	1		1	1	0	0					
1	0	0	0		0	0	0	0		1	1	0	0					
1	0	0	0		0	0	0	0		0	0	0	0					
1	0	0	0		0	0	0	0		0	0	0	0					
1	1	0	0		1	1	1	0		0	1	0	0		1	0	0	0
1	0	0	0		0	0	1	0		0	1	0	0		1	1	1	0
1	0	0	0		0	0	0	0		1	1	0	0		0	0	0	0
0	0	0	0		0	0	0	0		0	0	0	0		0	0	0	0
1	1	1	0		0	1	0	0		0	1	0	0		1	0	0	0
0	1	0	0		1	1	0	0		1	1	1	0		1	1	0	0
0	0	0	0		0	1	0	0		0	0	0	0		1	0	0	0
0	0	0	0		0	0	0	0		0	0	0	0		0	0	0	0

An array of arrays creates a multi-dimensional array. For example the following code:

```
fruits = new Array("oranges", "lemons", "apples");
veg = new Array("potatoes", "cabbages", "carrots");
food = new Array(fruits, veg);
```

```
    for(j=0; j<food[i].length; j++){
         trace("food[" + i + "][" + j + "]=" + food[i][j]);
    }
}
```

generates the following output:

```
food[0][0]=oranges
food[0][1]=lemons
food[0][2]=apples
food[1][0]=potatoes
food[1][1]=cabbages
food[1][2]=carrots
```

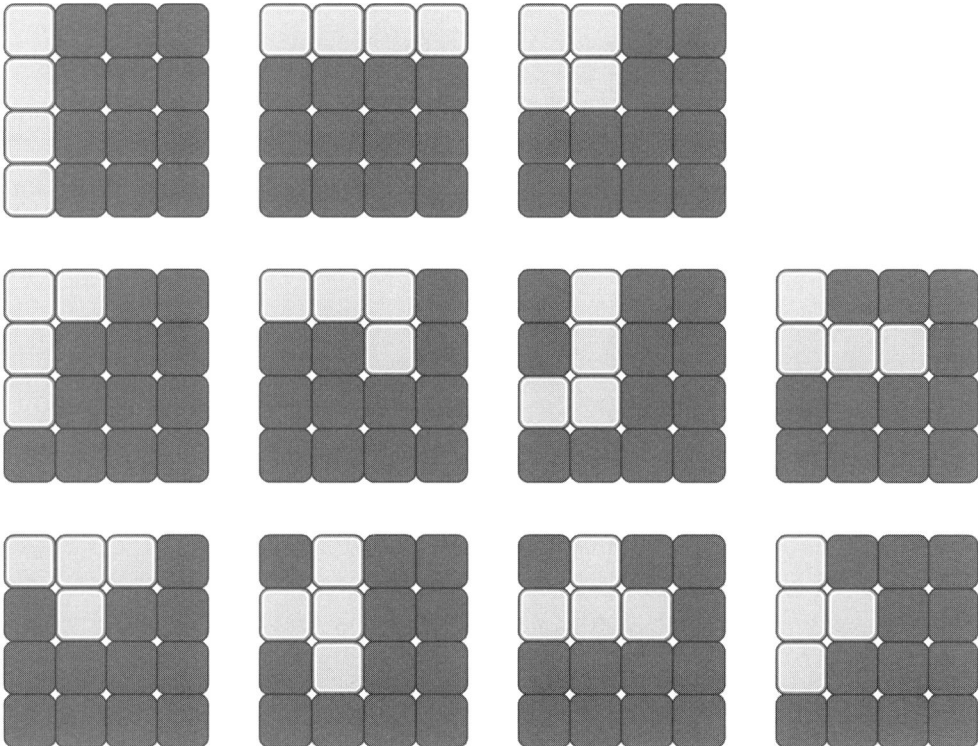

Figure 10.1 *How the values in Table 10.2 translate into images in the game*

Multi-dimensional arrays are very useful when a program lends itself to a grid-like structure. We are basing the code for the Tetris example on a grid-like structure using 21 rows and 14 columns. If we find a '1' in the grid then a tile should be displayed in that position, if we find a '0' then the grid is empty and no tile will be shown. To allow for row highlighting when a completed row occurs, '2' is used in the grid to indicate a highlighted tile. Figure 10.2 shows how the grid numbers translate to the displayed game board.

0	0	0	0	0	0	0	0	0	0	0	0	0	0
0	0	0	0	0	0	0	0	0	0	0	0	0	0
0	0	0	0	0	0	0	0	0	0	0	0	0	0
0	0	0	0	0	0	0	0	0	0	0	0	0	0
0	0	0	0	0	0	0	0	0	0	0	0	0	0
0	0	0	0	0	0	0	0	0	0	0	0	0	0
0	0	0	0	0	0	0	0	0	0	0	0	0	0
0	0	0	0	0	1	1	1	0	0	0	0	0	0
0	0	0	0	0	0	1	0	0	0	0	0	0	0
0	0	0	0	0	0	0	0	0	0	0	0	0	0
0	0	0	0	0	0	0	0	0	0	0	0	0	0
0	0	0	0	0	0	0	0	0	0	0	0	0	0
0	0	0	0	0	0	0	0	0	0	0	0	0	0
0	0	0	0	0	0	0	0	0	0	0	0	0	0
0	0	0	0	0	0	0	0	0	0	0	0	0	0
0	0	0	0	0	0	0	0	0	0	0	0	0	0
1	0	0	0	1	1	0	0	0	0	0	0	0	0
1	0	0	0	1	1	1	0	0	0	1	0	0	0
1	0	1	0	1	1	0	0	0	1	1	1	0	1
1	0	1	1	1	1	0	0	0	1	1	1	0	1
1	1	1	0	1	1	1	0	1	1	0	1	0	1

Figure 10.2 *How the multi-dimensional array is used to store the current game board position*

By breaking the game concept into a plan and a structure, we are already much closer to having a working game. It is imperative that new sections of a program do exactly what is intended. They should work like a little black box. We will translate the first of the two lists above into functions. A function should do exactly what it is supposed to do and nothing else. If the function is 'initGame' and the purpose of this function is to reset all the variables needed in the game, then this is what it should do and no more. If a function should return a value then this should be able to take any game condition and return an appropriate value with no exceptions. So let's look at how we can move forward from this specification to a finished game.

From a structure to a project

Each function that you create to build your game should be tested in isolation; this often means you will need to output debugging information or set up a game condition in order to test your function. Each cell in the game board grid can display a blank, a normal tile or a highlighted tile. Figure 10.3 shows how these will appear.

| Frame 1 | Frame 2 | Frame 3 |

Figure 10.3 *Possible displayed images for each cell in the game board grid*

The purpose of the function 'initBoard' will be to take a single movie clip based at the top left corner of the game board, which contains the images shown in Figure 10.3, and to duplicate it 21 × 14 times, less the original clip. Each new clip will be named so that the array that we will use to set the clip's frame has a similar structure. If the movie clip is called 'tile3_4', then the multi-dimensional array that contains the frame number for this clip is called 'board[3][4]'. To duplicate the movie clip we need to set up two loops, one nested inside the other. One loop deals with the rows while the other deals with the columns. If we call the original tile 'tile0_0' then we can duplicate all the clips we want using this simple code:

```
count = 0;
for (col = 0; col<14; col++){
    xpos = tile0_0._x + col * 18;
    for (row=0; row<21; row++){
        if (count!=0){
            name = "tile" + row + "_" + col;
            duplicateMovieClip("tile0_0", name, count);
            eval(name)._x = xpos;
            eval(name)._y = tile0_0._y + row * 18;
        }
        count++;
    }
}
```

The command 'duplicateMovieClip' takes as the third parameter the level where the new clip will be created. This needs to be a new level; the easiest way to achieve this is simply to have a variable that is incremented by one as each run through the loop is executed. The other thing to point out is that the first movie clip already exists so if count is equal to zero then the clip does not need duplicating. Having created this function we need to be sure it does the job for which it is intended. By running the movie using 'Ctrl + Enter' you should see the entire board displayed. But it would be useful to set up a connection between the game board array and the duplicated movie clips. For this purpose why not create a function called something like 'testGameBoardArray'. The purpose of the function is to populate the array and then to call the function 'updateGameBoard'. So the test function is dual purpose: it will check the 'initBoard' function and the 'updateGameBoard' function. The function will look something like this:

```
function testGameBoardArray(){
    for (row=0; row<21; row+=2){
        for(col=0; col<14; col++){
            gameBoard[row][col] = 1;
        }
        for(col=0; col<14; col++){
            gameBoard[row + 1][col] = 0;
        }
    }
}
```

> Notice that the incrementing term in a 'for' loop does not have to be just '++'. You can use any statement. In the above example we add 2 to the loop variable using 'row+ =2'.

This simple function will set alternate rows in the 'gameBoard' array to 1 or 0. Then the 'updateGameBoard' function needs to read this data and set the movie clips appropriately, something like:

```
function updateGameBoard(){
    for (row=0; row<21; row++){
        for(col=0; col<14; col++){
            name = "tile" + row + "_" + col;
            eval(name).gotoAndStop(gameBoard[row][col] + 1);
        }
    }
}
```

By making your program modular using functions you place complex functionality in a black box that you can test and then use elsewhere in your program. In the above example the function 'updateGameBoard' allows you to update the board at any time, simply by calling the function.

To call a function, simply place the name of the function in your script, along with any parameters the function needs. To call 'updateGameBoard' you would use

```
      ...
      updateGameBoard();
      ...
```

From a project to a game

Already the project is developing into a game. Remember that a function must do exactly what is intended, regardless of the current state of the game or passed parameters. If passed parameters are unsuitable then pass this information on either by using a 'trace' or by using an on-screen text box, that ultimately will be hidden from the player but will make creating the game easier for you as the developer. When you develop new functions you can place them all inside the same script. When developing Flash games we tend to place all functions on the first frame of the first scene. If you are calling the function from a '_root' level frame script then you just use the function name as indicated above. If, however, you are calling the function from a movie clip then you need to indicate a path to the function either by using '_root.myfunction()' or '_parent.myfunction()'. If you are using the '_parent' alternative then make sure that you have moved through the appropriate number of parents. If a movie clip is nested three down from the '_root' then you will need to use three '_parent's: '_parent._parent._parent.myfunction()'.

You will never succeed in creating complex games by writing the whole game and then hoping that it works. It simply doesn't work like that. Modularize the game. Write each individual component and then test the components using test data. When you set out to do the testing, try to break the function using extreme data parameters. In game play the extremes are likely to occur at some stage. Try to keep all the functionality for an aspect of your game in one place. Flash is very flexible; you could have a condition inside a movie clip that sets the playback for the '_root'. When you are returning to a project that is set up in this way it is very difficult to work out why the playback head is moving. An example may illustrate the problem more effectively. Imagine a kids' maths game. There is a cartoon character holding up a board on which you need to enter a value. If you get it wrong then the board is held up again, and if you get it wrong a second time then the cartoon character shows you the correct answer. We could put all the functionality into the cartoon character movie clip. The clip could initialize a 'wrongcount' variable at the start of a problem then increment the value if the child gets the sum wrong. That method would be fine. Problems are likely to occur if a '_root' level frame action controls the behaviour of the clip but the updating of the 'wrongcount' variable is done inside the movie clip. Although this method could certainly be made to work it is likely to confuse the developer when they return to the game to tweak it, some weeks later. Either control everything at the '_root' frame action level or control everything in the movie clip. If everything is controlled inside the movie clip then why not add a 'do nothing' script to the first frame of the scene?

```
//Functionality is control inside the Rhino Movie Clip
//The variable 'wrongcount' is update everytime the child
//enters an incorrect value. This is handled using the 'enterData' loop
//When the child presses the return key the Clip jumps to
//'validateData'. A correct answer jumps to 'correct'
//An incorrect answer and the Clip jumps to 'inCorrect'
//where the variable 'wrongcount' is incremented. If 'wrongcount'
//is equal to one then the clip jumps to 'showAnswer'
//where the correct answer is displayed for the child.
//Then the game moves on to the next problem by calling 'nextProblem'.
```

Believe me, if you do that you will feel a warm glow when you return to your own code, and other developers who read your code will think just one thing – respect!

One final tip: don't change a variable's value outside the current scope. If you find that you do need to change the value of a variable in several places then set the variable's value using a function, such as

```
function setMyVariable(newValue, calledFrom){
 trace("setMyVariable to " + newValue + " called from " + calledFrom);
 myVariable = newValue;
}
```

This will make tracking down any errors much easier. The 'trace' will show you who attempted to change the value of the variable. Often you can find that as you develop your programs there may be errant code that is left over from an earlier incarnation of the program and that this errant code is setting the values in a movie clip inappropriately. These type of errors are much easier to find if you follow the simple rule 'don't change the value of a variable directly outside the current scope. Always use a function call that says who was trying to change the value.'

Creating a new object

Object-oriented programming involves combining the data and the operations on the data within a single object. Flash allows you to create such an object. In this code snippet we create a new object by calling the 'point' function. This type of function is sometimes called a constructor. Inside the function variables are created and initialized. The variables 'x' and 'y' are both set to zero, but the variables 'init' and 'sum' are set to point to functions. We can use the functions from within the object. In this example 'pt1' calls the 'init' method which sets the values of 'x' and 'y' to 3 and 10 respectively and 'pt2' uses the same method to initialize the values. Then the function 'pt2' uses the method 'sum' to add the point 'pt1' to its own internal data. After running the program the output window will display 23 40.

```
1  pt1 = new point();
2  pt2 = new point();
3  pt1.init(3, 10);
```

```
4   pt2.init(20, 30);
5   pt2.sum(pt1);
6   trace(pt2.x + " " + pt2.y);
7
8   function point(){
9     this.x = 0;
10    this.y = 0;
11    this.init = setPoint;
12    this.sum = addPoint;
13  }
14
15  function setPoint(x, y){
16    this.x = x;
17    this.y = y;
18  }
19  function addPoint(pt){
20    this.x += pt.x;
21    this.y += pt.y;
22  }
```

Listing 10.1

Before Flash MX 2004 this was the only way to create purpose-made objects. Flash MX 2004 introduces the ability to create your own classes.

Creating your own classes

Object-oriented programming is definitely the robust technique for developing big projects. It is a technique that is proven and as such is well worth trying in your own projects. Don't worry about it – it isn't too difficult. If you have Flash MX 2004 Professional then start a new Flash document using 'File\New\Flash Document', and save the file in a suitable folder. Then use 'File\New\ActionScript File' and save this file as 'point.as' in the same folder.

If you have the standard version of Flash MX 2004 then you must create and edit the ActionScript file using a plain text editor.

Enter the code in Listing 10.2. Note that all classes start using the keyword class, followed by the class name. In this simple class there are just two variables, x and y. The function in line 5 is a constructor function; it is called when you create a new 'point' in this case and takes the name of the class. The function defined in lines 10 to 14 is the old favourite technique for finding

145

the distance between two locations. Finally we convert the 'point' into a string using the 'dump' function defined in lines 16 to 18.

```
1 class point{
2    var x:Number = 0;
3    var y:Number = 0;
4
5    function point(xx:Number, yy:Number){
6        x = xx;
7        y = yy;
8    }
9
10   function distanceTo(pt:point):Number{
11       var dx:Number = x - pt.x;
12       var dy:Number = y - pt.y;
13       return Math.sqrt(dx * dx + dy * dy);
14   }
15
16   function dump(){
17       return ("(" + x + ", " + y + ")");
18   }
19 }
```
Listing 10.2

Listing 10.3 shows how we use the 'point' class. Line 1 creates a new point with the *x* value set to 10 and the *y* value set to 10. By using the new keyword Flash knows to try to find a class definition of point in the current folder. It finds the definition in the ActionScript file 'point.as'. Flash then looks in the class for the constructor function, simply a function with the same name as the class, and uses the parameters passed to initialize the class. Lines 3 and 4 show how the output from the 'dump' function can be used within a 'trace' statement and the output from the 'distanceTo' is also used.

```
1 pt1 = new point(10, 10);
2 pt2 = new point(100, 50);
3 trace("Distance from " + pt1.dump() + " to " +
4      pt2.dump() + " is " + pt1.distanceTo(pt2));
```
Listing 10.3

In a complex project there could be several programmers working on different ActionScript class files. Another very useful feature of classes is their ability to inherit the characteristics of an existing class. Listing 10.4 shows the 'vector' class. A vector has the same data set as a point; namely, in the case of a two-dimensional vector, it has just two numeric values, but instead of representing a location in screen space, these represent a direction; a vector that has the values [3, 4] means go 3 units to the right and 4 units down. Notice also how they are usually surrounded by square brackets. By convention they are usually written vertically with the numbers above each other, but it is impossible for a string to output in this way so we will use what is called the 'transpose' of the vector, a horizontal representation. Notice that in line 1 of Listing 10.4 we use 'extends point'. This means that the class builds on what is already there in the point class, so we don't need to declare the variables, as they already exist from the point class. The class has its own constructor function defined in lines 2 to 5, and a 'duplicate' function. The purpose of the 'duplicate' function is to return a copy of the existing class instance. Line 8 creates a copy by using the keyword 'new' and then returns this, so to get a copy of an existing vector you can use the code

```
var v:vector = v1.duplicate(); //v1 is a vector
```

The function 'sum' simply adds two vectors together and returns the sum of the two. It does not affect either of the existing vectors. To use it you would call:

```
var v:vector = v1.sum(v2); //v1 and v2 are both vectors
```

The function 'dot' returns the dot product of two vectors. The dot product is simply defined as

$$v1.x * v2.x + v1.y * v2.y$$

Multiply the components together and then sum the products.

The function 'mag' returns the magnitude of a vector, or its length, which we can find using Pythagoras's famous theorem.

Finally the function 'angleBetween' returns the angle between two vectors using the information that

$$\cos \theta = \frac{\mathbf{a} \cdot \mathbf{b}}{||\mathbf{a}|| \; ||\mathbf{b}||}$$

This means that the cosine of the angle θ (angles are usually written using the Greek letter theta), equals the dot product of the two vectors divided by the magnitude of the two vectors; symbolically the magnitude function is written as the vector between double vertical lines. So to find the angle we can look for the inverse of the cosine function, which is acos. That is

$$\mathrm{acos} \left(\frac{\mathbf{a} \cdot \mathbf{b}}{||\mathbf{a}|| \; ||\mathbf{b}||} \right) = \theta$$

Line 29 of Listing 10.4 shows how the number in brackets is determined. We use the dot product of the two vectors first and divide this by the magnitude of the two vectors. Notice the use of the keyword 'this' to refer to the current instance. A vector can call the methods in its own class from within the class definition using the keyword 'this'. Finally we use the method of the built-in class 'Math' to return the results of the 'acos' function. This returns a number in radians, not degrees. This is easily converted to degrees by multiplying by $180/\pi$.

```
1   class vector extends point{
2     function vector(xx:Number, yy:Number){
3         x = xx;
4         y = yy;
5     }
6
7     function duplicate(vv:vector):vector{
8         var v:vector = new vector(vv.x, vv.y);
9         return v;
10    }
11
12    function sum(vv:vector):vector{
13        var v:vector = new vector(vv.x, vv.y);
14        v.x += x;
15        v.y += y;
16        return v;
17    }
18
19    function dot(vv:vector):Number{
20        var n:Number = vv.x * x + vv.y * y;
21        return n;
22    }
23
24    function mag():Number{
25        return Math.sqrt(x * x + y * y);
26    }
27
28    function angleBetween(vv:vector):Number{
29        var n:Number = vv.dot(this)/(this.mag() * vv.mag());
30        return Math.acos(n) * (180/Math.PI);
31    }
32
33    function dump(){
34        return ("[" + x + ", " + y + "]");
35    }
36 }
```
Listing 10.4

In Listing 10.5 we use the 'vector' class defined in Listing 10.4. We first create two vectors then print out the vectors and the angle between them using the methods in the class. Notice that the base class for the vector 'point' has a 'dump' method, lines 16–18 of Listing 10.2, but because an alternative one is defined in the 'vector' class, lines 33–35 of Listing 10.4, it is this latter one that is used in the trace statement, which we can tell because the square brackets are used.

```
1 v1 = new vector(0, 1);
2 v2 = new vector(1, 1);
3 trace("Angle between " + v1.dump() + " and " +
4       v2.dump() + " is " + v1.angleBetween(v2) + " degrees");
```

Listing 10.5

We will learn more about classes later in this book but for now there is just one more thing that is useful to know; that is, making the variables inside a class 'private' to that class. In this way you can stop users of the class accessing and changing the contents of variables. As the creator of the class you give the users access to the data and oversee how they manipulate the contents. Take a look at the triangle class, a section of which is shown in Listing 10.6. A triangle takes three points to define the corners and when it is created calculates the value of the area and stores this in the 'private' variable 'triarea'. This is something that can be read but it does not make sense to be able to set it, because it is dependent on the position of the corners. Instead we create an access function in lines 23 to 25. This returns the area of the triangle by returning the stored value for the variable 'triarea'.

```
1 class triangle{
...
5    private var triarea:Number = 0;
...
23   function get area():Number{
24       return triarea;
25   }
...
```

Listing 10.6

To use the area function we write code such as shown in Listing 10.7, line 3.

```
1 var tri:triangle = new triangle(new point(0, 0), new point(4, 0),
2                                 new point(0, 3));
3 trace ("The area of your triangle is " + tri.area);
4 //Using this will generate an error
5 //tri.area = 3;
```

Listing 10.7

In code it is just like accessing a variable. This code is available on the CD at 'Examples/Chapter10/modular04.fla'. If you uncomment line 5 then you get the error message shown in Figure 10.4.

This is because area does not have a 'set' function to match the 'get' function, so it cannot be used to the left of an assignment statement. If you wanted to allow for assigning then you would

```
**Error** Scene=Scene 1, layer=Layer 1, frame=1:Line 4:
Type mismatch in assignment statement: found Number where
 Function is required.
     tri.area = 3;


Total ActionScript Errors: 1     Reported Errors: 1
```

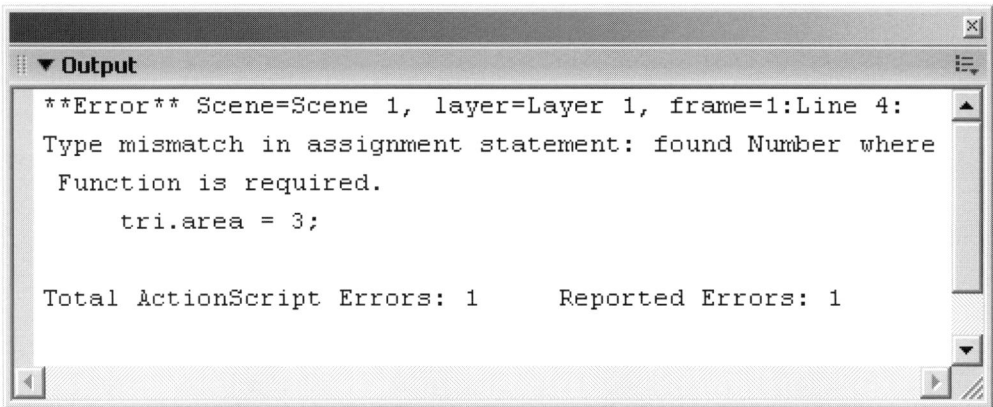

Figure 10.4 *Errors reported when 'set' and 'get' functions are missing*

create a function like:

```
function set area(a:Number){
    triarea = a;
}
```

You may think, why not set the variable directly such as:

```
tri.triarea = 3;
```

Because the member variable is private you cannot do this. Using classes allows you to expose just the variables you choose, to hide complexity and to make the code you have written easier to follow.

```
**Error** Scene=Scene 1, layer=Layer 1, frame=1:Line 5:
The member is private and cannot be accessed.
     tri.triarea = 3;


Total ActionScript Errors: 1     Reported Errors: 1
```

Figure 10.5 *Errors reported when trying to set a private variable*

That covers the most important aspects of classes. We will meet them again in later chapters.

Summary

In this chapter we looked at how to modularize your code so that you can write small chunks of functionality that can be used from anywhere in your game. We looked at how you can break down the way a game will be coded by splitting the game into small segments and identifying key variables. Functions are such a useful idea that they should form the basis of much of the more complex behaviour of your games. Movie clip frame actions are perfect for reading user input or navigation, but they should not be used for more complex testing such as collision detection or data formatting. This should always be put inside a function so that it can be called from different places in your game. Remember, write it once and use it lots of times. You will often find that developers place almost the same code in many places in a program; if the code needs tweaking then they must change all the instances of it, a technique prone to error. When designing your games try to keep all the functionality for a particular aspect of your game in one place. Many of the techniques in this chapter are designed to make your programs easier to write, easier to extend and easier to debug. This last aspect leads on to the next chapter where we look in detail at debugging techniques.

11 Debugging

No matter how experienced you get at writing code, there will be times when the code you write doesn't work the way you expect. Isolating and fixing the errors is called *debugging* and is a fascinating mental challenge, or a complete headache depending on how you are feeling that day! In this chapter we will look at many of the more common errors and look at techniques for isolating the problem and then fixing it.

Strings and numbers

You have created a game that allows the user to input a numeric value using an input box. Then you run this code:

```
on (release){
    num = num + userInput;
}
```

You have a *num* of 14, and a *userInput* of 10. You expect the *num* to be set to 24; instead it is set to 1410. Why? Simple really, *userInput* is a string; all input boxes store data as a string. The operation '+' can be applied to strings, so Flash converts *num*, 14, into the string '14' and 'adds' it to the string '10'. The string operation '+' is concatenation, the string to the left of the operator and the string to the right are joined together. This is not the method that was intended; in your code you wanted the string '10' to be used as a number. One solution is to make sure Flash realizes to use *userInput* as a number by using the 'Number' method:

```
on (release){
    num = num + Number(userInput);
}
```

The result will now be a number, 24, as you intended. If the combination operation were any other arithmetic operation then Flash would have realized that you intended to use *userInput* as a numeric quantity, because no other arithmetic operation applies to strings. Therefore:

```
on (release){
    num = num - userInput;
}
```

would give the result 4, if *num* was 14 and *userInput* was 10, with no requirement to force *userInput* to be a number. Flash 'knows' that if you are using the '−' operator then the value to the left and right of the operation is a number.

In many languages you are forced to define what type of variable you are using, then when you combine incompatible types you are warned. Flash up to MX 2004 was not a strongly typed language so you have to be careful that you are combining data types in the way intended. Now that strict data typing is available you are recommended to use it.

Declare your variables

Flash does not force you to declare variables. This is both a benefit and a problem. See if you can work out what will happen in the following code:

```
piece = 10;
trace("The current value of piece is " + getPiece());

function getPiece(){
    return peice;
}
```

Award yourself a prize if you thought that the value returned would be undefined. Instead of 10 being the return value, the value will be empty because there is a typo error. The function returns the value of the undefined variable 'peice' instead of the variable 'piece'.

Errors like this are quite hard to spot because Flash creates variables as you use them. In a strongly typed language you would get a compilation error because you are returning a value that does not exist.

Here's another one:

```
1   i=10;
2   trace(sumUpTo());
3   i--;
4   trace(sumUpTo());
5
6   function sumUpTo(){
7       total = 0;
8       while (i>0){
9               total += i;
10              i--;
11      }
12      return total;
13 }
```

Listing 11.1 *'Examples/Chapter11/debug03.fla'*

The output of this program, 'Examples/Chapter11/debug03.fla', is shown in Figure 11.1.

```
Output                                              ×
                                          Options  ◢
    55
    0
```

Figure 11.1 *Output of debug03 program*

The sum of the $10 + 9 + 8 + 7 + 6 + 5 + 4 + 3 + 2 + 1 + 0 = 55$. But looking at the code you would have thought that the second time the function was called, *i* would be 9 and so the returned value would be $9 + 8 + 7 + 6 + 5 + 4 + 3 + 2 + 1 + 0 = 45$. Instead we get a result of zero. The problem is that the function altered the value of the root level variable *i*. After the function was called, *i* was equal to zero. Then this value is decremented making *i* equal to -1. Because *i* is not greater than zero the function returns the initial value of the variable *total*, zero. A much better alternative would be

```
1   i=10;
2   trace(sumUpTo());
3   i--;
4   trace(sumUpTo());
5
6   function sumUpTo(){
7       n = i;
8       total = 0;
9       while (n>0){
10          total += n;
11          n--;
12      }
13      return total;
14  }
```

Listing 11.2 *'Examples/Chapter11/debug04.fla'*

Now we get the values we are aiming at, 55 and 45. However, we are still dealing with root level variables. What if the code used was:

```
1   n = 25;
2   i = 10;
3   trace("Sum = " + sumUpTo());
```

```
4   trace("n = " + n);
5
6   function sumUpTo(){
7      n = i;
8      total = 0;
9      while (n>0){
10         total += n;
11         n--;
12     }
13     return total;
14  }
```

Listing 11.3 *'Examples/Chapter11/debug05.fla'*

Again inside the black box function, the root level variable *n* has been set to a new value, zero. This can be a very difficult error to correct, because in looking through the code it is easy to overlook what is happening inside the function.

```
1   total = 0;
2   n = 25;
3   i = 10;
4   trace("Sum = " + sumUpTo());
5   trace("n = " + n);
6   trace("total = " + total);
7
8   function sumUpTo(){
9      var n = i, total = 0;
10
11     while (n>0){
12         total += n;
13         n--;
14     }
15     return total;
16  }
```

Listing 11.4 *'Examples/Chapter11/debug06.fla'*

This shows the simple fix. Declaring the variables *n* and *total* inside the function using 'var' means that we are using local and temporary versions of the variables, not the root level variables with the same name. If you intend to change the value of a variable inside a function then use local variables, not root level. There will be no problem reading root level variables but do not change their value. A finally improved version is shown in Listing 11.5 where we also use strict data typing to make our code even more robust.

```
1   n = 25;
2   i = 10;
3   total = 1;
4
5   trace("Sum = " + sumUpTo(i));
6   trace("n = " + n);
7   trace("total = " + total);
8
9   function sumUpTo(n:Number):Number{
10      var total:Number = 0;
11
12      while (n>0){
13          total += n;
14          n--;
15      }
16
17      return total;
18  }
```

Listing 11.5 *'Examples/Chapter11/debug07.fla'*

Again we create some variables in the old way of just assigning them values. The new function 'sumUpTo' is passed a parameter, in this case the contents of the variable *i*. The function declaration shows that this is supposed to be a number. If instead we pass a string then we get an error message. The function is expected to return a number. Within the function we declare a number type variable called 'total', which is not the same variable as created in line 3. The function decrements the variable passed in as the parameter *n*, but this has no effect on the variable *i* because it is a copy. Any attempt to manipulate it has no effect on the original. The end of the function returns the value of the local variable 'total'. Having returned from the function the original variables assigned in lines 1 to 3 have been unaffected; the trace statements in lines 5 to 7 show this to be the case.

Variable scope

'Examples\Chapter11\debug08.fla' illustrates another extremely common problem.

In this simple project we have a dynamic text box tracking the variable 'count' and a movie clip with the instance name 'counter'. The 'counter' clip has the following clip events.

```
1 onClipEvent(load){
2   count = 0;
3 }
4
```

```
5 onClipEvent(enterFrame){
6    count++;
7 }
```

Listing 11.6 *'Examples/Chapter11/debug08.fla'*

Figure 11.2 *Developing the debug08 project*

If you try running the program, however, the number stays stubbornly at zero. Why? It is because the text box is tracking the variable 'count', rather than the variable 'counter.count'. This very simple error is so common that you are advised to check for it as a first step in debugging your code. Always ensure that you are dealing with a variable that has the correct scope.

Figure 11.3 *Setting a variable for a dynamic text box*

Infinite loops

Flash Player

⚠ A script in this movie is causing Flash Player to run slowly. If it continues to run, your computer may become unresponsive. Do you want to abort the script?

Yes   No

Figure 11.4 *Error caused by infinite loop*

If you experience a long delay in the program and then get the message shown in Figure 11.4 the cause is almost certainly an infinite loop.

```
i = 0;
while (i<10){
    trace("Hello there");
}
```

The above code snippet is a classic infinite loop. The intention is almost certainly to print 10 instances of 'Hello there' to the output window. But instead of decrementing the variable *i* for each run through the loop, there is no change to *i*. Consequently the loop will never terminate. This loop is very easy to spot, but the following example is much more difficult to determine, especially if the function 'setBoxes' is declared on a different frame than the calling script. This gives another example of why it is so important not to alter root level variables inside a function. In this example the value of *i* is set to zero and incremented for each loop. In theory therefore the loop would terminate after 10 passes. But the variable *i*, is also used inside the function, as the function exits *i* is set to 5, it is then incremented to six, but this is less than 10 so the loop is permitted. For every loop after the first the value of *i* will be six and so the program enters an infinite loop. By declaring *i* local to the function 'setBoxes' this infinite loop can be avoided.

```
1   i = 0;
2   while (i<10){
3       setBoxes(i*50);
4       i++;
5   }
6   trace("Boxes set");
7
8   function setBoxes(n){
9       for (i=0; i<5; i++){
```

```
10              name = "Box" + i;
11              eval(name)._x = n;
12              eval(name)._y = 100;
13        }
14 }
```

Listing 11.7 *'Examples/Chapter11/debug11.fla'*

Program execution

Never assume you know what is going on under the hood. Some of the most stubborn bugs occur because of program execution order. You may be setting something inside a movie clip that is being overridden by another clip or a root level loop. Often the best way to discover the error is to trace every function call. The following code snippet from 'Examples\Chapter11\debug13.fla' illustrates how to track program execution. Each function call is headed by a 'trace'; the trace string is set to give the parameters passed to the function, which can often highlight an error.

```
1  count = 0;
2  while(count<10){
3      i = random(3);
4      switch(i){
5              Case 0:
6              red();
7              break;
8              Case 1:
9              green(random(100), random(100));
10             break;
11             Case 2:
12             blue(random(9));
13             break;
14     }
15     count++;
16 }
17
18 function red(){
19     trace(count + ":red");
20 }
21
22 function green(x, y){
23     trace(count + ":green (" + x + "," + y + ")");
24 }
25
```

```
26 function blue(i){
27     trace(count + ":blue " + i);
28     if (i>3){
29         trace("Calling red from blue");
30         red();
31     }
32 }
```

Listing 11.8 *'Examples/Chapter11/debug13.fla'*

Figure 11.5 *Running 'Examples\Chapter11\debug13.fla'*

Turning your debugging on and off

There will be times when you are tracking down a particularly annoying bug and will want to dump reams of information to the output window. Once you have tracked down the problem you can go through all the code and comment out the debugging code, or you could precede each debug code section with a condition that can be set globally. By changing one variable assignment you then effectively turn off detailed debugging. The benefit of this approach is that it can be turned on again just as easily.

```
1  _DEBUG = false;
2  count = 0;
3  while(count<10){
4      i = random(3);
```

```
5      switch(i){
6             case 0:
7             red();
8             break;
9             case 1:
10            green(random(100), random(100));
11            break;
12            case 2:
13            blue(random(9));
14            break;
15      }
16      count++;
17 }
18 trace("Finished");
19
20 function red(){
21     if (_DEBUG) trace(count + ":red");
22 }
23
24 function green(x, y){
25     if (_DEBUG) trace(count + ":green (" + x + "," + y + ")");
26 }
27
28 function blue(i){
29     if (_DEBUG) trace(count + ":blue " + i);
30     if (i>3){
31            if (_DEBUG) trace("Calling red from blue");
32            red();
33     }
34 }
```

Listing 11.9 *'Examples/Chapter11/debug14.fla'*

Using a debug layer

When your code runs, it will execute so fast that it becomes extremely difficult to work out what is happening. A debug layer is often useful for more stubborn run-time errors. You create a dynamic text box on its own layer, which tracks the variable 'info', or any other name that you prefer. Then for each movie clip create a 'dump' function. The dump function can be used to add some information to the 'info' variable.

```
1 //Frame 1 - Main timeline
2 info = Ball.dump();
```

```
1 //Frame 1 - Ball clip
2 function dump(){
3   return "Pos (" + _x + "," + _y + ")" + chr(13) +
4           "Target (" + tX + "," + tY + ")";
5 }
```

Listing 11.10 *'Examples/Chapter11/debug15.fla'*

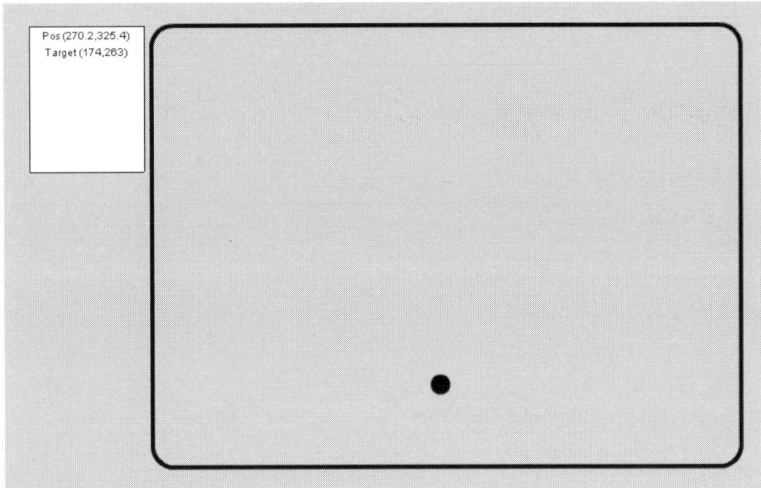

Figure 11.6 *Using an information layer*

By creating the text box on an independent layer you can instantly remove the layer, either by deleting the layer or by setting it to be a guide. Guides do not show at run-time.

Setting data with functions

You will greatly improve your code and minimize debugging if you set the values for a clip inside a function. The benefit of using a function is that you can check the integrity of the data passed to the function. For example if the value of 'sx' can vary between 0 and 500, then values outside this range are unsuitable. By using a function call you can test for unacceptable values and track down whereabouts in your code the out-of-range values are being set.

```
function setSX(n){
    if (n<0 || n>500){
        trace("Out of range error");
        return;
    }
    sx = n;
}
```

Using the Flash debugger

Flash MX 2004 includes a full breakpoint debugger. This tool can be very useful when tracking down difficult to locate bugs. To activate the debugger, either use the menu option 'Control\Debug Movie' or press 'Ctrl + Shift + Enter'. Flash parks at the start of a movie before playing the first frame. To continue, press the green arrow.

Figure 11.7 *The Flash MX 2004 debugger*

Take a look at 'Examples\Chapter11\DebugTest.fla'. Right-click on the 'Cat' sprite and choose 'Actions' in the script window. Right-click on the fourth line down, 'this.gotoAndPlay("StartRight")'. From the context menu choose 'Set Breakpoint'. A red circle appears in the blue band to the left of the script. This red circle indicates a breakpoint. When in debug movie mode, the script will halt whenever this line is executed. Now run the movie in debug mode by pressing 'Ctrl + Shift + Enter'. Press the green arrow to continue and move or resize the debug window so that the 'Cat' is visible. Press the right arrow key. Notice that the break line is within a code block that is only executed when the right arrow key is pressed. Code execution should halt and the debug window will look like the one shown in Figure 11.8.

Figure 11.8 *Debugging 'Examples\Chapter11\debug16.fla'*

Once the code is halted you can use the debug window to examine the state of every variable that is currently available in Flash. Move through the different clips and levels using the list box at the top left of the debugger. Clicking on the '_level0.Cat' level allows you to examine the 'properties' of this clip. Some of the properties can be altered by entering a new value: try altering the '_x' property as you move the debugger, and the cat will jump to a new location across the screen. Moving the debugger window is necessary in order to force Flash to repaint itself, when halted at a breakpoint Flash is not running any code and so no repainting is occurring. Other properties are read only and cannot be altered by the developer; these properties are greyed out so that the value can be read but not altered.

The variables tab lists the variables that are set in the clip. In this example this is just the 'action' and the value for 'moveX'. A right-click on the variable allows you to add this to the 'Watch' panel. To avoid moving through several movie clips and layers, you can add certain variables to the Watch window, then you can see how just these variables are behaving as you run through the code. There is also a 'locals' tab, which lists the variables that are declared in the current function.

The buttons above the script pane allow the developer to 'Continue', 'Stop Debugging', 'Toggle Breakpoint', 'Remove All Breakpoints', 'Step Over', 'Step In' and 'Step Out'. The last three allow the developer the ability to study at close quarters how the code behaves.

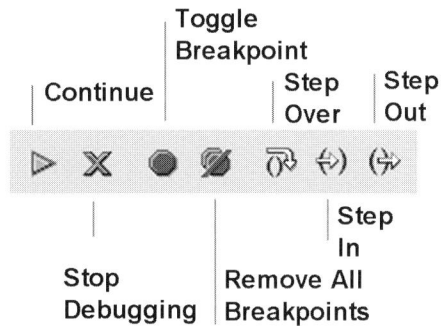

Figure 11.9 *Debugger toolbar*

Step Over executes a single line of code in the current function.

Step In will take the playback head into a user-defined function if there is such a call on the current line of code. Once inside the function you can use Step Over to examine how the code behaves a line at a time.

Step Out only applies to a user-defined function. If the code pointer is currently inside a user-defined function then that function is executed until there is a return from the function, at which time the program halts.

Stepping through the code can be a very effective way of tracking down a persistent problem.

Remote debugging

You can even use the debugger to analyse a remote file on a web server. To enable remote debugging you must ensure that you have taken two important steps.

Step 1

Enable remote debugging of the movie by selecting 'File/Publish Settings'. The dialog box shown in Figure 11.10 appears. Make sure that you have checked the box that says 'Debugging Permitted'.

If necessary you can enter a password in the dialog box to make your file more secure. Then publish your movie.

Step 2

When you publish the movie, Flash creates a file with the extension 'swd'; this file has the same name as the 'swf' file. It is essential that the 'swd' file be in the same location as the 'swf' file for remote debugging to work fully. Without the 'swd' file Flash will not be able to stop at a breakpoint or step through the code a line at a time.

Having made sure that you enabled debugging and that the 'swd' file resides at the same URL as the 'swf' file, you are now ready to use remote debugging. Open the Debugger window using 'Window/Development Panels/Debugger'. Click the options icon in the top right corner and make sure 'Enable Remote Debugging' is checked. Try running the file: 'Examples/Chapter11/Remote.html'.

Figure 11.10 *Enabling remote debugging*

Before the page launches you will see the dialog box in Figure 11.11, accept the default of 'Localhost'.

This example is the same as 'debug16'; there is a breakpoint set in the clip event for the 'cat' movie clip. The breakpoint occurs whenever the right arrow key is pressed. In this example a password of 'FlashMX2004Games' is used. Set the windows on the desktop so that you can see both the debug window and the browser. At the breakpoint you can check variables and step through the code as if

Figure 11.11 *The remote debugging confirmation box*

the file were local. When you have got the project working correctly, deleting the 'swd' and unchecking the 'Debugging Permitted' check box will ensure that your code is secure from prying eyes.

Figure 11.12 *Debugging remotely*

Summary

Debugging is something that is learnt by experience. Each project will require a different technique in order to detect where the code is in error. In this chapter we have looked at some tips and techniques that will help you get started when debugging your code.

12 Using external files

When you are using Flash, the target platform for your game is usually the web. Your game will be seen in a browser. In order for your game to be available on the web it will need to reside on a server that can be accessed from the web. In most cases this will mean that the game is on a computer belonging to an ISP (Internet Service Provider). If you work for a big company then you may well have one or more servers that are accessible from the web, but for home and small business users this accessibility is usual provided by a third party. Once your game is accessible to the world via the Internet you may want your game to have several levels or you may want the ability to easily change the game monthly, weekly or even daily. You may want the game to perform slightly differently for different users. To achieve these goals you may have the different versions of the game on the server or the behaviour of the game could be influenced using an external file. In this chapter we will look at using a simple text file containing variable data so that the game you have created behaves differently by using different configuration text files. Another popular method for setting the configuration data is to use ASP (Active Server Pages). ASP is often used to link to databases on the server. Using a link to the database the game can be easily updated or made to have a unique configuration for the current user.

A brief overview of the web

You probably already know about the web and how to use it but if not here's the briefest of brief introductions. The web was the brainchild of Tim Berners-Lee, who came up with a common standard for hyperlinked documents across a network. He invented the acronym that we have all come to love, HTML (Hyper Text Mark-up Language). We link to an HTML document using HTTP (Hyper Text Transfer Protocol). Everything on the web has a URL (Uniform Resource Locator). The URL for the home page for this book is

http://www.niklever.net/flash/index.html

'http' indicates the protocol, 'www.niklever.net' directs the browser to the appropriate folder on the appropriate server. Basically, the name is just a link into a big look-up table that finds the IP address of the computer. An IP address will have the form XXX.XXX.XXX.XXX, where XXX is a number up to 255. Although interesting, so far none of this is directly relevant to you as a developer. Where it gets more interesting is the document itself, the HTML page. In this example we have 'index.html', although because the server defaults to this file and because HTTP is presumed,

www.niklever.net/flash

will find the same file.

All HTML documents have the format

```
<HTML>
<HEAD>
<TITLE>A very simple web page</TITLE>
</HEAD>
<BODY>
This is the content of the web page.
</BODY>
</HTML>
```

Most HTML tags have the form <TAG>…</TAG> where 'TAG' is the start of a tag and '/TAG' is the end of that tag. Most tags can be nested inside other tags. You may well have your favourite program for creating HTML pages: 'Frontpage' and 'Dreamweaver' are just two. But it is useful to know what is being created when you author an HTML page. Essentially you just create a text file. Whenever an image is added the image is not part of the document; instead a URL is created. This can be a direct link to the image such as 'http://www.niklever.net/flash/images/masthead.jpg' or alternatively in the current example we can just use 'images/masthead.jpg' which is a relative link to the file, relative in respect of the current page, http://www.niklever.net/flash/index.html. We look in the image folder and find the file 'masthead.jpg'. When you create a Flash game you can choose to 'publish' the game. Figure 12.1 shows the 'Publish Settings' dialog box that is accessed from 'File/Publish Settings…'.

The check boxes that are checked by default are 'Flash' and 'HTML'. When you create a Flash game the project file is an 'FLA' file. When you publish this file it is in the compressed form of an swf file. In order to view this file on the Internet you will link to the HTML file, not the swf file. Linking to the swf file directly will simply bring up a file download box if you have the rights to download files from the folder. Here is an HTML file produced using Flash Publish.

```
1  <!DOCTYPE html PUBLIC "-//W3C//DTD XHTML 1.0 Transitional//EN"
2        "http://www.w3.org/TR/xhtml1/DTD/xhtml1-transitional.dtd">
3  <html xmlns="http://www.w3.org/1999/xhtml" xml:lang="en" lang="en">
4  <head>
5  <meta http-equiv="Content-Type" content="text/html;
6        charset=iso-8859-1" />
7  <title>remote</title>
8  </head>
9  <body bgcolor="#ffffff">
10 <!--url's used in the movie-->
11 <!--text used in the movie-->
```

```
12 <!-- Press Right arrow to start walking -->
13 <object classid="clsid:d27cdb6e-ae6d-11cf-96b8-444553540000"
14        codebase = "http://download.macromedia.com/
15                    pub/shockwave/cabs/flash/swflash.cab#version =
16                    7,0,0,0"
17        width="550" height="400"
18        id="remote" align="middle">
19        <param name="allowScriptAccess" value="sameDomain" />
20        <param name="movie" value="remote.swf" />
21        <param name="quality" value="high" />
22        <param name="bgcolor" value="#ffffff" />
23    <embed src="remote.swf" quality="high" bgcolor="#ffffff"
24        width="550" height="400" name="remote" align="middle"
25        allowScriptAccess="sameDomain"
26        type="application/x-shockwave-flash"
27        pluginspage = "http://www.macromedia.com/go/getflashplayer" />
28 </object>
29 </body>
30 </html>
```

Listing 12.1

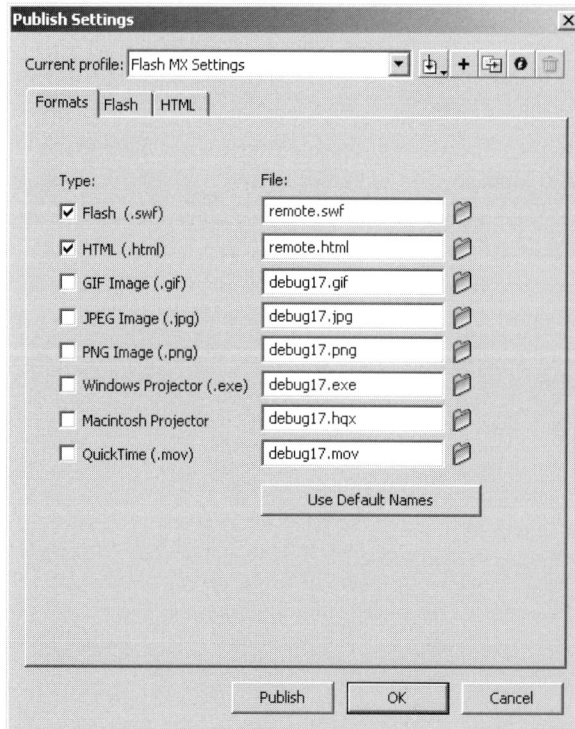

Figure 12.1 *Setting the Publish Settings in Flash*

The familiar HTML tags are all there but in addition within the 'BODY' tags are 'OBJECT' tags and with those are 'EMBED' tags. 'OBJECT' is used by Internet Explorer to insert an ActiveX control. When using Flash with IE, the user sees an ActiveX control, usually found in the 'System32' folder of the Windows folder. The strange numbered 'classid' is simply the Windows way of finding the control within Windows registry. If the control cannot be found then the 'codebase' option tells IE where to find the installation program for Flash on the Internet; this is a URL address. The final parameters for the 'OBJECT' tag define the width and height in pixels. Following the 'OBJECT' tag are several lines beginning with 'PARAM'. ActiveX technology can be passed in parameters via the HTML page. A parameter has a name and a value. The 'movie' parameter defines the name of the swf file. This is in URL format so it can reside in a different folder if necessary. The 'quality' parameter controls whether anti-aliasing is used on the display. Some slower computers struggle to display a high quality image and so the frame rate can drop. It is sometimes useful to give the player the option of a higher frame rate at the expense of a poorer display or vice versa. The final parameter in this example is 'bgcolor' which takes a value in hexadecimal notation.

Numbers do not have to use a base of 10. In the familiar place-value decimal notation when a column reaches 9 and is incremented the next column along has one added and the current column goes to zero:

100, 101, 102, 103, 104, 105, 106, 107, 108, 109, 110

In the binary system that has only two symbols for numbers once a column has the value one and is incremented the next column along becomes one and the current column becomes zero:

100, 101, 110

Translating the symbols into a value involves summing the values of the columns:

$1111 = 1 * 10^3 + 1 * 10^2 + 1 * 10 + 1$ in the decimal system (10^3 simply means $10 \star 10 \star 10$)
$1111 = 1 * 2^3 + 1 * 2^2 + 1 * 2 + 1$ in the binary system or 15 as a decimal value.

Hexadecimal uses 16 symbols; after 9 there are A,B,C,D,E and F. F is equivalent to 15 in decimal notation. When specifying colours in an HTML document they take the form '#RRGGBB' where 'RR', 'GG' and 'BB' are two hexadecimal values that specify a number between zero and 255 for red (RR), green (GG) and blue (BB). How is this the case? Take the hexadecimal value '00', this is simply,

$0 * 16 + 0 = 0$

At the maximum end we have the value 'FF' which means

$$15 * 16 + 15 = 255$$

Since each term red, green and blue can take a value between 0 and 255, the maximum number of colours that are possible is

$$256 * 256 * 256 = 16777216$$

A value of 255 in decimal is FF in hexadecimal and 11111111 in binary. That is, it takes 8 numbers to define the value in binary; each of these numbers is sometimes called a bit and a cluster of 8 bits is called a byte. Since the colour is defined using three 8-bit values there are in actual fact 24 bits used to define a colour, hence the term 24-bit colour.

Netscape uses a different method to insert a Flash file. This is where the 'EMBED' tags come in. As usual the tag has a closing '</EMBED>' tag. Within the tag the parameters are specified directly; 'src' gives the Flash movie name, 'quality' and 'bgcolor' are as previously described. Width and height are specified in the same way as used by the 'OBJECT' tag. The main difference is the way the application that will display the content is described. Instead of inserting an ActiveX control, Netscape uses a plug-in. The 'type' is defined; if this is not found on the client's machine then the 'pluginspage' defines where to find the plug-in.

Tell me about query strings

Suppose inside Flash you want to set the value for the variable 'configfile' to 'config/february.txt'. You can do this very easily by altering the specification for both the 'movie' parameter for IE and the 'src' parameter for Netscape.

```
. . .
   <PARAM NAME=movie↵
         VALUE="Publishing.swf?configfile=config/February.txt">
   <PARAM NAME=quality VALUE=high>
   <PARAM NAME=bgcolor VALUE=#FFFFFF>
   <EMBED
     src = "Publishing.swf?configfile=config/February.txt "
. . .
```

When specifiying several variables they must be separated using the '&' symbol, for example:

```
<PARAM NAME=movie↵
      VALUE = "Publishing.swf?configfile=config/February.txt&↵
                          audiofile=sounds/February.swf">
```

When Flash starts the value of the variables following the question mark is automatically set. Later in the chapter we will look at using query strings as part of the URL for the page. They are commonly used when using ASP.

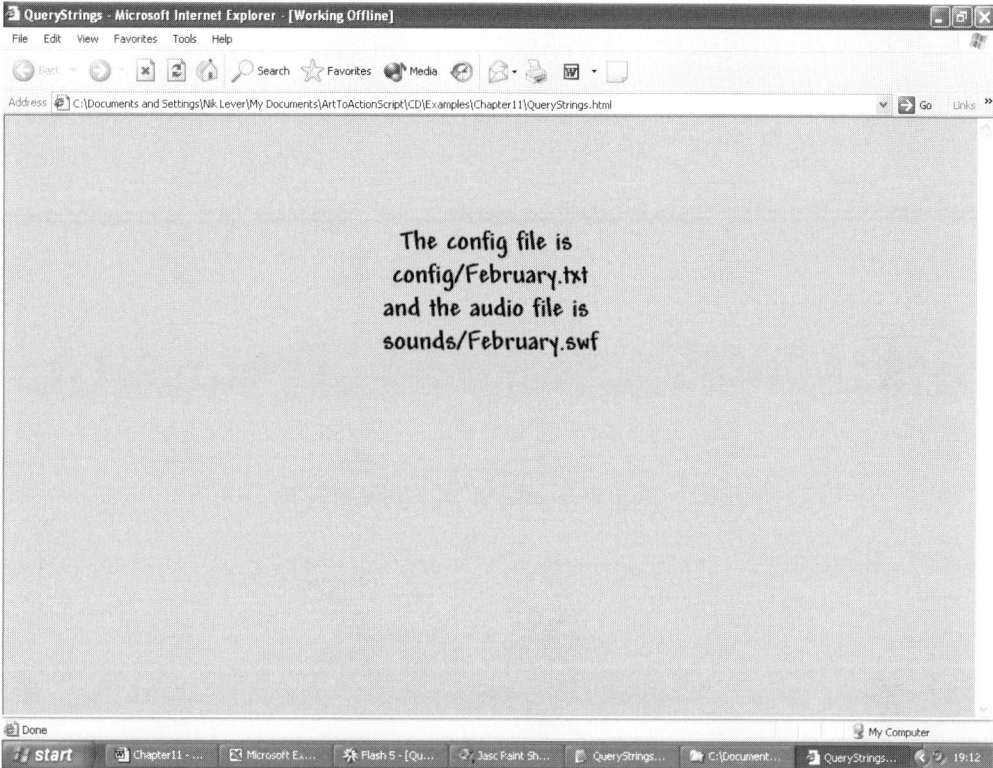

Figure 12.2 *Running 'Examples/QueryString.html' from the CD*

Try running 'Examples/QueryString.html' on the CD. Then open the file in a text editor (Notepad on the PC or Simple Text on the MAC). The file looks like this:

```
1   <HTML>
2   <HEAD>
3   <TITLE>QueryStrings</TITLE>
4   </HEAD>
5   <BODY bgcolor="#CCCC99">
6   <BR><BR>
7   <CENTER>
8   <!-- URL's used in the movie-->
9   <!-- text used in the movie-->
10  <OBJECT classid="clsid:D27CDB6E-AE6D-11cf-96B8-444553540000"
11  codebase="http://download.macromedia.com/pub/shockwave/cabs/flash/
```

```
12   swflash.cab#version=7,0,0,0"
13   WIDTH=550 HEIGHT=400>
14   <PARAM NAME=movie VALUE="QueryStrings.swf?configfile=config/↵
         February.txt&audiofile=sounds/February.swf">
15   <PARAM NAME=quality VALUE=high>
16   <PARAM NAME=bgcolor VALUE=#CCCC99>
17   <EMBED
18     src="QueryStrings.swf?configfile=config/February.txt&↵
     audiofile=sounds/February.swf"
19    quality=high bgcolor=#CCCC99
20    WIDTH=550    HEIGHT=400
21    TYPE="application/x-shockwave-flash"
22    PLUGINSPAGE="http://www.macromedia.com/go/getflashplayer">
23   </EMBED>
24   </OBJECT>
25   </CENTER>
26   </BODY>
27   </HTML>
```

Listing 12.2

Notice how the 'bgcolor' is set to '#CCCC99', that is a red value of 'CC' ($12 * 16 + 12 = 204$), a green value of 'CC' (204) and a blue value of '99' ($9 * 16 + 9 = 153$). But the most important aspect of this file is the values for 'configfile' and 'audiofile'; try changing the values and then re-running the HTML file. The display will change to show the new values. If you are running IE on PC then change the value for the 'PARAM NAME=movie'; if you are running Netscape or on a MAC then change the value for the '<EMBED src..'.

Query strings are very useful for getting information into Flash, but there is a limitation. The symbol that delimits (links together) the variables is '&', this effectively means you cannot use the '&' symbol within a variable. Another problem with query strings is the structure of the file. Query strings are just a single very long sentence. Creating them can lead to confusion. Compare the clarity of the first list:

```
date=23 February 2002
day=Saturday
time=9am
place=dobcross
temperature=-1C
weather=Snow and high winds
outlook=Winds dying, snow changing to sleet
font=Copperplate
map=UK
symbols=ukweathermap.swf
anim=1
webcam=1
webcamURL=http://www.dobcross.co.uk/webcam/cam1.html
```

with a query string version:

```
date=23 February 2002&day=Saturday&time=9am&place=dobcross&temperature=-
1C&weather=Snow and high winds&outlook=Winds dying, snow changing to
sleet&font=Copperplate&map=UK&symbols=ukweathermap.swf&anim=1&webcam=1&
webcamURL=http://www.dobcross.co.uk/webcam/cam1.html
```

On the CD you will find a small program, 'Utilities/MakeQueryString.exe', which takes a list in the first format and changes it into a query string format. If you have particularly complex query strings then I recommend using this program; sorry, it is PC only.

Using loadVariables

Query strings are useful for a one-off initialization of variables. If at launch you need to collect information from the user before knowing which set of variables to initialize then you will need to use a slightly different method, 'loadVariables'. The syntax to use is:

```
anyMovieClip.loadVariables(url, variables);
```

where 'url' is the absolute or relative URL for the external text file. It is essential that this file is in the same domain as the movie clip. The second parameter 'variables' defines the method for sending the variables. Despite the name of the function 'loadVariables' can be used for sending variables. You have one of two options for this; the first is 'GET' which appends the variables to the end of the URL, in other words, a query string. Please bear in mind that all variables local to the movie clip will be appended so if you have a lot of variables defined then this string is likely to be too long to work effectively.

```
myMovieClip.loadVariables("sendvariables.asp", "GET");
```

If the movie clip 'myMovieClip' has variables 'tom', 'dick' and 'harry' defined then the URL will actually be set to:

```
http://currentMoviePath/sendVariables.asp?tom=smart&
    dick=normal&harry=stupid
```

Notice how the variables have been added to the URL as a query string. The Flash documentation recommends using this method for small numbers of variables. The second method 'POST' sends the variables in a separate HTTP header and is recommend to be used for long strings of variables. But neither method is needed for loading variables from an external file into Flash. So if this is what you are doing then instead use:

```
myMovieClip.loadVariables("variables.txt");
```

Try running 'Examples/Chapter12/Weather.html'; this simple program loads data from a static text file into the current Flash movie. The action on frame 1 starts this happening:

```
loaded = 0;
_root.loadVariables("weather.txt");
```

Here we have set a '_root' level variable 'loaded' to zero. The reason for this is that 'loadVariables' returns immediately after the call, on many connections this does not mean that the variables are now set as expected. You must wait until they have been correctly set, by including a variable in the loading file that when loaded will have a know value you can detect when the loading has completed. Here is the file 'weather.txt'.

```
date=23 February 2002&day=Saturday&time=9am&place=dobcross&temperature=-
1C&weather=Snow and high winds&outlook=Winds dying, snow changing to
sleet&font=Copperplate&mapmode=UK&symbols=ukweathermap.swf&anim=1&webcam=
1&webcamURL=http://www.dobcross.co.uk/webcam/cam1.html&lastupdate=06:00
23/02/02&loaded=1&
```

Notice that the variable 'loaded' is included in the file and is set to the value 1. The variable does not have to be called 'loaded' – any variable will do as long as the file sets it to a known value; it could be 'Batman=Bruce Wayne', as long as before the call to 'loadVariable' the variable 'Batman' is set to some value other than 'Bruce Wayne'. Because we must wait for the external file to load we have a simple looping script that checks the value of the variable 'loaded' and continues to loop until the value is one. On some occasions because of server problems the file may never load; because of this it is useful to add a counter. Each loop in the wait script will increment the counter. If the counter exceeds a 30 second wait then you may choose to show a text box that explains that there are problems with the server at present, come back later. If the 'fps' for the current movie is 25, then 30 seconds will have elapsed when the counter is $25 * 30 = 750$. You may decide that two minutes is a better waiting time; this is dependent on your server and the traffic on the site. Simultaneous users all trying to access the file will greatly affect the load time.

When using 'loadVariables' the external file can be a static text file, but it can also be a text file generated by a CGI script, Active Server Pages (ASP), or PHP. Before you start reeling with the alternatives, we are only going to consider one, ASP. In the above example we used a static text file. But in a real application the data will be dynamic. You will be connecting to actual data that is current at the present time. This is where server side creation of the strings that load into your program becomes vital. Let's consider one of the most commonly used techniques.

So what is ASP?

An ASP page is simply a script page that when you access it from a URL runs as a program on the server, using either VBScript or JavaScript. This program can then generate the variable data that Flash requires, passing this information back to Flash dynamically. You can create an ASP page using any text editor. But to function it needs to be run from a Windows server. If you are

Figure 12.3 *Developing the Weather program*

using Win95, Win98, Win2000 or WinXP Professional then you can set up your own machine to function as a server by installing Internet Information Services (IIS).

To install Internet Information Services

1. Click **Start**, point to **Settings**, click **Control Panel** and start the **Add/Remove Programs** application.
2. Select **Add/Remove Windows Components** and then follow the on-screen instructions to install, remove, or add components to IIS.

If you are able to install IIS then you must create and run ASP pages in the 'inetpub/wwwroot' folder that IIS creates. If you are not able to install IIS because you are on a MAC platform or your version of Windows does not contain IIS then you will need to run the ASP pages from a remote server, uploading the pages using an FTP program to test them.

Later in the book we will study ASP pages in more detail. Here is a very simple example:

```
<%@ language="Javascript" %>
<%
    var a = Number(Request("A"));
```

```
var b = Number(Request("B"));
var op = Request("op");
var output = "answer=error";

Response.Expires = -1;

if (op == "add") {
    output = "answer=" + (a + b);
}else if (op == "subtract"){
    output = "answer=" + (a - b);
}

Response.Write(output);
%>
```

The first line tells ASP that the scripting language is JavaScript. Then the actual script is contained between the tags '<%...%>'. Because the language is JavaScript it is very similar to ActionScript. First we declare a few variables. 'Number(Request("A"))' extracts the variable A in the query string and turns it into a number rather than the default of a string. If the file is saved as 'calc.asp' in folder 'scripts' of server 'myserver' then we can call the page using

```
http://myserver/scripts/calc.asp?A=13&B=8&op=add
```

In this case the value for the variable a will be set to 13, b to 8 and op to 'add'. Using 'Response.Expires= −1' tells the browser not to cache the page. Then we test for the appropriate op; if either 'add' or 'subtract' is found then we build a string, 'output'. Finally this is sent to the browser using 'Response.Write(output)'. If we called this from Flash then the variable 'answer' would be set to one of '$a + b$', '$a - b$', or 'error'. The output can contain multiple values if each variable, value pair is connected to the rest using the ampersand character (&).

Using the LoadVars object

A new feature in Flash MX was the LoadVars object. This useful object is designed to make communicating with external data easier for the developer. The object uses callback functions. A callback function is simply a function that is called when a particular event occurs. You tell the object where to find the function and then this function will be called whenever a certain event takes place.

Suppose we have the following code on frame 1 of our main timeline:

```
lv = new LoadVars();
lv.onLoad = loaded;
lv.load("myvariables.txt");
stop();
```

```
function loaded(success){
    if (success){
        gotoAndStop("LoadedOK");
    }else{
        gotoAndStop("LoadFailed");
    }
}
```

Firstly a new LoadVars object is created and called 'lv'. The callback that will be used whenever the object has loaded some variables is set to the function called 'loaded'. A LoadVars object passes a single parameter into the onLoad function that indicates whether the load was successful or not. We can use this parameter to adjust the behaviour of the movie. We do not have to call this parameter 'success'; it is simply a Boolean variable (true or false) and can have whatever name we choose.

If the load is successful then the variables are not at the root of the movie, instead they are all inside the LoadVars object. For example if the file 'myvariables.txt' contained:

Apple=1&Pear=2&Orange=3

then the object lv would contain:

lv.Apples = 1

lv.Pear = 2

lv.Orange = 3

Chapters 14, 21 and 22 give more information about communicating with databases using Flash and ASP pages.

Using JavaScript on the current page

Flash can communicate with the current page using any JavaScript function that is placed on the page using the ActionScript function 'fscommand'. This function takes two parameters: the first is a string that can be used as a command name, the second is used for arguments. Because Internet Explorer uses VBScript as the default scripting language you need to put a VBScript version on the page and a JavaScript version. In example 'Examples\Chapter12\fscommand.html' we use a simple Flash movie 'fscommand.swf' which is created with the project file 'fscommand.fla'.

The 'Set' button calls a function 'onSet' which contains the following code:

```
function onSet(){
    fscommand("setSpan", str);
}
```

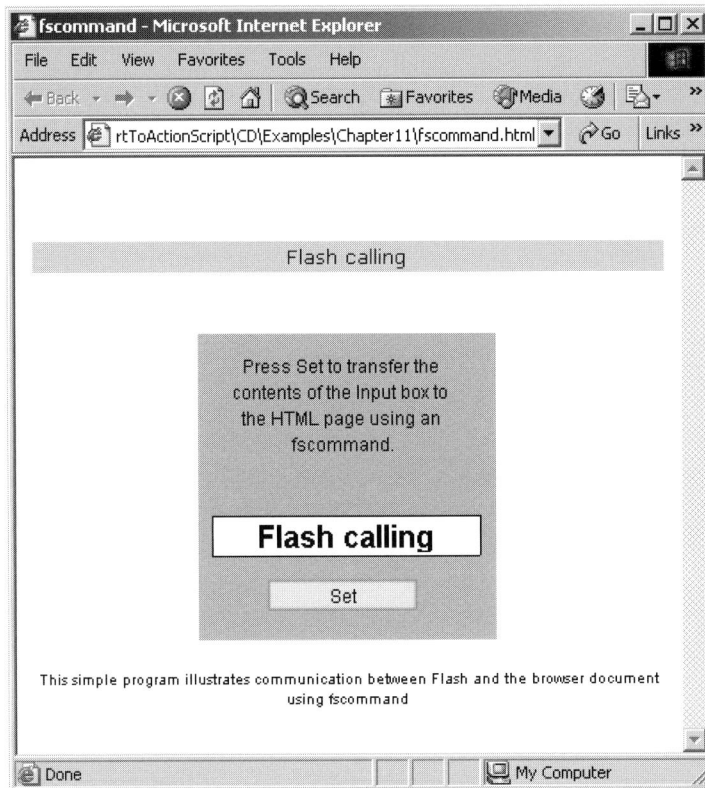

Figure 12.4 *Communication between Flash and the HTML page using fscommand*

The variable 'str' is the input box that you can see in Figure 11.4 displaying the string 'Flash calling'. When 'fscommand' is called for Internet Explorer, if the HTML page contains a VBScript Sub 'xxxx_FSCommand(cmd, args)' where 'xxxx' is the ID used for the Flash object, then this subroutine is called. When fscommand is called for Netscape, if the HTML page contains a JavaScript function 'xxxx_DoFSCommand(cmd, args)' where 'xxxx' is the name used for a Flash embed, then this function is called. A VBScript can call a JavaScript function on the same page using the form 'call functionname(parameter1, …)'. In the example the VBScript function 'flash_FSCommand' calls the JavaScript function 'flash_DoFSCommand' using the 'call' method.

In this instance Flash affects the actual page by setting the document object with the ID 'flashStr', which is the SPAN of the one item table, to the value passed in the variable 'args'.

```
...
<SCRIPT LANGUAGE=JavaScript>
function flash_DoFSCommand(command, args){
    if (command == "setSpan"){
        document.all.flashStr.innerHTML = args;
    }
}
</SCRIPT>
```

```
<SCRIPT LANGUAGE="VBScript">
<!--
//  Handle IE.
Sub flash_FSCommand(ByVal command, ByVal args)
    Call flash_DoFSCommand(command, args)
End Sub
//-->
</SCRIPT>

</HEAD>

<BODY bgcolor="#ffffff">
<CENTER><BR><BR>
<TABLE>
<tr bgcolor="#ccccff">
  <td width="450" height="20">
     <P align=center>
    <font face="Verdana, Arial, Helvetica, sans-serif" size="2"
             color="#0000ff"><span id="flashStr"> </span>
    </font></P></td>
</tr>
</TABLE>
...
<OBJECT
    id = flash
    ...
    <EMBED
       ...
       Name = "flash"
    </EMBED>
</OBJECT>
...
```

Summary

As your games get more sophisticated and your program skills develop you will often need to access data in external files. In this chapter we looked at using the 'loadVariables' method and the 'LoadVars' object. Sometimes the data needs to be created dynamically and we introduced the use of ASP pages for this purpose. Finally we looked at how Flash can use JavaScript on the page into which Flash is embedded by using the fscommand method. Often loading external data will involve databases and we will look at these methods in Chapters 14, 21 and 22.

Section 3

Putting it into practice

You know your stuff, so how about using this knowledge to make some games?

13 Small games to keep them loading

If your game is over a meg and most users access this via dial-up, then you will have lost your audience before they have even seen it. Another game site is just a click away. Your job is to entertain the user; one useful way of keeping the interest of your players while your latest one-meg epic loads is to provide a small game as a pre-loader that they can play while the main game loads. In this chapter we look at creating games that use 20 K or less; for the bandwidth of a small gif we have a game to entertain and sustain their interest.

How to keep a game small

There are a few golden rules for keeping a game small:

Minimize the use of bitmaps

ActionScript code is usually only a few K. But a single bitmap image can easily add 50 K to the download size of your game. Therefore when producing small games, you can effectively rule out the use of bitmaps.

Use Movie Clip symbols for anything that gets reused

There are several ways to group things in Flash. You can use a 'group' but the problem with this is that you are not creating a symbol in the library. Everything about the graphic is stored for each use of the 'group'. It is always preferable to use a symbol, since then you are only storing the complex object once. 'Tweens' make a huge impact on a file and should be used sparingly in small games. If you can duplicate a clip in code then the impact on the file size is negligible.

Minimize the use of sound

Even poor quality sound at 16 kbps adds 20 K to the file size for each 10 seconds. If we are going to fit the entire game in under 20 K then you will need to limit the audio to 4 K at the most. This will give four seconds of 8 kbps audio, suitable for impacts and clicks only.

Don't embed a font

Another common requirement is the use of embedded fonts. If you are only using the numbers for a score, for example, then only embed the numbers.

To select the font outlines that you intend to embed, make sure that the Properties panel is open, either by selecting the menu option 'Window/Properties' or Ctrl + F3. Click on a text box on the main stage and select 'Dynamic Text' from the options on the left of the Properties

Figure 13.1 *Embedding selected font outlines*

panel, and then click the 'Character. . .' button on the right. This will open a dialog box 'Character Options' as in Figure 13.1, giving you a list of the options for embedding fonts. For all capital letters click Uppercase [A..Z] and for all lower case click Lowercase [a..z]; for all numbers choose the Numerals [0..9] option and for all punctuation select Punctuation [!@#%...]. To select specific outlines enter them in the box 'Include these characters:'.

If you need to embed an entire font then the game will be too big. A single font is rarely less than 20 K. Just the numbers are usually around 1 K, so can easily be justified. If you need the odd word then select this using specific outlines or if the text is static then let Flash select just the outlines needed.

Working out where the size goes using a Publish report

Flash has several tools to help the developer determine how the size of their swf files relates to the project's content. The most detailed option is to generate a size report. The 'Publish Settings' dialog box contains the check box necessary to tell Flash to create a report. The 'Publish Settings' dialog box is accessed using the menu option 'File/Publish Settings. . .'.

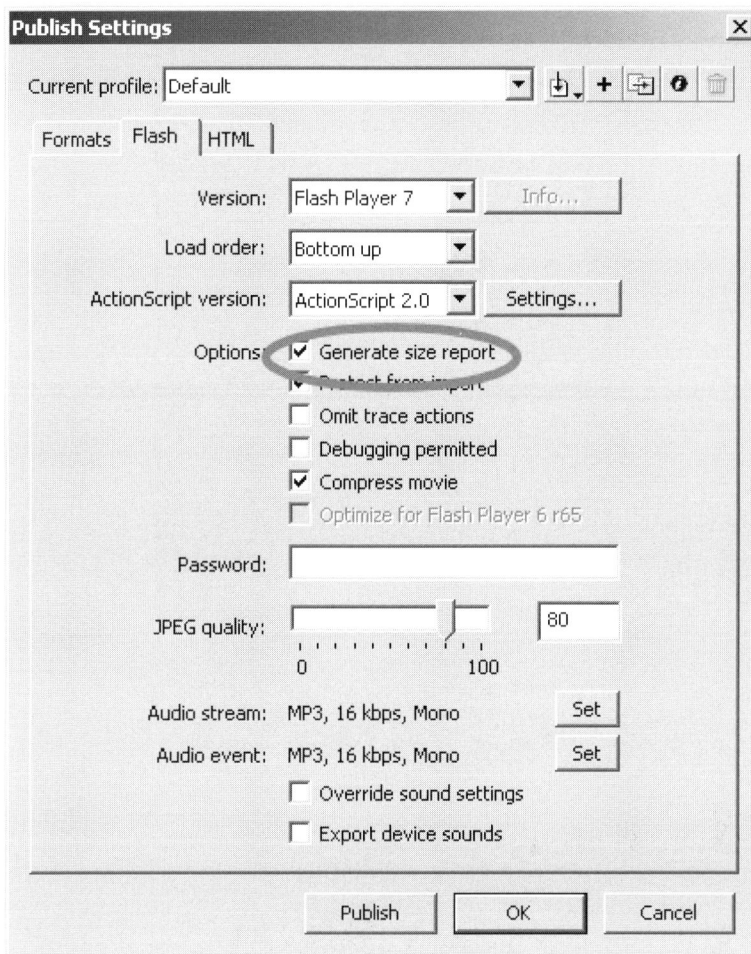

Figure 13.2 *Using the Publish Settings dialog box to generate a size report*

To see how this works open the Flash project file 'Examples/Chapter13/random.fla'. This is a very simple game in which you watch a random number generator and click a button when the displayed number is less than 100 000. Basically it is a reaction time tester. The displayed output shows the total number of times the random number generator created a number less than 100 000, the number of times the user pressed the stop button correctly and the number of times the user pressed the stop button incorrectly.

There is a considerable use of text in this game, but despite this the minimum total size for the game is just 3136 bytes or 3.06 K. Let's look at how this size can be affected by the incorrect use of fonts.

In the game the greatest single use of fonts involves the numbers displayed. For this reason the outlines for the numbers of the chosen font, Arial Narrow, are embedded. The text box settings for the dynamic text boxes that show the main 'randomnumber', 'total', 'right' and 'wrong' answers

Figure 13.3 *A simple reaction time tester*

Figure 13.4 *Dynamic text boxes used in the 'Examples/Chapter13/random.fla' project*

are all set to include just the number outlines. The word 'TOTAL' is a static text box using the same font and the label on the button 'STOP' is also static.

Flash can use either *embedded fonts* or *device font*. The large text area is set to be a device font by selecting '_sans' as the font. Flash includes three device fonts: '_sans', '_serif' and '_typewriter'. On a Windows machine these will default to 'Arial', 'Times' and 'Courier'.

The large text area is set to be a dynamic text box. Because it is dynamic the only way to put multiple font formatting into the box is to use the HTML option. This is set in the text Properties panel in the 'Var:' options box.

Figure 13.5 *Setting a dynamic text box to use HTML formatting*

When using HTML formatting you can set the font face, colour and size. You can include bold, underline and italic formatting. You can add a hyperlink and you can set the paragraph splits. In this example the formatting was all done in the action for frame 1 using the following ActionScript.

```
htmltext = "<P><FONT FACE='Arial' SIZE='10'>Press stop when the number is↵
        less than 100,000. </P><P></P>";
htmltext += "<P>Get more help using a HTML dynamic text box by </FONT>";
htmltext += "<FONT COLOR='#0000FF'><A HREF='randomhelp.html'>clicking↵
        here</A></FONT></P>";
htmltext += "<P><FONT FACE='Arial' SIZE='10' COLOR='#000000'>HTML↵
        formatting is flexible and very bandwidth friendly</FONT>";
htmltext += "<P><FONT FACE='Arial' SIZE='12'><B>This is Arial Bold size↵
        12</B></FONT></P>";
htmltext += "<P><FONT FACE='Times' SIZE='14' COLOR='#FF0000'><I>This is↵
        Times italic size 14 in red</I></FONT></P>";
htmltext += "<P><FONT FACE='Arial' SIZE='10' COLOR='#000000'>This is just↵
        the default text</FONT>"
```

HTML text formatting adds no resources to the size of your game, but it is a very flexible way to put up instructions or text that can change very dynamically. All this text is formatted within the game, or it could be loaded into the game using 'loadVariables'.

The tags you can use are

<A>

Used to create a hyperlink,

```
<A HREF='mylink.html'>This is the words you see on the page</A>
```

<P>

Used to set a paragraph break,

```
<P>This is new paragraph</P>
```

<B>

Used to set bold text,

```
This is ordinary text and <B>this is Bold text</B>
```

<U>

Used to set underlined text,

```
This is ordinary text and <U>this is underlined text</U>
```

<I>

Used to set italic text,

```
This is ordinary text and <I>this is Italic text</I>
```

<FONT FACE... COLOR... SIZE>

Used to set a font's face, colour and size,

```
This is ordinary text and <FONT FACE='Arial' COLOR='#FF0000'
SIZE='12'>this is 12 point Arial in Red </FONT>

FACE='...' takes a font name.
COLOR='...' takes a hexadecimal colour value see chapter 11 for an
explanation of hexadecimal use
SIZE='...' the point size for the font.
```

When using HTML text formatting remember that all HTML tags expect a closing tag that is the same as the opening tag but includes a forward slash character. To create a paragraph you would use:

```
<P>This is the first paragraph and will automatically word wrap to the↵
size of the text box.</P>
<P>This is the second paragraph and is guaranteed to start on a↵
newline.</P>
```

Once you set a tag, it remains active until the closing tag. So:

```
<P><FONT FACE='Arial' SIZE='10' COLOR='#000000'><B>HTML formatting is↵
    flexible and very bandwidth friendly</FONT>
```

```
<P><FONT FACE='Arial' SIZE='12'>This is a bigger font but it is still↵
    set to be bold</B></FONT></P>";
```

because of the position of the closing '</B>' bold tag.

Here is the Publish report for the game:

```
random.swf Movie Report
-----------------------
Frame #    Frame Bytes    Total Bytes    Scene
-------    -----------    -----------    ----------------
      1           3034           3034    Scene 1 (AS 2.0 Classes Export Frame)
      2             68           3102
      3              1           3103
      4              1           3104
      5              1           3105
      6              1           3106
      7              1           3107
      8              1           3108
      9              1           3109
     10              1           3110
     11              1           3111
     12              1           3112
     13              1           3113
     14              1           3114
     15             16           3130
```

```
Scene                        Shape Bytes    Text Bytes    ActionScript Bytes
-----------------------      -----------    ----------    ------------------
Scene 1                              324           406                   752
```

```
Symbol                       Shape Bytes    Text Bytes    ActionScript Bytes
-----------------------      -----------    ----------    ------------------
ResetButton                          122             0                     0
StopButton                            57            87                     0
RandomNumbers                          0            48                     0
```

```
Font Name                 Bytes       Characters
---------------------     ---------   --------------
_sans                        15
Arial Narrow               1087       .0123456789OPST
```

```
ActionScript Bytes    Location
-----------------     --------
            581    Scene 1:Control:1
             61    Scene 1:Buttons:1:No instance name
assigned(StopButton)
             49    Scene 1:Buttons:1:No instance name
assigned(ResetButton)
             51    Scene 1:Control:2
             10    Scene 1:Control:15
```

Pay particular attention to the font section. Here there are two fonts mentioned; '_sans' uses just 15 bytes. This is because the small text area at the bottom of the game is a static font that is set to be a device font by checking the box in the Properties panel.

Figure 13.6 *Using device fonts*

See what happens if this box is not checked.

Font Name	Bytes	Characters
Arial	2125	GLRUacdeghiklmnoprstuwx
Arial Narrow	1087	.0123456789OPST

This includes every font outline needed to display the line 'Get more help using static text with linked URL'. Rather than this using just 15 bytes it uses 2125 bytes, over 100 times the size, just because one simple check box was overlooked. Notice also that the font outlines included for the Arial Narrow font contain the numbers and 'OPST', just the outlines needed to display 'STOP' along with the number text boxes. When you are trying to keep the game small, device fonts make a huge difference to the file size.

Pong, one of our favourites

Before we look at how to code the game let's look at how the use of fonts can influence the size. You can see from the Movie Report for Pong that the game uses just 5854 bytes or around 5 K. But look where the bytes come from: 4688 of the 5854 come from the numbers in the 'JellybabyITC' font. If you are really strapped for bandwidth you could use a device font here. As you know, device fonts use just 15 bytes so the total size would come down from 5854 to just 1166. See what impact fonts can make on the file size of a small game. If we had chosen to embed the entire font instead of just the numbers, then the game would have used 42 131 bytes, nearly 40 K more than we could have used for a device font. My recommendation for these small loader games is to use device fonts unless you really cannot.

```
pong.swf Movie Report
---------------------
Frame #    Frame Bytes    Total Bytes    Scene
-------    -----------    -----------    ----------------
      1           5854           5854    Scene 1 (AS 2.0 Classes Export ..
```

Figure 13.7 *Developing the Pong game*

```
Scene                          Shape Bytes    Text Bytes    ActionScript Bytes
-----------------------        -----------    ----------    ------------------
Scene 1                                  0             0                     0


Symbol                         Shape Bytes    Text Bytes    ActionScript Bytes
-----------------------        -----------    ----------    ------------------
pong                                    44            25                   480
pongboard                               16             0                     0
pongball                                30             0                     0
pongSFX                                  0             0                     5


Font Name                   Bytes        Characters
---------------------       ---------    --------------
JellybabyITC TT Bold         4688        .0123456789


ActionScript Bytes      Location
----------------        -------
             44         pong:control:1
              1         pongSFX:Layer 1:1
              1         pongSFX:Layer 1:2
              3         pongSFX:Layer 1:5
```

```
        92      pong:control:5
         1      pong:control:9
       343      pong:control:10
```

Event Sounds: 11KHz Mono 16 kbps MP3

```
Sound name                  Bytes          Format
----------------------      ---------      ----------
Pulselec.wav                  639           11KHz Mono 16 kbps MP3
```

Another thing to notice in the Movie Report is the use of a small sound file. At less than 1 K the 'bip' sound when the ball hits the bat is well worth including.

When you are creating small loader games you want to be able to easily port them to another game. For this reason a loader game should be a self-contained movie clip. It is best not to access any '_root' level variable because then you can place this game anywhere. A new feature of Flash MX 2004 is the ability to localize a _root to within the current document. When loading the movie clip into a container use the following code:

```
onClipEvent (load){
        this._lockroot =true;
}
```

This ensures that references to _root in the game will refer the timeline of the original document, not the actual root timeline of the container.swf.

Pong uses seven layers:

sound: Used for the single sound effect, which is embedded inside the movie clip, sfx. This way it can be triggered easily from code. An alternative method would be to use a 'Sound' object, but movie clips work fine.

score: The score is just a dynamic text box that tracks the variable 'pongScore'.

mask: Used to contain the ball within the frame.

ball: Containing the ball movie clip.

board: Containing the board and the bat movie clip.

bg: Containing the background design.

control: Containing all the ActionScript that controls the game.

Graphically the game could not be simpler, but the design could easily be changed to reflect the main game for which Pong is being used as just an entertaining loader. The main interest then is in the coding. For this game all the code is contained in the main timeline. There are no 'onClipEvent's or nested movie clips that contain code. The code is set in four frame actions.

```
1 //The board clip is dragged horizontally across the base of the
2 //screen
3 startDrag ("board", true, -51, 24, 52, 24);
4 gotoAndPlay ("ballstart");
```
Listing 13.1 *Frame 1 – 'Examples/Chapter13/pong.fla'*

The purpose of the script on frame 1 is to simply allow the user to drag the board using the mouse. Flash contains a very useful command, 'startDrag', which takes up to six parameters:

```
startDrag(movieClip, [lockMouse], [left, top, right, bottom]);
```

movieClip:	The name of a movie clip instance.
lockMouse:	Whether the movie clip is locked to the centre of the mouse position (true) or where the user first clicks (false).
left, top, right, bottom:	Coordinates relative to the movie clip's parent; these specify a constraining rectangle.

In the script we set the drag to be locked to the mouse centre and the constraining rectangle to allow no vertical movement by setting the values for top and bottom to be the same. Then the playback jumps to the frame 'ballstart':

```
1  //Initialise the variables for a new ball and score
2  //The ball always starts at the top going directly down
3  ballY = -23;
4  ballX = Math.random() * 100 - 50;
5  ball._y = ballY;
6  ball._x = ballX;
7  moveX = 0;
8  moveY = 3;
9  pongScore = 0;
10 gotoAndPlay ("ballplay");
```
Listing 13.2 *Frame 'ballstart' – 'Examples/Chapter13/pong.fla'*

Again this is a very simple initialization script. The variables 'ballX' and 'ballY' store the 'ball' location. Initially these are set to −23, the top of the play area and a random location across the play width. Using these variables the location of the movie clip, 'ball', is set using the movie clip parameters '_x' and '_y'. The game uses a movement in the 'x' direction set to zero and a movement in the 'y' direction initially set to three. The two variables define the amount of horizontal and vertical movement of the ball in a single frame. Finally the score is set to zero and play jumps to the frame 'ballplay'.

```
1  ballX += moveX;
2  ballY += moveY;
```

195

```
3
4   //Bounce off the sides
5   if ((ballX>57 && moveX>0) || (ballX<-57 && moveX<0)) {
6        ballX = ballX - moveX;
7        moveX = -moveX;
8   }
9
10  //Bounce off top
11  if (moveY<0 && ballY <= -26) {
12       ballY = ballY - moveY;
13       moveY = 3;
14  }
15
16  ball._x = ballX;
17  ball._y = ballY;
18
19  //Bounce off bat or miss
20  if (moveY>0 && ballY == 19) {
21       boardTest = ballX - board._x;
22       if (boardTest>-8 && boardTest<8) {
23            pongScore++;
24            moveY = -3;
25            moveX += (boardTest * 0.625);
26            sfx.gotoAndPlay (2);
27       }
28  }
29
30  //If we are going down and the y>31 then we've missed
31  if (moveY>0 && ballY >= 31) {
32       gotoAndPlay ("ballstart");
33  } else {
34       prevFrame ();
35  }
```

Listing 13.3 *Frame 'ballplay' – 'Examples/Chapter13/pong.fla'*

Here is the 'meat' of the game. First we update the 'ballX' and 'ballY' variables by adding the values for 'moveX' and 'moveY'. Then we test to see if the ball has hit the side. This happens if the *x* value for the ball is greater than or less than 57. If we only test for the ball location then we could end up trapping the ball. What we need to do is detect for a collision with the side only when the ball is heading towards that side. This ensures that when the ball bounces off the wall it does not immediately set itself up to hit the wall, then bounce off, then hit in an infinite loop. If we test for the right side, when the 'ballX' variable is greater than 57 and only react if the 'moveX', the ball's direction, is greater than zero then we only react to the collision when the ball is heading right.

The code that is contained within the 'if' statement flips the 'moveX' variable and updates the value for 'ballX' so that it is at the position of the previous frame. It is possible that the next time this code is run the value for 'ballX' is still greater than 57, in which case if we had not added the further condition that 'moveX' has to be greater than zero then the code within the 'if' statement would be executed again, flipping 'moveX' a second time, so the ball would stick to the wall. But the test for 'moveX' ensures that the ball will bounce freely from the wall.

The next 'if' statement tests for a collision with the top wall and behaves identically to the test for the sides; this time we test for the value of 'ballY' only when the direction is up, 'moveY' is less than zero. At this point we update the ball. Then we test for a collision with the 'board' clip. This can only happen when the ball is moving down, 'moveX>0' and the y value of the ball is 19. The use of an exact value like this means that you cannot change the direction value or the initial start position without adjusting this value. I point this out because it is a coding technique to discourage. Because the initial y position for the ball is -23, and the increments are in threes the ball will eventually hit the value 19.

$$-23 + 14 * 3 = 19$$

But if you change anything it won't. Yuck! It would be much better to make 19 the goal value. If we want to make sure the test only occurs once then add in another test to make

```
if (moveX>0 && ballY>=19 && ballY<22){
```

But there is still a problem here; we are embedding into the code the increment in the 'y'. Because we 'know' that the movement in the 'y' is always three we have used this to test for the 'ballY' value being equal to or greater than 19 while also less than $19 + 3 = 22$. What if we want to scale the gameplay as the player gets a higher score by making the y increment four? The code would not work. It is a much better coding technique to use a variable for the y increment, 'incY'. Then wherever we have used the value '3' we can use 'incY' instead. Now the ball hitting the board test should be:

```
if (moveX>0 && ballY>=19 && ballY<(19 + incY)){
```

Wherever possible avoid the use of numeric equality in a conditional, as this is prone to errors. A test for zero is about the only one worth using.

If the condition for the y position of the ball passes the above test, the code within the 'if' statement executes. Firstly a convenience variable 'boardTest' is set to the position of the ball relative to the 'board'. If this is between plus and minus eight then the player has successfully hit the ball and so the score is incremented and a new deflection value is set. The y movement is simply going to be the y increment negated but the value for moveX reflects how central the bat is in relation to the board along with the current movement in the x. Finally the sound effect for a hit is triggered by moving the playback of the sound effect movie clip 'sfx' to the second frame where the sound is played.

197

A simple game, about an hour's work and just over 1 K; it may not be the latest hot game for the Playstation but it should keep them occupied for the seconds it takes to load your game.

Tetris – simple concept, terrific gameplay

Figure 13.8 *Developing Tetris*

The game of 'Tetris' uses five layers:

Control: Containing all the ActionScript.
KeyDetector: Containing a blank button to test for key presses.
Score&Time: Containing the text boxes that display score and time.
Tiles: Containing the main playing pieces.
Bg: Containing the background panels.

The coding for the game makes extensive use of arrays of game data. The game is initialized by duplicating movie clips containing a single tile and placing these all over the game board. The displayed frame for each of these movie clips is controlled by the game logic and the value is stored in the arrays. Reading these arrays controls all the collision detection. For more details on the coding strategy for this game read Chapter 10, where the concepts are discussed in detail. The game uses just 14 K and can be placed inside any Flash timeline.

Listing 13.4 is a small section from the main game loop that can be found on frame 22 ('MainLoop') of the 'tetris' clip in the project 'Examples/Chapter13/tetris.fla'.

We will just look at how the current time and level is set using the following code:

```
1   // Update time
2   milliSecs = getTimer() - startTime;
3
4   //Increment the speed as the time increases
5   if (milliSecs>30000) {
6       //At 30 secs set to level 1
7       level = 1;
8   } else if (milliSecs>60000) {
9       //At 60 secs set to level 1
10      level = 2;
11  } else if (milliSecs>90000) {
12      //At 90 secs set to level 1
13      level = 3;
14  }
15
16  secs = int(milliSecs/1000);
17  mins = int(secs/60);
18  secs -= (mins * 60);
19  if (secs<10) {
20      Time = mins + ":0" + secs;
21  } else {
22      Time = mins + ":" + secs;
23  }
```

Listing 13.4 *Frame 22 – 'Examples/Chapter13/tetris.fla'*

The Flash command 'getTimer' returns a time in milliseconds. Since we initialized a variable called 'startTime', using 'getTimer', when the game was launched, the time since the game began is simply the current timer value minus the starting value. This value is used to set the game level, so that the game scales as the player gets further into the game. Finally the on-screen display for time is set by first getting the number of elapsed seconds, by dividing the millisecond value by 1000. Then the number of minutes in this value is determined by dividing the seconds value by 60. The 'int()' command converts the number within the brackets into an integer value. Having determined the number of minutes, then seconds can be reduced by this value times 60. The on-screen display for 'Time' is in a dynamic text box; we want to ensure that the seconds part of the box always shows two characters, '01' not '1'. Consequently if 'secs' is less than 10 we need to insert a '0' into the string. The string handling is placed within the 'if' conditional to allow for this.

The remainder of the 'MainLoop' frame action involves fairly complex checking of the game state and collision testing; try reviewing it now and see if you can analyse how the game works.

Crosswords – make them read the instructions!

Figure 13.9 *Testing the crossword project*

One popular technique for loaders is to place the instructions in the loading screens. But who reads instructions? In my experience, hardly anyone does. Simple, low file size, animated instructions certainly help. But you could have a quiz, or a crossword that makes the user read the instructions. Without reading the instructions they cannot do the crossword or quiz. An interactive experience is the reason the user has visited your site, so they are willing and eager to get involved. Here is a simple crossword puzzle that could contain questions relating to the instructions for the game. For the example here the questions all relate to Flash programming so you should know all the answers. The layout is very simple: the crossword is on the left and the clues on the right. To avoid using too much screen space the clues are split into 'Across' and 'Down' which can be flipped using the button on the bottom right. If you are stuck then click the 'Answers' button. This reverts to a 'Clear' button when clicked. The crossword layout and questions are all loaded in from a text file using 'loadVariables' so the game is very easily adapted. The project file for this example can be found at 'Examples/Chapter13/crossword.fla'.

The 'crossword.txt' file contains variables of the form

rows:	An integer giving the total number of rows.
rowx:	Where *x* is an integer between 1 and 'rows'. Each of these is a string giving the letters for the row. To show a black square, enter a '0' in the appropriate place in the string. row1=variable00a0 would show as 8 blank squares, 2 black, a blank and a black.
cluetotal:	The total number of clues.
cluex:	Where *x* is an integer between 1 and cluetotal. Each of these indicates the square on which a clue starts.
cluesacross:	A string in HTML format.
cluesdown:	A string in HTML format.
loaded:	Set to 1 to indicate that loading of the file is complete.

The number of columns, 'cols', is determined by getting the length of the first row string. Then the on-screen clue display 'cluetext' is set to show the 'cluesacross' clues. The crossword is made up of duplicated movie clips to keep the formatting flexible and to maintain a small file size. Each square of the crossword contains a single movie clip that contains just two frames: the first frame is a black square and the second frame includes an Input text box connected to the variable 'letter' and a dynamic text box connected to the variable 'clueNum'. Using a little string parsing, the appropriate frame is chosen. If the current row string contains a '0' at the current column then the black square, frame one, is shown, if not then frame two is shown.

```
1   count=0;
2   cols = length(row1);
3   cluetext = cluesacross;
4
5   orgX = 27;
6   orgY = 24;
7
8   var mc:MovieClip;
9
10  for(row=0; row<rows; row++){
11   for (col=0; col<cols; col++){
12      name = "cell" + row + "_" + col;
13
14      if (count>0){
15              duplicateMovieClip("cell0_0", name, count);
16              mc = eval(name);
17              mc._x = orgX + col * 20;
```

```
18              mc._y = orgY + row * 20;
19         }else{
20              mc = cell0_0;
21         }
22
23         str = new String(eval("row" + (row + 1)));
24         if (str.charAt(col)=='0'){
25              mc.gotoAndStop(1);
26         }else{
27              mc.gotoAndStop(2);
28         }
29
30         mc.letter = "";
31         mc.number = "";
32         count++;
33     }
34 }
35
36 duplicateMovieClip("cell0_0", "extra", count);
37 extra.gotoAndStop(2);
38 extra.letter = "";
39 extra.number = "1";
40
41 for (i=1; i<=cluetotal; i++){
42   cell = eval("clue" + i);
43   cell--;
44   col = (cell % cols);
45   row = int(cell/cols);
46   name = "cell" + row + "_" + col;
47   eval(name).number = i;
48 }
49
50 stop();
```

Listing 13.5 *Frame 4 – 'Examples/Chapter13/crossword.fla'*

The remainder of the script sets the clue numbers in the crossword. The cell number is calculated from the value for the 'cluex' variables. Because these think of the top left cell as one, the value is decremented. To get the column we need the remainder after dividing by the number of columns. We get this using (cell % cols), which will give the integer value remaining after division by 'cols'. To get the 'row' we need to find the integer portion of division by 'cols'; 'int(cell/cols)' does just that. Then we can build up the name of this cell as one of the duplicated movie clips from the earlier part of the script. At this point we can assign the current loop value to the variable 'clueNum' inside the clip. That sets up the game, and then the player can enter the values as they wish. There is no checking involved in the game; I leave you to do this enhancing. But there is an Answers button that populates the crossword with the correct answer. After doing this, the button becomes a Clear button so that the player can try again. The code for the Answers button is fairly straightforward:

```
1  on (release){
2   if (answerbuttontext == "Answers"){
3        for (row=0; row<rows; row++){
4              str = eval("row" + (row + 1));
5              for (col=0; col<cols; col++){
6                    name = "cell" + row + "_" + col;
7                    if (str.charAt(col)!='0'){
8                          eval(name).letter = str.charAt(col);
9                    }
10             }
11       }
12       extra.letter = "v";
13       answerbuttontext = "Clear";
14  }else{
15       for (row=0; row<rows; row++){
16             for (col=0; col<cols; col++){
17                   name = "cell" + row + "_" + col;
18                   eval(name).letter = "";
19             }
20       }
21       extra.letter = "";
22       answerbuttontext = "Answers";
23  }
24 }
```

Listing 13.6 *Answers button – 'Examples/Chapter13/crossword.fla'*

If the displayed text on the button is 'Answers' then the values in the 'rowx' variables are parsed to get the current letter for the current cell and this is then assigned to the movie clip variable 'letter'. If the displayed value is not 'Answers' then the movie clip variable 'letter' is set to a blank string for each cell.

Summary

Small games to play while the main game loads are an important consideration for users on a dial-up connection. A 56 K modem connection means 56 kbps (56 000 bits per second), a byte uses 8 bits, and so you can immediately divide the value by 8. $56/8 = 7$, where 7 K is the theoretical maximum throughput with no error checking of a 56 K modem; in practice a 56 K modem usually delivers around 4 K per second. If you can get the player involved in a game within 5 seconds of viewing the page by introducing a simple game that is under 20 K then they are much more likely to stay while the 500 K game loads in around $500/4 = 125$ seconds or just over two minutes. When another site is only a click away, two minutes can seem like an eternity. On TV the broadcasters worry about losing their audience in the short time it takes for the credits to role and regularly put trailers for the programs that are coming later on the same screen as the credits to avoid losing audience share. Your users do not know how marvellous your game is until it loads; how many will you lose who get to the page and don't stay the distance? Your aim must be to minimize this haemorrhaging of users. In this chapter we covered some ideas about how you can 'keep 'em watching'.

14 Quizzes

Quizzes are a very popular form of entertainment on TV. In the UK, a quiz show called *Who Wants To Be a Millionaire?* rapidly became one of the highest rated programmes on TV. Quizzes are very simple to create, Flash MX 2004 even includes a template for creating them, but they are fairly demanding to maintain. In this chapter we will look at creating a database of questions using an SQL Server database. Because the questions are categorized by difficulty and topic we can use this database to access questions in a variety of ways. The chapter builds on some of the concepts presented in Chapter 12.

Multiple choice or free text?

The easiest way to write a quiz program is to use questions that have multiple-choice answers. The advantage of using multiple choice is that any answer the user gives is either *definitely* wrong or *definitely* right. There is no ambiguity. Computer programs hate ambiguity. The disadvantage is that the quiz compilers are required to create the alternative 'wrong' answers, which adds to their work. Free-text input is prone to errors. A quiz that allows free-text input for the answers must have answers that are very easy to input. Numeric answers are the least prone to error, but even here there are possible problems; if the answer is '3', how do you respond to an answer of 'three'? Both answers are correct but if the code is checking for '3' and finds 'three' then the player could easily be marked wrong. Free-text input is very demanding to code; many answers that are incorrectly spelt must be marked as correct. But how do you allow for that? One way is to compare the player's answer with the correct answer using a table of permissible, wrongly spelt answers. But however you approach it, the problem is complex and can result in 'obvious' wrong answers being marked correct and vice versa. In this chapter we are, therefore, only going to consider the multiple-choice option. In the database of quiz questions we will keep the correct answer and three incorrect ones for each question.

Creating a database

Databases come in many shapes and forms. In this chapter we will concentrate on using SQL Server. This is a relational database management system for Windows NT servers. If you intend to do much work using SQL Server then you will need to get a copy of the developer edition. Unfortunately this costs about the same as a copy of Flash although a trial evaluation version is available. A simpler alternative is to use an Access-based database. Access comes with a complete version of Microsoft Office, and much of the material in this chapter applies to both databases. The major difference between the two options is in the way the server implements the database access. The SQL Server route is much more flexible and results in a smoother experience for the user. In the end the cost difference is more than outweighed by the benefits.

Because most of this chapter involves the use of server-based techniques the examples do not run direct from the CD. They are on the CD so that you can examine the code, but to use them live you will need to be running the database on an SQL Server and the ASP code needs to be running on an IIS (Internet Information Server). If you are using a Windows platform it is easy to set up your own machine to operate as an IIS. Check out the documentation that comes with your version of Windows to learn how to do this. (Unfortunately the Home Edition of Windows XP does not allow you to set up your machine as an IIS.) If you are unable to set up your machine as an IIS either because your version of Windows is unsuitable or because you are developing on a MAC then you will need to upload the ASP stuff to an ISP and run the samples across the Internet.

Having installed your version of SQL Server, run the option called 'Enterprise Manager'. This is an application that allows you to create and manipulate databases.

Figure 14.1 *SQL Server Enterprise Manager*

First we will create a database. Connect to a database by clicking on one of the available servers. You can use SQL Server to connect to a remote database, assuming you have the access privileges.

For now we will assume that the server is local to your machine and that you are logged on as administrator. Right-click on the 'Database' folder and choose 'New Database'. For the examples in this chapter I have created a database called 'a2a'.

Figure 14.2 *Creating the database, stage 1*

By default the files for the database are stored in the 'C:\Program Files\Microsoft SQL Server\MSSQL\Data' folder. Each database uses two files, the data file and the transaction log. You can change the path to these files using the Database Properties dialog that is opened when you create a database.

Creating a user for the database

Having created the database we will now create a user. In this example the user is called 'quiz' and has access via SQL Server Authentication using a password. To create a new user expand the database folder and select the newly created database 'a2a', if you are following the example. Expand the 'a2a' folder and right-click on Users, select 'New Database User...' from the context menu. This brings up the dialog box that you can see in Figure 14.5.

Figure 14.3 *Creating the database, stage 2*

Figure 14.4 *Creating the database, stage 3*

Figure 14.5 *Creating a user*

Type in the name 'quiz' and the password you intend to use. Now set up the type of database access this user can have using the 'Database Access' tab. Check the 'db_datareader' and the 'db_datawriter' boxes as shown in Figure 14.6.

Creating a table

A database can contain several tables. For this example we will create a single table called 'Quiz'. To create a table right-click 'Table' in the 'a2a' drop down and select 'New Table...'. This brings up the table designer tool. For this example the table contains nine columns. Each column has a data type suitable for the information that will be stored in the column. Database design is a complex subject and if you intend to use a lot of database access then you are strongly advised to get a good SQL book; the bibliography lists a few of the best ones we have used.

Finally we set the permissions for the user 'quiz' we have created in this table (Figure 14.7). The user 'quiz' can 'SELECT', 'INSERT' and 'UPDATE' but they cannot 'DELETE'. Right-click on user 'quiz' and select properties, and then click the 'Permissions' button.

Figure 14.6 *Allocating the user's roles*

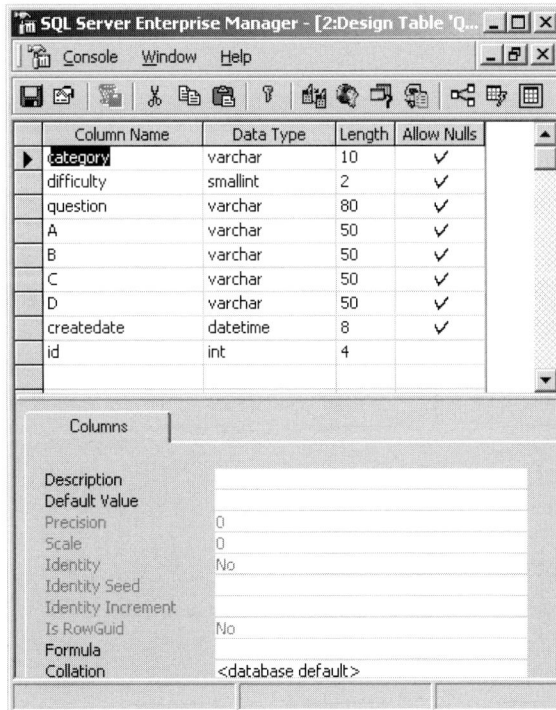

Figure 14.7 *Creating a table*

Figure 14.8 *Setting user permissions*

You now have a database that the user 'quiz' can access to select rows from the table 'quiz', update the data stored there and insert new rows.

Inputting the data

To make the inputting of data easy we will create a Flash-based input tool. Open 'Examples\Chapter14\createquiz.fla'. This project uses the new Flash components to create a tool that allows the developer to read and update the database. Access to the database is via ASP pages. ASP pages can run on your local machine if it is set up as an IIS, Internet Information Server, or you can run them on a remote server. Before we look at how the 'createquiz.fla' project works we will look at the ASP pages it uses.

Connecting to the database using ASP

When using a database the first thing we must do is to connect to it. Because all our pages will use it, we will put this code in a file that can be included in all the other files. As well as creating the connection to the database the code snippet includes the definitions of a few constants that will be used by other pages. 'adCmdText', 'adCmdTable' and 'adCmdStoredProc' are just useful constants to make the code more readable. To create a connection we declare several variables: 'dbUserID' which in this example is the user we have created to access the database, 'quiz'. The password is included; this must be exactly as entered into the SQL Authentication box when creating the user 'quiz'. We also include the database name that we are going to link to, in this case 'a2a', and the server on which the data resides; this can be a remote server. Once these details are provided we can create a connection string, which is simply a string containing all the information a database connection will require. Finally we can use the 'Server' object to create an 'ADODB.Connection', using the 'CreateObject' method. Although by this stage we have a connection object, it is not yet connected; to actually connect we must use the 'Open' method of the connection object passing the connection string as a parameter. Here is the code, which can be found as 'Examples\Chapter14\scriptsJS\dbconnect.asp'.

```
1   <%
2   //-----------------------------------------------------------------
3   //Connects to database
4   //-----------------------------------------------------------------
5
6   //***********DB connection************
7   var dbUserID, dbPassword, dbDatabaseName, dbServerName, dbConnectStr;
8   var conn;
9   var adCmdText = 1;
10  var adCmdTable = 2;
11  var adCmdStoredProc = 4;
12
13  dbUserID = "quiz";
14  dbPassword = "A2a!quiz";
15  dbDatabaseName = "a2a";
16  dbServerName = "NiksDell2";
17  dbConnectStr =    "Provider=SQLOLEDB.1;" +
18                    "Password=" + dbPassword + ";" +
19                    "Persist Security Info=True;" +
20                    "User ID=" + dbUserID + ";" +
21                    "Initial Catalog=" + dbDatabaseName + ";" +
22                    "Data Source=" + dbServerName;
23
24  conn = Server.CreateObject("ADODB.Connection")
25  conn.Open(dbConnectStr);
26  %>
```
Listing 14.1

Creating a new row

Now we have the script to create a connection, we can use it to create a new entry in the database or to update an existing entry. The details for the new entry are passed in via a querystring.

Remember that a querystring takes the form

```
varName1=varValue1&varName2=varValue2&varName3=varValue3&varName4=
   varValue4&...
```

Each variable name and value are linked using the ampersand character. To turn the string into variable data you can use the 'Request' command. The first section of the script turns the querystring into the variables 'category', 'difficulty', 'question', and 'A, B, C, D'.

An ASP page is cached by the browser so it is best to include the command 'Response.Expires=0;' at the beginning of the file to ensure that this caching does not take place, otherwise the page can only be used once.

Having parsed the string into usable variables the 'dbconnect.asp' file is included in the file. The effect of an include is as though the code in the file is actually part of this page. So if everything has worked at this stage in the file you will have the variables to define a record in the database and an open connection. Because the same ASP page is used for both updating and adding we must first find out whether this question appears in the database. To do this we will need another object, an 'ADODB.recordset', which is created in the same way as the connection. Having created a recordset we use the 'Open' method passing a string and the open connection. This time the string is an SQL query. To discover whether the record exists we simply ask for a list of records containing this question using the SQL query 'SELECT ★ FROM quiz WHERE question=' the current question. Here the table is 'quiz' and the only test is for the single parameter 'question'. The database engine then looks through all the records in the 'quiz' table for a match for the current question. Each time it finds a match it is added as a new record to the object 'rs'. We can move between records in the 'rs' object until we reach the end when rs.EOF (End Of File) evaluates to true. If rs.EOF is false after the SQL query then the question was not found. To allow us to use this information later in the code the variable 'found' is set to true or false based on the return value of the query: true if the question exists and false if not.

Part of the information stored in the database is the date the record was added. To do this we need to get the current date. Creating a variable using 'new Date( )' initializes the variable to a 'Date' object containing the current date. To use this with an SQL query we must convert the format into a string. The string should be of the form

```
Month/Date/Year
```

where 'Month' is a number between 1 and 12, 'Date' is a number between 1 and 31 (depending on the month) and the year is in the four-number format. The 'Date' object has methods for returning this information, although the month is returned as a number between 0 and 11, so 1 must be added to achieve the SQL formatting.

We are nearly ready to update or add to the database. First we must format a query string using the information we have discovered. If we are updating then we use the SQL command 'UPDATE'. The format is to follow 'UPDATE' with the table name, and then use 'SET' and a list of values to set separated by commas. So that SQL knows which record to update, the query is completed by adding 'WHERE' with the column name 'question' being equal to the current variable 'question'. If instead we are adding a new record then we use the SQL command 'INSERT INTO' followed by the table name and a list of column names separated by commas inside round brackets. The value of the column names follows the word 'VALUES' and is a list of values separated by commas inside round brackets in the same way as the column names. To actually send this information to the database we create the string then pass it to the 'Execute' method of the open connection. Finally we close the open connection and pass some data to Flash, either 'questionAdded=true' or 'questionUpdated=true' using the 'Response.Write' method. Inside Flash the values of these variables will be set directly as a result of the write. The code for this script is in the file 'Examples\Chapter14\scriptsJS\addQuestion.asp'.

```
1   <%@Language=JavaScript %>
2
3   <%
4   //-------------------------------------------------------------
5   //Script writes a new question to the database from a querystring
6   //-------------------------------------------------------------
7   //Strip data from the query string
8   Response.Expires = 0;
9   var category = Request("category");
10  var difficulty = Request("difficulty");
11  var question = Request("question");
12  var A = Request("A");
13  var B = Request("B");
14  var C = Request("C");
15  var D = Request("D");
16
17  //--------------DATABASE STUFF---------------------
18  %>
19  <!--#include file="dbconnect.asp"-->
20  <%
21  var rs=Server.CreateObject("ADODB.recordset");
22  var found = false;
23
24  rs.Open("SELECT * FROM quiz WHERE question=\'" + question + "\'", conn);
25  if (!rs.EOF) found = true;
26  rs.Close();
27
28  var sqlStr, date;
29  var d = new Date();
30  var dateStr = new String((d.getMonth()+1) + "/" + d.getDate() +
31                           "/" + d.getYear());
32
33  if (found) {
34      // The entry exists so we will amend it
35      sqlStr = "UPDATE quiz SET category=\'" + category +
```

```
36                "\', difficulty=" + difficulty + ", A=\'" + A +
37                "\', B=\'" + B + "\', C=\'" + C + "\', D=\'" + D +
38                "\' WHERE question=\'" + question + "\'";
39      Response.Write("questionUpdated=true&");
40  }else{
41      //No entry so add it
42      sqlStr = "INSERT INTO quiz " +
43              "(category, difficulty, question, A, B, C, D, createdate) " +
44              "VALUES (\'" + category + "\', " + difficulty + ", \'" +
45              question + "\', \'" + A + "\', \'" + B + "\', \'" + C +
46              "\', \'" + D + "\', \'" + dateStr + "\')";
47      Response.Write("questionAdded=true&");
48  }
49
50  conn.Execute(sqlStr);
51  conn.Close();
52
53
54  %>
```

Listing 14.2

Deleting a row

Sometimes we will need to delete a row. Here the method is similar to the above. First we parse the querystring to find the current question. Then we make a connection by including the 'dbconnect.asp' file. Then we build a query this time using 'DELETE FROM' and the table name 'WHERE question=' the current value of the variable question. We can execute this directly on the database without the need for any recordsets. The code for this is in the file 'Examples\Chapter14\scriptsJS\deleteQuestion.asp'.

```
1   <%@Language=JavaScript %>
2
3   <%
4   //--------------------------------------------------------------
5   //Script writes a new question to the database from a querystring
6   //--------------------------------------------------------------
7   //Strip data from the query string
8   Response.Expires = 0;
9   var question = Request("question");
10
11  //--------------DATABASE STUFF---------------------
12  %>
13  <!--#include file="dbconnect.asp"-->
14  <%
15  var sqlStr = "DELETE FROM quiz WHERE question=\'" + question + "\'";
```

```
16
17 conn.Execute(sqlStr);
18 conn.Close();
19
20 Response.Write("questionDeleted = true");
21 %>
```

Listing 14.3

Deleting an entire category

For convenience another ASP page deletes an entire category. This is done in the same way as deleting a single question, except multiple records can be deleted. The code for this is in the file 'Examples\Chapter14\scriptsJS\deleteCategory.asp'.

```
1   <%@Language=JavaScript %>
2
3   <%
4   //------------------------------------------------------------
5   //Script writes a new question to the database from a querystring
6   //------------------------------------------------------------
7   //Strip data from the query string
8   Response.Expires = 0;
9   var category = Request("category");
10
11  //--------------DATABASE STUFF--------------------
12  %>
13  <!--#include file="dbconnect.asp"-->
14  <%
15  var sqlStr = "DELETE FROM quiz WHERE category=\'" + category + "\'";
16
17  conn.Execute(sqlStr);
18  conn.Close();
19
20  Response.Write("questionDeleted = true");
21  %>
```

Listing 14.4

Accessing a category

The input engine will require data from the records in a category. So that the user can access an entire category the script 'Examples\Chapter14\scriptsJS\getCategory.asp' was included. Here a connection is made to the database in the usual way and the variable 'category' is tripped from the query string. The recordset is made using the SQL query 'SELECT ★ FROM' the table 'Quiz' 'WHERE category=' the value of the variable category. Then we create a string from the records to pass back to Flash. The value of the columns in a record can be accessed using 'Fields.Item(x)' where 'x' is the number of the column. To set up the string suitable for Flash the variable data must be in the MIME-encoded form of variable name equals variable value connecting each assignment pair with the ampersand character. To move through the records in the recordset object use the 'moveNext' method. So that Flash knows how many records have been sent, the value of the variable 'questionTotal' is added to the string and a 'loaded=1' value so that Flash knows that the data has been passed. An alternative method for passing data is to use the 'LoadVars' object which has something called a call back function, to inform the program when the data has been correctly received. You will learn more about the 'LoadVars' object in Chapter 19.

```
1   <%@ Language=JavaScript%>
2
3   <%
4   //-------------------------------------------------------------
5   //Script writes card data to db and sends ecards
6   //-------------------------------------------------------------
7   Response.Expires = 0;
8   var category;
9
10  //Strip data from the query string
11  category = Request("category");
12
13  //---------------DATABASE STUFF---------------------
14  %>
15  <!--#include file="dbconnect.asp"-->
16  <%
17  var rs = Server.CreateObject("ADODB.Recordset");
18  var str = "SELECT * FROM Quiz WHERE category =\'" + category + "\'";
19
20  rs.Open( str, conn);
21
22  var i=0;
23  str = "";
24
25  while (!rs.EOF){
26      //Set string
27      str += ("question" + i + "=" + rs.Fields.Item(2).Value + "&");
28      str += ("difficulty" + i + "=" + rs.Fields.Item(1).Value + "&");
29      str += ("A" + i + "=" + rs.Fields.Item(3).Value + "&");
30      str += ("B" + i + "=" + rs.Fields.Item(4).Value + "&");
31      str += ("C" + i + "=" + rs.Fields.Item(5).Value + "&");
```

```
32      str += ("D" + i + "=" + rs.Fields.Item(6).Value + "&");
33      rs.moveNext();
34      i++;
35 }
36 str += ("questionTotal=" + i + "&loaded=1&");
37 Response.Write(str);
38
39 rs.Close();
40 conn.Close();
41
42 %>
```

Listing 14.5

Getting a list of all categories

The last script we will look at returns all the categories in the database, useful for creating the input engine. Much of the methodology will be familiar. The new feature is the use of the term 'DISTINCT' which ensures that only one record for each instance is returned; if there are 25 records in the 'sport' category only a single record 'sport' is returned to the recordset. The data is passed back to Flash using the MIME-encoded string method.

```
1  <%@Language=JavaScript %>
2
3  <%
4  //--------------------------------------------------------------
5  //Script gets all the distinct category names from the database
6  //--------------------------------------------------------------
7  //--------------DATABASE STUFF--------------------
8  %>
9  <!--#include file="dbconnect.asp"-->
10 <%
11 Response.Expires = 0;
12 var rs = Server.CreateObject("ADODB.Recordset");
13 var str = "SELECT DISTINCT(category) FROM Quiz";
14
15 rs.Open( str, conn);
16
17 var i=0;
18 str = "";
19
while(!rs.EOF){
      str += ("category" + i + "=" + rs.Fields.Item(0).Value + "&");
      rs.moveNext();
      i++;
}
str += ("categoryTotal=" + i + "&loaded=1&");
```

```
rs.Close();
conn.Close();

Response.Write(str);

%>
```

Listing 14.6

Creating the front end

Figure 14.9 *Creating an input application*

Now we have the ASP scripts we can use them with a front end for inputting the data. In this example we will make use of the UI components that come with Flash MX 2004. The input screen has a combo box in the top left corner to select the category; buttons to move through the questions within a category are placed to the right of the category combo. There are four buttons on the right, 'Delete category', 'Delete question', 'Reset' and 'Enter question'. There are five radio buttons to select the level of difficulty and finally five text boxes to enter and display the question, the correct answer and three alternative answers. To initialize the data the script 'scriptsJS/getCategories.asp' is called using the 'LoadVariables' method. This occurs on

ActionScript for frame 1. Then the movie goes into a mini loop waiting for the value of 'loaded' to be set to 1 by the ASP script.

```
1   loaded = 0;
2   count = 0;
3   resetQuestion();
4   loadVariables("scriptsJS/getCategories.asp", "");
5   status = "Loading category list";
6
7   function resetQuestion(){
8       categoryCombo.setValue("");
9       question = "";
10      difficulty = "";
11      correctAnswer = "";
12      option1 = "";
13      option2 = "";
14      option3 = "";
15      questionInfo = "";
16  }
```
Listing 14.7

Once the categories are loaded we can load them into the combo box using the 'addItem' method. Remember to clear the combo box first using 'removeAll'. Because the data is passed in as 'category0', 'category1', 'category2' etc., we access the values of these variables using the 'eval' command. The second parameter passed to the 'addItem' method is a data value for this entry. In this example we do not use this so the second parameter is always zero. Once the combo box is populated we load the questions for the first category in the list using the 'getCategory.asp' script with the value for category set to the value the variable 'category0'.

```
1   for (i=0; i<categoryTotal; i++){
2       categoryCombo.addItem(eval("category" + i), 0);
3   }
4   loaded = 0;
5   loadVariables("scriptsJS/getCategory.asp?category=" + category0, "");
6   status = "Loading category " + category0;
7   nextFrame();
```
Listing 14.8

Again the engine enters a waiting loop until the value for 'loaded' is set to one by the ASP script. Finally the first question can be displayed using the 'setQuestion' function. This function is passed the index of the required question and the values of the displayed variables are updated using the variables set by the ASP page.

```
1   function setQuestion(i){
2       questionIndex = i;
3       question = eval("question" + i);
4       difficulty = eval("difficulty" + i);
5       eval("diff" + difficulty).setState(true);
6       correctAnswer = eval("A" + i);
7       option1 = eval("B" + i);
8       option2 = eval("C" + i);
9       option3 = eval("D" + i);
10      questionInfo = (i+1) + "\\" + questionTotal;
11      prevBtn.setEnabled((i!=0));
12      nextBtn.setEnabled((i!=(questionTotal-1)));
13      debug = question + chr(13) + correctAnswer + chr(13) +
14              option1 + chr(13) + option2 + chr(13) + option3 + 15 chr(13);
15  }
```

Listing 14.9

Whenever there is a change of category the following script is run, which makes a call to the 'getCategory.asp' script.


```
1   function changeCategory(){
2       category = categoryCombo.getSelectedItem().label;
3       loaded = 0;
4       loadVariables("scriptsJS/getCategory.asp?category=" + category, "");
5       status = "Loading " + category;
6       gotoAndPlay("loadCategory");
7   }
```

Listing 14.10

Whenever the enter button is pressed the following script is used. Here the current value of the category is accessed using the combo box method 'getValue'. If a combo box is editable then this value is the text string that is entered by the user and displayed in the combo box when the drop-down options are not shown. If this is a new entry then we should place it in the combo box drop-down list. To check this we look through every entry in the combo box list to see if it is the same as the current category value. If it is then we do not need to update the combo box, if not then an update is required using the 'addItem' method.

To get the difficulty level we need to go through each radio button in turn, they have been given the instance names 'diff1' to 'diff5'. As soon as we find the one that is set we can set the difficulty level to the index for that button and jump out of the repeat loop. It just remains to create the MIME-encoded query string, by combining all the elements needed to add or update a question and call the 'addQuestion.asp' script. Then playback jumps to a loop that is waiting for the variables either 'questionAdded' or 'questionUpdate' to be set to true.

```
1   function enterQuestion(){
2       category = categoryCombo.getValue();
3       //Update the combo box if this is a new category
4       found = false;
5       for (i=0; i<categoryCombo.getLength(); i++){
6               if (category==categoryCombo.getItemAt(i).label){
7                       found = true;
8                       break;
9               }
10      }
11      if (!found) categoryCombo.addItem(category, 0);
12      str = "category=" + category;
13      //Get the difficulty level from the radio buttons
14      for (i=1; i<=5; i++){
15              if (eval("diff" + i).getState()){
16                      difficulty = i;
17                      break;
18              }
19      }
20      str += "&difficulty=" + difficulty;
21      str += "&question=" + question;
22      str += "&A=" + correctAnswer;
23      str += "&B=" + option1;
24      str += "&C=" + option2;
25      str += "&D=" + option3;
26      questionAdded = false;
27      questionUpdated = false;
28      loadVariables("scriptsJS/addQuestion.asp?" + str, "");
29      resetQuestion();
30      status = "Adding or updating question";
31      gotoAndPlay("addQuestion");
32  }
```

Listing 14.11

When deleting a question it was found necessary to add a random variable to avoid the caching issue. That is the purpose of 'killcache='+ random(100000); it simply makes each call to the page unique. If any readers know of a better way to avoid the caching problem then please get in touch via the web page for this book: www.niklever.net/flashmx2004games.

```
1   function deleteQuestion(){
2       loadVariables("scriptsJS/deleteQuestion.asp?question=" + question +
3                               "&killcache=" + random(100000), "");
4       resetQuestion();
```

```
5        status = "Question deleted";
6  }
```

Listing 14.12

Deleting a category involves updating the combo box, by first finding the category that is currently displayed and then using the combo box method 'removeItemAt'.

```
1  function deleteCategory(){
2      category = categoryCombo.getValue();
3      //Update the combo box
4      for (i=0; i<categoryCombo.getLength(); i++){
5              if (categoryCombo.getItemAt(i).label==category){
6                      categoryCombo.removeItemAt(i);
7                      break;
8              }
9      }
10     loadVariables("scriptsJS/deleteCategory.asp?category=" +
11                     category, "");
12     status = "Category deleted";
13     resetQuestion();
14 }
```

Listing 14.13

Moving through the questions is easily achieved using these two simple functions that are called by the forward and back buttons.

```
1  function previousQuestion(){
2      if (questionIndex>0){
3              setQuestion(questionIndex - 1);
4      }
5  }
6
7  function nextQuestion(){
8      if (questionIndex<(questionTotal-1)){
9              setQuestion(questionIndex + 1);
10         }
11 }
```

Listing 14.14

Figure 14.10 *Using the input application*

Ideas for the implementation

At this stage you have an engine to enter and update quiz questions. The actual implementation of the quiz is left to the developer. You can access the questions based on category and difficulty. An interactive quiz should include some scaling of the difficulty and certain hurdles that the player must get over in order to move on to an extra life. Maybe you can offer some useful lifelines initially by reducing the number of possible answers, or making suggestions that are often but not always correct. The quiz could be made funny by including a cartoon character that responds to correct and incorrect answers in an amusing way. The quiz could use a high score table that offers prizes on a daily, weekly or monthly basis. Maybe the quiz could be part of an email program, where players could send 10 questions to a friend. However it is implemented, a quiz is a popular form of entertainment and easily updated. Because we have included the input date in the database we could easily offer the player the opportunity just to select from the new questions. This breathes new life into a website and encourages more visits.

Summary

Most of this chapter dealt with database access. This is a very important subject, because on even the simplest site you probably want to collect some data from the users, even if it is only email addresses and current high score. Flash MX 2004 has an alternative way of passing data using the 'LoadVars' object and if the topics in this chapter may prove useful to you then you are recommended to read through Chapters 21 and 22 where other important methods of passing data are explained.

15 Mazes

Mazes form the basis of many games. The maze structure may be obvious, as in the example in this chapter, or subtle like the movement from room to room in a first-person shooter. In this chapter we are going to look at creating a first-person maze. Graphically the imagery will be computer generated, created using Lightwave 3D. The process has three stages. First we will create a program using Flash to generate the data that a maze game will need. Then we will create the graphics using in this instance Lightwave, but any CGI application will suffice. Finally we will learn how to import the data and how to move around the maze using the constraints implied by the maze data.

Storing a maze in a computer readable form

People like pictures, computers like numbers. The imagery we will show to the player of our maze game will be pictorial, but internally the computer will only understand numbers. To store the maze in a computer readable form we will first ensure that the maze is effectively a grid. Each cell in the grid can have an entrance to the North, South, East or West, or any combination of these. There are 16 possible combinations of four elements.

Table 15.1 *Storing the paths into a cell*

North (1)	South (2)	East (4)	West (8)	Total
0	0	0	0	0
1	0	0	0	1
0	2	0	0	2
1	2	0	0	3
0	0	4	0	4
1	0	4	0	5
0	2	4	0	6
1	2	4	0	7
0	0	0	8	8
1	0	0	8	9
0	2	0	8	10
1	2	0	8	11
0	0	4	8	12
1	0	4	8	13
0	2	4	8	14
1	2	4	8	15

The strategy used to store the paths is to assign a number to each exit; North will be 1, South is 2, East is 4 and West is 8. If a cell has no paths then the value stored for this cell will be zero. If a cell has four paths then the value stored will be 15. Table 15.1 shows all the possible values. Because a path can either be on or off, choosing powers of two to provide the value for a column ensures that we have enough information to store every possible value. If a cell is the entrance then we will add 16 to the value and if the cell is an exit we will add 32. To create a maze we need to generate the values for each cell and store this in a MIME-encoded form so that we can easily load the variable values into Flash. To do this we will create a maze maker program.

Maze maker

Figure 15.1 *Creating the maze generator program*

The maze maker program, 'Examples\Chapter15\mazeMaker.fla', contains a movie clip called 'cell'. This has 16 frames to represent the 16 different possible values for the paths coming into a cell. It also contains a transparent button, i.e. a button with only a hit area, no graphics. The one release action for the button is to step to the next frame; on frame 17 the playback head is set to frame one. The maze maker program also contains input boxes to set up the number of rows and columns in the maze. There are three command buttons and a dynamic text area.

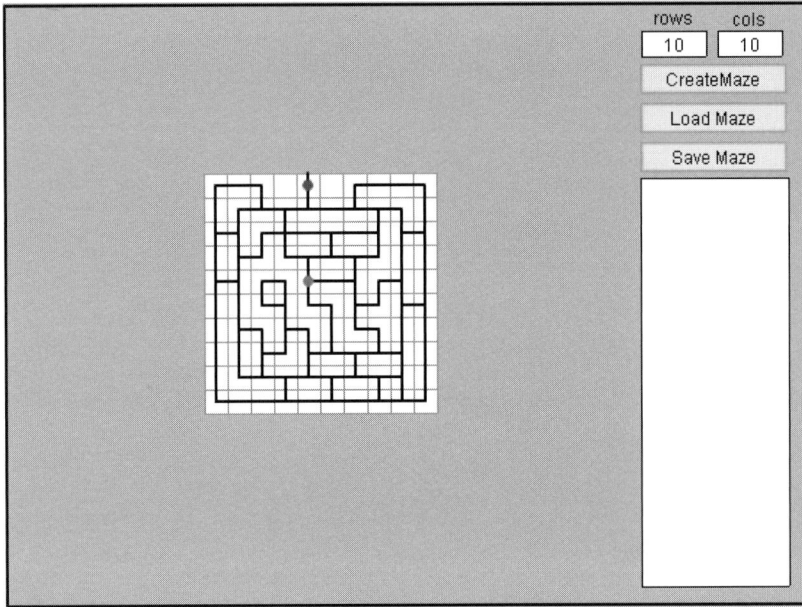

Figure 15.2 *Using the maze generator program*

When the movie starts, a new 'LoadVars' object is created on line 5 of Listing 15.1. A 'LoadVars' object is an alternative to using the ActionScript function 'loadVariables'. It has an 'onLoad' callback function. A callback function happens whenever the relevant event takes place; in this instance because in line 6 of Listing 15.1 we assign the 'onLoad' callback to 'mazeLoaded', Flash looks for a function called 'mazeLoaded' and if it finds one then it will call this function whenever new data has been loaded. The use of callbacks makes the execution of the program much easier to handle. Previously a waiting loop would have been necessary after a call to 'loadVariables', because the program needs to know when the data has been downloaded from the Internet. Now the program can continue immediately and will be informed about a successful or unsuccessful load at the earliest opportunity. The 'LoadVars' object even has facilities for estimating the length that a download will take so that you can inform the player with a progress bar. This code is placed on frame 1 of the main timeline.

```
1   ENTRANCE = 16;
2   EXIT = 32;
3   cellH = 0;
4   cellV = 0;
5   lv = new LoadVars();
6   lv.onLoad = mazeLoaded;
7   createMaze();
8   stop();
```

Listing 15.1

Notice that the frame 1 code contains a call to a function called 'createMaze'. The purpose of this function is to dynamically create the duplicated movie clips that show a maze grid. To ensure that a previous maze grid is deleted the function calls 'clearCells'. The number of duplicated movie clips in the vertical direction is stored in the variable 'cellV' and the number in the horizontal direction in the variable 'cellH'. These two variables are used by the 'clearCells' function in the two loops, for 'row' and 'col'. Having duplicated a clip it is positioned based on a grid centred on the middle of the movie. To centre something you can use the code snippet

```
left = (movieWidth - clipWidth)/2;
top = (movieHeight - clipHeight)/2;
```

The 'orgX' and 'orgY' variables, Listing 15.2, lines 6 and 7, are set in a similar way, only rather than using the value for a clip's width and height we take the value of the number of rows and columns multiplied by a cell width and height, giving the total width of the maze on screen.

```
1   function createMaze(){
2       var name, row, col, count = 1, orgX, orgY;
3
4       if (cellH>0 || cellV>0) clearCells();
5
6       orgX = (450 - cols * 16)/2;
7       orgY = (400 - rows * 16)/2;
8
9       for (row=0; row<rows; row++){
10              for (col=0; col<cols; col++){
11                      name = "cell" + row + "_" + col;
12                      duplicateMovieClip("cell", name, count++);
13                      eval(name)._x = col * 16 + orgX;
14                      eval(name)._y = row * 16 + orgY;
15              }
16      }
17      cellH = cols;
18      cellV = rows;
19  }
20
21  function clearCells(){
22      var row, col;
23
24      for (row=0; row<cellV; row++){
25              for (col=0; col<cellH; col++){
26                      removeMovieClip("cell" + row + "_" + col);
27              }
28      }
```

```
29    cellH = 0;
30    cellV = 0;
31 }
```
Listing 15.2

When the 'Load Maze' button is pressed the movie uses the 'LoadVars' object 'lv' to load the variables contained in the text file 'maze.txt'. Because we set the callback for the 'lv' object to 'mazeLoaded' this function is called when the variables are loaded or have failed to load. If the load was successful then the parameter passed to the function will be set to true. This is used in the function. Then the function 'createMaze' is used to create a new maze set to the size indicated by the 'maze.txt' file. The frame for each cell is then set using the values in the file. Finally for each cell the nested movie clip 'Entrance' is set to a frame indicating whether this is an entrance or exit frame or whether it is an ordinary cell. The value for a cell is stored as in Table 15.1. To get the cell value, however, we must strip out the effect of the addition of a possible value for EXIT or ENTRANCE. This is achieved using the bitwise And operator, &. The code snippet

```
low4bits = (src & 0xF);
```

0xF refers to the hexadecimal value 'F'. Hexadecimal uses 16 symbols for each column while decimal uses 10. The symbol 9 is followed by A, then B, C, D, E and F. F is the same as 15. The binary value for 15 is 1111 as you can see from Table 15.2. For the number 15 the lowest four bits are all set to one. Suppose we have the number 234. The binary representation of this is 11101010. Here the lowest four bits are 1010, or A using hexadecimal notation or 10 using the familiar decimal notation. To quickly separate the value stored in the lowest four bits from the rest we And the number with 00001111. Recall that each of the separate numbers, or bits, in the binary representation is set only if both numbers are set. So we have

$$00001111 \quad \& \quad 11101010 = 00001010$$

The top four bits being set to zero using this method. By ANDing in this way we ensure that any higher bits are excluded.

```
next4bits = (src & 0xF0);
```

The effect of ANDing with 0xF0 is to test the next four bits, that is the bits that represent 16, 32, 64 and

Table 15.2 *Decimal, hexadecimal and binary chart*

Decimal	Hexadecimal	Binary
0	0	0000
1	1	0001
2	2	0010
3	3	0011
4	4	0100
5	5	0101
6	6	0110
7	7	0111
8	8	1000
9	9	1001
10	A	1010
11	B	1011
12	C	1100
13	D	1101
14	E	1110
15	F	1111

128, and exclude the effect of lower bits. Using this method we can easily extract just the value we want from a variable that may contain multiple bits of information. For example, because we know that the information for the SOUTH path is stored in the second bit we can use

```
southPath = (src & 0x2)
```

to access just this bit.

```
1   function loadMaze(){
2       lv.load("maze.txt");
3   }
4
5   function mazeLoaded(success){
6       var row, col, cell, valname, val;
7
8       if (success){
9               rows = lv.rows;
10              cols = lv.cols;
11              createMaze();
12              for(row=0; row<rows; row++){
13                  for(col=0; col<cols; col++){
14                      cell = eval("cell" + row + "_" + col);
15                      valname = "lv.val" + row + "_" + col;
16                      val = (eval(valname) & 0xF);
17                      cell.gotoAndStop(val);
18                      val = (eval(valname) & 0xF0);
19                      switch(val){
20                          case ENTRANCE:
21                          cell.Entrance.gotoAndStop(2);
22                          break;
23                          case EXIT:
24                          cell.Entrance.gotoAndStop(3);
25                          break;
26                          default:
27                          cell.Entrance.gotoAndStop(1);
28                      }
29                  }
30              }
31      }
32  }
```

Listing 15.3

Because of security implications across the Internet, Flash does not contain any code for saving a file – but a user can select the characters in a dynamic text box. In this example we use a text box in this way. After pressing the 'Save Maze' button the text box is populated. To save the text, select and copy it and paste it into a text editor. The text is simply a MIME-encoded file. The value for each cell is stored in the file as 'valx_y' where *x* is the row and *y* the column.

```
1   function saveMaze(){
2       var row, col, cell, valname, val;
3
4       mazeStr = "rows=" + rows + "&cols=" + cols;
5       for (row=0; row<rows; row++){
6               for (col=0; col<cols; col++){
7                       cell = eval("cell" + row + "_" + col);
8                       valname = "val" + row + "_" + col;
9                       val = cell.value;
10                      if (cell.Entrance._currentframe == 2){
11                              val += ENTRANCE;
12                      }else if (cell.Entrance._currentframe == 3){
13                              val += EXIT;
14                      }
15                      mazeStr += ("&" + valname + "=" + val);
16              }
17      }
18 }
```

Listing 15.4

Creating the graphics

In the example 'Examples\Chapter15\maze.fla', we use a first-person view of the maze. This is created using the 3D application program Lightwave. This is not a real-time 3D program; all the images are pre-rendered. Every cell has an animation that takes you into the cell in 10 frames and then a left, forward, right and spin action that is dependent on the current cell type. A cell with four paths would have each action while a straight will have just a forward and spin action. Every animation sequence has a common frame at the beginning of the animation. This is achieved using fogging so that the path in the distance is hidden from the viewer as it disappears into darkness. There are 18 different animations pre-rendered in 10 frame sequences, making a total of 180 bitmap images. The total would be greater if it were not for symmetry. This ensures that the corners and T-junctions to the right can be flipped to give the corners and T-junctions to the left. Because the mid position of the animations needs to be common across all animations, the modelling and animating must be done using numeric values.

The basic model used is a cross. This allows for every possible path. Each exit from the central cross can be blocked using an extra polygon whose surface can be set to 100 per cent transparent. The distance fogging is set so that the end of the tunnel disappears.

Figure 15.3 *Creating the tunnel model*

Figure 15.4 *Setting camera paths for the tunnel*

The camera motion is set to move the camera exactly three cells forward and rotate right if necessary. The end of the motion matches the beginning exactly so that each animation sequence can be joined with any other.

Creating the maze game

Figure 15.5 *Developing the maze game*

At this stage we have 18 ten-frame animation sequences. These are used in several different movie clips. There is a 'T_Both', 'T_Right', 'T_Left', 'Cross', 'Straight', 'CornerR', 'CornerL', 'End', 'Block' and 'Exit'. The allowed paths from the different cells are as follows

Table 15.3 *Exit paths from cells*

Clip	moveForward	turnLeft	turnRight	SpinAround	Value
T_Both		✓	✓	✓	14
T_Right			✓	✓	7
T_Left		✓		✓	11
Cross	✓	✓	✓	✓	15
Straight	✓			✓	3
CornerR			✓	✓	6
CornerL		✓		✓	10
Exit				✓	8

Open 'Examples\Chapter15\maze.fla' and double-click the tunnel to see the embedded movie clips.

Figure 15.6 *Playing the maze game*

In addition to the images in the 'Tunnel' clip there is an overview of the maze, which is created in an identical way to that used in the 'mazeMaker' project, and a 'Start Again' button.

The ActionScript for frame 1 simply defines a few constants and loads in the maze using a 'LoadVars' object.

```
1   NORTH = 1;
2   SOUTH = 2;
3   EAST = 4;
4   WEST = 8;
5   ENTRANCE = 16;
6   EXIT = 32;
7   lv = new LoadVars();
8   lv.onLoad = mazeLoaded;
9   lv.load("maze.txt");
10  stop();
```
Listing 15.5

When the data for the maze is loaded the 'mazeLoaded' function is called, where the values for the entrance and exit are extracted and the overview map is created, in much the same way as the mazeMaker project and the current cell is entered.

```
1   function mazeLoaded(success){
2       var found = false, exitRow, exitCol, name;
3
4       //trace("Maze loaded: (" + lv.rows + "," + lv.cols + ") " + success);
5
6       for (row=0; row<lv.rows; row++){
7           for (col=0; col<lv.cols; col++){
8               if (eval("lv.val" + row + "_" + col) & EXIT){
9                   exitRow = row;
10                  exitCol = col;
11                  found = true;
12                  break;
13              }
14          }
15      }
16
17
18      found = false;
19
20      for (row=0; row<lv.rows; row++){
21          for (col=0; col<lv.cols; col++){
22              if (eval("lv.val" + row + "_" + col) & ENTRANCE){
23                  found = true;
24                  break;
25              }
26          }
27          if (found) break;
28      }
29
30      if (!found){
31          //Create default entrance
32          row = 0;
33          col = 0;
34      }
35
36      entranceRow = row;
37      entranceCol = col;
38
39      dir = NORTH;
40      showMap();
41      enterCell();
42  }
```

Listing 15.6

The purpose of the 'enterCell' function is to set up the correct images sequence to show. A player's direction influences the behaviour. If a player is pointing in a northerly direction then the current value of the cell gives the information necessary to show the current images sequence. If, however, the player is facing south, then the images we should show are different. The images sequence to show is based on the values of the paths from that cell. For example if we have a 'T_Right' junction when facing north, the value for this cell would be 7, made up of North (1), South (2) and East (4). If we faced south at the same cell then the image sequence should be 'T_Left'. Facing east we should show 'Straight' and facing west we should show 'T_Both'. What we need is a mapping for each direction. When facing south, north maps to south and south maps to north, while west maps to east and east maps to west; so the value changes as shown in Table 15.4.

Table 15.4 *How mapping from a north to a south direction affects the value*

	North	South	East	West	Total
Original	1	2	4	0	7
Mapped	1	2	0	8	11

This maps a T_Right to a T_Left as you can see from the values displayed in Table 15.2.

It is important that the program knows when an animation is playing and when to wait for user input. The movie clip 'Tunnel' contains a 'mode' variable that can take the values 'STATIONARY', 'EXITING', 'EXITED', 'ENTERING' or 'NOTLOADED'. These constants are declared on frame 1 of the Tunnel clip. It is customary to define constants using upper-case letters.

```
1   function enterCell(){
2       var val, tmp, exitcell, nm, path = new Array(4);
3
4       nm = "lv.val" + row + "_" + col;
5       val = eval(nm) & 0xF;
6       exitcell = eval(nm) & 0x20;
7
8       cell = eval("cell" + row + "_" + col);
9       Location._x = cell._x;
10      Location._y = cell._y;
11
12      switch(dir){
13          case NORTH:
14          //Already correct value
15          Location.gotoAndStop(1);
16          break;
17          case SOUTH:
18          tmp = 0;
19          if (val & SOUTH) tmp += NORTH;
20          if (val & NORTH) tmp += SOUTH;
```

```
21          if (val & WEST) tmp += EAST;
22          if (val & EAST) tmp += WEST;
23          val = tmp;
24          Location.gotoAndStop(2);
25          break;
26          case EAST:
27          tmp = 0;
28          if (val & EAST) tmp += NORTH;
29          if (val & WEST) tmp += SOUTH;
30          if (val & NORTH) tmp += WEST;
31          if (val & SOUTH) tmp += EAST;
32          val = tmp;
33          Location.gotoAndStop(3);
34          break;
35          case WEST:
36          tmp = 0;
37          if (val & EAST) tmp += SOUTH;
38          if (val & WEST) tmp += NORTH;
39          if (val & SOUTH) tmp += WEST;
40          if (val & NORTH) tmp += EAST;
41          val = tmp;
42          Location.gotoAndStop(4);
43          break
44  }
45
46  trace("enterCell: (" + row + "," + col + ") = " + val);
47
48  Tunnel.gotoAndStop(1);
49  //Store the current direction rotated path value
50  paths = val;
51  if (exitcell == EXIT) val = 1;
52
53  switch (val){
54          case 1:
55                  Tunnel.gotoAndPlay("exit");
56                  break;
57          case 3:
58                  Tunnel.gotoAndPlay("straight");
59                  break;
60          case 6:
61                  Tunnel.gotoAndPlay("cornerR");
62                  break;
63          case 7:
```

```
64                    Tunnel.gotoAndPlay("T_Right");
65                    break;
66         case 10:
67                    Tunnel.gotoAndPlay("cornerL");
68                    break;
69         case 11:
70                    Tunnel.gotoAndPlay("T_Left");
71                    break;
72         case 14:
73                    Tunnel.gotoAndPlay("T_Both");
74                    break;
75         case 15:
76                    Tunnel.gotoAndPlay("cross");
77                    break;
78    }
79    Tunnel.mode = Tunnel.ENTERING;
80 }
```
Listing 15.7

Responding to user input

If the mode for the 'Tunnel' clip is STATIONARY then during the 'onClipEvent', enterFrame for this clip we read the keyboard. The arrow keys all call a different function declared on frame one of the main timeline. The same clip event is used to trigger the changeover from an exiting animation to an entering animation. Exiting animation is triggered by user input, but entering events are called from this event alone.

```
1   onClipEvent(enterFrame){
2       switch(mode){
3            case EXITED:
4            _root.enterCell();
5            break;
6            case STATIONARY:
7            if (Key.isDown(Key.UP)){
8                    _root.moveForward();
9            }else if (Key.isDown(Key.LEFT)){
10                    _root.turnLeft();
11            }else if (Key.isDown(Key.RIGHT)){
12                    _root.turnRight();
13            }else if (Key.isDown(Key.DOWN)){
14                    _root.spinAround();
15            }
16            break;
```

```
17        }
18  }
```
Listing 15.8

Each of the functions called from a keyboard press tests for a suitable exit in the required direction. The variable 'paths' is the user-rotated view of the maze. If you are pointing east and there is a path to the east then this will have been mapped to a north direction using the enterCell function. The purpose of each of these functions is to move the player around the maze legally. Each function updates the 'row' and 'col' variables and adjusts the direction variable 'dir' if a turn is involved. Each function completes by setting the 'mode' variable and playing the appropriate animation to exit a cell.

```
1   function moveForward(){
2       if (paths & NORTH){
3               //Only allowed if a NORTH movement is available
4               switch (dir){
5                       case NORTH:
6                       row--;
7                       break;
8                       case SOUTH:
9                       row++;
10                      break;
11                      case EAST:
12                      col++;
13                      break;
14                      case WEST:
15                      col--;
16                      break;
17               }
18              Tunnel.mode = Tunnel.EXITING;
19              Tunnel.anim.gotoAndPlay("Forward");
20       }
21  }
22
23  function turnLeft(){
24      if (paths & WEST){
25              //Only allowed if a WEST movement is available
26              switch (dir){
27                      case NORTH:
28                      dir = WEST;
29                      col--;
30                      break;
31                      case SOUTH:
```

```
32                     dir = EAST;
33                     col++;
34                     break;
35                     case EAST:
36                     dir = NORTH;
37                     row--;
38                     break;
39                     case WEST:
40                     dir = SOUTH
41                     row++;
42                     break;
43                 }
44             Tunnel.mode = Tunnel.EXITING;
45             Tunnel.anim.gotoAndPlay("Left");
46     }
47 }
48
49 function turnRight(){
50     if (paths & EAST){
51             //Only allowed if a EAST movement is available
52             switch (dir){
53                     case NORTH:
54                     dir = EAST;
55                     col++;
56                     break;
57                     case SOUTH:
58                     dir = WEST;
59                     col--;
60                     break;
61                     case EAST:
62                     dir = SOUTH;
63                     row++;
64                     break;
65                     case WEST:
66                     dir = NORTH
67                     row--;
68                     break;
69             }
70             Tunnel.mode = Tunnel.EXITING;
71             Tunnel.anim.gotoAndPlay("Right");
72     }
73 }
74
```

```
75 function spinAround(){
76     if (paths & SOUTH){
77             //Only allowed if a SOUTH movement is available
78             switch (dir){
79                     case NORTH:
80                     dir = SOUTH;
81                     row++;
82                     break;
83                     case SOUTH:
84                     dir = NORTH;
85                     row--;
86                     break;
87                     case EAST:
88                     dir = WEST;
89                     col--;
90                     break;
91                     case WEST:
92                     dir = EAST;
93                     col++;
94                     break;
95             }
96             Tunnel.mode = Tunnel.EXITING;
97             Tunnel.anim.gotoAndPlay("Spin");
98     }
99 }
```

Listing 15.9

Each exit sequence completes by setting the mode variable to 'EXITED'; this is used by the onClipEvent to trigger an 'Into' sequence. This in turn completes by setting the mode variable to STATIONARY. Using this code you can move around any maze at will. Try creating a new maze using the mazeMaker and then saving this as 'maze.txt' in the same folder as 'maze.swf'. Running the 'maze.swf' movie will load the new maze.

Suggestions for enhancement

The example is only the basis for a program; you can improve it by randomly blocking an exit, or having a timer so that the user must move quickly. Maybe the map is usually hidden with just a quick glance every now and then. Maybe you are being chased and have to avoid the cells that contain baddies. You could work out a value for every cell as a distance to exit value. By comparing this with the previous cell you could provide a 'getting warmer' or 'getting colder' bar to help find the way out of the maze without a map. There are so many additions to the basic idea that I leave it to the interested reader to add some excitement to the basic game.

Summary

In common with many computer-programming exercises, creating a maze is all about data structures and navigating them. In this chapter we looked at using Flash to create a tool to help produce the raw data that a game needs. We also showed that Flash games do not always need to have a cartoon look. Flash is quite capable of displaying bitmap images and does a reasonable job of keeping their sizes within Internet-friendly constraints. Just look at the fact that the project file is over 11 MB in size while the published game is just 273 K!

16 Board games

There are many two-player board games that convert readily to being played by a solo player and a computer. Chess programming in particular played a significant role in the history of computer programming. In this chapter I hope to introduce some of the ideas necessary to create a two-player strategy game that involves some programmed intelligence on the part of the computer.

Two-player board games

The simplest game is noughts and crosses. Even this game presents several challenges but with only a 3 × 3 playing grid it can be thought of as a game that could be analysed to a finish. Connect 4 is a variation on noughts and crosses limiting the player's possible moves to filled columns only, and the game is made more difficult since a line of four is required. The classic two-player board game is chess, but programming a full chess implementation is beyond a one-chapter tutorial. The game of Go is such an easy game to learn and such a difficult one to master. The game we are going to concentrate on in this chapter is a simple game to learn and yet again quite tricky to play well, but it does have some very useful ground rules that makes it easier to teach a computer to play at least reasonably well.

The game of Reversi

The traditional game of Reversi is sold today as the game 'Othello'. It has very simple rules, yet the game has all the hallmarks of a game of skill, namely that a good player will always beat a poor player; luck does not play any role. Each player uses the same counters that are coloured differently on each side, black and white being two obvious choices; one player always places their counters on the board with the black side facing up and the other player uses the opposite side. The board is a grid of 64 squares, eight in each direction. At the start of the game each player takes it in turn to place a counter on the board in any vacant one of the four central squares. After these first four pieces are placed, play continues with each player in turn placing a piece on the board to sandwich any number of their opponent's pieces between their own coloured pieces in a line. A line can be horizontal, vertical or diagonal. Any opponent's piece that is in a line between the current player's new piece and any of the current player's existing pieces is flipped over, thus becoming the same colour as the current player's pieces.

Figure 16.2 shows how placing a white piece at the lower right corner has the effect of creating two lines thus flipping two black pieces over to white. A line of opposing pieces can be of any length. The game is completed when either all the squares on the board are filled or a player cannot

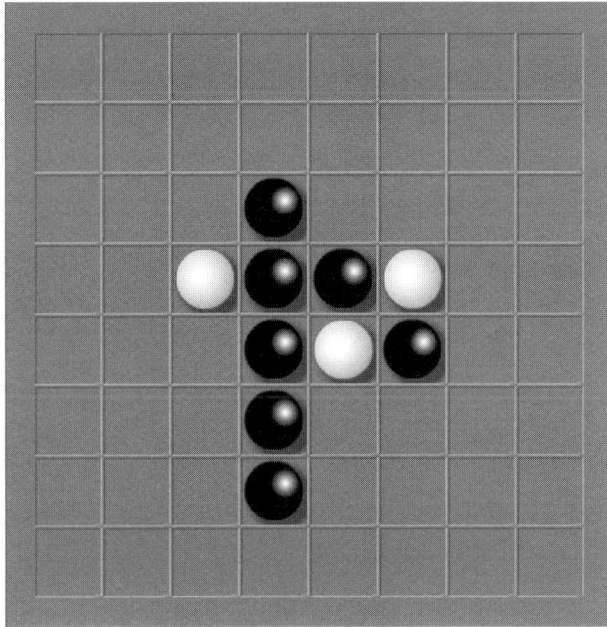

Figure 16.1 *The traditional game Reversi*

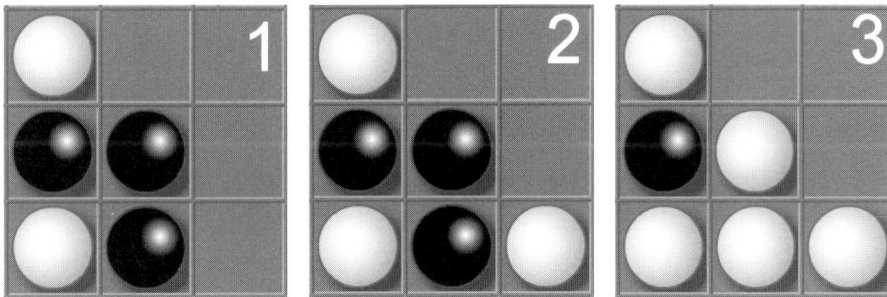

Figure 16.2 *Placing a new piece*

go. So that's the basic game. Where do we begin programming this game as a solo player against the computer game?

Methods for board games

First we need to reduce the problem into manageable chunks. How are we going to play the game?

1   Build and display the board.
2   Check for user input.
3   If the user places his piece legally, update the placed square and then update the board.

245

4   Scan the board for legal computer moves.
5   Work out the best move for the computer.
6   Place computer piece in the best calculated square and then update the board.
7   Repeat steps 2–6 until the game ends.
8   Show the number of player pieces and computer pieces and declare a winner.

So we will need an initialization function to build a clear board, a legal move generator and an evaluation function to determine the best computer move. By far the hardest part of this is the evaluation function. Such a function could in fact look ahead to the end of the game and work out which move from the current position would give the computer the best result. We are only going to look ahead two moves; the idea for the two moves is to maximize the computer's result and minimize the player's. If you are interested in the technical background to this type of game then try a search for 'Combinatorial Game Theory' in your favourite web search engine.
http://www.ics.uci.edu/~eppstein/cgt/ is a good starting point.

Building and initializing the board

Without question this is the easiest part of the programming. The game is a simple 8×8 grid and the images that can appear in this grid are limited to just three possibilities: a blank square, a white piece or a black piece. Figure 16.3 shows the images needed. To achieve this we will create a three-frame movie clip that is duplicated to form the 8×8 grid. The movie clip contains a blank button that has an event that responds to the user's input.

Figure 16.3 *Three frames are used to display the pieces*

Here is the simple code used on frame 1 of the main timeline. Take a look at 'Examples\Chapter16\reversi.fla' to examine the code.

```
1 PLAYER = 3;
2 COMPUTER = 2;
3 flip = new Array(8);
4 board = new Array(64);
```

```
5 cBoard = new Array(64);
6 pBoard = new Array(64);
7 makeBoard();
8 initGame();
9 stop();
```

Listing 16.1

The arrays are used throughout the program to store the data needed. The array 'flip' stores which directions from a given square have a line that can be flipped after executing a legal move. 'board' contains the current view of the board in a computer-friendly manner. 'cBoard' stores the temporary board after the computer has made a possible move and is used in the code for evaluating the computer's best option. 'pBoard' stores the player's move following the computer's move and is used for evaluating the player's least best move after the computer has made a temporary move. We will look at the use of these arrays in more detail later in the chapter. Then we have a call to a simple function that duplicates and positions the single movie clip 'piece'.

```
1   function makeBoard(){
2       var row, col, name, mc, count=1;
3
4       for(row=0; row<8; row++){
5               for(col=0; col<8; col++){
6                       name = "board" + row + "_" + col;
7                       duplicateMovieClip("piece", name, count++);
8                       mc = eval(name);
9                       mc._x = col * 45 + 36;
10                      mc._y = row * 45 + 36;
11                      mc.row = row;
12                      mc.col = col;
13              }
14      }
15 }
```

Listing 16.2

The code on the first frame of the main timeline also initializes a first game with a call to the function 'initGame'.

```
1   function initGame(){
2       var row, col, name, count=1;
3
4       for(row=0; row<8; row++){
5               for(col=0; col<8; col++){
6                       name = "board" + row + "_" + col;
```

```
7                        eval(name).gotoAndStop(1);
8               }
9        }
10      curGo = 0;
11      playersMove();
12 }
```
Listing 16.3

The initialization function makes use of one of two functions that swap the current player and update the move counter 'curGo'. Two movie clips use the variable 'whoseGo' to check for the next player; they are visually the lozenges behind the word 'Computer' and 'Player'.

```
1   function playersMove(){
2        computerHL.gotoAndStop(1);
3        playerHL.gotoAndStop(2);
4        whoseGo = PLAYER;
5        curGo++;
6  }
7
8  function computerMove(){
9        computerHL.gotoAndStop(2);
10       playerHL.gotoAndStop(1);
11       whoseGo = COMPUTER;
12       curGo++;
13 }
```
Listing 16.4

Tracking the player's move

A player's move is legal if the square they clicked is empty, if in one of eight directions stemming from this square there is an opponent's piece and if continuing in the same direction there is a player's piece. This checking is all done using the 'checkBoard' function. Either the player or the computer can call this function; the caller is contained in the variable 'piece'. The function calls a further function 'scanBoard' a total of eight times. For each call the direction that is being scanned is contained in the fifth and sixth parameters. Parameters one and two contain the starting square and parameters three and four the current player and opponent. For each direction the array 'flip' is set to either true or false, and a variable 'legal' dictates whether this is an acceptable square.

```
1   function checkBoard(row, col, piece){
2        var legal = false, opponent;
3
4        if (piece==PLAYER){
5              opponent = COMPUTER;
```

```
6      }else{
7            opponent = PLAYER;
8      }
9
10     if (scanBoard(row, col, piece, opponent,  1,  0)){
11           legal = true;
12           flip[0] = true;
13     }else{
14           flip[0] = false;
15     }
16     if (scanBoard(row, col, piece, opponent,  0,  1)){
17           legal = true;
18           flip[1] = true;
19     }else{
20           flip[1] = false;
21     }
22     if (scanBoard(row, col, piece, opponent, -1,  0)){
23           legal = true;
24           flip[2] = true;
25     }else{
26           flip[2] = false;
27     }
28     if (scanBoard(row, col, piece, opponent,  0, -1)){
29           legal = true;
30           flip[3] = true;
31     }else{
32           flip[3] = false;
33     }
34     if (scanBoard(row, col, piece, opponent, -1, -1)){
35           legal = true;
36           flip[4] = true;
37     }else{
38           flip[4] = false;
39     }
40     if (scanBoard(row, col, piece, opponent,  1, -1)){
41           legal = true;
42           flip[5] = true;
43     }else{
44           flip[5] = false;
45     }
46     if (scanBoard(row, col, piece, opponent,  1,  1)){
47           legal = true;
48           flip[6] = true;
```

```
49       }else{
50            flip[6] = false;
51       }
52       if (scanBoard(row, col, piece, opponent,  -1,  1)){
53            legal = true;
54            flip[7] = true;
55       }else{
56            flip[7] = false;
57       }
58
59       return legal;
60  }
```
Listing 16.5

As you can see from Listing 16.5 the meat of the legal move checker is the function 'scanBoard'. Listing 16.6 shows the function in full. Notice how parameters five and six are used in a repeat loop checking for the existence of an opponent's piece. There must be at least one piece so if none is found the function returns false. If there is an opponent's piece then the values for 'incX' and 'incY' are added repeatedly until the condition fails. At this point we check that the end of the line contains a player's piece; if this is true then this direction contains a line that is suitable.

```
1   function scanBoard(row, col, piece, opponent, incX, incY){
2       var x, y, name;
3
4       x = col + incX;
5       y = row + incY;
6       name = "board" + y + "_" + x;
7
8       //Must be at least one
9       if (eval(name)._currentframe != opponent) return false;
10
11      while(eval(name)._currentframe==opponent){
12            x += incX;
13            y += incY;
14            name = "board" + y + "_" + x;
15      }
16
17      //Next piece must be a piece frame
18      if (eval(name)._currentframe == piece) return true;
19
20      return false;
21  }
```
Listing 16.6

Once the player's chosen square has been checked and found to be legal we need to update the display. The function 'adjustBoard', Listing 16.7, does that. The start location and current player are passed to the function and then the values stored in the 'flip' array set by the 'scanBoard' function calls are used. Again we use eight calls to another function with the direction passed to each call.

```
1  function adjustBoard(row, col, piece){
2      var opponent;
3
4      if (piece==PLAYER){
5          opponent = COMPUTER;
6      }else{
7          opponent = PLAYER;
8      }
9
10     if (flip[0]) flipLine(row, col, piece, opponent,  1,  0);
11     if (flip[1]) flipLine(row, col, piece, opponent,  0,  1);
12     if (flip[2]) flipLine(row, col, piece, opponent, -1,  0);
13     if (flip[3]) flipLine(row, col, piece, opponent,  0, -1);
14     if (flip[4]) flipLine(row, col, piece, opponent, -1, -1);
15     if (flip[5]) flipLine(row, col, piece, opponent,  1, -1);
16     if (flip[6]) flipLine(row, col, piece, opponent,  1,  1);
17     if (flip[7]) flipLine(row, col, piece, opponent, -1,  1);
18 }
```
Listing 16.7

As you can see from Listing 16.7, the function 'flipLine' does the actual work of manipulating the display.

```
1  function flipLine(row, col, piece, opponent, incX, incY){
2      var x, y, name;
3
4      x = col + incX;
5      y = row + incY;
6      name = "board" + y + "_" + x;
7
8      while(eval(name)._currentframe==opponent){
9          eval(name).gotoAndStop(piece);
10         x += incX;
11         y += incY;
12         name = "board" + y + "_" + x;
13     }
14 }
```
Listing 16.8

Figure 16.4 *Developing the Reversi game*

Evaluating the computer's best move

The evaluation function for the computer's best move is the most complex part of the game to code efficiently. The aim of the function is to derive the computer's best move based on a look-ahead of two moves. Because we do not want to affect the display we first copy the on-screen board into a one-dimensional array called 'board'. This array starts in the top left corner and scans the board one row at a time; index 8 is therefore row 1 column 0.

After storing the board position in a format that is easily readable by the computer we then process every square of the board looking for a legal move. The function used is 'computerScore'; this function returns −1 if the position is an illegal move and a score for the computer if the square is a legal move. We will look a little later at how this score is derived. If the move is legal then we use the position following this move that is stored in the single dimension array 'cBoard' in a further function 'playerScore'; the purpose of this function is to calculate the player's best score from the board position stored in the array 'cBoard'. Then we subtract the player's best score from the computer's best score and work out which move will give the computer the best advantage. Finally, having discovered the best move on the basis of this simple algorithm, we calculate the row and column that the move implies. Because the arrays are single dimensional to map to row and column we use the code snippet:

```
row = int(best/8);
col = best % 8;
```

Here 'row' is the integer value after dividing the index 'best' by 8, which will place 'row' between 0 and 7. The value of 'col' is determined using the modulus operator '%'. This operator returns the remainder, after dividing the left of the operator by the right. Again this will return a value between 0 and 7. We update the 'flip' array by calling 'legalMove' again and set the current square directly, and it only then remains to update the on-screen display using the 'adjustBoard' function we looked at earlier.

```
1  function doComputerMove(){
2      var diff=-100000, c, p, i, row, col, best=-1, count=0, name;
3
4      //Get current board
5      for (row=0; row<8; row++){
6          for (col=0; col<8; col++){
7              name = "board" + row + "_" + col;
8              board[count++] = eval(name)._currentframe;
9          }
10     }
11
12     count = 0;
13
14     for (i=0; i<64; i++){
15         c = computerScore(i);
16         if (c > -1){
17             p = playerScore();
18             if (diff < (c - p) || best==-1){
19                 diff = c - p;
20                 best = i;
21             }
22         }
23     }
24
25     row = int(best/8);
26     col = best % 8;
27
28     legalMove(best, COMPUTER);
29     name = "board" + row + "_" + col;
30     eval(name).gotoAndStop(COMPUTER);
31
32     adjustBoard(row, col, COMPUTER);
33
34     playersMove();
35 }
```
Listing 16.9

The function shown in Listing 16.9 calls several functions that we will look at in detail. The first function to consider is the 'computerScore' function. This function uses the 'legalMove' generator to test whether the current square is legitimate for the current board and player. If it is then we set the array 'cBoard' to be a duplicate of 'board' which you will recall is simply the current displayed board. Then we update the current board using the function 'adjustArray'. Finally, we count how many COMPUTER pieces are on the new board, stored in the array 'cBoard'.

```
1   function computerScore(i){
2       var n, count = 0;
3
4       if (!legalMove(i, COMPUTER)) return -1;
5
6       for (n=0; n<64; n++) cBoard[n] = board[n];
7       cBoard[i] = COMPUTER;
8       adjustArray(i, COMPUTER);
9
10       count = 0;
11       for (n=0; n<64; n++){
12               if (cBoard[n]==COMPUTER) count++;
13       }
14       return count;
15  }
```
Listing 16.10

The 'legalMove' function works in much the same way as the function 'checkBoard' only this function operates on the single dimensional arrays rather than using the frame values of the movie clips in the on-screen display. The function in turn calls the 'scanArray' function, which is a mirror of 'scanBoard', operating on arrays.

```
1   function legalMove(i, piece){
2       var legal = false;
3
4       if (scanArray(i, piece, 1,  0)){
5               legal = true;
6               flip[0] = true;
7       }else{
8               flip[0] = false;
9       }
10       if (scanArray(i, piece,  0,  1)){
11               legal = true;
12               flip[1] = true;
13       }else{
14               flip[1] = false;
15       }
16       if (scanArray(i, piece, -1,  0)){
17               legal = true;
18               flip[2] = true;
```

```
19      }else{
20              flip[2] = false;
21      }
22      if (scanArray(i, piece,   0, -1)){
23              legal = true;
24              flip[3] = true;
25      }else{
26              flip[3] = false;
27      }
28      if (scanArray(i, piece, -1, -1)){
29              legal = true;
30              flip[4] = true;
31      }else{
32              flip[4] = false;
33      }
34      if (scanArray(i, piece, 1, -1)){
35              legal = true;
36              flip[5] = true;
37      }else{
38              flip[5] = false;
39      }
40      if (scanArray(i, piece, 1,  1)){
41              legal = true;
42              flip[6] = true;
43      }else{
44              flip[6] = false;
45      }
46      if (scanArray(i, piece, -1,  1)){
47              legal = true;
48              flip[7] = true;
49      }else{
50              flip[7] = false;
51      }
52
53      return legal;
54 }
```

Listing 16.11

To calculate the index based on the values for 'incX' and 'incY' in a single dimensional array requires the use of a new increment value.

```
inc = incY*8 + incX;
```

The function can operate either on the 'board' array if the value for 'piece' is COMPUTER, or the 'cBoard' array if the value for 'piece' is PLAYER. Again when scanning a row the first square must be empty, the next must contain an opponent piece and the final must be a player piece. If all the conditions are passed then true is returned; otherwise false is returned.

```
1   function scanArray(i, piece, incX, incY){
2       var name, n, inc;
3
4       inc = incY*8 + incX;
5       n = i + inc;
6
7       //Must be at least one
8       switch (piece){
9           case PLAYER:
10          if (cBoard[i]!=1 || cBoard[n]!=COMPUTER) return false;
11          do{
12              n += inc;
13          }while(cBoard[n] == COMPUTER);
14          //Next piece must be a PLAYER piece
15          if (cBoard[n] == PLAYER) return true;
16          break;
17
18          case COMPUTER:
19          if (board[i]!=1 || board[n]!=PLAYER) return false;
20          do{
21              n += inc;
22          }while(board[n] == PLAYER);
23          //Next piece must be a COMPUTER piece
24          if (board[n] == COMPUTER) return true;
25          break;
26      }
27
28      return false;
29  }
```
Listing 16.12

Once the best computer score is evaluated the function 'adjustArray' is called:

```
1 function adjustArray(i, piece){
2       if (flip[0]) flipArrayLine(i, piece,  1,  0);
3       if (flip[1]) flipArrayLine(i, piece,  0,  1);
4       if (flip[2]) flipArrayLine(i, piece, -1,  0);
5       if (flip[3]) flipArrayLine(i, piece,  0, -1);
6       if (flip[4]) flipArrayLine(i, piece, -1, -1);
7       if (flip[5]) flipArrayLine(i, piece,  1, -1);
```

```
8       if (flip[6]) flipArrayLine(i, piece,  1,  1);
9       if (flip[7]) flipArrayLine(i, piece, -1,  1);
10 }
```
Listing 16.13

which uses the function 'flipArrayLine'.

```
1  function flipArrayLine(i, piece, incX, incY){
2      var n, inc;
3
4      inc = 8*incY + incX;
5      n = i + inc;
6
7      switch (piece){
8              case PLAYER:
9              while(pBoard[n]==COMPUTER){
10                     pBoard[n] = PLAYER;
11                     n += inc;
12             }
13             break;
14
15             case COMPUTER:
16             while(cBoard[n]==PLAYER){
17                     cBoard[n] = COMPUTER;
18                     n += inc;
19             }
20             break;
21     }
22 }
```
Listing 16.14

This leaves just the 'playerScore' function to consider from the main function 'doComputer-Move', shown in Listing 16.9. This works in much the same way as calculating the computer's best move. Each square in the board stored in the array 'cBoard' is tested for a legal PLAYER move. Subject to this test evaluating to true, we update the 'pBoard' array and count the number of PLAYER squares; if this is a higher value than the stored value for 'score' then the variable 'score' is updated. After considering every square the final value for 'score' is returned.

```
1  function playerScore(){
2      var i, n, score=0, count;
3
4      for (i=0; i<64; i++){
```

```
5                if (legalMove(i, PLAYER)){
6                        for(n=0; n<64; n++) pBoard[n] = cBoard[n];
7                        adjustArray(i, PLAYER);
8                        pBoard[i] = PLAYER;
9                        count = 0;
10                       for(n=0; n<64; n++){
11                               if (pBoard[n]==PLAYER) count++;
12                       }
13                       if (count>score) score = count;
14               }
15       }
16
17       return score;
18 }
```

Listing 16.15

Figure 16.5 *Debugging the game*

Using this code gives a reasonable game. Problems do occur stemming from the evaluation function using array values out of range. This is an important point. Whenever you use arrays in this way, it is always best to ensure that the bounds are within the constraints of the array. A call to an array with an index below zero or above the length of the array minus one returns an undefined value. It is easy to mistake this for useful data and so it is always best to check that the index for an array is within the bounds of the array.

Improving the evaluation function

The score derived in this function is all about the pieces on the board after two look-ahead moves. Although this gives some semblance of intelligence a good Reversi player knows that certain rules improve their play. In the early game, controlling the four centre squares is a useful extra so you could add to your evaluation function by scoring these squares higher in the return value for a position. Also a border square means that your opponent cannot get a piece to the other side of you so they are more valuable; again using this positional information you could add to the score in these circumstances. The three squares that surround a corner are very poor squares to play in because your opponent will almost certainly then get a corner and corner pieces can never be flipped. You could improve the evaluation function greatly by scoring these squares very low regardless of the short-term gain they may achieve. Finally, getting a corner is the strongest move you can play and should be given a very high score. These improvements in the evaluation function will make a huge difference to the chances of a poor player ever beating the computer. When creating this type of game the method is always to look for ways to improve the evaluation function while not performing an exhaustive search. In many games an exhaustive search is well beyond the power of today's computers. The number of possible game options from a single game position is enormous and working through the game to the end for each of these is not a realistic possibility.

The presentation

Although the presentation of the game in this chapter was quite traditional, it doesn't have to be that way. For example, the game of Reversi could be presented using a cat and mouse theme; you place a cat and all the mice in a line runoff and a cat takes their place. A cartoon effect on the changeover would make the game strikingly different while the gameplay remains the same.

Summary

One surprise about the example in this chapter is that the final game is only 2 K, so could have been included in Chapter 13. In this chapter you were given an overview of the techniques required to create a two-player board game where the computer is a reasonable opponent. The techniques we learnt were board initialization, legal move generation and evaluation function. The final technique is where your skills as a programmer and all your creativity will be used. After the mind games in this chapter you will find the manual dexterity of the next a welcome break.

17 Platformers

Creating a platform-based game is quite a challenge, but by this stage in the book you should have acquired all the necessary skills. In this chapter we are going to look at the problems of controlling the behaviour of a sprite in a platform world. First we will look at an example in which we move the sprite whilst the background remains stationary and then we will look at using a multi-layered scrolling background. Platform games often use dynamically created sprites; we will look at creating sprites on the fly and removing them when they are no longer in use.

The basics of platform games

Platform games involve two fundamental concepts. Firstly, user control of a sprite character that can usually perform several actions: walk, run, jump fall etc. Secondly, collision detection to ensure that the character remains anchored to the world that is presented to the player. Both parts of creating a platform game need careful coding to ensure success. You may prefer to start with the collision testing or with the user control, but either way they are two separate problems and should be tested and debugged separately as far as possible. Here we will start with the problem of user control.

Responding to user input

Usually the only control the user has over the gameplay will be via a few key presses or use of the mouse. Often the control is context sensitive. For example, if a character is falling then the player cannot set a new direction until the character has landed and the player regains control. For this reason always use a control flag. If the character is under player control then set the flag to 'true' and if the character is under computer control then set the control flag to 'false'. Because wherever possible we want to keep the data pertaining to a movie clip within that movie clip, place this flag as a variable inside the clip. The actions a sprite can perform are often limited both by its placement on screen and the action that is currently being performed, so for this reason use a variable that stores the current action. Responding to keyboard input is easier to handle than mouse input for a platform game. Usually keyboard control will mean reading the arrow keys, space bar and possibly the control and shift keys. Reading the keyboard is easy using the 'Key.isDown()' construct. To clarify the principles let's look at an example. Open 'Examples/Chapter17/FatCat01.fla'. Press 'Ctrl + Enter' to run the program. Using the arrow keys you can move the cat around the screen, jumping and landing on the various platforms that you can see on the screen.

A simple example

Figure 17.1 *Developing 'Examples/Chapter17/FatCat01.fla'*

The code for this example is mainly located in three places. An initialization script on frame 1 of the main timeline contains the following code:

```
1 //Set initial parameters
2 DEBUG_GAME = true;
3 Cat.orgX = Cat._x;
4 Cat.orgy = Cat._y;
5 Cat.tracemotion = false;
6 stop();
```

Listing 17.1

Notice that here we are just setting some initial values and some debug parameters. As you will know from the chapter on debugging, getting feedback information as your game plays is vital to creating a stable game. By setting a simple Boolean value to true or false we can quickly set the debugging level of a game.

The second main code location is a clip event for the 'Cat' movie clip.

```
1  onClipEvent(enterFrame){
2     if (_root.DEBUG_GAME){
3        if (Key.isDown(Key.SHIFT)){
4           moveY = 1;
5        }else if (Key.isDown(Key.CONTROL)){
6           moveY = -1;
7        }else if (Key.isDown(Key.SPACE)){
8           moveY = 0;
9        }else if (Key.isDown(Key.TAB)){
10          initAction(STOPRIGHT);
11          userControl = true;
12       }
13       if (Key.isDown(Key.CAPSLOCK)){
14          tracemotion = true;
15       }else{
16          tracemotion = false;
17       }
18       dump();
19    }
20
21    if (usercontrol){
22       if (Key.isDown(Key.RIGHT)){
23          userKey = "Right";
24          userAction(WALKRIGHT);
25       }else if (Key.isDown(Key.LEFT)){
26          userKey = "Left";
27          userAction(WALKLEFT);
28       }else if (Key.isDown(Key.UP)){
29          userKey = "Up";
30          userAction(JUMP);
31       }else{
32          userKey = "none";
33          userAction(HALT);
34       }
35    }
36
37    move();
38 }
```

Listing 17.2

Notice that the first section of this code is conditional on the flag 'DEBUG_GAME'; this allows you to quickly turn off features that are unsuitable to the finished game but make debugging the game much easier. When in debug mode several extra keys are used. The shift key causes the sprite to move up the screen by one pixel for each screen redraw. The control key works in the opposite direction. The space bar fixes the up and down movement set by the shift and control keys. The tab key forces the character into a distinct mode and reactivates 'usercontrol', a variable that is used to activate and deactivate keyboard input. If the caps lock key is down then the variable 'tracemotion' is set to true. This causes dump of the location of the sprite to be sent to the output window. The value of the variable is used within another function that actually does this work, which we will examine later.

The bulk of the code is inside the 'Cat' clip on frame 1. Before we examine that, take a look at the timeline for the 'Cat' movie clip. There are 14 labels, each one indicating the first frame of an animation. Within the Control layer there are a few small ActionScripts that set variables specific to certain actions or reset the action; we will examine these later. The labels used are:

WalkRight, FallRight, JumpRight, LandRight, StopRight, StartRight, TurnRight
WalkLeft, FallLeft, JumpLeft, LandLeft, StopLeft, StartLeft, TurnLeft

The code on frame 1 starts with some simple initialization, but most of the code defines functions that are used to control the character. Both 'userAction' and 'move' are called by the 'onClipEvent' ActionScript.

```
1   //Init variables
2   JUMP = 1;
3   TURNLEFT = 2;
4   STARTRIGHT = 3;
5   WALKRIGHT = 4;
6   FALLRIGHT = 5;
7   JUMPRIGHT = 6;
8   LANDRIGHT = 7;
9   STOPRIGHT = 8;
10  TURNRIGHT = 9;
11  STARTLEFT = 10;
12  WALKLEFT = 11;
13  FALLLEFT = 12;
14  JUMPLEFT = 13;
15  LANDLEFT = 14;
16  STOPLEFT = 15;
17  HALT = 16;
18  actionNames = new Array(
19               "No action", "Jump", "TurnLeft", "StartRight",
20               "WalkRight", "FallRight", "JumpRight", "LandRight",
21               "StopRight", "TurnRight", "StartLeft", "WalkLeft",
22               "FallLeft", "JumpLeft", "LandLeft", "StopLeft",
23               "Halt");
24  x = 0;
25  y = 0;
26  jumping = false;
```

```
27 platform = "";
28 initAction(STOPRIGHT);
```

Listing 17.3

In the initialization section the values of certain constants are defined so that we can write 'WALKLEFT' in the code rather than '11'. When you are reading through the code it is much easier to understand if you use names in this way rather than numbers. To facilitate easier debugging the initialization also creates a string array that contains the names of the possible actions. Using this array we can get the name of an action using the code:

```
actionNames[action];
actionNames[WALKRIGHT]
```

would return 'WalkRight'.

Now we will look at the functions defined on frame 1.

'userAction' is called by the keyboard reader in the onClipEvent for the cat. A 'switch' statement is used to select which code to run.

```
1  //===============userAction=====================================
2  //This is called by the onClipEvent of the Cat instance
3  //parameters===================================================
4  //index    Possible values WALKRIGHT, WALKLEFT and JUMP
5  //===============================================================
6  function userAction(index) {
7     switch (index) {
8     case WALKRIGHT :
9        userWalkRight();
10       break;
11    case WALKLEFT :
12       userWalkLeft();
13       break;
14    case JUMP :
15       userJump();
16       break;
17    case HALT :
18       if (action == WALKLEFT) {
19          initAction(STOPLEFT);
20       } else if (action == WALKRIGHT) {
21          initAction(STOPRIGHT);
22       }
23       break;
24    }
25 }
```

Listing 17.4

If the cat calls 'userRight' then we need to decide what to do based on the current action. The cat action could be 'STOPRIGHT', 'STOPLEFT' or 'WALKLEFT'. The current action dictates what the cat action should be set to.

```
1   //==============userRight==================================
2   //This is called by the userAction function
3   //parameters===============================================
4   //none
5   //=========================================================
6   function userRight() {
7      switch (action) {
8      case STOPRIGHT :
9         initAction(STARTRIGHT);
10        break;
11     case STOPLEFT :
12        initAction(STARTLEFT);
13        break;
14     case WALKLEFT :
15        initAction(TURNRIGHT);
16        break;
17     }
18  }
```
Listing 17.5

'userLeft' works in a similar way with the directions reversed.

```
1   //==============userLeft===================================
2   //This is called by the userAction function
3   //parameters===============================================
4   //none
5   //=========================================================
6   function userLeft() {
7      switch (action) {
8      case STOPLEFT :
9         initAction(STARTLEFT);
10        break;
11     case STOPRIGHT :
12        initAction(STARTRIGHT);
13        break;
14     case WALKRIGHT :
15        initAction(TURNLEFT);
16        break;
17     }
18  }
```
Listing 17.6

'userJump' is called if the cat is under user control and the UP arrow is pressed.

```
1   //===============userJump=====================================
2   //This is called by the userAction function
3   //parameters================================================
4   //none
5   //==========================================================
6   function userJump() {
7      //Only possible if we are walking or stopped
8      switch (action) {
9      case STOPLEFT :
10        initAction(JUMPLEFT);
11        break;
12     case STOPRIGHT :
13        initAction(JUMPRIGHT);
14        break;
15     case WALKLEFT :
16        initAction(JUMPLEFT);
17        break;
18     case WALKRIGHT :
19        initAction(JUMPRIGHT);
20        break;
21     }
22 }
```

Listing 17.7

All three of the above functions use 'initAction' to set the actual action to show and set up variables specific to that action. Notice that this function uses another debugging technique: the variable 'TRACE_ACTIONS' is set to false, causing the current action 'trace' statements to be ignored. If when debugging you want to quickly see the order of action assignment, then by setting 'TRACE_ACTIONS' to true the 'trace' statements are all used.

```
1   function initAction(index) {
2      TRACE_ACTIONS = false;
3      switch (index) {
4      case WALKRIGHT :
5         if (TRACE_ACTIONS) trace("initAction WalkRight");
6         action = index;
7         usercontrol = true;
8         moveX = -5;
9         moveY = 0;
10        gotoAndPlay("WalkRight");
```

```
11       break;
12   case FALLRIGHT:
13       if (TRACE_ACTIONS) trace("initAction FallRight");
14       action = index;
15       usercontrol = false;
16       moveY = -2;
17       gotoAndPlay("FallRight");
18       break;
19   case JUMPRIGHT :
20       if (TRACE_ACTIONS) trace("initAction JumpRight");
21       action = index;
22       usercontrol = false;
23       moveY = 0;
24       moveX = 0;
25       gotoAndPlay("JumpRight");
26       break;
27   case LANDRIGHT :
28       if (TRACE_ACTIONS) trace("initAction LandRight");
29       action = index;
30       usercontrol = false;
31       moveX = 0;
32       moveY = 0;
33       gotoAndPlay("LandRight");
34       break;
35   case STOPRIGHT :
36       if (TRACE_ACTIONS) trace("initAction StopRight");
37       action = index;
38       usercontrol = false;
39       moveX = 0;
40       moveY = 0;
41       gotoAndPlay("StopRight");
42       break;
43   case STARTRIGHT :
44       if (TRACE_ACTIONS) trace("initAction StartRight");
45       action = index;
46       usercontrol = false;
47       moveX = 0;
48       moveY = 0;
49       gotoAndPlay("StartRight");
50       break;
51   case TURNRIGHT :
52       if (TRACE_ACTIONS) trace("initAction TurnRight");
53       action = index;
```

```
54        usercontrol = false;
55        moveX = 0;
56        moveY = 0;
57        gotoAndPlay("TurnRight");
58        break;
59    case WALKLEFT :
60        if (TRACE_ACTIONS) trace("initAction WalkLeft");
61        action = index;
62        usercontrol = true;
63        moveX = 5;
64        moveY = 0;
65        gotoAndPlay("WalkLeft");
66        break;
67    case FALLLEFT:
68        if (TRACE_ACTIONS) trace("initAction FallLeft");
69        action = index;
70        usercontrol = false;
71        moveY = -2;
72        gotoAndPlay("FallLeft");
73        break;
74    case JUMPLEFT :
75        if (TRACE_ACTIONS) trace("initAction JumpLeft");
76        action = index;
77        usercontrol = false;
78        moveX = 0;
79        moveY = 0;
80        gotoAndPlay("JumpLeft");
81        break;
82    case LANDLEFT :
83        if (TRACE_ACTIONS) trace("initAction LandLeft");
84        action = index;
85        usercontrol = false;
86        moveX = 0;
87        moveY = 0;
88        gotoAndPlay("LandLeft");
89        break;
90    case STOPLEFT :
91        if (TRACE_ACTIONS) trace("initAction StopLeft");
92        action = index;
93        usercontrol = false;
94        moveX = 0;
95        moveY = 0;
```

```
96          gotoAndPlay("StopLeft");
97          break;
98      case STARTLEFT:
99          if (TRACE_ACTIONS) trace("initAction StartLeft");
100         action = index;
101         usercontrol = false;
102         moveX = 0;
103         moveY = 0;
104         gotoAndPlay("StartLeft");
105         break;
106     case TURNLEFT:
107         if (TRACE_ACTIONS) trace("initAction TurnLeft");
108         action = index;
109         usercontrol = false;
110         moveX = 0;
111         moveY = 0;
112         gotoAndPlay("TurnLeft");
113         break;
114     }
115 }
```

Listing 17.8

For each call to the cat onClipEvent the function 'move' is called. The purpose of move is to set the on-screen position of the sprite. The position is based on the value of x and y, which in turn are updated using the values of moveX and moveY. 'move' must test based on the current action to ensure that the position is legal. As the game starts the value of the variable 'platform' is set to an empty string. If this is the case then the cat is on the floor. The switch statement uses the value for 'platform' if the cat action is currently WALKRIGHT, STOPRIGHT, STARTRIGHT, WALKLEFT, STOPLEFT or STARTLEFT. The variable 'platform' contains the name of the platform on which the cat is standing or walking. The variable is set by the 'land' function that we will examine next. If this is set then we need to know whether we have reached the limit of the platform; the limits are reached when the '_x' position of the platform minus the current value for 'x' is less than 60 or greater than 120. If this is the case then a fall is initialized using the 'initAction' function. The other special case occurs if the cat is jumping. When a jump is occurring we need to constantly update the moveY value. Initially this is set to 23, a value that was found simply by trying out the action. For each call, the value is reduced by multiplying the current value by 0.7. When the current value is less than 4 and greater than minus 4, the value is reduced by subtracting 2 from the value. Finally the negative value is increased, by multiplying by 1.3. The effect of this curve is to create a curved motion of sorts. However, if your maths can cope with it I recommend following the physics calculations in the box.

Instead of using lots of if conditions we can use a simple physics calculation. The Y value for a projectile motion is defined as:

$$y = ut + gt^2$$

where u is the launch value, t is the time in seconds and g is the value of gravity. If time, t, is less than a second the value for t^2 will be less than t, but above one second, t^2 will overtake. If g operates in the opposite direction to u then the increase in the values for y will decrease and eventually reverse. But this may seem all very hit and miss. Actually it is easy to calculate. Suppose that you want a jump to occur over one second and the starting and ending values for y are zero, then you want:

$$ut = -gt^2$$

when $t = 0$ and $t = 1$. To do this you need to solve a quadratic equation. Whoops, that sounds like maths! But believe me, it is not that hard. You want:

$$ut + gt^2 = 0$$

But you also want to control the maximum height of the jump. This occurs when the derivative of the curve has a value of zero. The derivative of the curve is:

$$u + 2gt$$

OK, so let's fiddle with the figures. If we want a maximum height for the curve of 150 and if the total jump takes one second then the maximum height is going to be at 0.5 seconds; in other words, half way through the jump. At $t = 0.5$ we want:

$$u + 2gt = 0 \text{ and } ut + gt^2 = 150$$

Replacing t with 0.5 gives:

$$u + g = 0 \text{ and } 0.5u + 0.25g = 150$$

Two equations with two unknowns can be solved: $u = -g$ from the first equation therefore we can substitute u for $-g$ in the second equation giving $-0.5g + 0.25g = 150$ or $0.25g = 150$; which means that $g = -600$ and $u = 600$.

If you are working in metres rather than pixels then the usual value for g is $-9.81\,ms^2$ but for convenience we will call this $-10\,ms^2$. Imagine that the cat is about one metre tall and can jump just a metre. Therefore

$$u - 20t = 0 \text{ and } ut - 10t^2 = 1$$

From the first equation we know that $u = 20t$, we can pump this into the second equation and see that

$$20t^2 - 10t^2 = 1 \text{ or } t^2 = 1/10$$

or t is approximately 0.32 seconds. So the peak of the curve will occur at around about one third of a second.

If you are able to follow this then it is without doubt the best way to get the curved motions that you want. But if it is all totally baffling then just try changing the values until you get the result you want. Trial and error never hurt. Physics can, however, be a very useful way of creating very smooth animations and it is well worth trying to get your head around some simple manipulation of equations. You are unlikely to need more than some simple trigonometry, a little basic algebra and enough calculus to understand how to work out the derivative of a curve when working with Flash games.

To work out the derivative of a polynomial, simply multiply the coefficient by the power and reduce the power by one. Therefore x^2 becomes $2x$, $4x^3$ becomes $(3) * 4x^{(3-1)} = 12x^2$, $5x$ becomes just 5 and a constant drops out to zero. Consequently the derivative of:

$$4x^3 + x^2 + 5x + 3 \text{ is } 12x^2 + 2x + 5$$

The derivative gives the slope of a curve. The maximum or minimum of a quadratic curve (a curve where the highest power is two) occurs when the derivative has the value zero because this indicates that the slope of the curve at this point is horizontal.

Lecture over; let's make some games!!

```
1   function move() {
2     var i, name, dx;
3
4     x -= moveX;
5     y -= moveY;
6
7     switch (action){
8     case WALKRIGHT:
9     case STOPRIGHT:
10      case STARTRIGHT:
11         if (platform!=""){
12            dx = eval(platform)._x - x;
```

```
13          if (dx<60 || dx>120){
14              platform = "";
15              initAction(FALLRIGHT);
16          }
17      }
18      break;
19  case WALKLEFT:
20  case STOPLEFT:
21  case STARTLEFT:
22      if (platform!=""){
23          dx = eval(platform)._x - x;
24          if (dx<60 || dx>120){
25              platform = "";
26              initAction(FALLLEFT);
27          }
28      }
29      break;
30  case FALLRIGHT:
31  case JUMPRIGHT:
32      if (jumping){
33          if (moveX>0) moveX-=0.5;
34          if (land()){
35              initAction(LANDRIGHT);
36          }else{
37              if (moveY > 4){
38                  moveY *= 0.7;
39              }else if (moveY<=4 && moveY>-4){
40                  moveY -= 2;
41              }else if (moveY < 0){
42                  moveY *= 1.3;
43              }
44          }
45      }
46      break;
47  case FALLLEFT:
48  case JUMPLEFT:
49      if (jumping){
50          if (moveX<0) moveX+=0.5;
51          if (land()){
52              initAction(LANDLEFT);
53          }else{
54              if (moveY > 4){
55                  moveY *= 0.7;
```

```
56              }else if (moveY<=4 && moveY>-4){
57                  moveY -= 2;
58              }else if (moveY < 0){
59                  moveY *= 1.3;
60              }
61          }
62      }
63      break;
64  }
65  _x = x + orgX;
66  _y = y + orgY;
67 }
```
Listing 17.9

One of the most important parts of the code in this example is the collision detection involved in the 'land' function. There are two possible landings: either on the floor at $y > 0$, or on a platform. To decide if the cat has landed on a platform we must go through each platform in turn. There are 11 boxes and 3 bins, and each of these must be tested. To achieve a landing the cat must be in a legal position both horizontally and vertically. We determine this position using the debug box. On screen for debugging purposes you can see a multi-line dynamic text box which tracks the value of the variable '_root.debug'. A considerable quantity of debugging values is displayed using string functions. To work out the values needed to land on a platform, simply move the cat using the control keys and the debug keys and work out the values for the upper left and lower right of the rectangle that defines a legal landing area.

Figure 17.2 *Legal area for a landing*

The vertical range must use the current value for moveY to ensure that the platform is not missed. It is remarkably easy when checking for a collision with a platform to check on one frame where the sprite will be above the platform and the check on the following frame where the sprite is below the platform. A collision must have occurred between the two frames but if the movement in the vertical direction is not part of the calculation then this collision can be missed.

```
1   function dump(){
2     var dx, dy;
3
4     _root.debug = actionNames[action] + chr(13);
5     _root.debug += "(x,y): (" + int(x) + "," + int(y) + ")" + chr(13);
6     _root.debug += "(mX,mY): (" + int(moveX) + "," +
7                                   int(moveY) + ")" + chr(13);
8     _root.debug += "userControl: " + usercontrol + chr(13);
9     _root.debug += "jumping: " + jumping + chr(13);
10    _root.debug += "Platform: " + platform + chr(13);
11    _root.debug += "userKey: " + userKey + chr(13);
12    name = "_root.Box1";
13    dx = eval(name)._x - x;
14    dy = eval(name)._y - y;
15    if (tracemotion) trace("moveY, dy: " + moveY + ", " + int(dy));
16    _root.debug += "Box1: (" + int(dx) + "," + int(dy) +
17                         ")" + chr(13);
18    //_root.debug += "landing: " + landing + chr(13);
19  }
```

Listing 17.10

In the calculations we first calculate a delta distance from the current platform to the current value for x. If this is in the range 60 to 120 then the platform is in a possible collision location. Next we test the y location, again using a delta distance. The condition must conform to two tests, one that includes the current movement in the y direction. If each of the four tests evaluates to true then the cat has landed on a platform. The cat is set to an exact fit in the y direction, otherwise the cat could seem too low in relation to the platform, and the name of the platform is stored in the platform variable.

```
1   function land(){
2     var i, name, dx, dy;
3
4     if (moveY>0) return false; //Must be going down to land
5     //Main floor
6     if (y>0){
7        y = 0;
8        return true;
9     }
10    //Check platforms
11    for (i=1; i<12; i++){
12       if (i<=3){
```

```
13          name = "_root.Bin" + i;
14          dx = eval(name)._x - x;
15          if (dx>60 && dx<120){
16              dy = eval(name)._y - y;
17              if (dy<475 && dy>(475+moveY)){
18                  //Align to exact fit
19                  y = eval(name)._y - 475;
20                  platform = name;
21                  return true;
22              }
23          }
24      }
25      name = "_root.Box" + i;
26      dx = eval(name)._x - x;
27      if (dx>60 && dx<120){
28          dy = eval(name)._y - y;
29          if (dy<460 && dy>(460+moveY)){
30              //Align to exact fit
31              y = eval(name)._y - 460;
32              platform = name;
33              return true;
34          }
35      }
36  }
37  return false;
38 }
```

Listing 17.11

Although there are a great number of conditions to test when creating a platform game, keeping the code as modular as possible and carefully considering every possible location and action make the exercise possible.

Using a scrolling background

Most players expect a platform game to scroll. Unfortunately, scrolling games are not handled well by Flash and the software can often struggle to maintain frame rate when using a scrolling environment. On a fast machine the second example should maintain a reasonable frame rate, but on a slow machine it will probably be dire. As machines get generally faster Flash scrollers will become more acceptable so with a nod to the future let's look at some of the problems. In a scrolling game the main character stays central and everything else moves. We can use most of the code from the previous example with a few exceptions. Open 'Examples/Chapter17/FatCat02.fla'. Take a look at the game first so you can see how it behaves. Notice that we have what is called parallax scrolling; that is, things further away scroll less than things nearer to the camera. To achieve this, the initial parameters are set in frame 1 of the main timeline.

Figure 17.3 *Testing 'Examples/Chapter17/FatCat02.fla'*

```
1 //Set initial parameters
2 DEBUG_GAME = true;
3 var mc;
4
5 for (i=1; i<12; i++){
6 if (i<=3){
7        mc = eval("Bin" + i);
8        mc.orgX = mc._x;
9        mc.orgY = mc._y;
10             mc.scale = 1.0;
11      }
12
13       mc = eval("Box" + i);
14       mc.orgX = mc._x;
15       mc.orgY = mc._y;
```

```
16       mc.scale = 1.0;
17 }
18
19 House.orgX = House._x;
20 House.orgY = House._y;
21 House.scale = 0.6;
22
23 Fence.orgX = Fence._x;
24 Fence.orgY = Fence._y;
25 Fence.scale = 0.8;
26
27 stop();
```
Listing 17.12

Notice that in addition to storing a starting location (orgX, orgY) we also store a scale for each movie clip. In this example even the fence and the houses are movie clips. The scale value does not relate to the standard movie clip parameter '_scale'; we do not use it to resize the clip, we use it to work out how far it should move. Take a look at the revised 'move' function.

```
1    function move() {
2      var i, name, dx, mc;
3
4      x += moveX;
5      y += moveY;
6
7      switch (action){
8      case WALKRIGHT:
9      case STOPRIGHT:
10     case STARTRIGHT:
11        if (platform!=""){
12           dx = eval(platform)._x - _x;
13           if (dx<-30 || dx>30){
14              platform = "";
15              initAction(FALLRIGHT);
16           }
17        }
18        break;
19     case WALKLEFT:
20     case STOPLEFT:
21     case STARTLEFT:
22        if (platform!=""){
23           dx = eval(platform)._x - _x;
24           if (dx<-30 || dx>30){
```

```
25              platform = "";
26              initAction(FALLLEFT);
27          }
28      }
29      break;
30  case FALLRIGHT:
31  case JUMPRIGHT:
32      if (y<0){
33          y = 0;
34          initAction(LANDRIGHT);
35          break;
36      }
37      if (jumping){
38          if (moveX>0) moveX-=0.5;
39          if (land()){
40              initAction(LANDRIGHT);
41          }else{
42              if (moveY > 4){
43                  moveY *= 0.7;
44              }else if (moveY<=4 && moveY>-4){
45                  moveY -= 2;
46              }else if (moveY < 0){
47                  moveY *= 1.3;
48              }
49          }
50      }
51      break;
52  case FALLLEFT:
53  case JUMPLEFT:
54   if (y<0){
55          y = 0;
56          initAction(LANDLEFT);
57          break;
58      }
59      if (jumping){
60          if (moveX<0) moveX+=0.5;
61          if (land()){
62              initAction(LANDLEFT);
63          }else{
64              if (moveY > 2){
65                  moveY *= 0.7;
66              }else if (moveY<=2 && moveY>-2){
67                  moveY--;
```

```
68                }else if (moveY < 0){
69                    moveY *= 1.3;
70                }
71            }
72        }
73     break;
74    }
75    for (i=1; i<12; i++) {
76        if (i<=3) {
77            mc = eval("_root.Bin" + i);
78            mc._x = x*mc.scale + mc.orgX;
79            mc._y = y*mc.scale + mc.orgY;
80        }
81        mc = eval("_root.Box" + i);
82        mc._x = x*mc.scale + mc.orgX;
83        mc._y = y*mc.scale + mc.orgY;
84    }
85    _root.House._x = x*_root.House.scale + _root.House.orgX;
86    _root.House._y = y*_root.House.scale + _root.House.orgY;
87    _root.Fence._x = x*_root.Fence.scale + _root.Fence.orgX;
88    _root.Fence._y = y*_root.Fence.scale + _root.Fence.orgY;
89 }
```
Listing 17.13

The only real difference is the end of the function where all the clips are moved. Each clip is moved using the value of *x* or *y*, which is in turn scaled by the scale value for the clip and then the original location is added to the result. This simple code gives perfect parallax scaling and the elements retain their original relationship because every element is moved using the same code. The 'land' code must take into consideration the value of scale, because this affects the on-screen location.

```
1        function land(){
2        var i, name, dx, dy, mc;
3
4        if (moveY>0) return false; //Must be going down to land
5        //Main floor
6        if (y<0){
7        y = 0;
8        return true;
9 }
10       //Check platforms
11       for (i=1; i<12; i++){
12       if (i<=3){
```

```
13                  name = "_root.Bin" + i;
14                  mc = eval(name);
15                  dx = mc._x - _x;
16                  if (dx>-30 && dx<30){
17                          dy = mc._y - _y;
18                          if (dy>67 && (67-dy)>moveY){
19                                  //Align to exacxt fit
20                                  y = (67 - mc.orgY + _y)/mc.scale;
21                                  platform = name;
22                                  return true;
23                          }
24                  }
25          }
26      name = "_root.Box" + i;
27              mc = eval(name);
28      dx = mc._x - _x;
29      if (dx>-30 && dx<30){
30                      dy = mc._y - _y;
31                      if (dy>55 && (55-dy)>moveY){
32                              //Align to exacxt fit
33                              y = (55 - mc.orgY + _y)/mc.scale;
34                              platform = name;
35                              return true;
36                      }
37              }
38      }
39  return false;
40  }
```
Listing 17.14

Creating sprites dynamically

Often a platform game will involve a central character jumping on elements or head butting them to get power up sprites or tokens. This means that you must be prepared to create sprites dynamically during the course of the game. This could not be easier than it is in Flash. Simply use the ActionScript command

```
duplicateMovieClip(target, name, level);
```

where *target* is the movie clip that is being duplicated, *name* is the name that will be used for the new clip and *level* is the unique number that indicates where the clip will be located, rather like the layers on the timeline. When you create a new clip, store the name of the clip in a global level array, 'dynamicClips', so that at a later stage you will be able to remove it. In order to add a new element to an array, simply use 'push'.

```
dynamicClips.push(newclip); //newclip is the name that will be stored
```

Suppose that when the cat lands on a certain box you want to set off an animation that includes a fish power-up token. First you create the graphics and animation and store this in a clip that is off-screen. Make sure that the animation in the clip stops at the end rather than loops back and have it set a flag at the start, something like 'clipFinished=false' which is set to true at the end of the animation. On the main ticking loop for the game, either a clip event or a main timeline loop, run through every clip in the dynamicClips array. If you find that the variable 'clipFinished' is true then remove the clip using:

```
removeMovieClip(clipname);
```

then update the array so that it is not removed again. A single element can be removed from an array using the 'splice' method. This method takes the starting index in the array and then a parameter that defines how many elements to delete. The same method can take a third and subsequent parameters; these subsequent parameters define elements that are added to the array. These parameters are optional and when missing, the method operates just by removing elements rather than removing and replacing.

If the second parameter is missing then the array is deleted from the number index indicated by the first parameter up to the end of the array.

```
for (i=0; i<dynamicClips.length; i++){
   if (eval(dynamicClips[i]).clipFinished){
        removeMovieClip(dynamicClips[i]);
        dynamicClips.splice(i, 1);
   }
}
```

Summary

Platform games can be quite difficult to code but if you are methodical and prepared to rigorously test each part of your script then they can be great fun to produce and certainly great fun to play. The two examples in this chapter give you the basis for a game. Hopefully you will create a functional game using these as a template and if you do then please send a URL of the game to me at niklever.net. I look forward to seeing the results. I hope to create a page of readers' examples at www.niklever.net/flash.

18 Sports simulations

Some of the most successful commercial games are sports simulations. Golf has been a popular game on computer since the beginning of the computer games industry and tennis sometimes makes the bestsellers. Downhill skiing and snowboarding are popular in the retail games arena and in the arcades. But one of the bestsellers worldwide is undoubtedly football. In this chapter we are going to look at how to create a football game. One of the central problems is gathering user input when potentially there could be 11 players to control. Another feature of the game is the use of a roving camera to simulate TV coverage. Although a 3D game would certainly give a more realistic view of the game, the Flash presentation can still be very involving.

An overview of the game

Essentially the aim of the game from a programming perspective is to keep the game as object orientated as possible. We want the players to move themselves because most of them will be under computer control. Only a single player will be under user control, and this player will be moved using the arrow keys and will kick the ball using the space bar. For each step of the game the computer will move all the other players and decide which opposing player is nearest to the ball, making this player the one with ball focus. If the ball has been kicked by the user's team then the computer calculates the nearest team player and they become the new player under user control. The ball is hit using simple physics calculations and the camera tracks the player from each team with the ball focus and the ball itself, centring the display in the middle of this triangle. If any one of the elements of the triangle, player team A, player team B and ball, is out of shot then the scale of the view switches to wide so that an overview of the game is shown. Each team has just five players and the game is played in the manner of five-a-side football where the players can bounce the ball off the walls.

Initializing the game

As usual the first code section we will review is game initialization. Each instance of a player uses the same movie clip, 'Blue0'. The movie clip contains just two frames; all the actions for the blue player are stored in a movie clip on frame 1 and all the actions for the red player on frame 2. In all other respects the players perform identically, so the purpose of this initialization is just to duplicate the clips, set their index value, set the appropriate colour for the team by moving to either frame 1 or 2 and to tell the clip which team they belong to. At this stage we are ready to call the root level function 'startGame' that is defined on frame 1 of the movie, which is the 'Loader' scene.

Figure 18.1 *Developing the football game*

```
1   count = 1;
2   for (i=0; i<5; i++){
3       name = "Blue" + i;
4   if (i>0) duplicateMovieClip ("Blue0", name, count++);
5   eval(name).index = i;
6   eval(name).Team.gotoAndStop(1);
7   eval(name).teamno = _root.BLUE;
8
9   name = "Red" + I;
10      duplicateMovieClip ("Blue0", name, count++);
11      eval(name).index = i;
12      eval(name).Team.gotoAndStop(2);
13      eval(name).teamno = _root.RED;
14 }
15 _root.startGame();
16 stop();
```

Listing 18.1

Frame 1 of the loader is also used to define several constants that will be used throughout the program. As usual I define all the constants using upper case to make them stand out in the source code. Because Flash does not have a constant definition they are in actual fact just variables.

```
1   //Constants
2   BALLDIAMETER = 16;
3   BALLDIAMETER2 = BALLDIAMETER * 2;
4   BALLDIAMETER3 = BALLDIAMETER * 3;
5   BALLDIAMETER4 = BALLDIAMETER * 4;
6   BALLDIAMETER5 = BALLDIAMETER * 5;
7   PI = Math.PI;
8   ROTATIONFRAMES = 64;
9   PLAYERFRAMES = 16;
10  PLAYERROTATESTEP = ROTATIONFRAMES/PLAYERFRAMES;
11  FRAMETORADIANS = (2 * PI)/ROTATIONFRAMES;
12  PANFRAMES = 20;
13  RED = 0;
14  BLUE = 1;
15  MINSPEED = 0.2;
16  MAXSPEED = 10;
17  STARTSPEED = 2.5;
18  ACCELERATION = 0.05;
19  MAXSPEEDB = 6;
20  ACCELERATIONB = 0.03;
21  PASS = 0;
22  SHOOT = 1;
23  SHOOTDISTANCE = 150;
24  MAXKICKSTRENGTH = 80;
25  BALLFRAMES = 100;
26  TARGETMIN = 10;
27  PLAYERSIZESQ = 2 * BALLDIAMETER * BALLDIAMETER;
```
Listing 18.2

The 'startGame' function initializes the scores for each team and defines which team the computer controls, and which the player. The direction in which the teams are playing is defined using the movie clip variable 'playleft'. This allows a half-time break when the players' direction will change. The movie clip function 'enableuser' is called to define which of the players the keyboard controls.

```
1   function startGame(){
2       starttime = getTimer();
3
4       ScoreA = 0;
```

```
5        ScoreB = 0;
6        playerTeam = RED;
7        for (i=0; i<5; i++){
8                eval("Blue" + i).playleft = false;
9                eval("Red" + i).playleft = true;
10       }
11       eval("Pitch.Red0").enableuser();
12       kickoff();
13   }
```
Listing 18.3

The 'startGame' function completes by calling the function 'kickOff'. The purpose of this function is to reposition the players to the kick off locations and enable and disable keyboard control. Notice how each and every team member is positioned and set a target.

```
1    function kickoff(){
2        Pitch.Ball._x = 0;
3        Pitch.Ball._y = 10;
4
5        Pitch.Blue0._x = -32;
6        Pitch.Blue0._y = 0;
7        if (playerTeam!=BLUE){
8                Pitch.Blue0.disableuser();
9        }
10
11       Pitch.Red0._x = 34;
12       Pitch.Red0._y = 0;
13       if (playerTeam!=RED){
14               Pitch.Red0.disableuser();
15       }
16
17       for (i=1; i<4; i++){
18               name = "Pitch.Blue" + i;
19               eval(name)._y = Pitch.Blue0._y - 40 + (i-1)*40;
20               eval(name)._x = Pitch.Blue0._x - 40;
21               eval(name).disableuser();
22               name = "Pitch.Red" + i;
23               eval(name)._y = Pitch.Red0._y - 40 + (i-1)*40;
24               eval(name)._x = Pitch.Red0._x + 40;
25               eval(name).disableuser();
26       }
27
28       //Goalies
29       Pitch.Blue4._x = -199;
30       Pitch.Blue4._y = 0;
```

Figure 18.2 *Player animation frames*

```
31        Pitch.Blue4.disableuser();
32        Pitch.Red4._x = 190;
33        Pitch.Red4._y = 0;
34        Pitch.Red4.disableuser();
35
36        Pitch.Blue0.targetx = -135;
37        Pitch.Blue0.targety = -108;
38        Pitch.Blue1.targetx = 41;
39        Pitch.Blue1.targety = 105;
40        Pitch.Blue2.targetx = 96;
41        Pitch.Blue2.targety = -120;
42        Pitch.Blue3.targetx = 151;
43        Pitch.Blue3.targety = 83;
44        Pitch.Blue4.targetx = -192;
45        Pitch.Blue4.targety = 0;
46        Pitch.Red0.targetx = 135;
47        Pitch.Red0.targety = 108;
48        Pitch.Red1.targetx = -41;
49        Pitch.Red1.targety = -105;
```

```
50        Pitch.Red2.targetx = -96;
51        Pitch.Red2.targety = 120;
52        Pitch.Red3.targetx = -151;
53        Pitch.Red3.targety = -83;
54        Pitch.Red4.targetx = 192;
55        Pitch.Red4.targety = 0;
56 }
```
Listing 18.4

The main game loop

The main game loop is in the clip event for the 'Pitch' movie clip. Step one is to update the timer. The purpose of storing the 'startTime' is so that it can be used to calculate the elapsed time using

```
    secs = int((getTimer() - startTime)/1000);
```

The 'getTimer' returns the system time in milliseconds; by subtracting the start time and dividing by 1000, the elapsed seconds can easily be calculated. This can then be stripped into minutes and seconds using the integer value after division by 60 and the remainder after division by 60, the modulus operator '%'. The values for these two numbers are then converted in strings of two characters and built into a string to display the time.

```
1   function SetTimeStr(){
2        secs = int((getTimer() - startTime)/1000);
3        mins = int(secs/60);
4        secs %= 60;
5
6        secstr = String(secs);
7
8        while (length(secstr)<2){
9               secstr = "0" + secstr;
10       }
11
12       minstr = String(mins);
13
14       while (length(minstr)<2){
15              minstr = "0" + minstr;
16       }
17
18       TimeStr = minstr + ":" + secstr;
19 }
```
Listing 18.5

The next step in the main game loop is to determine the player from each team that is nearest to the ball. This is done using the function 'nearestPlayer'. The function sets up the team name using the passed in team number. Then for each of the five players in the team the x and y distance to the ball is calculated. The actual distance to the ball is then the square root of the x distance square plus the y distance square. This is just Pythagoras's theorem about the sides of a triangle. The square root function is actually quite a slow function to calculate and you could improve this code by just calculating the squared distance, because we are only interested in the nearest not the actual distance. If the loop is being run for the first time, namely i equals zero, then the variables 'player' and 'dist' are set to the current values of 'i' and 'balldist' respectively. If the loop is in the second or higher passes then the values for 'player' and 'dist' are only set if the 'dist' value is greater than the value for 'balldist' in the current pass. Finally the 'Direction' clip inside the player's clip is set if the current team is not the player's team. The direction clip is an arrow indicator showing the player's direction and indicating to the player that this player has the ball focus.

```
1   function nearestplayer(teamno){
2       var i, dist, dx, dy, name, player;
3
4       if (teamno==BLUE){
5           teamname = "Pitch.Blue";
6       }else{
7           teamname = "Pitch.Red";
8       }
9
10      for (i=0; i<5; i++){
11          name = teamname + i;
12          if (teamno != playerTeam) eval(name).disableuser();
13          dx = eval(name)._x - Pitch.Ball._x;
14          dy = eval(name)._y - Pitch.Ball._y;
15          eval(name).balldist = Math.sqrt(dx*dx + dy*dy);
16          if (i==0){
17              player = i;
18              dist = eval(name).balldist;
19            }else if (eval(name).balldist<dist){
20              player = i;
21              dist = eval(name).balldist;
22          }
23      }
24
25      if (teamno != playerTeam){
26          name = teamname + player;
27          eval(name).Direction.gotoAndStop(2);
28      }
29
30      return player;
31  }
```

Listing 18.6

Having calculated the nearest player to the ball for both teams, these are stored in the variables 'a' and 'b'. The code is designed so that a player can choose which team to use, then the choice is stored in the variable 'playersTeam'. If the opponent closest to the ball has changed after calling the 'nearestPlayer' function then root level variables 'opponentNo' and 'movecount' are updated, the function 'opponentMove' is executed on the opponent nearest to the ball and the current team member nearest to the ball is stored in the root level variable 'closestplayer'.

The opponentMove function

This function is quite complex and needs some careful study. The basic idea is that the player wants to move towards the ball in such a direction that they can have a direct kick towards the correct goal. The function starts by creating a vector from the goal to the ball. This vector needs to be of length 1. To convert an arbitrary vector to a vector of length 1 in the same direction we must normalize the vector; that is we must divide both the values by the same number, so it is then still in the same direction, in such a way that if we draw the diagonal vector connecting the start of the vector to the end the length will be 1. First we find out what the current length is using the famous Pythagoras theorem. This value is stored in the variable 'mag'. Now we divide both the elements in the vector by this value, and hey presto we have a unit length vector. Next we move along this vector three times the ball's diameter and create a new target stored in the variables 'gx' and 'gy' which will be the perfect spot for our player to run and hit the ball to get a terrific goal kick. Now we create two ramp values 'a' and 'b'. 'a' is how much we want our player to run towards our perfect spot to kick the ball, 'b' is how much we want our player to just run at the ball. If we are within three times the ball's diameter then we want the player to be more targeted at hitting the ball the nearer they are. To make sure we show the appropriate images of the player we must calculate the angle that the player will be running now that we have the information needed. The player graphics contains 32 separate two-frame run cycles, rotating around a full 360 degrees. We can decide which to show on the basis of this angle. The angle is calculated using the 'atan' function, which takes two sides of a triangle and returns an angle. This angle can be converted into which frame to show using a division by the constant FRAMETORADIANS.

The player must avoid kicking the ball towards their own goal so if they are positioned in a line comprising player, ball, own goal then they must run around the outside of the ball. This is done by adjusting their angle; if this is the case, aiming towards the outside of a circle that is three times the player's diameter.

```
1  function opponentmove(){
2      //Create a vector from the goal to the ball
3      x = _root.Pitch.Ball._x - 260;
4      y = _root.Pitch.Ball._y - 0;
5      //Normalise this vector
6      //mag is the distance from the ball to the goal
7      mag = Math.sqrt(x*x + y*y);
8      x /= mag;
9      y /= mag;
```

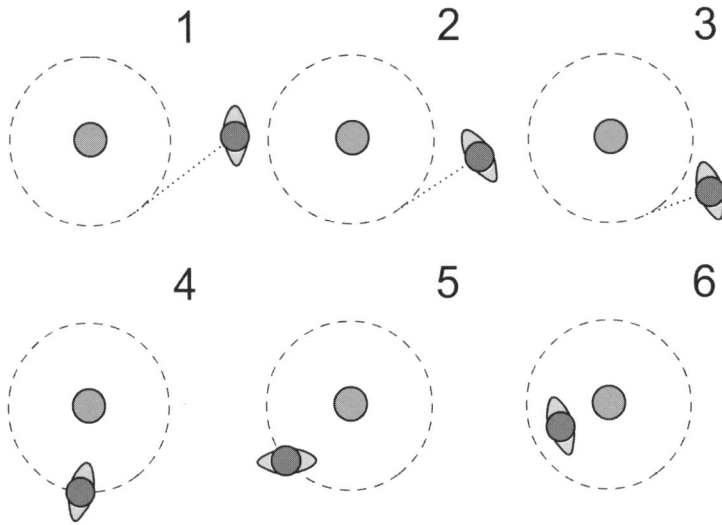

Figure 18.3 *The effect of ramping between moving the player to the ball and to three times the ball's diameter*

```
10        //Move out by 3 times ball diameter
11        x *= _root.BALLDIAMETER3;
12        y *= _root.BALLDIAMETER3;
13        gx = x + _root.Pitch.Ball._x;
14        gy = y + _root.Pitch.Ball._y;
15        //Create a ramp between the outer target and the ball
16        //a is target proportion
17        //b is ball proportion
18        if (balldist>_root.BALLDIAMETER3){
19                a = 1;
20                b = 0;
21        }else{
22                a = (balldist - _root.BALLDIAMETER)/_root.BALLDIAMETER3;
23                b = 1 - a;
24        }
25
26        c = _root.ROTATIONFRAMES/3;
27        x = a * (_x - gx) + b * (_x - _root.Pitch.Ball._x);
28        y = a * (_y - gy) + b * (_y - _root.Pitch.Ball._y);
29        angle = Math.atan2(y, x) + _root.PI;
30        frame = int(angle/_root.FRAMETORADIANS) + 1;
31
32        if ( balldist<_root.BALLDIAMETER){
33                if (frame > c && frame < (_root.ROTATIONFRAMES - c)){
34                        //Test whether the player is running back
35                        //If so and the balldist less than the ball
36                        //diameter then kick ball
```

```
37                      kickball(_root.PASS);
38            }else if (a<b && mag<_root.SHOOTDISTANCE){
39                      //Test for shoot
40                      //Condition is goal distance is less than
41                      //SHOOTDISTANCE and direction is based on a<b
42                      kickball(_root.SHOOT);
43            }
44      }else{
45            if (frame > c && frame < (_root.ROTATIONFRAMES - c)){
46
47                      //Try to run around outside of ball
48                      //First set b equal to the ball angle
49                      x = _x - _root.Pitch.Ball._x;
50                      y = _y - _root.Pitch.Ball._y;
51                      b = Math.atan2(y, x) + _root.PI;
52                      //Get deflection angle
53                      if (balldist < _root.BALLDIAMETER3){
54                            y = balldist;
55                      }else{
56                            y = _root.BALLDIAMETER3;
57                      }
58                      x = Math.sqrt(balldist * balldist - y * y);
59                      a = Math.atan2(y, x);
60                      //Move towards the closest deflection angle
61                      //to the target
62                      i = angle - (b - a);
63                      j = angle - (b + a);
64                      i *= i;
65                      j *= j;
66                      if (i<j){
67                            angle = b - a;
68                      }else{
69                            angle = b + a;
70                      }
71                      frame = int(angle/_root.FRAMETORADIANS) + 1;
72            }
73      }
74
75      setframe(frame);
76      if (speed<0.2){
77            speed=1;
78      }else{
79            speed += ((_root.MAXSPEEDB - speed)*_root.ACCELERATIONB);
80      }
81 }
```

Listing 18.7

Reading the keyboard

The 'checkKeys' function is used to both read the keyboard and set up movie clip parameters that are affected by user input. The name of the movie clip under user control is calculated and stored in the variable 'name'. If the left key is pressed then the player is rotated anticlockwise, similarly the right key rotates the clip clockwise. The rotation is virtual, in that the movie clip itself is never rotated; it is simply the display frame that suggests the rotation. The 'setFrame' function does the work of setting the appropriate frame. The up arrow adjusts the speed for the clip and the space bar kicks the ball if it is close enough to the player.

```
1   function checkKeys(){
2       var name;
3
4       if (_root.playerTeam == _root.BLUE){
5               name = "Blue" + _root.playerNo;
6       }else{
7               name = "Red" + _root.playerNo;
8       }
9
10      if (Key.isDown(Key.LEFT)){
11              //Left arrow
12              if (rotateleft<3) rotateleft *= 1.4;
13              frame = int(eval(name)._currentframe - rotateleft);
14              if (frame<1){ frame += _root.ROTATIONFRAMES; }
15              eval(name).setFrame(frame);
16      }else{
17              rotateleft = 1;
18      }
19
20      if (Key.isDown(Key.UP)){
21              //Up arrow
22              eval(name).uparrow = true;
23              if (eval(name).speed < _root.MINSPEED){
24                      eval(name).speed = _root.STARTSPEED;
25              }else{
26                      eval(name).speed += ((_root.MAXSPEED-
27                                      eval(name.speed))*_root.ACCELERATION);
28              }
29      }
30
31      if (Key.isDown(Key.RIGHT)){
32              //Right arrow
33              if (rotateright<3){
34                      rotateright *= 1.4;
35              }
36              frame = int(eval(name)._currentframe + rotateright);
```

```
37                  if (frame>_root.ROTATIONFRAMES){
38                  frame -= _root.ROTATIONFRAMES;
39                  }
40                  eval(name).setFrame(frame);
41          }else{
42                  rotateright = 1;
43          }
44
45      if (Key.isDown(Key.SPACE)){
46              //Space Bar
47              if (eval(name).balldist<_root.BALLDIAMETER){
48                  eval(name).kickBall(_root.SHOOT);
49              }
50              eval(name).disableUser();
51              if (_root.playerTeam == _root.BLUE){
52                  name = "Blue" + _root.closestplayer;
53              }else{
54                  name = "Red" + _root.closestplayer;
55              }
56              eval(name).enableUser();
57              if (_root.closestplayer != _root.playerNo){
58                  if (_xscale>100){
59                      movecount = _root.PANFRAMES;
60                  }else{
61                      movecount = 0;
62                  }
63              }
64          }
65 }
```

Listing 18.8

The 'setFrame' function determines whether the player is actually already on the best frame to display the current angle, because in this example we only have 32 different display angles but the clip can be set to any angle. We only need to update the frame when we move into a new angle display. By finding the integer of the current frame after division by the step value and comparing this with the requested frame divided in the same way, we can see whether we have stepped into a new display block. Then we test for the current speed and set the player's display frame to either a stationary rotate frame or a running display frame.

```
1  function setFrame(frame){
2      a = int(_currentframe/_root.PLAYERROTATESTEP);
3      b = int(frame/_root.PLAYERROTATESTEP);
4      if (a!=b){
5              //Need to rotate our player
6              b++;
```

```
7                    if (speed<1){
8                            Team.Player.gotoAndStop(b);
9                    }else{
10                           Team.Player.gotoAndPlay("Rotate" + b);
11                   }
12        }
13        gotoAndStop(frame);
14 }
```
Listing 18.9

The other function called by the keyboard reader is 'kickBall'. Firstly the strength of the kick is calculated based on the player's current distance from the ball's centre. The ball in turn is informed that a kick has occurred and is required to start bouncing, using the ball function 'startKick'.


```
1    function kickBall(type){
2         //Calculate the strength of the kick based on
3         //players distance from the ball
4         //balldist = BALLDIAMETER max strength
5         //balldist = BALLDIAMETER*2 min strength
6
7         a = (1 - balldist/_root.BALLDIAMETER)*5;
8         //Calculate players movement vectors
9         x = Math.cos(angle) * speed;
10        y = Math.sin(angle) * speed;
11        _root.Pitch.Ball.startKick(a, x, y);
12 }
```
Listing 18.10

The 'startKick' function is very simple; using the parameters passed from the 'kickBall' function, the movement vector and power are calculated.


```
1    function startKick(strength, x, y){
2         strength /= 10;
3         moveX = x * strength;
4         moveY = y * strength;
5         if (strength>1) strength = 1;
6         power = int(strength * _root.BALLFRAMES)/2.5;
7         bouncing = true;
8         bouncestart = getTimer();
9    }
```
Listing 18.11

Updating the players

By the time the 'update' function is called for the players, all user input has been gathered and the nearest player to the ball has been stored. There are two different update methods; either the player is under keyboard control in which case the movement has taken place, or the player is the computer-controlled player nearest the ball, in which case the function 'opponentMove' has already been called to update their position. If neither of these possibilities applies to the current player then the function 'moveToTarget' is used. Each player has a target position at which they are aiming, which is a simple mechanism to get the players to work as a team, rather than every player heading towards the ball. The function works by first creating a vector from the current position of the player to the target position. If the target has been achieved then the square of this vector will be less than the constant 'TARGETMIN'. If this is the case then a new target is calculated. Some players are set to be attacking players and the others are defenders. The new target is calculated taking into consideration an arbitrary location on the pitch and the current ball position; attacking players use more of the ball position in deciding on a new target, whereas defenders tend to stay inside their own half. The function closes with a call to 'setDirection'.

```
1   function moveToTarget(){
2       x = _x - targetx;
3       y = _y - targety;
4       if ((x*x + y*y)<_root.TARGETMIN){
5               //At target so run towards the ball
6               a = random(100)/100;
7               b = 1 - a;
8               if (index<3){
9                       //Attacking players
10                      b = -b;
11              }
12              x = random(100) + 140;
13              if (playleft){
14                      x = -x;
15              }
16              y = 75 - random(100);
17              targetx = a * _root.Pitch.Ball._x + b * x;
18              targety = a * _root.Pitch.Ball._y + b * y;
19
20      }
21      setDirection(targetx, targety);
22  }
```
Listing 18.12

In the 'setDirection' code a vector from the current position to the target is used to calculate the current direction and then the 'setFrame' function is called to update the current frame for the player.

```
1   function setDirection(x1, y1){
2       x = _x - x1;
3       y = _y - y1;
4       angle = Math.atan2(y, x) + _root.PI;
5       frame = int(angle/_root.FRAMETORADIANS) + 1;
6       setFrame(frame);
7       if (speed<0.2){
8               speed=1;
9       }else{
10              speed += ((_root.MAXSPEEDB - speed)*_root.ACCELERATIONB);
11      }
12  }
```

Listing 18.13

Having executed either a keyboard-controlled move, a computer-controlled move or a move to target move, we need to test for any collisions with other players. The 'update' function uses the functions 'playerCollide' and 'collision' to do just this.

```
1   function update(){
2       if (_root.playerTeam == teamno){
3               if (_root.playerNo!=index){
4                       //Move player using location tactics
5                       moveToTarget();
6               }
7       }else{
8               if (_root.opponentNo!=index){
9                       //Move player using location tactics
10                      movetotarget();
11              }
12      }
13      angle = getAngle();
14      if (!Key.isDown(38)){
15              speed *= 0.95;
16      }
17      vecx = Math.cos(angle) * speed;
18      vecy = Math.sin(angle) * speed;
19
20      //Test for collisions with other players
21      for (i=0; i<5; i++){
22              if (i!=index){
23                      name = "_root.Pitch.Blue" + i;
24                      if (playerCollide(name)){
25                              clearCollision(name);
```

```
26                         break;
27                     }
28                 }
29             name = "_root.Pitch.Red" + i;
30             if (playerCollide(name)){
31                     clearCollision(name);
32                     break;
33                 }
34         }
35 }
```
Listing 18.14

Testing for collisions

A collision occurs if the squared value of the vector between the two players is greater than the constant PLAYERSIZESQ. The 'playerCollide' returns true if a collision occurs and false otherwise.

```
1  function playerCollide(name){
2      x = (_x + vecx) - (eval(name)._x + eval(name).vecx);
3      y = (_y + vecy) - (eval(name)._y + eval(name).vecy);
4      if ((x*x + y*y)<_root.PLAYERSIZESQ){
5              return true;
6      }
7      return false;
8  }
```
Listing 18.15

   Clearing the collision is much more complex. The aim of the function is to calculate a vector in the direction of the collision then bounce the player off like a snooker ball. The normal for the collision is the direction vector of the current object minus the direction vector of the collision object plus the current object's location minus the collision object's location. These values are stored in the two variables 'cnx' and 'cny'. This vector is then normalized. The relative velocity of the two objects is found by subtracting the collision object's movement vector 'vecx, vecy' from the current object's movement vector. The relative velocity is stored in the two variables 'vabx' and 'vaby'. The dot product of the two vectors is the sum of the products of the components of the vector.

$$\mathbf{a} \cdot \mathbf{b} = a.x * b.x + a.y * b.y$$

if **a** and **b** are both vectors containing two components x and y. The function 'dotproduct' is designed to return this value.

```
function dotproduct(x1, y1, x2, y2){
        return (x1 * x2 + y1 * y2);
}
```

But the dot product of two vectors has another definition:

$$\mathbf{a} \cdot \mathbf{b} = |\mathbf{a}||\mathbf{b}| \cos \theta$$

This means that the dot product is the magnitude of one vector times the magnitude of the other times the cosine of the angle between them. If each has magnitude 1, they are unit vectors, and then the dot product is the cosine of the angle between the two vectors. If this value is less than or equal to zero then we can calculate the new velocities for the objects involved in the collision. If the value is positive then the collision has occurred with the opposite side of the object, that is the objects totally overlap; if we allow such a collision then the effect will be to bounce in the opposite direction to the desired result.

```
1   function collision(name){
2         //Get the normal of the collision
3         cnx = (_x + vecx) - (eval(name)._x + eval(name).vecx);
4         cny = (_y + vecy) - (eval(name)._y + eval(name).vecy);
5         //Get magnitude of normal and normalise
6         mag = Math.sqrt(cnx * cnx + cny * cny);
7         cnx /= mag;
8         cny /= mag;
9         //Set masses for collision objects
10        ma = 20;
11        mb = 20;
12        //Coefficient of restitution value,
13        //how much force is lost in collision
14        e = -(1 + 0.8);
15        //Components of player's velocity are already known
16        vax = vecx;
17        vay = vecy;
18        //Calculate components of player b velocity
19        if (eval(name).speed!=0){
20                vbx = eval(name).vecx;
21                vby = eval(name).vecy;
22        }else{
23                vbx = 0;
24                vby = 0;
25        }
26        //Calculate relative velocity
```

```
27      vabx = vax - vbx;
28      vaby = vay - vby;
29      //Get magnitude of relative velocity and normalise
30      mag = Math.sqrt(cnx * cnx + cny * cny);
31      vabx /= mag;
32      vaby /= mag;
33
34      //Check collision direction
35      vdotn = _root.dotproduct(vabx, vaby, cnx, cny);
36
37      if (vdotn<=0){
38              //Only react to a collision if negative
39              //relative normal velocity
40              a = _root.dotproduct(vabx*e, vaby*e, cnx, cny);
41              b = _root.dotproduct(cnx, cny, cnx, cny);
42              b *= (1/ma + 1/mb);
43              j = a/b;
44              a = j/ma;
45              vecx += a*cnx;
46              vecy += a*cny;
47              //At this point we can calculate the deflection for player b
48              //using vb' = vb - (j/mb)n
49              eval(name).vecx -= a*cnx;
50              eval(name).vecy -= a*cny;
51      }
52 }
```

Listing 18.16

It is time to move the players and the ball

The main game loop is now ready to move the players and the ball by calling the 'move' functions of the movie clips. Moving the players is easy; the new location for the clip is calculated by adding 'vecx' and 'vecy' to the current position as long as the player stays within the room. If the player goes beyond the room boundaries then the speed for the player is set to zero and the position is not updated.

```
1   function move(){
2       i = _x + vecx;
3       if (i > -271 && i<256){
4               _x = i;
5       }else{
6               speed = 0;
7       }
8       i = _y + vecy;
```

```
9        if (i > -171 && i<154){
10               _y = i;
11       }else{
12               speed = 0;
13       }
14  }
```
Listing 18.17

Moving the ball is much more complex and involves testing for collisions with any of the players or the walls. Step 1 is to slow the ball down, by multiplying the movement vector by 0.95. Then we test for a goal subject to the *x* value exceeding plus or minus 230 and the *y* position being within acceptable bounds. If a goal is scored then the score is updated and the root level function 'kickOff' is called to reposition all the players at their starting positions. If the '_currentframe' for the ball is greater than 1 then the ball must be bouncing. If the '_currentframe' is greater than 5 then the ball is considered too high to be played by any player and so only collisions with walls are considered. If the ball is on the ground then we test for and respond to collisions with all players in the same way as we responded to collisions between players. The ball movie clip contains a bounce animation that takes place over 100 frames. If the ball is bouncing because of a kick then the 'bounce' function is called. This uses a simple physics function; the displayed frame is calculated using the time since the bounce began and the current power. If the value calculated is less than 1 then a new bounce is initialized subject to a new power calculation staying above 1.

```
1   function bounce(){
2        time = (getTimer() - bouncestart)/150;
3        frame = time * ( power - 5 * time) + 1;
4        if (frame<1){
5                power *= 0.8;
6                if (power<1){
7                        bouncing = false;
8                        gotoAndStop(1);
9                   }else{
10                       bouncestart = getTimer();
11                }
12       }else{
13               gotoAndStop(int(frame));
14       }
15  }
```
Listing 18.18

The final step in the 'move' function is to update the current position for the ball by adding the final value for 'movex' and 'movey' to the current position.

```
1   function move(){
2       movex *= 0.95;
3       movey *= 0.95;
4       //Test for collisions with goal posts
5       if (x < -230){
6           //Blue team goal
7           if ((_y<-53 && y>-53)||(_y > 43 && y < 43)){
8               //Hit top or bottom side
9               movey *= -0.8;
10          }else if (y > -53 && y < 43){
11              //Red team have scored
12              _root.ScoreB++;
13              _root.kickOff();
14          }
15      }else if (x > 230){
16          //Red team goal
17          if ((_y<-53 && y>-53)||(_y > 43 && y < 43)){
18              //Hit top or bottom side
19              movey *= -0.8;
20          }else if (y > -53 && y < 43){
21              //Blue team have scored
22              _root.ScoreA++;
23              _root.kickOff();
24          }
25      }
26
27      if (_currentframe<5){
28          //Test for collisions with other players
29          for (i=0; i<5; i++){
30              name = "_root.Pitch.Blue" + i;
31              if (eval(name).balldist<_root.BALLDIAMETER){
32                  collision(name);
33                  if (_root.playerTeam == _root.BLUE){
34                      break;
35                  }
36              }
37              name = "_root.Pitch.Red" + i;
38              if (eval(name).balldist<_root.BALLDIAMETER){
39                  collision(name);
40                  if (_root.playerTeam == _root.RED){
41                      break;
42                  }
43              }
44          }
45      }
46
47      //Test for collisions with the room
48      x = _x + movex;
```

```
49        y = _y + movey;
50        if (x<-250 || x>250){
51                movex *= -0.6;
52                x = _x + movex;
53        }
54        if (y<-140 || y>140){
55                movey *= -0.6;
56                y = _y + movey;
57        }
58
59        if (bouncing) bounce();
60
61        _x += movex;
62        _y += movey;
63 }
```

Listing 18.19

Adjusting the camera location and scale

Figure 18.4 *Testing the game*

For much of the time the camera is scaled as in Figure 18.4 with the centre located in the middle of a triangle that includes the two players with focus and the ball. This movement is achieved using the 'move' function for the 'Pitch' clip. All the players and the ball are children of the 'Pitch' clip. Because the players with focus change regularly and yet we do not want the camera view to jump, we calculate a ramp between the positions using the 'movecount' variable. Whenever the player with focus changes the 'movecount' variable is set to the value of the constant PANFRAMES. A first call to the 'move' function with 'movecount' equal to PANFRAMES gives a value for a of 1 and a value for b of 0. The x and y values are calculated using the ramp value.

```
1    function move(){
2         //Position the pitch so that it is centred around
3         //the ball and the nearest player and opponent
4         if (_root.playerTeam==_root.RED){
5             x = eval("Red" + _root.playerNo)._x;
6             x += eval("Blue" + _root.opponentNo)._x;
7             y = eval("Red" + _root.playerNo)._y;
8             y += eval("Blue" + _root.opponentNo)._y;
9         }else{
10            x = eval("Red" + _root.playerNo)._x;
11            x += eval("Blue" + _root.opponentNo)._x;
12            y = eval("Red" + _root.playerNo)._y;
13            y += eval("Blue" + _root.opponentNo)._y;
14        }
15
16        scale = _xscale/100;
17
18        x = (x + Ball._x)/3;
19        x = 270 - x *scale;
20
21        if (movecount>0){
22            a = movecount/_root.PANFRAMES;
23            b = 1 - a;
24            x = b * x + a * _x;
25        }
26
27        if (x>-247 && x<795){
28            _x = x;
29        }
30
31        y = (y + Ball._y)/3;
32        y = 220 - y * scale;
33
34        if (movecount>0){
```

```
35                  y = b * y + a * _y;
36                  movecount--;
37          }
38
39      if (y>-104 && y<537){
40              _y = y;
41      }
42 }
```
Listing 18.20

The onClipEvent(enterFrame) function for the Pitch movie clip

That completes the analysis of the main game loop. Here is the function by which that operates:

1   Find the nearest player to the ball for each team.
2   Update the stored values if step 1 involved a change of player.
3   Read the keyboard.
4   Update the players if any have collided.
5   Move the players now that their final positions have been determined.
6   Move the ball by responding to the new player locations.
7   Position the camera to centre on the players with focus and the ball, or to show the full pitch.

```
1   onClipEvent (enterFrame) {
2       _root.SetTimeStr();
3       frametime = getTimer() - frametime;
4
5       //Find closest player and calculate ball distances
6       a = _root.nearestPlayer(_root.RED);
7       b = _root.nearestPlayer(_root.BLUE);
8
9       if (_root.playerTeam==_root.RED) {
10              if (_root.opponentNo!=b) {
11                      movecount = _root.PANFRAMES;
12                      _root.opponentNo = b;
13              }
14              eval("Blue" + b).opponentMove();
15              _root.closestplayer = a;
16      }else{
17              if (_root.opponentNo!=a) {
18                      movecount = _root.PANFRAMES;
19                      _root.opponentNo = a;
20              }
21              eval("Red" + a).opponentMove();
```

```
22              _root.closestplayer = b;
23          }
24
25      checkkeys();
26
27      //Update players
28      for (i=0; i<5; i++){
29              name = "Blue" + i;
30              eval(name).update();
31              name = "Red" + i;
32              eval(name).update();
33      }
34
35      //Move players
36      for (i=0; i<5; i++){
37              name = "Blue" + i;
38              eval(name).move();
39              name = "Red" + i;
40              eval(name).move();
41      }
42
43      //Move ball
44      Ball.move();
45
46      if (_root.playerTeam == _root.BLUE){
47              name = "Blue" + _root.playerNo;
48      }else{
49              name = "Red" + _root.playerNo;
50      }
51
52      //Move camera
53      if (eval(name).balldist>100){
54              //If ball is getting near to out of shot
55              //then track back
56              _xscale = 90;
57              _yscale = 90;
58              _x = 273.5;
59              _y = 225;
60      }else{
61              _xscale = 200;
62              _yscale = 200;
63              move();
64      }
65
66      frametime = getTimer();
67 }
```

Listing 18.21

305

Enhancements

As 'Examples\Chapter18\Football.fla' stands, there are many enhancements that could be made to greatly improve the game. The game needs a team strip chooser to enable the user to choose a team. There is no defined end to the game, and there should be a change of ends at half time and a final whistle. Running into an opponent could be regarded as a foul and a free kick given. The game needs crowd noises and music.

The collision code is all the code necessary to create a snooker game; the balls can be made to bounce off each other using the collision function in the ball object. It is left to the interested reader to create a snooker, pool or pinball game based on this collision code.

Summary

The code in this chapter presents the greatest challenge to the reader. Some of the tests involved in the collision detection use vector math results that are likely to push many readers' maths to the limit. By all means just strip out the code and get it working for you without worrying unduly how the code achieves its results. If you are interested in the methods then read up more on vector math, because there is a lot of interesting stuff out there for you to make use of in your games. In the next section we look at how you can create Flash games for players on the move.

Section 4

Flash for mobiles

The mobile games market is growing exponentially. With Flash MX 2004 developers have a new target platform, Flash Lite. This new section shows the limitations and possibilities of the new platform.

19 Flash Lite – how does it affect game developers?

With Flash MX 2004 Professional it is now possible to create Flash games that will run on mobile phones. These devices are greatly limited in their memory, screen and processors when compared to a modern desktop computer. For this reason Macromedia have created a Flash player that is scaled to suit the limited capabilities. In this chapter we will walk through the limitations inherent in the new player and examine how the ActionScript you write has to be different in style from the script you use to target the latest Flash player for desktop machines.

Flash Lite features

With Flash MX Professional 2004 there are two versions of the Flash player installed on your desktop development PC. When developing with Flash Lite it is essential that you set the player version to 'Flash Lite 1.0' in the Publish Settings dialog. One feature of Flash Lite is that it is device dependent. Some features differ on different devices. So the first step in creating any content is to get hold of the latest content development kit (CDK) for the device that you are developing for.

Kerning, spacing, bold and italic styles are not supported in Flash Lite when using Dynamic or Input text fields, so be careful when creating content not to use these features. Most Flash Lite devices have no mouse-based navigation. Lacking a mouse there is no support for 'dragOver', 'dragOut' and 'releaseOutside', and draggable movie clips ('startDrag' and 'stopDrag') are not supported.

Sound support is very limited: only MIDI and MFi (Melody Format for i-mode) are supported. Consequently special techniques have to be used when testing the content on a desktop PC. See the section on Using Sound for details.

Flash Lite string methods

Strings are not handled using the JavaScript methods; instead they use the Flash 4 implementation (Table 19.1).

Starting with Flash Lite

The easiest way to get started with Flash Lite is to use a template. Open Flash MX 2004 Professional and click on the 'Create from Template/Mobile Devices' button. If other projects are already open then simply choose 'File>New...' and select the 'Template' tab. Try any of the NTT DoCoMo options.

Table 19.1 *Syntax difference between standard ActionScript and ActionScript Lite for string operations*

ActionScript	Lite	Notes
+	add or &	Concatenate two strings
==	eq	Compare two strings
>=	ge	Greater than or equal to for two strings
>	gt	Greater than for two strings
<=	le	Less than or equal to for two strings
<	lt	Less than for two strings
!=	ne	Not equal to for two strings

Figure 19.1 *Using the Flash MX 2004 Professional Templates panel*

Using the template, your movie size is automatically set and a guide layer is provided with a photo of the phone you are developing for. If you check the 'Publish Settings' panel you will see that the 'Version:' setting is 'Flash Lite 1.0'. When you publish, the swf created will be in this form.

Using sound

The only sound support in Flash Lite is for MIDI files and MFi (Melody Format for i-mode). To enable sound on the desktop you need to import a placeholder 'wav' or 'mp3' file then open the Sound Properties panel by right-clicking on the sound file from the Library panel. In the

Figure 19.2 *Developing a Flash Lite game using Flash MX 2004 Professional*

Figure 19.3 *Specifying a device sound*

'Device sound:' box enter the path to a MIDI or MFi file by clicking on the folder icon. If the file is of the right format it should be heard when using either 'Control > Test Movie' or the 'Standalone Flash Lite Player'.

When using 'Test Movie' the compiler sends compilation information to the 'Output' window. If a sound is successfully embedded then you should see an SWFS045 message as shown in Figure 19.4.

Figure 19.4 *Flash Lite compilation messages*

It should be noted that the 505i phones only support the Mfi sound format, which are saved as files with the 'mld' extension. http://smaf-yamaha.com/what/other.html provides a tool that allows you to create mld files from an mp3 or wav file. As is the nature of the Internet this page is likely to have moved so if this is the case do a search for 'mld authoring tools' to find the current best ones.

Testing content using the i-mode HTML Simulator

One of the quickest ways to test your games that target mobile devices is to use the i-mode HTML Simulator. This can be downloaded from https://www.nttdocomo.co.jp/imode_sim/dl.html. Unfortunately this page was only available in Japanese at the time of writing; however, if it is available when you are downloading then Figure 19.5 shows what to enter and which button to press. The details shown are found at the bottom of the page.

Figure 19.5 *Downloading the i-mode HTML Simulator from the Japanese website*

Unzip the file then run the 'setup.exe' program. Having installed the simulator you should find a new icon on your desktop. Click this to run the simulator. Two windows are opened, the simulator and a log window. To run your game simply use the 'Function > OpenURL' menu option and then select 'Browse'. Go straight to the swf file. I-mode phones can open swf files directly; they do not need a host HTML page but they can use one if required. Listing 19.1 shows how it can be done.

```
1   <HTML>
2   <TITLE>Pong Lite</TITLE>
3   <BODY>
4   <object declare id="swf1" data="pongLite.swf"
5           type="application/x-shockwave-flash" >
6   <param name="bgcolor" value="#ffff00">
7   <param name="quality" value="medium">
8   </object>
9   <a iswf="swf1" href="pongLite.swf">PongLite</a>
10  </BODY>
11  </HTML>
```
Listing 19.1

A practical example

'Examples/Chapter19/ponglite.fla' is a simple Flash Lite game. Figure 19.6 shows the game running in the i-mode HTML Simulator.

Figure 19.6 *Testing 'Examples/Chapter19/ponglite.swf' in the i-mode HTML Simulator*

The game uses keys 1 and 3 to control the 'Bat'. The left, right, up and down keys are reserved for the i-mode browser so you cannot receive key information from these. The keys available are 0, 1, 2, 3, 4, 5, 6, 7, 8, 9, * and #. To receive keyboard input you must use a Flash button. You cannot target key messages to a movie clip or use the 'Key' object; these techniques are unavailable on Flash Lite. The syntax for detecting key presses is shown in Listing 19.2.

```
1   on(keyPress "1"){
2       if (dx>0) dx=0;
3       if (dx>-5) dx--;
4       if (board._x>-51) board._x += dx;
5   }
6
7   on(keyPress "3"){
8       if (dx<0) dx=0;
9       if (dx<5) dx++;
10      if (board._x<52) board._x += dx;
11  }
```

Listing 19.2

In Flash Lite there is no such thing as an 'onClipEvent' so you will find that you will have to use the main timeline to control the movie far more. In this example, Pong, we have to support a new game, a new ball and the main game loop. A new game occurs as the playhead runs the script at frame 1. A new ball is created whenever the script at frame 5 is executed and the main loop is frames 9 and 10. Frame 9 is simply a play event, while frame 10 is the code shown in Listing 19.3.

```
1   ballX += moveX;
2   ballY += moveY;
3   //Bounce off the sides
4   if ((ballX>57 && moveX>=0) || (ballX<-57 && moveX<0)) {
5       ballX = ballX - (moveX*2);
6       moveX = -moveX;
7   }
8   //Bounce off top
9   if (moveY<0 && ballY == -26) {
10      ballY = ballY - moveY;
11      moveY = 3;
12  }
13  ball._x = ballX;
14  ball._y = ballY;
15  //Bounce off bat or miss
16  if (moveY>0 && ballY == 19) {
17      boardTest = ballX - board._x;
```

```
18      if (boardTest>-8 && boardTest<8) {
19          pongScore++;
20          moveY = -3;
21          moveX += (boardTest * 0.625);
22          //sfx.gotoAndPlay (2);
23      }
24 }
25 //If we are going down and the y>31 then we've missed
26 if (moveY>0 && ballY >= 31) {
27    gotoAndPlay ("ballstart");
28 } else {
29    prevFrame ();
30 }
```

Listing 19.3

As you can see from the listing a lot of the ActionScript that you are familiar with is available in Flash Lite. Table 19.2 is a summary of what is available in Flash Lite 1.0.

Table 19.2 *ActionScript supported in Flash Lite 1.0*

ActionScript	Comment
//	Comment
,	Separator for two expressions
.	Navigate hierarchies
""	String
− −	Decrement
++	Increment
+	Add
+ =	Add and assign
−	Subtract
− =	Subtract and assign
*	Multiply
* =	Multiply and assign
/	Divide
/=	Divide and assign
=	Test two expressions for equality
<	Less than
<=	Less than or equal to
>	Greater than
>=	Greater than or equal to
<>	Not equal
%	Remainder after integer division
%=	Remainder and assign
||	Or
!	Not
&&	And
?:	Conditional assignment

Table 19.2 *Continued*

ActionScript	Comment
&	String concatenation
add	String concatenation
break	Exit a 'for' or 'while' loop
call	Jump to a function
switch case	Conditional jumping
chr()	ASCII to character
continue	Move to next loop of a 'for'
do – – while	Looping
duplicateMovieClip	Create new movie clip instance
if else	Conditional coding
eq	String equality
eval()	Access variables via names
ge	String greater than or equal to
getProperty()	Not all properties see list that follows
getTimer()	Time in milliseconds since movie started
getURL()	Not fully supported. Only one call per action
gotoAndPlay()	Moves playback head
gotoAndStop()	Stops playback head
gt	String greater than
ifFrameLoaded()	Used to test streaming of a movie
int()	Converts decimal to nearest integer
le	String less than
length()	Returns the length of a string
lt	String less than
mbchr()	ASCII to multibyte character
mblength()	Returns length a multibyte string
mbord()	Character to multibyte code
mbsubstring()	Extracts a multibyte character string from a multibyte string
ne	String inequality
nextFrame()	Moves playback head on a frame and stops
nextScene()	Moves playback head on a scene and stops
on(...)	Partially supported event handlers
ord()	Character to ASCII
play()	Starts playback
prevFrame()	Moves playback head back a frame and stops
prevScene()	Moves playback head back a scene and stops
random()	Returns a random integer between 0 and the number passed
removeMovieClip()	Deletes a clip created with duplicateMovieClip
set()	Used to assign a value to a variable
setProperty	Partially supported property assignment
stop()	Stops playback
stopAllSounds()	Stops all sounds playing
substring()	Extracts a section of a string
tellTarget()	Used to send ActionScript to a particular movie clip
toggleHighQuality()	Turns anti-aliasing on or off
trace()	Debug method

Only a limited subset of properties is available for movie clips:

```
_alpha, _currentframe, _focusrect, _framesloaded, _height, _level, _name,
_rotation, _target, _totalframes, _visible, _width, _x, _xscale, _y and
_yscale.
```

Summary

Flash Lite allows you as a Flash developer to target mobile devices. With 400 million units sold each year this has got to make sense! Although these devices are greatly limited in terms of screen space and processor capabilities, an ingenious developer will milk some amazing results. I look forward to seeing your handiwork on a mobile near me soon!

20 Using Flash on a PocketPC

PocketPCs are selling like the proverbial hot cakes now that the prices are more in line with people's ability to pay. The little beasts are quite capable of running games. Macromedia has created a highly optimized Flash player engine for the PocketPC. In this chapter we look at tips and advice when creating content for a PocketPC.

Starting with Flash on PocketPC

The first step is to install Flash Player on your PocketPC. Flash Player is freely available from Macromedia at http://www.macromedia.com/software/devices/products/pocketpc/. At the time of writing the version number was 6 and this was available for PocketPC 2002 and 2003. You should also download the development kit that is available on the same page. This gives example project files and lots of tips and advice. Flash Player for PocketPC runs inside Pocket Internet Explorer although it is possible to create stand-alone movies either using the software available from Macromedia for a charge or following the instructions in Chapter 24, which you should be able to do for free. That alone should make buying this book worth the money!

A quick introduction to PocketPC 2003

A PocketPC comes with Pocket Internet Explorer (PIE) already installed in the ROM. Figure 20.1 shows the default out of the box screen for a Dell Axim X3. To use the device a stylus is supplied. The screen is touch-sensitive and allows you to click on the screen at any location. A rollover event does not occur. The default setup for PIE has a navigation and address bar at the top, taking up 48 pixels and a command bar at the base of the screen occupying 26 pixels. The main display area starts at (0, 49) and extends to (240, 293) giving a maximum size for a Flash movie of 240 × 245 pixels. When textual input is required the Soft Input Panel (SIP) screen is shown which allows the user to enter text from an on-screen keyboard or via handwriting recognition. This panel takes up a further 80 pixels. So if you want to accommodate for this then the available area for a Flash movie is just 240 × 165 pixels. In many games you will not require the SIP so for most purposes you should make your movies 240 × 245 pixels.

Figure 20.3 shows a simple animation embedded into PIE; the HTML required is very similar to that for a desktop machine. Some of the details required on a desktop can be eliminated – no EMBED is required – but it is recommended to set the quality to 'medium'. On the small screen of a PocketPC a quality setting of 'high' is virtually indistinguishable from that of 'medium', yet the processor has to do a lot more work. One thing you must get used to when developing for a PocketPC is to optimize wherever possible. One of the simplest ways to achieve this is by setting quality to medium.

Figure 20.1 *Pocket Internet Explorer on a PocketPC 2003*

Figure 20.2 *The effect of showing the SIP screen*

```
1   <html>
2   <head>
3   <title>Conker</title>
4   </head>
5   <body leftmargin="0" topmargin="0" bgcolor="#ffffff">
6   <center>
7   <object classid="clsid:D27CDB6E-AE6D-11cf-96B8-444553540000"
8           width="240" height="320" border = 0>
9     <param name="movie" value="conker.swf" />
10    <param name="quality" value="medium" />
11    <param name="menu" value="false" />
12    <param name="scale" value="noborder">
13    <param name="wmode" value="opaque" />
14    <param name="bgcolor" value="#ffffff" />
15  </object>
16  </center>
17  </body>
18  </html>
```

Listing 20.1

Figure 20.3 *A Flash animation embedded into PIE*

Scroll bars

Pocket Internet Explorer has two view settings. You can choose 'Fit to Screen' in which case a document is resized to fit into the 240 width of the PPC. If 'Fit to Screen' is disabled then a document will have a default virtual size of 640 × 480 pixels. Consequently the bottom scroll bar will always be on, which occupies 11 pixels above the Command bar. If this is the case and your user also has the Address bar active then the available screen height goes down from 320 to 234 pixels. This makes the ideal size for a Flash movie that is viewed in PIE to be 240 × 234 pixels. This will be visible on all user setups.

Server side detection

More and more PPCs are capable of a direct connection to the web. So what do you do when you have multiple versions of your game available, one for the PPC and one for desktop machines? The best option is to use a server side detection script. When Pocket Internet Explorer sends a request to your HTTP server, the following specific information is included in the HTTP request header:

```
1   UA-pixels: {i.e. 240x320}
2   UA-color: {mono2 | mono4 | color8 | color16 | color24 | color32}
3   UA-OS: {Windows CE (POCKET PC) - Version x.x}
4   UA-CPU = {}
```
Listing 20.2

Using the following server side JScript (ASP) lines you can create specially optimized pages as soon as a Pocket Internet Explorer attempts to access games from your site.

```
1   // Check for Windows CE (Pocket PC, Palm-size PC,
2   // Handheld PC, Handheld PC Pro)
3   var strNav = navigator.userAgent;
4   var isCE = strNav.indexOf("Windows CE");
5   if(isCE > -1) {
6       //add Windows CE specific code
7   }else {
8       //add code for other platforms
9   }
```
Listing 20.3

```
1   'Check for Pocket PC
2   var isPPC = strNav.indexOf("240x320");
3   if(isPPC > -1) {
4       // add Pocket PC specific code
```

```
5  }else {
6       // add code for other platforms
7  }
```
Listing 20.4

So what's missing?

In truth, for a game developer, not a lot is missing from the PPC version of Flash Player rather than the desktop one. The main features that are missing are links to the Flash Communication Server, printing and support for monochrome displays. Whenever you refer to the absolute location of a file you must include the 'file://' protocol. So if a text file used to store variable values is at '/Program Files/FlashMX2004Games/variables.txt' and you wish to use absolute file names in a call to 'loadVariables' then the code to use would be:

```
loadVariablesNum("file:///Program%20Files/FlashMX2004Games/
                 variables.txt", 0);
```

PPCs use / as the root of all files. So a file stored at the root would still require '/myfile.txt' to access. When calling files using ActionScript convert the backslash to a forward slash and replace spaces with '%20'. PIE does not support percentage sizes for document elements. Therefore if you used

```
<OBJECT Width="100%" ...
```

the width would be set to 100 pixels instead of the full width of the screen.

Let's get a game installed and loaded

I can see you are ready to go, so let's take a game we have developed and port it to the PocketPC. We met the game Reversi in Chapter 16. The game used a playing area of the standard 550×240. Within PIE we should be aiming at a movie size of 240×245. There are three approaches we can make. The first two options involve taking the original game and just using the HTML page in which it is embedded to shape it for the PPC. We can just use the game as is or make the game scale to the screen area (Figure 20.4), in which case the board would not be square. Neither of these options is particularly satisfactory.

The final option involves adjusting the layout in Flash to accommodate for the different screen area. This is by far the preferred alternative. Flash is very accommodating when changing layout because each movie clip has its own coordinate space. Simply convert the frames on the main timeline to a movie clip.

1 Copy all the frames on the main timeline by highlighting the top left corner and shift-clicking the bottom right.
2 Create a new symbol by using 'Insert > New Symbol...' from the main menu.

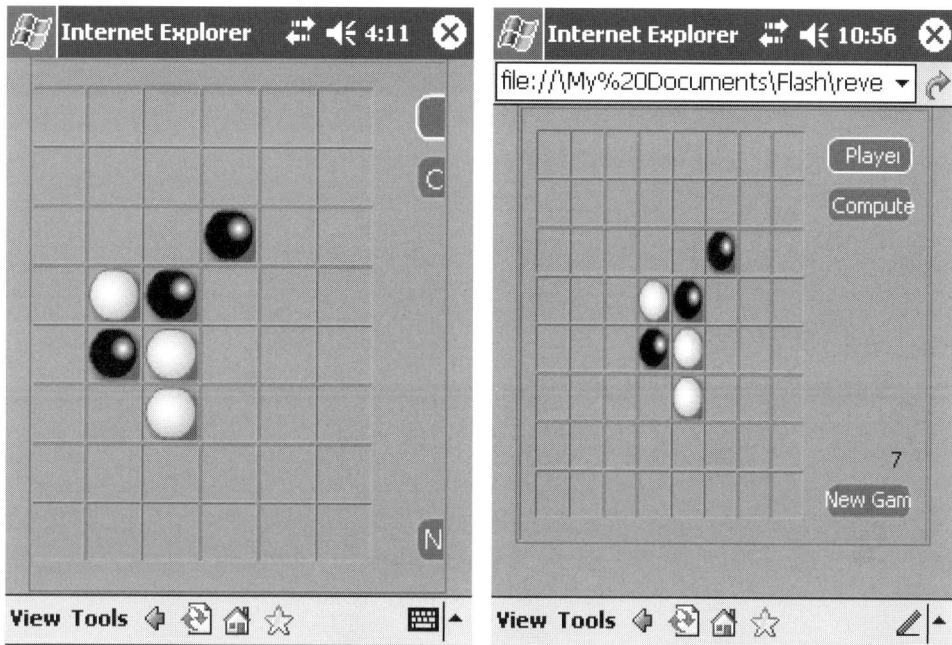

Figure 20.4 *Layout problems from a direct port of a desktop game*

3 Edit the new symbol by selecting it from the Library or the drop-down 'Edit Symbols' button.

4 Paste the frames into the new symbol.

5 Place your new symbol on the root-level timeline and resize while maintaining the aspect ratio by clicking on the 'Scale' option button for the 'Free Transform Tool (Q)'.

You should now resize your movie to 240 × 234 using the Document Properties panel, which is accessed by clicking in a non-occupied part of the stage and pressing the Size button in the Properties window.

In the original version of the game we had just one button on screen and two highlighting panels displaying who the current player is. The aim of the reshaping is to maximize the board area. If users have the Address bar hidden then the layout shown on the left in Figure 20.5 is ideal. This uses a movie area of 240 × 268 pixels allowing room for the buttons below the board. Unfortunately surveys indicate that the majority of users have the Address bar active, therefore it is recommended that the shape of the game is restricted to 240 × 234. The screenshot on the right of Figure 20.5 shows how we achieved this.

Using panels to display additional data

The screen space available on a PPC is easily big enough for a crossword puzzle. In Chapter 13 we looked at developing a crossword puzzle game. The game used the additional screen space available

Figure 20.5 *'Examples/Chapter20/Reversi.html' seen on a PocketPC 2003*

on a desktop machine to display the crossword and the clues side by side. On the restricted space of a PPC it is impossible to display both the crossword and the clues simultaneously. The strategy adopted on a mobile phone is to use the deck of cards analogy. Content is displayed as a card from the deck and it is possible quickly and efficiently to switch the card. The Flash timeline makes this easy to do. You can support each 'card' on a different frame on the timeline. Switching cards is simply an exercise in jumping to an alternative frame.

Another change we made when converting the crossword puzzle was to make the type size larger. Figures 20.6 to 20.8 show how the crossword puzzle appears on the PocketPC screen. When working with type on a PPC the anti-aliasing feature of Flash can sometimes make the small type difficult to read. To avoid this, try using pixel fonts. These

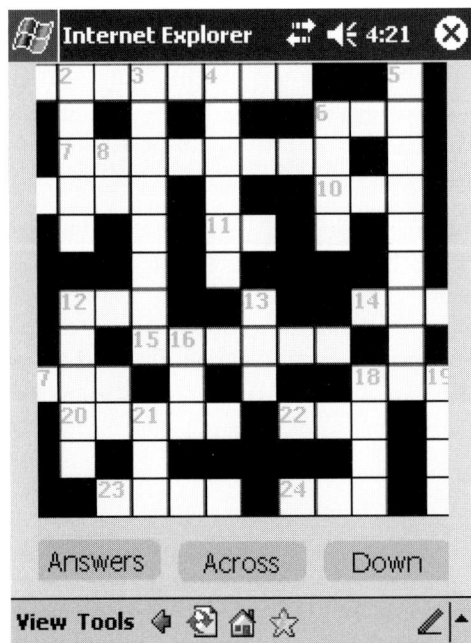

Figure 20.6 *Layout for Crosswords example*

must be placed on a pixel boundary. Click on the text and adjust the X: and Y: values in the Properties window so that the values are whole numbers with no decimal part. Another feature of pixel fonts is the need to be a multiple of 8 in size (8, 16, 24 etc.). More information is available on the web, a good source being http://www.bestflashanimationsite.com/tutorials/2/.

Figure 20.7 *Showing the clues as an overlay screen*

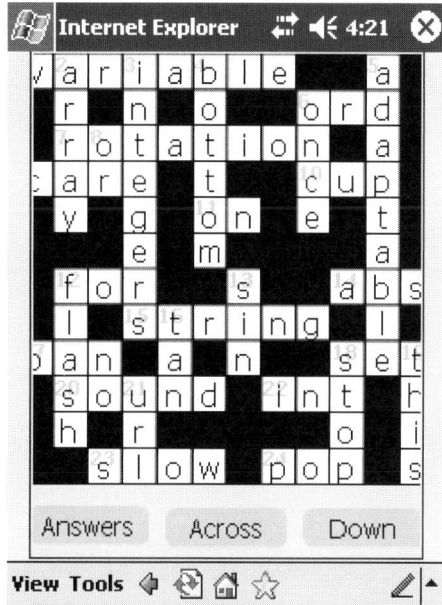

Figure 20.8 *Displaying the answers*

Reading the keyboard

For full textual input the PPC uses a Soft Input Panel (SIP). If you use the stand-alone player or the embedding solution given in Chapter 24 you can turn this panel on and off in ActionScript. Unfortunately this feature is not available to swf files that are hosted in PIE. To turn the panel on use

```
fscommand("_sip", true);
```

and to turn it off use

```
fscommand("_sip", false);
```

Any text entered into an input box works in much the same way as text returned from the keyboard. The transcribe option for the SIP, where handwriting is converted into text input, is unreliable in the Flash Player.

Reading the main button is simply a case of reading for LEFT, UP, RIGHT, DOWN and ENTER. In most games targeting a PPC this should provide sufficient user input options. Listing 20.5 shows how a movie clip can be moved around using the main button control.

```
1 onClipEvent(enterFrame){
2       if (Key.isDown(Key.LEFT))  _x -= 2;
3       if (Key.isDown(Key.RIGHT)) _x += 2;
4       if (Key.isDown(Key.UP))    _y -= 2;
5       if (Key.isDown(Key.DOWN))  _y += 2;
6       if (Key.isDown(Key.ENTER)) _parent.entercount++;
7 }
```

Listing 20.5

Summary

PocketPCs are a growing market for Flash games. Although more suited to turn-based games it is possible to create simple action games. It is very likely that the processors in these machines will soon be more than capable of action game displays. There has never been a better time to start developing mobile content with Flash. In this chapter you were introduced to the key features.

Section 5

Flash for boffins

Sometimes you will need to extend what you can do in Flash using external methods. In previous chapters we have looked at using external files. These last four chapters introduce you to other things you should be thinking about.

21 High score tables

High score tables encourage users to stay online in order to see their name appear in the high score list, or to win a prize if they are the highest scorer for a prize winning game. The high score tables are usually stored in a database and then loaded into Flash when a call to a high score table is required. This chapter explores the options. The information extends what you have learnt in Chapters 12 and 14. In contrast to Chapter 14, where we concentrated on using an SQL Server database, in this chapter we will use an Access database. Access is part of the Office package and can be accessed from all Windows servers. To make high score tables work you will need a registration and login form and you will need to keep track of information as you move from page to page. Session variables provide this vehicle or cookies if you want the information to persist even after the user has logged off the site. We will look at using session variables and cookies to store information as we navigate a multi-page site. On a big site the Webmaster will need tools to examine traffic and users; we will look at creating pages in Flash to review the database, update and delete records.

Creating a registration page

If a user has never visited a site then the first thing we want them to do is register. You probably want them to have some access to find out what the site has to offer, but you will constantly remind them that they should register. Registered users bring a database to help you to promote the site as new features and games are added. Some users will gladly register and are happy to receive information via email; others will deliberately give a fake address in order to remain anonymous. High score tables are the most effective encouragement to register, particularly when linked to a prize-winning game. There would be no point winning a prize-winning game if the player had given a fake email address!

On the registration page we are going to create we will collect the name, password, email, company, address, telephone number and fax number of the user. Only the name, password and email will be made mandatory. When you are creating form-based web pages it is recommended that you set the focus to the first field that you want the user to enter, and ensure that the user can tab through the different fields. Flash MX 2004 has a property of an instance called 'tabIndex'. If you set the tabIndex property then automatic tab ordering is disabled and only the instances with a specifically set tabIndex are included in the tab ordering. A text field can be given an instance name in the properties box for a text field and then this instance can be given a tabIndex in code. In 'Examples\Chapter21\Register.fla', the focus is set to the variable with the name 'name'. Assuming this variable is an input box and that this box is visible, the caret (the flashing line that indicates where text input will be directed) will be set to that field and will flash. Be warned that

Figure 21.1 *Creating a registration page*

Flash does not allow the caret colour to be set to any other colour than black so if your input box has a black background the caret will not be visible, which can be very confusing for the user.

The first few frames of the 'register.fla' project are all loading frames. By frame 5 we know that the form and all its resources are loaded. Take a look at the frame action on the main timeline for frame 5.

```
1   //Frame 5 main timeline
2   A.tabIndex = 1;
3   B.tabIndex = 2;
4   C.tabIndex = 3;
5   D.tabIndex = 4;
6   E.tabIndex = 5;
7   F.tabIndex = 6;
8   G.tabIndex = 7;
9   Selection.setFocus("name");
10  stop();
```

Listing 21.1

Notice here that the 'tabIndex' is set for each of the input box text fields and the focus is set to 'name'.

The functionality for the form is basically handled by Flash. A text field input box allows for keyboard input, character deletion, copying and pasting without a single line of code. The place where some ActionScript is required is for the 'register' button. This has a simple 'on (release)' method.

```
1   //Register button action
2   on (release) {
3       if (emailcheck(email) && name!="" && password!="") {
4           loadVariables("scripts/register.asp","","POST");
5           nextFrame();
6       } else {
7           warning.gotoAndPlay(2);
8       }
9   }
```
Listing 21.2

First we make a check for a legitimate email using a function call; assuming this is OK we then check for a name and password entry. If everything is in order, then we can send all the variables in the current Flash movie to an ASP page, using the POST action, and then move to the next frame. If the data entered is invalid, however, then we display a warning message that is embedded in the movie clip 'warning'.

The 'emailcheck' function works by testing for the presence of both the '@' symbol and a dot character, ultimately returning true only if they are both present in the email string passed to the function.

```
1   function emailcheck (str) {
2       at = false;
3       dot = false;
4       for (i=0; i<str.length; i++) {
5           if (str.charAt(i) == '@') {
6               at = true;
7           }
8           if (str.charAt(i) == '.') {
9               dot = true;
10          }
11      }
12      return (at && dot);
13  }
```
Listing 21.3

The ASP page 'register.asp' will handle most of the work in the register.fla project. We will look at how this works later in the chapter.

Creating a login page

Figure 21.2 *The login page*

A user may have already registered and simply wishes to log in. To allow for this we create a login page, 'Examples\Chapter21\login.fla'. This is a very simple project in which the login button calls the 'login.asp' script and either moves on to the 'highscore.html' page if login is successful or to the 'register.html' if the user cannot be found in the database.

Creating an Access database to store the data

The program Access comes with a complete Office package. To create a new database, simply run the program and select 'File/New'. Before you can make use of the database you will need to create two tables. Access does not have the same level of security as an SQL Server database so you will not need to create users and permissions. In some respects this makes life easier but at the expense of lower security. The speed with which records can be retrieved from the database is also noticeably slower than SQL Server, but sometimes, and particularly if your server does not have a version of SQL Server running, Access provides a good second-best alternative.

To create a table just use the 'Create a table in Design view' or one of the two other table creation tools.

Figure 21.3 *Creating an Access database*

Figure 21.4 *Creating a table in Access using the Design view*

To create a table in Design view, simply give the field a name and a data type. In the sample database 'Examples\Chapter21\Site\scripts\register.mdb' there are two tables, 'Scores' and 'Users'. *Scores* contains *gameID*, *playerID* and *score* fields. *Users* contains *name*, *password*, *email*, *company*, *address*, *telephone number* and *fax number* fields. In the example there are 10 users entered and 30 scores, one score for each user for each of three different games.

Using cookies for persistent data

When a user arrives at our site the first thing we will do is see if they have registered already by checking to see if a cookie exists. Cookies are a persistent form of data that can be saved on our computer by a web page. Reading and writing to the cookie is restricted to the domain from which the cookie originated. The existence or otherwise of the cookie is handled by the ASP page 'cookies.asp' which is stored in the 'scripts' subfolder of the folder 'Site'. To get a cookie we use the 'Request' object.

```
var name = Request.Cookies("name");
```

This code snippet will set the variable 'name' to the value of the cookie 'name' for this domain if it exists. If it does exist then we set two session variables, 'loggedIn' and 'playerID', to true and the player's name respectively. A session variable exists only while a user is connected to a particular site; when they disconnect the variable is deleted. The final task if the cookie exists is to update the expiry data by setting the 'Expires' property to a string that is formatted month dd, yyyy where month is the full month name, dd is the date using two characters, so the fourth would be 04 and yyyy is the year using four characters. The function 'getExpireString' formats the string by first getting the current time using the Date object, then adding 10 days in milliseconds to the millisecond value of the current time. This time is converted into another Date object 'expdate'. The 'expdate' object is used to build the expiry string.

If the cookie turns out to be empty then the session variable 'loggedIn' is set to false and the playerID is set to an empty string. The calling program can use the value for 'playerID' to choose how to behave. A 'playerID' of 'nocookie' will force the login or register screen to appear. In the example this is all handled by the 'index.fla' project.

```
1   <%@Language=JavaScript %>
2
3   <%
4
5   Response.Expires = -1;
6
7   var name = Request.Cookies("name");
8
9   if (name!=""){
10      Response.Write("playerID=" + name);
11      Session("loggedIn") = true;
```

```
12    Session("playerID") = String(name);
13    Response.Cookies("name").Expires = getExpireString();
14  }else{
15    Session("loggedIn") = false;
16    Session("playerID") = "";
17    Response.Write("playerID=nocookie");
18  }
19
20  function getExpireString(){
21    var nowdate = new Date();
22    var ms = nowdate.getTime() + (10 * 24 * 60 * 60 * 1000);
23    var expdate = new Date(ms);
24    var str, m, d, y, tmp;
25
26    m = expdate.getMonth();
27
28    switch(m){
29    case 0:
30      str = "January ";
31      break;
32    case 1:
33      str = "February ";
34      break;
35    case 2:
36      str = "March ";
37      break;
38    case 3:
39      str = "April ";
40      break;
41    case 4:
42      str = "May ";
43      break;
44    case 5:
45      str = "June ";
46      break;
47    case 6:
48      str = "July ";
49      break;
50    case 7:
51      str = "August ";
52      break;
53    case 8:
54      str = "September ";
```

```
55        break;
56    case 9:
57        str = "October ";
58        break;
59    case 10:
60        str = "November ";
61        break;
62    case 11:
63        str = "December ";
64        break;
65    }
66
67    d = expdate.getDate();
68
69    if (d<10) str += "0";
70    str += String(d) + ", " + expdate.getYear();
71
72    return str;
73 }
74 %>
```
Listing 21.4

Shared objects for persistent data

A great feature of Flash MX 2004 is the object 'SharedObject'. This operates in a very similar way to cookies and can be used without any external scripting. To use the SharedObject you first create an object from the 'getLocal' method of the SharedObject. This takes a single string parameter, which is the name to use for the shared data file. Unless you want to read this file from another program then you do not need to know where the data is actually stored; on a PC it is in the Documents and Settings folder: C:\Documents and Settings\[User Name]\Application Data\Macromedia\Flash Player\[path to swf]\swfname.swf. In the file the data for each stored element is saved as a string. Having created a shared object from this file, the object contains the data in the file. If the file does not exist then the object is essentially empty. To use the object you can use the 'data' property and the 'flush' method. The data property contains any data that you want to store up to the file limit that is settable, but should be fairly small. In this short snippet, we create a shared object called 'so' then trace the value of the data property 'favoriteColor'; this could be any name that you find useful. Then we assign to this property the value 'orange'. If the property does not exist then it is created by an assignment. Then we access the data property 'possibleColors'. If this exists then the data will be listed in the output window and if it does not then 'undefined' will be displayed. If the array is missing then we create it as a new Array and assign values to it, then assign this array to the data property 'possibleColors'. Finally we ensure that the data is written to the file using SharedObject method 'flush'. If 'flush' returns false then writing to the file is prohibited by security limits or file size.

```
1   so = SharedObject.getLocal("myInfo");
2   trace(so.data.favoriteColor);
3   so.data.favoriteColor = "orange";
4   trace(so.data.possibleColors);
5   if (so.data.possibleColors==NULL){
6       colors = new Array("red", "blue", "green", "blue");
7       so.data.possibleColors = colors;
8   }
9
10  if (!so.flush()){
11      //Did not work
12  }
13  stop();
```

Listing 21.5

SharedObjects are a useful and quick way to guarantee persistence between one run of the page and another for the user.

Logging in via ASP

The first job of the login ASP page is to strip out the elements of the query string, 'name' and 'pw' (password could not be used as a column name in the database because it is a keyword). Then we make a connection to the database using the connection string shown in Listing 21.6. Connection strings are very unforgiving; get them wrong and you will get nowhere. Once we have a connection we create a recordset object 'rs' and an SQL string. We are looking for a record in the database of the current user. To do this we look in the 'Users' table for a record where the 'name' field matches the value of the variable 'name' and the 'pw' field matches the value of the variable 'pw'. If a record is found then the 'rs' object will not be at the end of the file, EOF. Using this condition we set a string to write back to Flash, set the session variables 'loggedIn' and 'playerID' and write the name as a cookie just in case it has been deleted. The expiry date for the cookie is set using the same 'getExpireString' function we looked at earlier.

If the player cannot be found then we write a message back to Flash to indicate this fact and set the session variables to indicate that we have not yet logged in.

```
1   <%@Language=JavaScript %>
2
3   <%
4
5   Response.Expires = -1;
6
7   var name = Request("name");
8   var pw = Request("pw");
9
```

```
10 //Connect to the database
11 var conn = Server.CreateObject("ADODB.Connection");
12 var connStr = "PROVIDER=Microsoft.Jet.OLEDB.4.0; DATA SOURCE=" +
13         Server.Mappath("register.mdb") + ";" + "Password=;";
14 conn.Open(connStr);
15
16 var rs = Server.CreateObject("ADODB.Recordset");
17 var sqlStr = "SELECT * FROM Users WHERE name=\'" + name +
18         "\' AND pw=\'" + pw + "\'";
19
20 rs.Open( sqlStr, conn);
21
22 var str;
23
24 if (!rs.EOF){
25     str = ("loggedIn=true&message=Welcome back " + name);
26     Session("loggedIn") = true;
27     Session("playerID") = String(name);
28     Response.Cookies("name") = name;
29     Response.Cookies("name").Expires = getExpireString();
30 }else{
31     str = "loggedIn=false&message=Can't find you in our database";
32     Session("loggedIn") = false;
33     Session("playerID") = "";
34 }
35
36 Response.Write(str);
37
38 rs.Close();
39 conn.Close();
```

Listing 21.6

Registering via ASP

First we parse all the data sent to the page and store it in several variables. Then we connect to the database and build an SQL string. This time the string is an INSERT string that takes the form

INSERT INTO table (field1, …) VALUES(val1, …)

This is executed on the current connection. To make a full registration application we should really check for the existence of a user with the same name, because the 'name' field is required to be unique. We can find out whether a user with the same name exists simply by creating a recordset from the Users table based on the name value being the same; if this recordset has any entries then the name has already been used and so we can write back a message to indicate this and the Flash application can require the user to choose a different name. The function 'getExpireString' is again used to set the Expires property of the 'name' cookie if registration was successful.

Figure 21.5 *Registering*

```
1   <%@Language=JavaScript %>
2
3   <%
4
5   Response.Expires = -1;
6
7   var name, password, email, company, address, tel, fax;
8
9   name = Request("name");
10  password = Request("password");
11  email = Request("email");
12  company = Request("company");
13  address = Request("address");
14  tel = Request("tel");
15  fax = Request("fax");
16
```

```
17 //Connect to the database
18 var conn = Server.CreateObject("ADODB.Connection");
19 var connStr = "PROVIDER=Microsoft.Jet.OLEDB.4.0; DATA SOURCE=" +
20         Server.Mappath("register.mdb") + ";" + "Password=;";
21 conn.Open(connStr);
22
23 var sqlStr =
24     "INSERT INTO Users (name, pw, email, company, address, tel, fax)" +
25     " VALUES (\'" + name + "\',\'" + password + "\',\'" + email +
26     "\',\'" + company + "\',\'" + address + "\',\'" + tel + "\',\'" +
27     fax + "\')";
28
29 conn.Execute(sqlStr);
30 conn.Close();
31
32 Session("loggedIn") = true;
33 Session("playerID") = String(name);
34 Response.Cookies("name") = name;
35 Response.Cookies("name").Expires = getExpireString();
36 Response.Write("loggedIn=true");
```

Listing 21.7

Saving the user's score

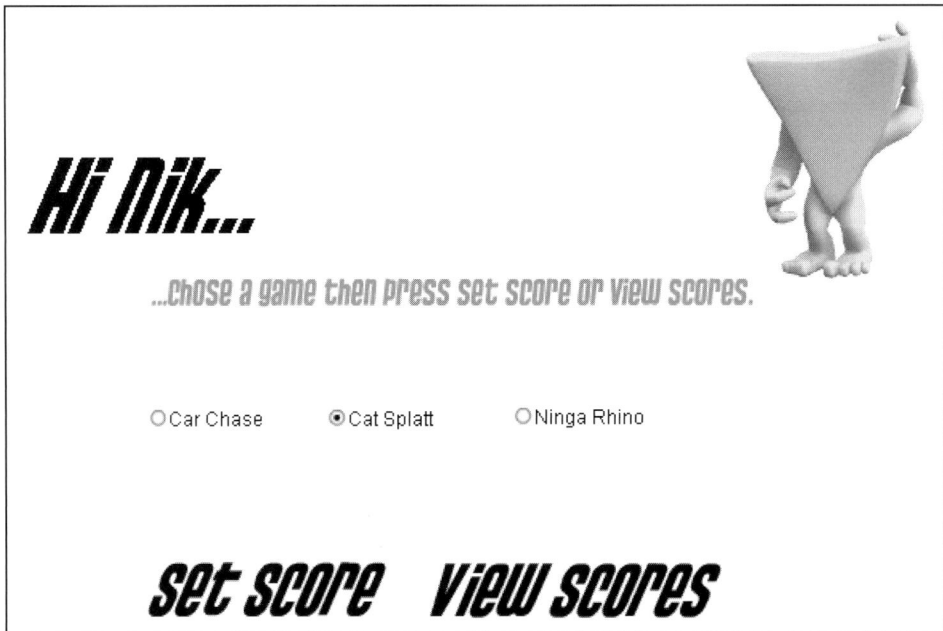

Figure 21.6 *Running the high scores page*

Assuming the player is successfully logged in via either an existing cookie, the login page or registration then the page is set to 'highscores.html' which contains the swf from the project 'Examples\Chapter21\highscores.fla'. When this loads it shows a menu screen from which you can select one of three games, 'Car Chase', 'Cat Splatt' on 'Ninga Rhino'. This screen also contains two buttons, 'Set Score' and 'View Scores'. The message displayed also shows the user's name because this is known by the time the screen is displayed.

The action for the 'Set Score' button first works out which game is selected by getting the state of the three radio buttons. Only one button in a radio button group can be active. This value is used to choose the name of the game from an array of game names. The score is arbitrarily set to a random value between 0 and 9999, then this data is sent to the ASP page 'setscore' via a query string. The playback head is set to the 'wait' frame, where playback loops until either 'setscore' or 'viewscores' is set to 'true'.

```
1   on (release){
2       var i, game=0, score;
3
4       for (i=1; i<=3; i++){
5               if (eval("game" + i).getState()){
6                       game = games[i-1];
7                       break;
8               }
9       }
10      score = random(10000);
11      loadVariables("scripts/setscore.asp?gameID=" + game +
12       "&score=" + score, "");
13      gotoAndPlay("wait");
14 }
```
Listing 21.8

The ASP page works by stripping the query string into variables, connecting to the database in the usual way and creating an SQL string. The SQL string is a SELECT statement, seeking to find a record from the Scores table for the current player and game. If this record exists then it is updated with the new score; ideally we should check to see if the existing score is higher than the new score that we are going to use to overwrite, but I leave this to the interested reader to develop further. If the record does not exist then it is inserted. Recall that the INSERT statement takes the form:

> INSERT INTO table (fieldname1, ...) VALUES (value1, ...)

When an existing entry is updated you use the form:

> UPDATE table SET fieldname1 = value1 [AND ...] WHERE fieldName2 = value2 [AND ...]

This method can be used to update several records simultaneously. Notice that Flash is informed that the page has completed successfully using the Response.Write method. Anything in brackets will be sent back to Flash, using a MIME encoded string format, and multiple variables can be returned in the form:

variable1 = value1&variable2 = value2 etc.

Each variable value pair is connected to the rest using an ampersand character.

```
1   <%@Language=JavaScript %>
2
3   <%
4
5   Response.Expires = -1;
6
7   var gameID = Request("gameID");
8   var playerID = Session("playerID");
9   var score = Number(Request("score"));
10
11  //Connect to the database
12  var conn = Server.CreateObject("ADODB.Connection");
13  connStr = "PROVIDER=Microsoft.Jet.OLEDB.4.0; DATA SOURCE=" +
14          Server.Mappath("register.mdb") + ";" + "Password=;";
15  conn.Open(connStr);
16
17  var sqlStr = "SELECT * FROM Scores WHERE playerID=\'" +
18          String(playerID) + "\' AND gameID=\'" + gameID + "\'";
19  var rs = Server.CreateObject("ADODB.recordset");
20
21  rs.Open(sqlStr, conn);
22
23  if (!rs.EOF) {
24     //No entry so add it
25     sqlStr = "INSERT INTO Scores " + "(gameID, playerID, score) " +
26          "VALUES (\'" + gameID + "\', \'" + playerID + "\', " + score +
27          ")";
28  }else{
29     // The entry exists so we will amend
30     sqlStr = "UPDATE Scores SET score=" + Number(score) +
31          " WHERE gameID=\'" + gameID + "\' AND playerID=\'" +
32          playerID + "\'";
33  }
34
35  conn.Execute(sqlStr);
36  Response.Write("setscore=true&message=Your score for " + gameID +
```

```
37    " has been set to " + score);
38 rs.Close();
39 conn.Close();
40
41 %>
```

Listing 21.9

Accessing the high score table

Figure 21.7 *The high score table*

When the 'View Scores' button is pressed in the 'highscores.fla' project the following code is executed. The game name is derived from the selected radio button and this is sent to the ASP page 'gethighscores.asp'.

```
1  on (release){
2      var i, game=0, score;
```

```
3
4      for (i=1; i<=3; i++){
5              if (eval("game" + i).getState()){
6                      game = games[i-1];
7                      break;
8              }
9          }
10     loadVariables("scripts/gethighscores.asp?gameID=" + game, "");
11     gotoAndPlay("wait");
12 }
```
Listing 21.10

The ASP page operates by first getting a total of all the scores for the current game. Then using this value we ask for a maximum of 10 scores. But we want the top 10. To do this we must ask for only 10 records and we must sort the record set using the score value.

```
SELECT TOP x fieldName1, ... FROM table
WHERE fieldNamex=value ORDER BY fieldNamex DESC
```

Using the condition TOP x, we can set how many records we want returning. ORDER BY lets us set the field to use for any sorting and DESC means that the highest values go first. Having got the data out of the database it is passed to Flash using the familiar MIME-encoded string formatting. In this instance the Flash variables 'hs1', 'hs2', ..., 'hs10' are set to the player's name and score strings.

```
1   <%@Language=JavaScript %>
2
3   <%
4
5   Response.Expires = -1;
6
7   function getScoreCount (gameID, conn)
8   {
9       var rs=Server.CreateObject("ADODB.recordset");
10      var scoreCount = 0;
11
12      rs.Open ("SELECT COUNT(gameID) FROM Scores WHERE gameID=\'"
13              + gameID + "\'", conn);
14      scoreCount = rs.Fields.Item(0).value;
15      rs.Close();
16      return scoreCount;
17  }
18
```

```
19 function getScore (playerID, gameID, conn)
20 {
21    var rs=Server.CreateObject("ADODB.recordset");
22    var score = 0;
23
24    rs.Open ("SELECT score FROM Scores WHERE playerID=\'" + playerID +
25            "\' AND gameID=\'" + gameID + "\'", conn);
26
27    if (!rs.EOF) score = rs.Fields.Item(0).value;
28    rs.Close();
29    return score;
30 }
31
32 var gameID = Request("gameID");
33 var playerID = Session("playerID");
34 var scoreCount = 0;
35
36 //Connect to the database
37 var conn = Server.CreateObject("ADODB.Connection");
38 connStr = "PROVIDER=Microsoft.Jet.OLEDB.4.0; DATA SOURCE=" +
39          Server.Mappath("register.mdb") + ";" + "Password=;";
40 conn.Open(connStr);
41
42 scoreCount = getScoreCount(gameID, conn);
43
44 // We may have to return less than they ask.
45 if (scoreCount > 10) scoreCount = 10;
46
47 var rs = Server.CreateObject("ADODB.recordset");
48 rs.Open ("SELECT TOP " + scoreCount +
49         " playerID, score FROM Scores WHERE gameID=\'" + gameID +
50         "\' ORDER BY score DESC", conn);
51
52 var count = 1, str;
53
54 while (!rs.EOF) {
55    str = "hs" + String(count++) + "=" + rs.Fields.Item(0).value + " " +
56          rs.Fields.Item(1).value + "&";
57    Response.Write(str);
58    rs.moveNext();
59 }
60 rs.Close();
61
62 score = getScore(playerID, gameID, conn);
63 str = "message=Your best score for " + gameID + " is " +
64        String(score) + "&viewscores=true";
```

```
65 Response.Write(str);
66
67 conn.Close();
68
69 %>
```
Listing 21.11

ASP pages are an easy way to link between Flash and a database. Because you can write ASP pages in JavaScript and that is the syntax used in ActionScript, you are already well on your way to becoming a JavaScript expert.

Creating administrative pages

The administrator for your site will want to be able to read and manipulate the database. SQL Server is very good for maintaining a remote database, Access is more limited. Sometimes the best way to create an easy-to-maintain site is to create admin pages. Such pages are designed to allow the administrator to check such features as traffic and users. We have found that cunning players often find ways to fake a high score, sometimes by sending a score directly to the database using the ASP pages that Flash uses. This happens particularly on prize-winning games. To avoid this happening we have taken to using encryption techniques for most data that we send by ASP. The Webmaster can often spot someone cheating simply by checking his or her records in a database. Flash is a good tool for creating user-friendly front ends to allow a Webmaster to check out the database. The 'admin.fla' project shows how you can tie a Flash application to a database. The 'Grid' component has three parameters, rowCount, colCount and colNames – an array of strings. These can be set directly at design time or you could create ASP pages to get the total number of columns and the names from a table in the database. Having accessed this information you can use it to initialize the grid to the appropriate column headers and the appropriate data in the cells. You could create a button that allows users to delete or update records. You could even let users write their own SQL strings and then use these to update the database. By linking Flash and ASP pages in this way you can provide all the functionality a Webmaster could ever need.

Summary

Flash MX 2004 is a great tool for linking to server-side scripts. Because we can get data out of Flash using a query string or the POST method, we can easily send this to a server-side script. On the server we can use the data to manipulate a database then send this information back to Flash using a MIME-encoded string. We can send as many variables in this way as are needed for a particular task. There are many books on ASP, a lot of which use VBScript as the scripting language, so you may find them unfamiliar at first but a lot of the detail will be the same if you use JavaScript as your scripting language.

In this chapter we explored more fully some of the features of ASP and SQL. If you are manipulating databases then it well worth learning more about SQL. The language offers you a great many tools for selecting records from databases and linking together tables. Check out the bibliography for some interesting SQL books.

22 Multi-player games using sockets

Although multi-player games are possible using ASP pages or another server-based script engine, the best technique to use is a server-side listening program that exploits the use of sockets. From Flash 5 sockets have been supported and provide the fastest and most reliable way to pass and process real-time data. In this chapter we are going to look at creating the server-side program using MFC, Microsoft Foundation Classes, on a Windows server. For many readers this will be unfamiliar territory, but we are in the 'Flash for boffins' section! The first part of this chapter assumes a reasonable knowledge of C++. There are lots of good C++ books available, a few of which are listed in the bibliography. To use a server-based socket listener the developer will need to have the ability to run an executable program on a server with a static IP address. Finally we will implement a very simple multi-player game across the Internet.

Moving boxes on a remote computer

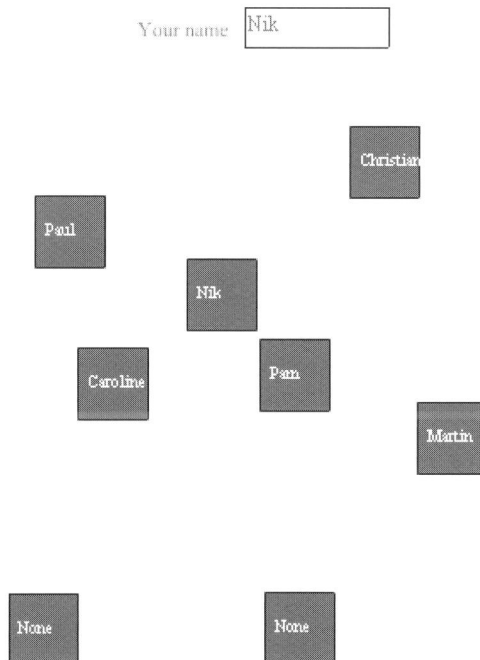

Figure 22.1 *Moving boxes on a remote computer*

The example we are going to study in this chapter is deliberately kept very simple. There is a lot to learn when understanding sockets and so your time is better spent understanding the principles rather than getting bogged down in the intricacies of the game design. In the example there are up to eight boxes. A user can click and drag any unused box. When a box is being dragged, it will be seen moving on the screen of every other computer connected to the site. If a user has entered their name in the box at the top, then their name will be displayed in the box. Very simple maybe, but it illustrates the concepts of multiple users receiving and passing data in real-time across a remote network. Before we can create the Flash application we need a program to be running on the server. This program acts as the conductor for all the connected computers. We are going to create this program using Visual C++.

Sockets on a Windows server

This section is going to use C++ code. The syntax for C++ is very similar to the JavaScript syntax you are familiar with from using Flash ActionScript. We are going to use something called Microsoft Foundation Classes. This is a library of C++ classes (another word for objects) that make programming Windows applications easier and more robust. To make use of the example on the CD, you will need a copy of Visual C++ on a PC. If you can, open the file 'Examples\Chapter22\ SockListener\SockListener.dsw'. This file is a Visual C++ project file. A C++ project uses several files to store the source code and other information required by the IDE (Integrated Development Environment) to compile the program. The source we will examine is in the file 'Sock-ListenerDlg.cpp', which is simply a text file; so if you don't have Visual C++ then just open this in a text viewer. MFC applications come in several flavours; this one uses a dialog box as the main window. Figure 22.2 shows the application running. Visually the program is just a list box where we can add text information that makes

Figure 22.2 *The SockListener application*

understanding the program's operation easier. The purpose of the program is to open a server socket on a defined port on a computer with a static IP address and listen for users across the Internet who want to connect to this socket. Whenever there is a new connection it is stored in a list and the program sees to it that all the current listeners to this socket get fed with information. The example program allows remote users to move boxes on another user's computer and vice versa.

Initializing the dialog box

Whenever a new dialog box is created, MFC calls the function 'OnInitDialog' in the dialog box class. Most of this is standard to all dialog boxes; a menu is created and the icon for the application is set. For the SockListener application we want to initialize a server socket. The dialog will only ever contain one of these, but first we need the IP address of the server. To get this we create a function called 'GetServerIP'. This uses the API (Application Programming Interface) function, 'gethostname'. The purpose of this function is to return the host name in string format. Notice that unlike Flash, every variable has to be of a specified type, and every variable must be declared before use.

After getting the name of the server, a structure HOSTENT is returned using the function 'gethostbyname' passing the host name as a parameter. The HOSTENT structure contains details about the server including the IP address, which is stored in the member h_addr. The host name is stored in the member variable 'm_cshostname' for future use.

```
1   BOOL CSockListenerDlg::GetServerIP()
2   {
3       HOSTENT *hs;
4       UCHAR ch[4]={0};
5       CString csInfo;
6
7       ::gethostname((LPSTR)(LPCTSTR)m_cshostname, 50);
8       hs = gethostbyname((LPSTR)(LPCTSTR)m_cshostname);
9
10      memcpy(ch, hs->h_addr, 4);
11      csInfo.Format("%s  %d.%d.%d.%d", m_cshostname,
12              ch[0], ch[1], ch[2], ch[3]);
13      GetDlgItem(IDC_TEXT)->SetWindowText(csInfo);
14
15      return TRUE;
16  }
```
Listing 22.1

Assuming that the IP address was successfully found, the server socket is created using the PORT defined by the constant PORT; in this example this is set to 5001 and the fact that the type of socket is a stream. The value of the PORT is set in file 'stdafx.h' which is part of this application and the value for the constant SOCK_STREAM is defined in the file 'winsock.h' which is a standard file included with Visual C++. Having created the server socket it is set to listening mode using the member function 'Listen'.

```
1   ////////////////////////////////////////////////////////////////
2   //
3   // CSockListenerDlg message handlers
4
5   BOOL CSockListenerDlg::OnInitDialog()
6   {
```

```
7
8      CDialog::OnInitDialog();
9
10     ASSERT((IDM_ABOUTBOX & 0xFFF0) == IDM_ABOUTBOX);
11     ASSERT(IDM_ABOUTBOX < 0xF000);
12
13     CMenu* pSysMenu = GetSystemMenu(FALSE);
14     if (pSysMenu != NULL)
15     {
16             CString strAboutMenu;
17             strAboutMenu.LoadString(IDS_ABOUTBOX);
18             if (!strAboutMenu.IsEmpty())
19             {
20                     pSysMenu->AppendMenu(MF_SEPARATOR);
21                     pSysMenu->AppendMenu(MF_STRING,
22                                     IDM_ABOUTBOX, strAboutMenu);
23             }
24     }
25
26     // Set the icon for this dialog.  The framework does this
27     // automatically
28     //  when the application's main window is not a dialog
29     SetIcon(m_hIcon, TRUE);                      // Set big icon
30     SetIcon(m_hIcon, FALSE);         // Set small icon
31
32     if(!GetServerIP()){
33             AfxMessageBox("Unable to get IP", MB_OK|MB_ICONERROR);
34     }
35     else{
36             m_ServerSocket.m_ptrDlg = this;
37             m_ServerSocket.Create(PORT, SOCK_STREAM);
38             m_ServerSocket.Listen();
39     }
40     return TRUE;
41 }
```

Listing 22.2

Establishing a connection

Every time a new connection needs to be made the server socket calls the dialog box function 'ProcessPendingAccept'. This function creates a new client socket and then calls the server function 'Accept' using a pointer to this new client socket. If you are new to pointers then think of it as a variable that points to the position in memory where the actual data that you are interested in resides. If the server function 'Accept' returns true then this socket is added to the list of sockets being handled by the server socket, if not then the client socket is deleted and no connection is made.

```
1  void CSockListenerDlg::ProcessPendingAccept()
2  {
3      TRACE("CSockListenerDlg::ProcessPendingAccept\n");
4      CString csSockAddr;
5      CString csInfo;
6      UINT nSockPort;
7
8      CClientSocket *pSocket = new CClientSocket(this);
9
10      if (m_ServerSocket.Accept(*pSocket))
11      {
12          if(pSocket->GetSockName(csSockAddr, nSockPort)){
13              csInfo.Format("%s : %u - Connected", csSockAddr,
14              nSockPort);
15              m_list1.InsertString(-1, csInfo);
16          }
17          m_connectionList.AddTail(pSocket);
18      }
19      else
20          delete pSocket;
21  }
```

Listing 22.3

Closing a connection

When a client socket is ready to close down the socket calls the dialog box function 'OnClose-Connection'; this function prints a message to the dialog's list box and builds an XML message string.

> XML, eXtensible Mark-up Language, is called extensible because it is not a fixed format like HTML (a single, predefined mark-up language). Instead, XML is actually a 'meta-language' – a language for describing other languages – which lets you design your own customized mark-up languages for unlimited different types of documents. XML can do this because it is written in SGML, the international standard meta-language for text mark-up systems (ISO 8879).

The format for Flash XML tag is a less-than symbol, name, data, forward slash and a greater-than symbol. The OnCloseConnection function sends the message

    <DROPBOX ID=x/>

where *x* is the index value for the box being controlled.

All sockets being controlled by this server socket are sent the message that a box has been dropped using the XML form and the client socket is removed from the list of sockets being handled by the server socket. Finally the socket is closed and deleted.

```
1    BOOL CSockListenerDlg::OnCloseConnection(CClientSocket *pSocket)
2    {
3        CString csSockAddr;
4        CString csInfo;
5        static int nIndex = 0;
6        char xmlmsg[1000];
7        UINT nSockPort;
8
9        if(pSocket->GetSockName(csSockAddr, nSockPort)){
10           csInfo.Format("%s : %u - DisConnected", csSockAddr, nSockPort);
11           m_list1.InsertString(-1, csInfo);
12       }
13
14           sprintf(xmlmsg, "<DROPBOX ID=\"%i\"/>", pSocket->boxid);
15
16       POSITION pos,temp;
17
18       for(pos = m_connectionList.GetHeadPosition(); pos != NULL;){
19           temp = pos;
20           CClientSocket* pSock =
21               (CClientSocket*)m_connectionList.GetNext(pos);
22
23           if (pSock == pSocket){
24               m_connectionList.RemoveAt(temp);
25               break;
26           }else{
27               pSock->Send(xmlmsg, strlen(xmlmsg)+1);
28           }
29       }
30
31       pSocket->Close();
32       delete pSocket;
33
34       return TRUE;
35   }
```

Listing 22.4

What happens when a client socket requests information?

A client socket calls the dialog box function 'ProcessPendingRead' whenever a socket wants information. First we read the information requested. XML syntax is used to pass information.

The possible tags in this example are:

QUERYBOXES – used to find out which boxes are currently under remote user control.
No parameters are passed. For each connection in the connection list the ID of the connection is stored in the array 'userids'. This array is initially set to eight zeros. If a connection is being used then the array for this index is set to one. Then we build a string using the XML tag QUERYBOXES and the value of each of the eight members of the 'userid' array is passed to it. This message is then sent back to the socket that asked for it.

PICKBOX – used to tell the server which box this connection is controlling and the name to use.
The name and ID are stripped out of the string that is passed. This information is then passed on to each connection in the server's connection list.

MOVEBOX – informs the server that the box has moved, which then passes the details onto each connection.
The ID, XPOS and YPOS of the box are stripped from the passed message and passed on to every connection.

DROPBOX – a user has stopped dragging the box. This information is passed to each connection.
The ID of the dropped box is stripped from the string and passed on to each connection in the server's connection list.

```
1  void CSockListenerDlg::ProcessPendingRead(CClientSocket *pSocket)
2  {
3     char msg[1000], xmlmsg[1000], *cp;
4     int id, xpos, ypos, usedids[]={0,0,0,0,0,0,0};
5     POSITION pos = m_connectionList.GetHeadPosition();
6     CClientSocket *socket;
7
8     memset(msg, 0, 1000);
9     pSocket->Receive( msg, 1000);
10
11    if (strncmp(msg, "QUERYBOXES", 5)==0){
12         while(pos){
13              socket = (CClientSocket*)m_connectionList.GetNext(pos);
14              if (socket->boxid) usedids[socket->boxid-1] = 1;
15         }
16
17         sprintf(xmlmsg, "<QUERYBOXES ID1=\"%i\" ID2=\"%i\" ID3=\"%i\"
18 ID4=\"%i\" ID5=\"%i\" Id6=\"%i\" ID7=\"%i\"/>",
19              usedids[0], usedids[1], usedids[2], usedids[3],
20              usedids[4], usedids[5], usedids[6]);
21
22         pSocket->Send(xmlmsg, strlen(xmlmsg)+1);
```

```
23
24          return;
25     }
26
27     if (strncmp(msg, "PICKBOX", 4)==0){
28            cp = strstr(msg, "ID=");
29            if (!cp) return;
30            cp+=3;
31            pSocket->boxid = atoi(cp);
32
33            cp = strstr(msg, "NAME=");
34            if (!cp) return;
35            cp+=5;
36            pSocket->name = cp;
37
38            sprintf(xmlmsg, "<PICKBOX ID=\"%i\" NAME=\"%s\"/>",
39                   pSocket->boxid, pSocket->name);
40
41            while(pos){
42                   socket = (CClientSocket*)m_connectionList.GetNext(pos);
43                   if (socket!=pSocket)
44                          socket->Send(xmlmsg, strlen(xmlmsg)+1);
45            }
46
47            return;
48     }
49
50     if (strncmp(msg, "MOVEBOX", 4)==0){
51            cp = strstr(msg, "ID=");
52            if (!cp) return;
53            cp+=3;
54            id = atoi(cp);
55
56            cp = strstr(msg, "XPOS=");
57            if (!cp) return;
58            cp+=5;
59            xpos = atoi(cp);
60
61            cp = strstr(msg, "YPOS=");
62            if (!cp) return;
63            cp+=5;
64            ypos = atoi(cp);
65
66            //Pass it on
67            sprintf(xmlmsg, "<MOVEBOX ID=\"%i\" XPOS=\"%i\" YPOS=\"%i\"/>",
68                   id, xpos, ypos);
```

```
69
70          while(pos){
71                  socket = (CClientSocket*)m_connectionList.GetNext(pos);
72                  if (socket!=pSocket)
73                          socket->Send(xmlmsg, strlen(xmlmsg)+1);
74          }
75
76          return;
77      }
78
79      if (strncmp(msg, "DROPBOX", 4)==0){
80          sprintf(xmlmsg, "<DROPBOX ID=\"%i\"/>", pSocket->boxid);
81          pSocket->boxid = 0;
82
83          while(pos){
84                  socket = (CClientSocket*)m_connectionList.GetNext(pos);
85                  if (socket!=pSocket)
86                          socket->Send(xmlmsg, strlen(xmlmsg)+1);
87          }
88
89          return;
90      }
91
92  }
```
Listing 22.5

Now we have a program that is going to handle the connections and pass the data around each connected user.

Creating the Flash application

Open the project 'Examples\Chapter22\MoveBox.fla'. The code in frame 1 is as follows:

```
sock = new XMLSocket();
sock.onXML = gotMessage;
sock.onConnect = onSockConnect;
usedids = new Array(0, 0, 0, 0, 0, 0, 0, 0);
dragbox = 0;
sock.connect("192.168.0.1", 5001)
stop ();
```

The root level variable 'sock' is set as a new XML Socket object and the two callback functions for this object 'onXML' and 'onConnect' are set to 'gotMessage' and 'onSockConnect' respectively. The 'onSockConnect' function gets called when a connection is made and is passed a Boolean variable that indicates whether the connection was successfully made. The XMLSocket member

Figure 22.3 *Creating the MoveBox.fla*

function 'connect' is called using the static IP address of the computer that is running the listening program, which is why the program must be running on a server that is available on the web and that uses a static IP address, and the second parameter in the function call 'connect' is the port to connect to. In the MFC application this was set to 5001. If the connection is made successfully, we create a new XML message that contains just the tag QUERYBOXES. Recall that the listening program handles this function by passing a message to all the connected computers indicating which boxes are currently being moved.

```
function onSockConnect (success) {
  if (success) {
        connected = true;
        xmlmsg = new XML("QUERYBOXES");
        sock.send(xmlmsg);
        gotoAndPlay("MainLoop");
  } else {
        connected = false;
  }
}
```

Whenever Flash receives a message via the connected socket it calls the function 'gotMessage'. This function handles any XML data that is passed by the server program. Firstly we create a variable out of the first child of the document object that is the only parameter of the function and then search for a node name of QUERYBOXES, PICKBOX, MOVEBOX or DROPBOX. If we find QUERYBOX then we search for the attributes ID1–8 that are passed from the SockListener application. In this simple case there is only ever one node to parse, so we do not need to loop through multiple layers. But an XML object in Flash has all the methods necessary to process a very complex document with multiple layers of embedded data. Each node can have an unlimited number of attributes that are accessed using the name used.

```
1    function gotMessage (doc) {
2        var name;
3
4        xmlObj = doc.firstChild;
5
6        if (xmlObj.nodeName == "QUERYBOXES") {
7            msg = xmlObj.attributes.USEDIDS;
8            usedids[1] = xmlObj.attributes.ID1;
9            usedids[2] = xmlObj.attributes.ID2;
10           usedids[3] = xmlObj.attributes.ID3;
11           usedids[4] = xmlObj.attributes.ID4;
12           usedids[5] = xmlObj.attributes.ID5;
13           usedids[6] = xmlObj.attributes.ID6;
14           usedids[7] = xmlObj.attributes.ID7;
15       }
16
17       if (xmlObj.nodeName == "PICKBOX") {
18           id = Number(xmlObj.attributes.ID);
19           clientname = xmlObj.attributes.NAME;
20           eval("Box"+id).Name = clientname;
21           usedids[id] = 1;
22           Debug = "Pickbox " + id + " " + clientname;
23       }
24
25       if (xmlObj.nodeName == "MOVEBOX") {
26           id = Number(xmlObj.attributes.ID);
27           xpos = xmlObj.attributes.XPOS;
28           ypos = xmlObj.attributes.YPOS;
29           if (usedids[id]!=0){
30               name = "Box" + id;
31               eval(name)._x = xpos;
32               eval(name)._y = ypos;
33           }
```

357

```
34        }
35
36        if (xmlObj.nodeName == "DROPBOX") {
37               id = Number(xmlObj.attributes.ID);
38               usedids[id] = 0;
39               name = "Box" + id;
40               eval(name)._x = id * 50 - 15;
41               eval(name)._y = 364);
42               eval(name).Name = "None";
43               Debug = "Dropbox " + id;
44        }
45 }
```

Listing 22.6

Figure 22.4 *The application running on the server*

The main loop

All that is necessary in the main loop is to pass the current on-screen location and ID of the box that is being dragged.

```
if (dragbox!=0){
    msg = "MOVEBOX ID=" + dragbox + "XPOS=" + _xmouse +
        "YPOS=" + _ymouse;
    sock.send(msg);
}
```

Whatever game you create, you can pass and handle data in this way. You will simply change the way you handle requests from clients in the SockListener and the way you handle messages in Flash; most of the other details will be the same across whatever the application in question.

Summary

Sockets provide a great way to handle multiple users if you have the ability to run server-side programs. The details can be a little tedious and you should never expect data to arrive in a pre-defined order. If you do an analysis of the way messages are passed, you will regularly be surprised to find that a message sent subsequent to another may be received in the opposite order.

23 Using Flash Communication Server

If multi-user connectivity is where you want to go then there is an easier way than the one featured in the previous chapter. The Flash Communication Server has all the robustness and tools that you will ever need and what's more the development version is free. In this chapter we are going to look at downloading, installing and configuring the Flash Communication Server and then creating a simple application to show it in use.

Where do I get it?

At the time of writing the main download page at Macromedia's website is

http://www.macromedia.com/downloads/

If you scroll down the page you will find Flash Communication Server; choose the 'Try' option, which will take you to a registration or login page and from there you can choose the version that suits your platform, Windows, MAC or Linux. This chapter focuses on the Windows version running on a Windows 2000 machine with IIS installed. Windows is the only platform available where you can author applications and run the server. Authoring is available on both MAC and Windows while the server is available on both Windows and Linux. Unfortunately Internet Information Services (IIS) are not available on Windows XP Home, but they are highly recommended when creating server-side solutions. You can run Flash Communication Server without IIS, but you will not be able to run any server-side scripting. To add IIS to a computer that is able to run it but where it is not yet installed:

1   Place the Windows 2000 Professional CD in the drive.
2   Select 'Add/Remove Programs' from the Control Panel options.
3   Select the 'Add/Remove Windows Components' button.
4   Make sure that the check box for 'Internet Information Services' is checked.
5   Once installed configure IIS by selecting 'Administration Tools' from the Control Panel.
6   Double-click the 'Personal Web Manager' option.

Installing Flash Communication Server

Having downloaded Flash Communication Server simply run the 'exe' to install it to your machine. You will be asked for a user name and password so that you can maintain the server. Once installed

Figure 23.1 *Select Add/Remove Programs in the Control Panel*

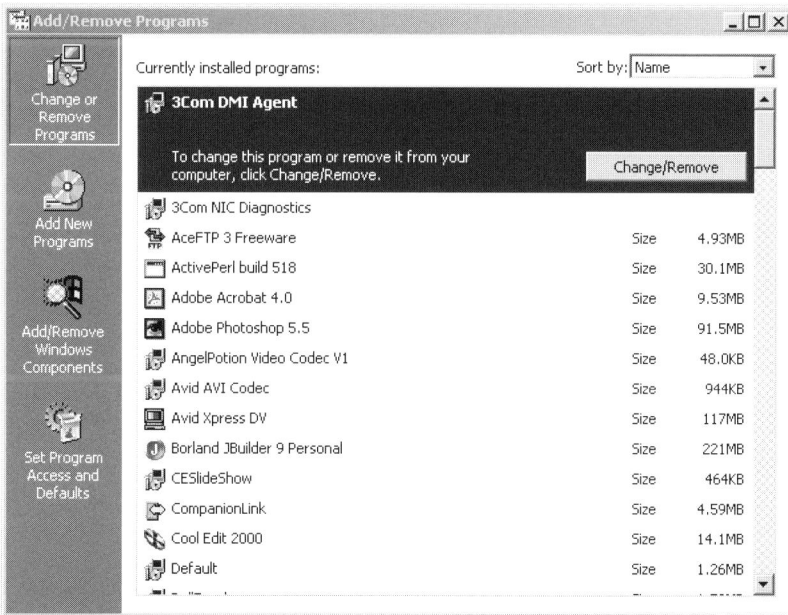

Figure 23.2 *Press the Add/Remove Windows Components button*

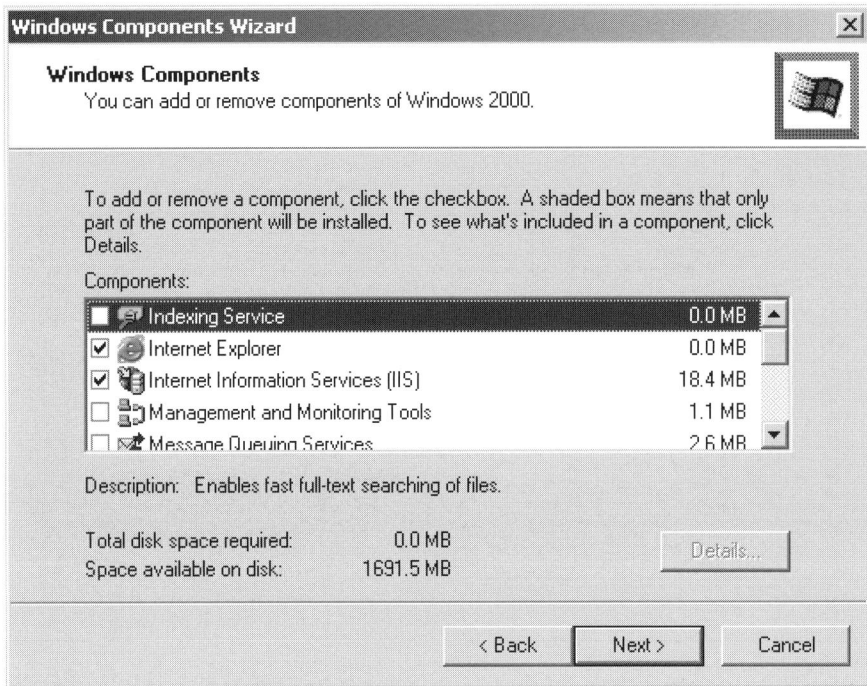

Figure 23.3 *Check the Internet Information Services box*

Figure 23.4 *Select Personal Web Manager to configure IIS*

Figure 23.5 *Configuring IIS*

Figure 23.6 *Flash Communication Server Welcome page*

you will find several new shortcuts under 'Start/Programs/Macromedia/Flash MX Communication Server…'. Macromedia offer a lot of online support for Flash Communication Server so check out http://www.macromedia.com/devnet/mx/flashcom/ to learn more. The first thing to do once FCS is installed is to select the shortcut 'Start/Programs/Macromedia/Flash MX Communication Server/Welcome'.

As an application developer you are probably best to choose the 'Developer' button. The following slides explain that Flash Communication Server has both a client side, i.e. what your users see, and a server side, which is a script running on the server that adds functionality to the communication between simultaneously connected users. Before you can do anything you will need to start the server. Simply choose 'Start/Macromedia/Flash MX Communication Server/Start Server'. A command prompt window will open indicating that Flash Communication Server is starting. Once the server is running you can start to run content. Try running 'Examples/Chapter23/Multiuser.swf'.

Figure 23.7 *'Examples/Chapter23/multiuser.swf'*

Open three copies of the swf file and type in a different name for each one. With all three copies visible on screen notice how a change to one is echoed in another.

A simple example

Let's look at how the communication in this simple example is achieved. Open 'Examples/Chapter23/multiuser.fla'. The code for this example is all on frame 1 of the main timeline. Listing 23.1 shows most of the ActionScript; there are two gaps, between lines 24 and 49, where the code

Figure 23.8 *Running several simultaneous copies*

in lines 19 to 23 is repeated for each of the five different avatars and between 93 and 186 where the code shown for avatar one between lines 71 and 92 is repeated again for avatars 2,3,4 and 5. The example has five avatars; in this case just a simple silhouette of a person. You enter a name in the Input text field and then click on an unnamed avatar to take control of it. You can drag your avatar around and other connected users will see you move. When you have finished click the 'Disconnect' button. So how does it work? First we have line 1; this is only there to allow for debugging later and can be safely removed or commented out when the project is working satisfactorily. A global variable 'avatar' is set to null in line 3. To create a new connection we call 'new NetConnection( )' as in line 6. Then we can define callback functions for the connection. Lines 9 to 11 show the code that will be executed when the connection sends an 'onStatus' event. We simply take the data passed and display the member variables 'level' and 'code'. Line 14 connects the empty connection to an actual area. In this case it is 'rtmp:/multiuser/room_01'. Connections are handled by 'instanceName'. You can have as many 'instances' for a server application as required. All your 'connect' calls will start with 'rtmp', Real-time Messaging Protocol, an optional port, the application name and finally the instance name. This combined string is called the Uniform Resource Identifier or URI.

```
rtmp://host[:port]/appName[/instanceName]
```

In line 17 we create a remote 'SharedObject'. This is the principal method for maintaining shared data across a network. The SharedObject resides on the server, but the client can get and set the data for it. When you create a remote shared object you pass the name of the data, the URI for the connection object, which is a member variable for the object, and a flag that governs the persistence for the data. By default, the shared object is not persistent on the client or server; that is, when all clients close their connections to the shared object, it is deleted. To create a shared object that is saved locally or on the server, you need to pass a value for persistence. If the default is 'null' or 'false' then no data is saved at either the server or the client. If you pass 'true' then the data is saved on the server. The final option is to pass a path. In this case the data is saved on the client and the server.

```
1   #include "NetDebug.as"
2
3   avatar = null;
4
5   // Open connection to the server
6   client_nc = new NetConnection();
7
8   // Show connection status in output window
9   client_nc.onStatus = function(info) {
10    trace("Level: " + info.level + newline + "Code: " +  info.code);
11  };
12
13  // Connect to the application
14  client_nc.connect("rtmp:/multiuser/room_01");
15
16  // Create a remote shared object
17  avatars_so = SharedObject.getRemote("avatars", client_nc.uri, false);
18
19  if (avatars_so.data.used1){
20      avatar1.gotoAndStop(3);
21  }else{
22      avatars_so.data.name1 = "";
23  }
24

...
49  // Update avatar positions when another participant moves
50  avatars_so.onSync = function(list) {
51      avatar1._x = avatars_so.data.x1;
52      avatar1._y = avatars_so.data.y1;
53      avatar1.name = avatars_so.data.name1;
54      avatar2._x = avatars_so.data.x2;
55      avatar2._y = avatars_so.data.y2;
56      avatar2.name = avatars_so.data.name2;
57      avatar3._x = avatars_so.data.x3;
```

```
58    avatar3._y = avatars_so.data.y3;
59    avatar3.name = avatars_so.data.name3;
60    avatar4._x = avatars_so.data.x4;
61    avatar4._y = avatars_so.data.y4;
62    avatar4.name = avatars_so.data.name4;
63    avatar5._x = avatars_so.data.x5;
64    avatar5._y = avatars_so.data.y5;
65    avatar5.name = avatars_so.data.name5;
66 };
67
68 // Connect to the shared object
69 avatars_so.connect(client_nc);
70
71 // Manipulate the avatar
72 avatar1.onPress = function() {
73    if (avatar==null && !avatars_so.data.used1){
74           //Connect to this avatar
75           _root.gotoAndStop(3);
76           avatar = avatar1;
77           avatars_so.data.name1 = _root.name;
78           avatars_so.data.used1 = true;
79    }
80    if (avatar==avatar1){
81           //Move connected avatar
82           this.onMouseMove = function() {
83                  avatars_so.data.x1 = this._x = _root._xmouse;
84                  avatars_so.data.y1 = this._y = _root._ymouse;
85           };
86    }
87 };
88
89 // Release control of the avatar
90 avatar1.onRelease = avatar1.onReleaseOutside=function () {
91    delete this.onMouseMove;
92 };
93
...
186 function disconnectAvatar(){
187    avatar._x = avatar.org.x;
188    avatar._y = avatar.org.y;
189    switch(avatar.id){
190           case 1:
191           avatars_so.data.name1 = "";
192           avatars_so.data.used1 = false;
193           avatars_so.data.x1 = avatar.org.x;
194           avatars_so.data.y1 = avatar.org.y;
```

```
195              break;
196              case 2:
197              avatars_so.data.name2 = "";
198              avatars_so.data.used2 = false;
199              avatars_so.data.x2 = avatar.org.x;
200              avatars_so.data.y2 = avatar.org.y;
201              break;
202              case 3:
203              avatars_so.data.name3 = "";
204              avatars_so.data.used3 = false;
205              avatars_so.data.x3 = avatar.org.x;
206              avatars_so.data.y3 = avatar.org.y;
207              break;
208              case 4:
209              avatars_so.data.name4 = "";
210              avatars_so.data.used4 = false;
211              avatars_so.data.x4 = avatar.org.x;
212              avatars_so.data.y4 = avatar.org.y;
213              break;
214              case 5:
215              avatars_so.data.name5 = "";
216              avatars_so.data.used5 = false;
217              avatars_so.data.x5 = avatar.org.x;
218              avatars_so.data.y5 = avatar.org.y;
219              break;
220      }
221   avatar = null;
222   gotoAndStop(2);
223 }
224
225 Selection.setFocus("entername");
```

Listing 23.1

Once we have got a remote shared object we can get and set the data in that object. Line 19 shows how by reading the value of the shared object data value 'used1' we can decide where to park up the first of the five avatars.

Lines 50 through 66 update the position and names of the avatars every time a sync message is sent from the server. This occurs as data stored within the shared object is modified. In this instance we simply update our avatar movie clips with the information. This callback function is invoked when we connect to the server at line 69. For each avatar we define onPress, onRelease and an onReleaseOutside functions. The 'onPress' function is defined between lines 72 and 87. First in line 73 we test to see if we have already defined an avatar, if so then we must disconnect before we can select an alternative avatar. We also need to test if the avatar is available, in which case the value for the shared object used parameter with the index of the avatar will be set to true. Assuming that we are currently disconnected and that the avatar we have clicked is available, then the code from line 75 is executed. Here we make the value of the variable 'avatar' point at the avatar just clicked and set the used and name values for the shared object. The same function is used to initiate a dragging by creating an 'onMouseMove' function. Lines 83 and 84 pass the value of the mouse to the shared object. The definition of the 'onRelease' and 'onReleaseOutside' functions is defined in lines 90 to 92.

Finally in lines 186 to 223 we use the value of 'id' in the variable 'avatar' to update the shared object as the user disconnects.

Examining what is happening on the server

You can see from the code that most of the communication is handled by the shared object. It is possible to do many of the things that you will want to do as a game developer by concentrating solely on the client-side scripting. But even then it is useful to see what is going on behind the scenes. Use 'Start/Macromedia/Flash Communication Server MX/Administration Console' to open up the admin screens.

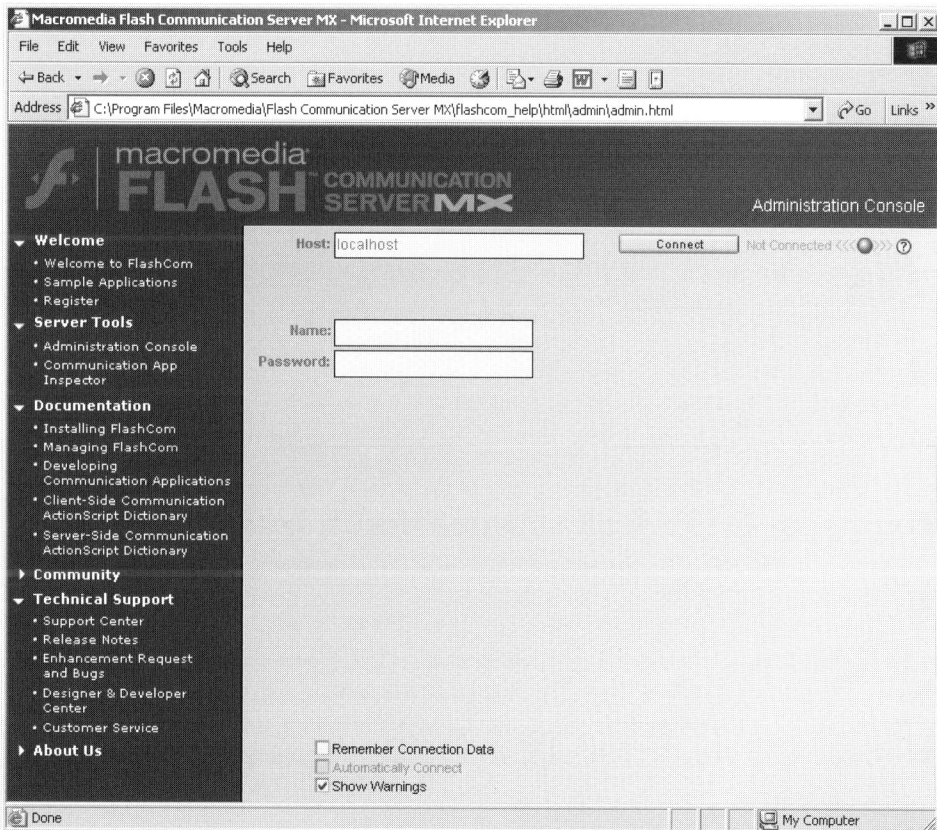

Figure 23.9 *Connecting to the server for administrative tasks*

To enter the admin area enter the name and password you used when installing and press the connect button.

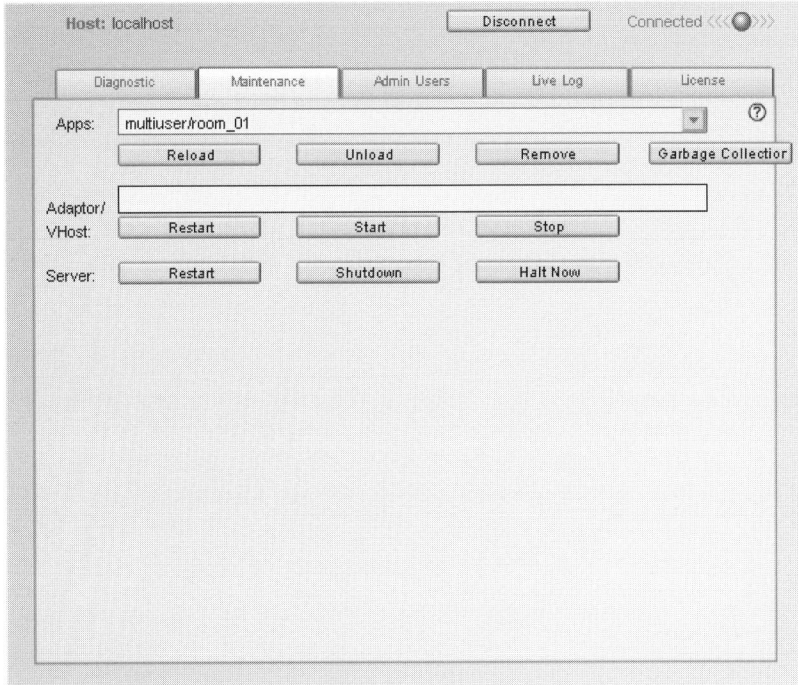

Figure 23.10 *Maintenance of running applications*

Under the 'Maintenance' tab you can use the drop-down box to look at any running applications. These can be restarted, unloaded or removed. If you experience any problems then the admin pages let you get to the bottom of the problem.

Debugging Flash Communication Server

Inevitably when creating client/server games you are going to want good debugging tools. To enable debugging you need to:

1. Add the statement in line 1 of Listing 23.1. You should delete this when the application is finished.
2. Choose 'Window/NetConnection Debugger' in Flash MX 2004. This will open the debugger.
3. Click Filters to display additional interface elements.
4. Enter your user name and password.

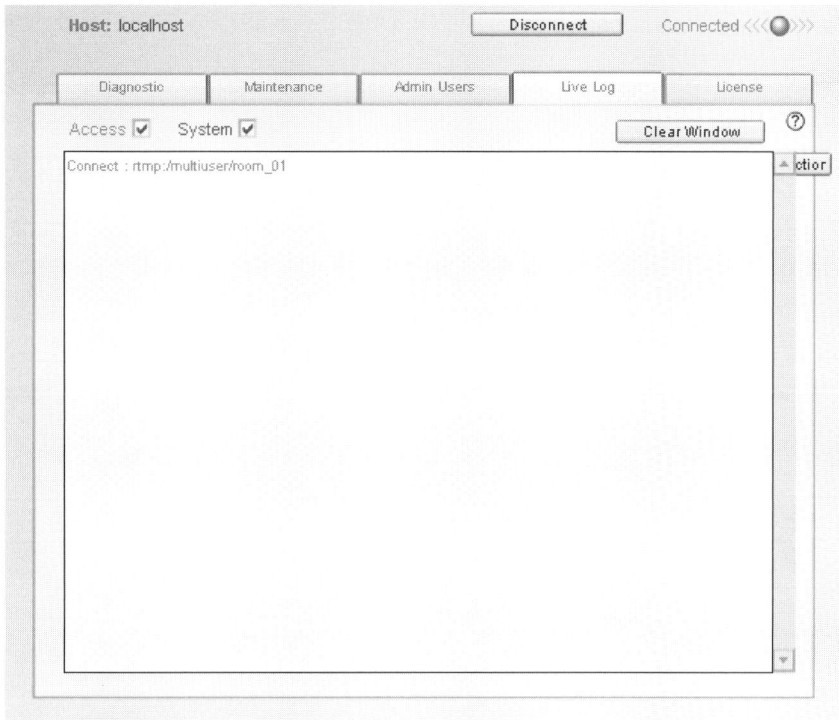

Figure 23.11 *Live Log tab of the admin pages*

Figure 23.12 *Using the NetConnection Debugger without setting a user name and password*

Using the NetConnection Debugger you can track the communication between the client and the server.

Adding server-side scripting

If the simple communication of shared data is not enough then you can add server-side scripting. The scripts are stored in a folder with the same name as the application in the folder 'C:\Program Files\Macromedia\Flash Communication Server MX\applications'.

```
1   application.onConnect = function(newClient, name) {
2
3       // Give this new client the same name as the user name
4       newClient.name=name;
5
6       // Accept the new client's connection
7       application.acceptConnection(newClient);
8
9       // Create a customized "Hello [client]" message
10      // that the server will send to the client
11      var msg = "Hello! You are connected as: " + newClient.name;
12
13      // Print out status message in the application console
14      trace("Sending this message: " + msg);
15
16      // Call the client function, 'message,' and pass it the 'msg'
17      newClient.call("msgFromSrvr", false, msg);
18  }
```
Listing 23.2

Listing 23.2 shows the server-side code for the sample project 'tutorial_hello' that is installed with Flash Communication Server. It is the simplest server-side script possible and it is saved as 'main.asc' in the folder. The only function defined is the 'onConnect' function. When a new connection is initiated in this instance two parameters are passed, the client and their name. We use this information to create a message string and then send this out to all connections using the code in line 17.

```
1   #include "NetDebug.as"
2
3   stop();
4
5   // Open connection to the server
6   client_nc = new NetConnection();
7
8   // Handle status message
9   client_nc.onStatus = function(info) {
```

```
10       trace("Level: " + info.level + newline + "Code: " +  info.code);
11 }
12
13 // Event handler for Connect_Btn
14 function doConnect() {
15
16       // If user wants to connect...
17       if (Connect_btn.getLabel() == "Connect") {
18
19               // Connect to the hello application
20               client_nc.connect("rtmp:/tutorial_hello/room_01", User.text);
21
22               // Update button label
23               Connect_btn.setLabel("Disconnect");
24
25       // If user wants to disconnect...
26       } else if (Connect_btn.getLabel() == "Disconnect") {
27
28               // Close connection
29               client_nc.close();
30
31               // Reset button label
32               Connect_btn.setLabel("Connect");
33
34               // Reset the text fields
35               user.text = "";
36               message.text = "";
37
38       }
39 }
40
41 // Callback function server calls to send message back to
42 // this client.
43 client_nc.msgFromSrvr = function(msg) {
44
45     var msg;
46     _root.Message.text = msg;
47
48 }
```
Listing 23.3

Listing 23.3 shows how the message is handled using the 'msgFromSvr' function; the parameter passed as 'msg' in listing 23.2 is received by this function as the only parameter and this is then used to populate a text field. You can see this code by opening 'tutorial_hello.fla' from the installed samples.

Summary

Flash Communication Server is a robust way to add multi-user connectivity to your game. It is simple to use and easy to set up. The communication is handled using a server-side shared object that all connections can write to and read. Using this simple technique most of the multi-user problems that you are likely to face as a game developer can be handled without having to write any server-side code. If you do need to write server-side code then you can leverage your ActionScript knowledge.

24 Embedding Flash

In this chapter we look at how programmers using other languages can add Flash to their executable programs. By creating a specialized wrapper we can get all the dynamic animation facilities that Flash can provide together with the excellent development environment and we can extend it to use operating system features such as the file system and purpose-made non-rectangular skins. Flash operates as an ActiveX control in the Windows environment and as such is fairly easily embedded into Visual Basic, C# and C++ executables. We also look at communication between the parent program and Flash.

Embedding Flash into a Visual Basic program

On the CD you can find 'Examples/Chapter24/VB/vbflash.vbp', a Visual Basic 6 project file. Using this you can examine how the code works. Alternatively, if starting from scratch, follow these simple steps.

1 Run your copy of Visual Basic and start a new Standard Exe.
2 Choose 'Project/Components...' from the main menu and select 'Shockwave Flash' from the list box.
3 Click on the new icon added to the Tools palette and drag a window on the form.
4 To add an 'swf' to this, place the following code in your Form_Load event:

```
flash.Movie = App.Path & "\yourmovie.swf"
```

It's as simple as that.

In the sample project we take it a stage further by communicating between the Flash and the VB wrapper.

Setting variables in the Flash movie

To set variables in the Flash movie use the following syntax:

```
Flash1.SetVariable "variablename", "content"
```

Setting the frame for the Flash movie

To set the frame for the Flash movie use the following syntax:

```
Flash1.GotoFrame frameNum
```

Figure 24.1 *Selecting the Shockwave Flash ActiveX control*

Receiving messages from Flash

To send messages from Flash to the VB wrapper:

1 Open the code window.
2 Select the Flash object from the left combo box.
3 Select FSCommand from the right combo box.

VB creates a function for you like the one shown in Listing 24.1:

```
1  Private Sub flash_FSCommand(ByVal command As String, ↵
                          ByVal args As String)
2
3  End Sub
```

Listing 24.1

In Flash whenever you use the following syntax in ActionScript, the 'command' parameter and the 'args' parameter are passed to the VB function.

```
fscommand(command, args);
```

You can react to different commands in different ways by first testing the value of 'command' passed into the function.

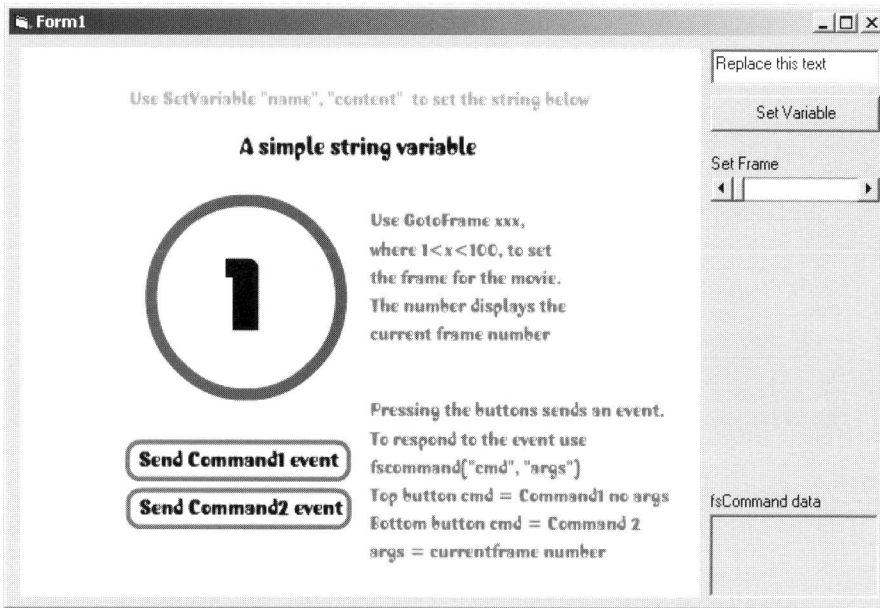

Figure 24.2 *'Examples/Chapter24/VB/vbflash.exe'*

Embedding Flash into C++

Although a little more difficult than VB, embedding Flash into C++ programs is still relatively easy.

Step 1 is to run Visual C++ and choose 'File/New'. Click the 'Projects' tab in the dialog box that opens and select 'MFC AppWizard (exe)' as the project type. You must also select a location and name for the project.

In the next dialog choose 'Dialog based' for the type of application you want to create.

The default file names for the source files will probably suffice, but you have the option to change them if you wish. Then click 'Finish'; all the project files are automatically created and you are ready to add the Flash object.

Inserting a Flash ActiveX control

To add the Flash object click on the 'ResourceView' tab in the workspace panel. If the dialog template is not open then expand the Dialog folder and click on the single template that is in the folder. You should see a dialog template that is the same as that shown in Figure 24.6. Right-click on the template and select 'Insert ActiveX Control. . .' from the context menu.

Figure 24.3 *Creating a new Visual C++ project*

Figure 24.4 *Selecting a dialog-based project*

Figure 24.5 *Choosing the source file names*

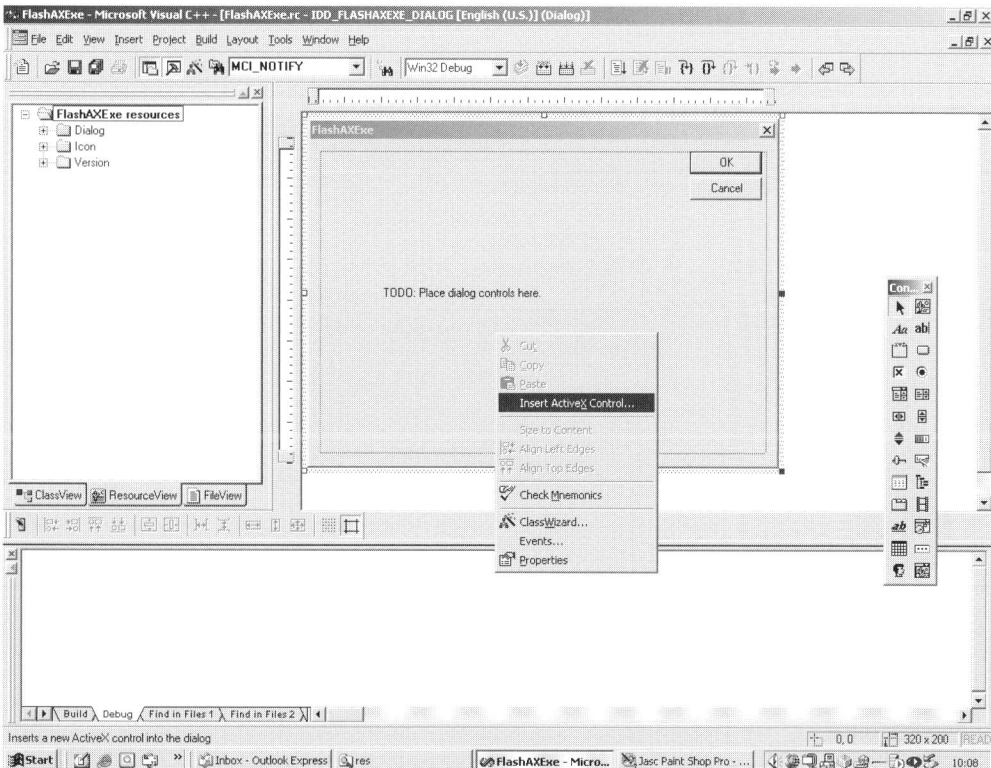

Figure 24.6 *Inserting an ActiveX control*

Figure 24.7 *Select Shockwave Flash Object from the list*

Figure 24.8 *Drag and size on the dialog box template*

A dialog box opens offering a list of ActiveX controls that appear on your PC. Scroll down to 'Shockwave Flash Object'. If you haven't got Flash installed then it will not appear in the list, but this book wouldn't be much use to you either!

A black box appears; this is the Flash Object without a movie embedded. You can drag and position this if you wish, or you can do this in code.

Figure 24.9 *Inserting a member variable for the dialog box*

To use the Flash Object in your source code open Class Wizard and select the 'Member Variables' tab. Click on the ID name you have chosen for the Flash Object. Press the 'Add Variable...' button.

Visual C++ warns you that the object does not have a source file in the current project and automatically generates one from the information found inside the ActiveX control.

The source files created can be renamed from the defaults if you choose.

Give the member variable a name that you will use to manipulate the Flash Object. You now have a project that contains a Flash ActiveX control.

Embedding the Flash movie as a resource

At this stage the Flash movie is empty. In this example we want to create a single exe file, so we need to embed the swf file in the exe. To do this you need to add a custom resource. In the Resource View panel, right-click and choose 'Import...'; in the import dialog select 'Custom' as the import type and select an swf file. In the Custom Resource Type dialog type in FLASH as the

Figure 24.10 *Choosing the source file names for the wrapper*

Figure 24.11 *Selecting the name of the Flash member variable*

resource type. A new folder will appear in the Resource View panel labelled 'FLASH'. Inside this folder will be the new resource. Give this a useful name by right-clicking and choosing 'Properties'.

Turning the resource into a temporary swf file

Before you can assign the custom resource to Flash you need to open it and store it as a temporary file. The function 'CreateTmpSwf' does this work for you. If you are interested in how this function works then you will need to get several books on the Windows platform to better understand the memory management and API calls.

```
1   BOOL CFlashAXExeDlg::CreateTmpSwf()
2   {
3       HINSTANCE hInst = AfxGetResourceHandle();
4       HRSRC hrsrc = ::FindResource(hInst,
5                         MAKEINTRESOURCE(IDR_FLASH), "FLASH");
6       if (!hrsrc) {
7         TRACE("BINARY resource not found");
8         return FALSE;
9       }
10      HGLOBAL hg = LoadResource(hInst, hrsrc);
11      if (!hg) {
12          TRACE("Failed to load BINARY resource");
13          return FALSE;
14      }
15      BYTE* pRes = (BYTE*) LockResource(hg);
16      ASSERT(pRes);
17      int iSize = ::SizeofResource(hInst, hrsrc);
18
19      // Mark the resource pages as read/write so the mmioOpen
20      // won't fail
21      DWORD dwOldProt;
22      BOOL b = ::VirtualProtect(pRes,
23                             iSize,
24                             PAGE_READWRITE,
25                             &dwOldProt);
26      ASSERT(b);
27
28      GetTempPath(MAX_PATH, m_tmp);
29      strcat(m_tmp, "\\tmp.swf");
30
31      CFile file(m_tmp, CFile::modeWrite|CFile::modeCreate);
32      file.Write(pRes, iSize);
33      file.Close();
34      return TRUE;
35  }
```

Listing 24.2

383

Initializing the Flash Control

Having called 'CreateTmpSwf', if the function was successful a movie exists in your temporary folder called 'tmp.swf'. We can set this as the movie for the Flash Object using the 'SetMovie' method of the ActiveX control. The 'OnInitDialog' function is called to initialize the dialog box and is also used to set the shape of the dialog box to a round rectangle using the 'SetWindowRgn' method for a window.

```
BOOL CFlashAXExeDlg::OnInitDialog()
{
        CDialog::OnInitDialog();

        SetIcon(m_hIcon, TRUE);                  // Set big icon
        SetIcon(m_hIcon, FALSE);          // Set small icon

        CScrollBar *bar = (CScrollBar*)GetDlgItem(IDC_SCROLLBAR1);
        bar->SetScrollRange(1, 100);

        if (CreateTmpSwf()) m_flash.SetMovie(m_tmp);

        return TRUE;  // return TRUE  unless you set the focus to a control
}
```

Removing the temporary swf

Whenever a temporary file is saved to the file system remember to remove it when the application closes. The API call 'DeleteFile' does this for you.

```
void CFlashAXExeDlg::OnDestroy()
{
        CDialog::OnDestroy();
        DeleteFile(m_tmp);
}
```

Communicating between the Flash Object and the wrapper

If you are doing anything more than just creating an exe wrapper then you will probably want to respond to events that take place inside Flash. To do this you need to respond to fscommand events. Flash sends an fscommand using this syntax:

```
fscommand("click", "");
```

The first parameter is the command name and the second any arguments you want to send at the same time. You can send an fscommand at any time in your ActionScript. The command name can be any string that is useful for the context. To respond to all fscommand events we need to add a member function to the main window of our wrapper.

```
void CFlashTalkDlg::OnFSCommandFlash(LPCTSTR command, LPCTSTR args)
{
        if (_stricmp(command, "click")==0){
            AfxMessageBox("Flash passed click fscommand");
        }
}
```

You test for the command string using the function 'strcmp' for a case-sensitive comparison or '_stricmp' if you want it to be case insensitive. If the strings are the same then the string comparison function is set to zero. In this way you can send any message from Flash. Having sent a message your wrapper may want to query the current state of variables in Flash.

If you need to get the value of a variable in Flash then use:

```
m_flash.getVariable(variablename)
```

Regardless of the type of the variable this function returns a string.

If you want to set a variable in Flash then use:

```
m_flash.setVariable(variablename, variablevalue)
```

where both 'variablename' and 'variablevalue' are both passed as strings.

You will be able to see from the list of exposed methods in the Flash ActiveX control that there are a considerable number of other ways that you can communicate between the wrapper and Flash. The wrapper can control the playback by setting the frame and the play mode for both the main timeline and any Movie Clips, but the principal methods you will use are 'setMovie', 'setVariable', 'getVariable' and the event callback 'OnFSCommand'.

Embedding Flash on a PocketPC 2003

The 2003 version of PocketPC software brought some changes to the platform. To embed Flash you will need to create an HTML View window and then populate this with an HTML file that accesses your Flash file. It is perfectly possible to embed both the HTML file and the Flash file so you can create a single executable that will appear to the user to be a self-contained executable. To do this you will need a copy of Embedded Visual C++ 4, which is freely available from Microsoft. The URL at the time of writing is http://msdn. microsoft.com/vstudio/device/embedded/download.aspx. After installing you should install any service packs and finally install the SDK for PocketPC 2003. Having successfully installed all the development tools you should be able to compile and execute on your PocketPC the program 'HTMLHost.exe'; the project file for this is found on the CD at 'Examples/Chapter24/PocketPC/ppcflash.vcw'. This code is just a slightly amended version of the 'HTMLHost' sample that comes with the PocketPC 2003 SDK. The default installation puts this at 'C:\Program Files\Windows CE Tools\wce420\POCKET PC 2003\Samples\Win32\ Htmlhost'. The program is a standard Windows application. The application starts by calling the WinMain function. Here is a listing of the 'HTMLHost.cpp' file.

```
1   #include "stdafx.h"
2
3   #define MENU_HEIGHT 26
4
5   #define WC_HTMLCONTAINER TEXT("HTMLContainer")
6   LRESULT TestWndProc(HWND hwnd, UINT uMsg, WPARAM wParam, LPARAM lParam);
7
8   ////////////////////////////////////////////////////////////////////////
9   // RegisterTestClass
10  ////////////////////////////////////////////////////////////////////////
11  HRESULT RegisterTestClass
12  (
13      HINSTANCE hInstance
14  )
15  {
16      WNDCLASS    wc = { 0 };
17      HRESULT     hrResult;
18
19      if (!GetClassInfo(hInstance, WC_HTMLCONTAINER, &wc))
20      {
21          wc.style            = CS_HREDRAW | CS_VREDRAW;
22          wc.lpfnWndProc      = TestWndProc;
23          wc.hInstance        = hInstance;
24          wc.lpszClassName    = WC_HTMLCONTAINER;
25          wc.hCursor          = LoadCursor(NULL, IDC_ARROW);
26          wc.hbrBackground    = (HBRUSH)(COLOR_WINDOW + 1);
27
28          hrResult = (RegisterClass(&wc) ? S_OK : E_FAIL);
29      }
30      else
31          hrResult = S_OK;
32
33      return hrResult;
34  }
35
36  ////////////////////////////////////////////////////////////////////////
37  // WinMain
38  ////////////////////////////////////////////////////////////////////////
39  int WINAPI WinMain
40  (
41      HINSTANCE   hInstance,
42      HINSTANCE   hPrevInstance,
43      LPWSTR      lpCmdLine,
44      int         nCmdShow
45  )
```

```
46 {
47    HWND hwndParent;
48    HWND hwndHTML;
49
50    VERIFY(SUCCEEDED(RegisterTestClass(hInstance)));
51
52    hwndParent = CreateWindow(  WC_HTMLCONTAINER,
53                                NULL,
54                                WS_VISIBLE,
55                                CW_USEDEFAULT, CW_USEDEFAULT,
56                                240, 280,
57                                NULL,
58                                NULL,
59                                hInstance,
60                                0);
61
62    RECT rc;
63    GetWindowRect(hwndParent, &rc);
64
65    SHFullScreen(hwndParent, SHFS_HIDETASKBAR | SHFS_HIDESIPBUTTON);
66
67    MoveWindow( hwndParent,
68                rc.left,
69                rc.top - MENU_HEIGHT,
70                rc.right,
71                rc.bottom + MENU_HEIGHT,
72                TRUE);
73
74    VERIFY(InitHTMLControl(hInstance));
75
76    hwndHTML = CreateWindow(WC_HTML,
77                            NULL,
78                            WS_CHILD
79                                | WS_BORDER
80                                | WS_VISIBLE,
81                            5,
82                            5,
83                            (rc.right - rc.left) - 10,
84                            (rc.bottom - rc.top) - 10,
85                            hwndParent,
86                            NULL,
87                            hInstance,
88                            NULL);
89
90    if (hwndHTML != NULL)
91    {
92        // Navigate to pocketpc.com
93        BSTR bstrURL = SysAllocString(TEXT("file://\\test.html"));
94        SendMessage(hwndHTML, DTM_NAVIGATE, 0, (LPARAM)bstrURL);
95        SysFreeString(bstrURL);
```

```
96
97        MSG msg;
98        while (GetMessage(&msg, NULL, 0, 0))
99        {
100             TranslateMessage(&msg);
101             DispatchMessage(&msg);
102        }
103   }
104
105   return 0;
106 }
```

Listing 24.3

In common with any Windows application it starts by registering the class in line 50; this in turn calls the function listed between lines 11 and 34. Then in line 52 we create the main window for this program and size it to 240 by 280 pixels. Then in line 65 we use the new Shell function 'SHFullScreen' to declare this as a full screen application that hides both the task bar and any buttons. This allows us to move the window, which is accomplished in line 67. The app size is now greater. In line 74 we call 'InitHTMLControl' which is declared in the 'htmlctrl.h' header file and is found in the 'htmlview.lib' so please ensure that this library is added to your project. Then we create the HTMLView in line 76. Note in this instance that the positioning of the control is inset. Changing these parameters allows you to bleed off your Flash entirely. Also removing the WS_BORDER, window style will remove the box surrounding Flash in the example. Finally, in lines 93 to 103 we set the HTML file to load. By using the embedded resource ideas set out earlier you could save this in a resource and then load it out to a temporary file along with the Flash swf so that the entire exe is self-contained. To use the HTMLView you use 'SendMessage'. Space is limited so if you intend to use a more sophisticated application then I suggest reading the documentation that comes with Embedded Visual C++ 4. In the sample you can see how communication between Flash and the host is achieved.

Summary

If you have ever done any Windows programming then much of the information in this chapter will be familiar and you may be pleasantly surprised how easy it is to incorporate Flash into your application. If you have never done any Windows programming then the whole lot probably seems totally confusing. You can actually use the source code without understanding it, if you wish, but if you do intend to create a wrapper for a Flash movie then I recommend getting to grips with at least the basics of Windows programming.

Using the Flash ActiveX control in this way allows you as a developer to create desktop characters, email virals and screensavers. It is certainly worth looking into how the control can be used to extend your applications.

Appendix A:
Integrating Flash with Director

Director is starting to make a more significant impact on the Internet with the addition of Shockwave 3D. As an experienced Flash developer you will probably find it easier to control the 3D world using a Flash interface. In this appendix you will find an introduction to controlling a 3D world using Flash.

As I write, Director MX 2004 is the latest version. Director MX 2004 can import Flash MX 2004 or below movies. This appendix will use two examples; the first is available at 'Examples\AppendixA\boxesinterface.fla' on the CD. This simple example uses just two buttons. One button is labelled 'Add Box' and the other 'Remove Box'. Each has a very simple ActionScript attached to the release event.

```
on (release){
        getURL("event:addBox");
}
```

To communicate between Flash and Director we use the Flash 'getURL' method. For each link we use 'event:*myeventName*', where 'myeventName' can be any name you like that is not a keyword in Director. On the Flash side that is all you need to do, the action is similar to passing an *fscommand* to a parent window.

In Director you can import the Flash interface that you have created. The Director project 'Examples\AppendixA\boxes.dir' is a working example. If you set the Filename property under the Flash tab of the Property Inspector to the 'fla' for the Flash interface, then double-clicking the Flash in Director will open Flash MX 2004 where you can edit the content, then press the 'Done' button to return to Director MX.

In the 'Boxes' example we use the terrific 3D physics engine Havok to add and remove boxes in a 3D world. You can pick up the boxes with the mouse and throw them around. The boxes all interact with each other, bounce off one another and react to the collisions. If you are interested then study the code.

For now, though, we are only interested in the way that Flash can be used to initiate the actions. For each 'event:myeventName' you need to add a function to a movie script in Director. The script must be a movie script, not a behaviour script or a parent script. The form for the code will be

```
on myeventName
--Code that will run when called
end
```

Figure A.1 *Developing the boxes interface*

If you place a 'put' in the code you will see that each time that Flash sends a 'getURL("event:myeventName")', Director catches the event within the function. 'put' is the Director equivalent to 'trace'. In the current example the function 'addBox' is used to create a new box and initiate the physical behaviour; 'removeBox' is used to delete the last box that has been added.

The movie can be published suitable for the Internet by setting the appropriate values in the Publish Settings dialog box. Director creates a compressed file with a 'dcr' extension. This file contains the Flash interface; you do not need to have a version of the swf file available on the site.

Sometimes you will want to pass on the 'event' to the 3D world. Director uses the same layered-design as Flash and in the next example, 'Examples\AppendixA\road.dir', you will find that the 3D world is on layer 2. In this example the arrows are Flash buttons, each button sending a different event to Director. In addition, Director sets two variables in Flash that display the current position and orientation. Each event is handled in the same way:

```
on turnleft
  sendsprite(2, #turnleft)
end
```

Figure A.2 *Importing the Flash interface*

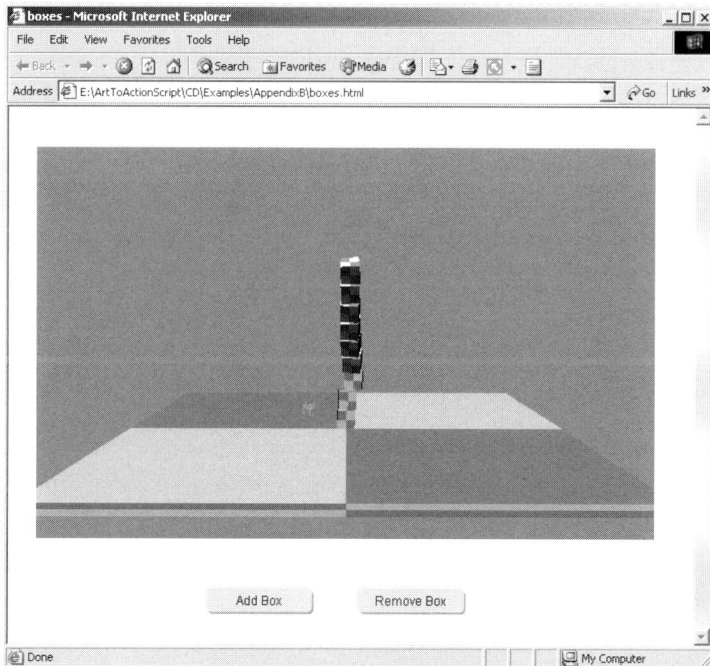

Figure A.3 *Running the project in a browser*

The first parameter in the 'sendsprite' method is the layer number for the sprite, and the second parameter is the name of a function for an attached behaviour for the sprite. Director uses a syntax that prefixes the name of a function with the '#' character to denote a symbol. The 3D world has a script behaviour attached that contains the code that will be called

```
on stopmotion
  moveZ = 0
  rotY = 0
end
```

In this example the code is used to set the value of two variables that are used to update the position of the camera in the 3D world for each step of the timer. Director uses the 'enterFrame' event for each beat of the timer:

```
on enterFrame
  vec = cam.transform.position
  x = integer(vec.x/10)
  y = integer(vec.y/10)
  z = integer(vec.z/10)
  str = string(x) & ":" & y & ":" & z
  sprite(1).setVariable("position", str)
  vec = cam.transform.rotation
  x = integer(vec.x)
  y = integer(vec.y)
  z = integer(vec.z)
  str = string(x) & ":" & y & ":" & z
  sprite(1).setVariable("orientation", str)

  cam.rotate(0, rotY, 0)
  cam.translate(0, 0, moveZ)
end
```

The 'enterFrame' event is used to update the value of a string containing information about the camera position and orientation. This is sent to Flash using the syntax:

```
sprite(n).setVariable(variableName, variableValue)
```

where *n* is the layer where the Flash sprite resides, *variableName* is the name of the Flash variable and *variableValue* is string value to set. If you have a variable within a movie clip that you need to set then you can use the following syntax:

```
sprite(n).telltarget(clipName)
        sprite(n).setVariable(variableName, variableValue)
sprite(n).endtelltarget()
```

where 'clipName' is the name of the movie clip instance from the '_root' level. You can use the same technique to move the frame within a Flash clip.

```
sprite(n).telltarget(clipName)
        sprite(n).gotoFrame(5)
sprite(n).endtelltarget()
```

You can set the properties of a clip using:

```
sprite(n).setFlashProperty(clipName, #propertyName, value)
```

For example,

```
sprite(2).setFlashProperty("Cat", #x, 180)
```

Figure A.4 *Developing the road example in Director MX*

To retrieve the value of a property use:

```
value = sprite(n).getFlashProperty(clipName, #propertyName)
```

For example,

```
CatX = sprite(2).getFlashProperty("Cat", #x)
```

Using these simple methods you can create a complex interface in Flash for controlling a 3D world.

Appendix B:
Tweening in code

The easiest way to tween a graphic or a movie clip is by right-clicking on a frame layer in the timeline and choosing 'Create Motion Tween'. Unfortunately the results are not always fantastic. In this appendix we look at how you can use ActionScript to provide dynamic tweening that gives a much smoother and more flexible result. In the first part we will simply look at how ramping (easing) in and out of a move gives a more natural feel. Later we will look at how several keyframes can be linked together to create a smooth and curved motion, the same kind of motion you would get in a CG animation package.

A bit of background

Traditional cell animation was, until relatively recently, shot on a camera that was mounted to point vertically down. This setup was called a rostrum camera or an animation stand. The only movement the camera could do was to move up and down a very rigid column. The artwork was placed on a bench underneath the camera and this bench could move north, south, east and west in relation to the camera. On most animation stands the bench could also rotate through 360 degrees. By moving the bench the artwork could move in a controlled fashion beneath the camera, and by moving the camera up and down the column the camera could be made to zoom in or out of the artwork. In the early days of rostrum cameras the movement of each axis was linked to a manual counter. The counter would often count up in thousandths of an inch. To create a smooth motion from one position to another on such a camera would require the use of a lookup table for each axis. The cameraman would first calculate the movement for each axis, and then find the nearest lookup table to achieve this movement in the desired number of frames. The lookup tables incorporated an acceleration from a stationary position and a deceleration to a stop at the end. If the cameraman had a move that went through several positions they would have to use some kind of smoothing to make the movement through a middle position seem smooth. Most of the tables that were used to give these camera moves used a sine curve as a ramp in and out. A rostrum cameraman's life was transformed when computers became available to control the motion of each axis. Many years ago I was involved in creating the software to drive the motors for an animation stand. The maths used to control the stand is the same as you will find in this appendix and the curved motion is still used to provide the movement of many motion control stands that are the big brother of an animation stand.

Options for easing in and out

When you move a clip from one location to another over time you have several options over the look of the motion. Each time interval could be used to move the clip exactly the same distance. This is called linear interpolation and it is the default for Flash motion tweening. The result is fine for an object that is already moving but looks stiff and artificial if the object either starts from stationary or stops while in view. An alternative is to ease in to the motion; the first time interval would move the clip only a small amount and this would be increased for each successive time interval, either until a certain speed is achieved or the ramping could continue throughout the motion. Similarly at the end of a motion the amount of motion for each successive time interval could be reduced to bring the clip to a smooth stop. When you start to play about with the speed of a clip in this way you will find that accelerating and then abruptly stopping has a dynamic that may be suitable for a particular application. Motion is as important to the success of a game as the look and feel. Controlling the speed of a clip can be done using simple mathematics, the simplest option being linear.

Linear interpolation

If a clip moves from location A to location B in time T, then linear interpolation is simply

```
var dt = time/duration;
_x = offset.x * dt + start.x;
_y = offset.y * dt + start.y;
```

Here we use a point object to store the start position and the total movement that is required. A motion is usually relative to the starting position. In this instance we simply create a variable *dt* and set it to the current time since the start of the motion divided by the duration of the motion. This number will vary over time between 0 and 1. At the start no time will have elapsed so the value for *dt* will be 0, in which case the *x* and *y* value is simply set to the starting position. As the variable time approaches the duration value, *dt* will get close to one so that *x* and *y* will be set to the starting value plus the value for offset.

Quadratic interpolation

The graph of $y = x^2$ is shown in Figure B.1. As you can see this is not a straight line but a curve. We will let the *x* value represent a number between 0 and 1, being the elapsed time in proportion to the total duration of a move. The *y* parameter will be the total distance moved. As you can see from the shape of the curve there will be a smaller movement at first, gaining speed throughout the move. This will give an ease in to the motion.

Such a motion is achieved using this code snippet.

```
var dt = time/duration;
_x = offset.x * dt * dt + start.x;
_y = offset.y * dt * dt + start.y;
```

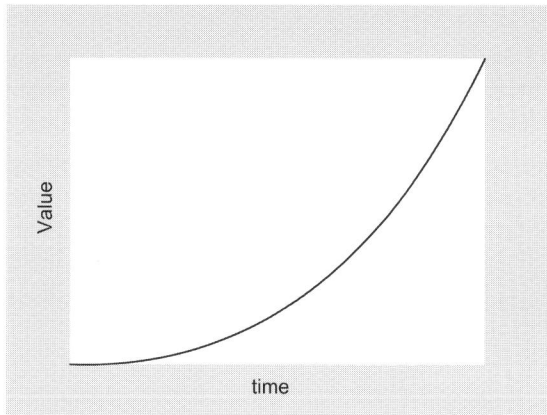

Figure B.1 *The graph of* $y = x^2$

If an ease out is required then we need a different shape to the curve. In fact we need to flip the curve for both values. Flipping the time value will give a parameter moving by $1 - dt$ (if dt is a value between 0 and 1 as described above). The quadratic of $1 - dt$ is simply $(1 - dt)(1 - dt)$ which can be multiplied out to give $1 - 2dt + dt^2$. We also want to flip the value parameter so the result is $1 - (1 - 2dt + dt^2)$ which simplifies to $2dt - dt^2$. So the curve we want is $y = 2x - x^2$, which is shown in Figure B.2.

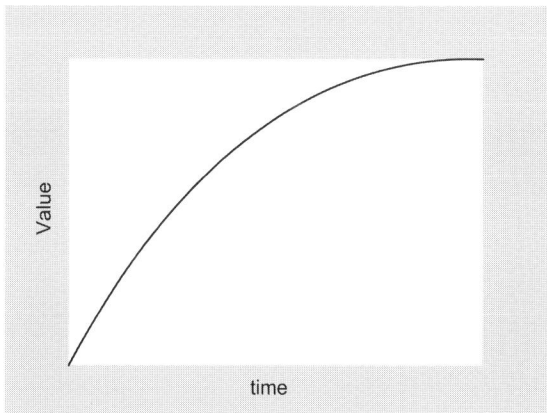

Figure B.2 *The graph of* $2x - x^2$

Such a curve is created with the code snippet:

```
var dt = time/duration;
_x = offset.x * dt *(2 - dt) + start.x;
_y = offset.y * dt *(2 - dt) + start.y;
```

In all the curves we shall study, we are using a delta time parameter dt that varies over the range 0 to 1, to create a curve whose maximum value is also 1. We use the value of the curve multiplied by the offset required for the actual move to place the moving item in the correct place for both the x and y directions. When we are considering the ease-in and -out option for a quadratic we need to join together the two previous curves. We want the ease-in curve to be used for the first half of the motion and the ease-out curve to be used for the second half. This time, however, we need to scale the result of the ease-in calculation by a half; we want the maximum value for this curve to happen when dt is 0.5 and for the result to be 0.5 likewise. To do this we must multiply the time value by 2, but halve the final answer. We get

```
var dt = time/duration;
dt *= 2;
if (dt < 1){
        _x = offset.x/2 * dt * dt + start.x;
        _y = offset.y/2 * dt * dt + start.y;
}
```

If dt is past the halfway mark then we need to apply the second curve with dt starting from 0 at the halfway stage and again we must half the final result and add 0.5, because the first part of the curve has already got to this point. We get:

```
var dt = time/duration;
dt *= 2;
if (dt >= 1){
        dt--;
        _x = offset.x * dt *(2 - dt) + 0.5 + start.x;
        _y = offset.y * dt *(2 - dt) + 0.5 + start.y;
}
```

In this way we can join together the two curves seamlessly at the point (0.5, 0.5) on the curve.

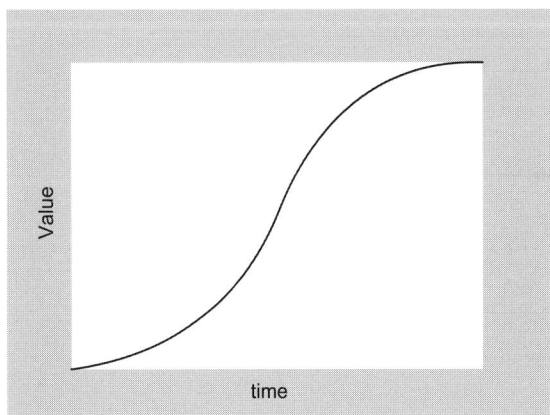

Figure B.3 *Joining* x^2 *and* $2x - x^2$

Joining together curves in this way can give very interesting motion. The Excel spreadsheet 'Examples\AppendixB\quadratic tweening.xls' allows you to play about with curves to see the results in the charts.

Figure B.4 *Using Excel to chart the curves*

Quadratic tweening can be extended to cubic or higher polynomials. A cubic curve is simply $y = x^3$. The higher the power the faster the ramping will be.

Sinusoidal tweening

A totally different method for generating motion curves is to use the sine curve. Figure B.5 shows a section of a cosine curve between PI and 2PI. Trigonometric functions use radians as the parameter not degrees, 180 degrees being the equivalent of PI radians, so the curve shown is actually between 180 and 360 degrees. Notice that the curve ramps up and ramps down between the two values and that the range for the function is plus and minus 1.

The curve is very similar to the joined quadratic curve. To use the curve to ease in we need the section between PI and 3PI/2. This will give a result between −1 and 0 so we will need to add 1 to get the values we want, which are between 0 and 1.

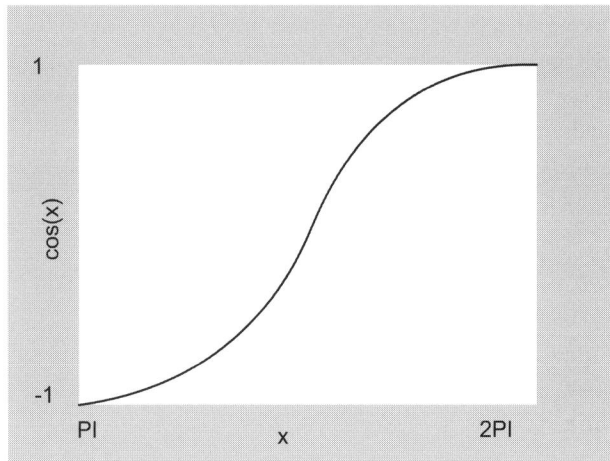

Figure B.5 *A section of the cosine curve*

```
var n, dt = time/duration;
n = Math.cos(Math.PI/2 * dt + Math.PI) + 1;
_x = offset.x * n + start.x;
_y = offset.y * n + start.y;
```

For an ease out we will use the curve between 3PI/2 and 2PI; this section of the curve already gives values between 0 and 1 so we do not need to scale or shift the values.

```
var n, dt = time/duration;
n = Math.cos((Math.PI * (dt + 3))/2);
_x = offset.x * n + start.x;
_y = offset.y * n + start.y;
```

The final option is to use the full curve to give both an ease in and out. For this we must use the full curve between PI and 2PI, the returned values will vary between plus and minus 1 so we must add 1 then divide by 2 to give returned values between 0 and 1.

```
var n, dt = time/duration;
n = (Math.cos(Math.PI * dt + Math.PI) + 1)/2;
_x = offset.x * n + start.x;
_y = offset.y * n + start.y;
```

Exponential tweening

Another curve that can give a very fast ramp is the curve $y = 2^x$. Any number raised to the power zero is equal to 1. As you know, the value of *dt* ranges between 0 and 1, but we want the result to start at 0 and ramp up to 1 for an ease-in curve. If we used 2^{dt} the result would start at 1 and ramp up to 2 with very little curve in the motion. In fact we want the tangent to the curve at time zero to have a zero gradient. This implies that before time zero the curve was flat indicating a static object. If we use the curve $y = 1/2^x$, then for large values of x, y tends to 0. If we make the starting value for x equal to 10 then $y = 1/1024$ which is fairly small. $1/2^x$ is the same as 2^{-x}. So we want the power values to range between -10 and 0.

```
var n, dt = time/duration;
n = Math.pow( 2, 10 * (dt - 1) );
_x = offset.x * n + start.x;
_y = offset.y * n + start.y;
```

The ease-out curve needs to start fast and decelerate so we flip the curve, and reverse the direction.

```
var n, dt = time/duration;
n = 1 - Math.pow( 2, -10 * dt ) - 1 ;
_x = offset.x * n + start.x;
_y = offset.y * n + start.y;
```

For an ease in and out we do a piecewise interpolation using the ease in for values up to dt equal 0.5 and the ease-out curve for dt above 0.5. The curves need to be scaled in both directions and the ease-out curve needs translating so that dt equal 0.5 gives a result of 0.5.

```
var n, dt = time/duration;
dt *= 2;
if (dt < 1){
    n = Math.pow( 2, 10 * (dt - 1))/2;
    _x = offset.x * n + start.x;
    _y = offset.y * n + start.y;
}else{
    dt--;
    n = -(Math.pow( 2, -10 * dt) - 2 )/2;
    _x = offset.x * n + start.x;
    _y = offset.y * n + start.y;

}
```

If you find the maths confusing then just copy the stuff into your project and use it like a black box. It works!

Figure B.6 *Using Excel to chart exponential curves*

The tweening example project

In addition to the Excel spreadsheets of the curves, there is the Flash project 'Examples\ AppendixB\tweening.fla' to help you to understand how this stuff works and what the results look like.

The tweening project consists of a screen that contains two check boxes to select easing in and easing out, and four radio buttons to choose the curve type. If you deselect both the ease-in and -out options then you will get a linear interpolation. The aim of the application is to allow you to click anywhere in the white area and then the yellow dot will move from its current location to the new location in one second, leaving behind a trail that gives an indication of how the speed of the motion accelerates and decelerates over time. Try running the application now and you will get a feel for the different curves involved. The code inside the project uses the code snippets already outlined and introduces a *point* class. As you know from Chapter 10, keeping data and the manipulation of data together is a very useful technique; it makes your code more robust and easier to modify and is highly recommended. To create a new point, simply use the 'new' keyword. The function 'point' assigns values to the data and sets up pointers to function calls. Then to set a point you can use the method 'set' and to add and subtract you can use the methods 'add' and 'sub'. The results of the code snippet here would be to set 'offset' to the point $(2, -18)$.

Figure B.7 *Creating the tweening project*

```
start = new point();
end = new point();
offset = new point();
start.set(12, 34);
end.set(10, 52);
offset.copy(start);
offset.sub(end);

function point(){
        this.x = 0;
        this.y = 0;
        this.set = setPoint;
        this.add = addPoint;
        this.sub = subPoint;
        this.copy = copyPoint;
}
```

```
function setPoint(nx, ny){
        this.x = nx;
        this.y = ny;
}

function addPoint(pt){
        this.x += pt.x;
        this.y += pt.y;
}

function subPoint(pt){
        this.x -= pt.x;
        this.y -= pt.y;
}

function copyPoint(pt){
        this.x = pt.x;
        this.y = pt.y;
}
```

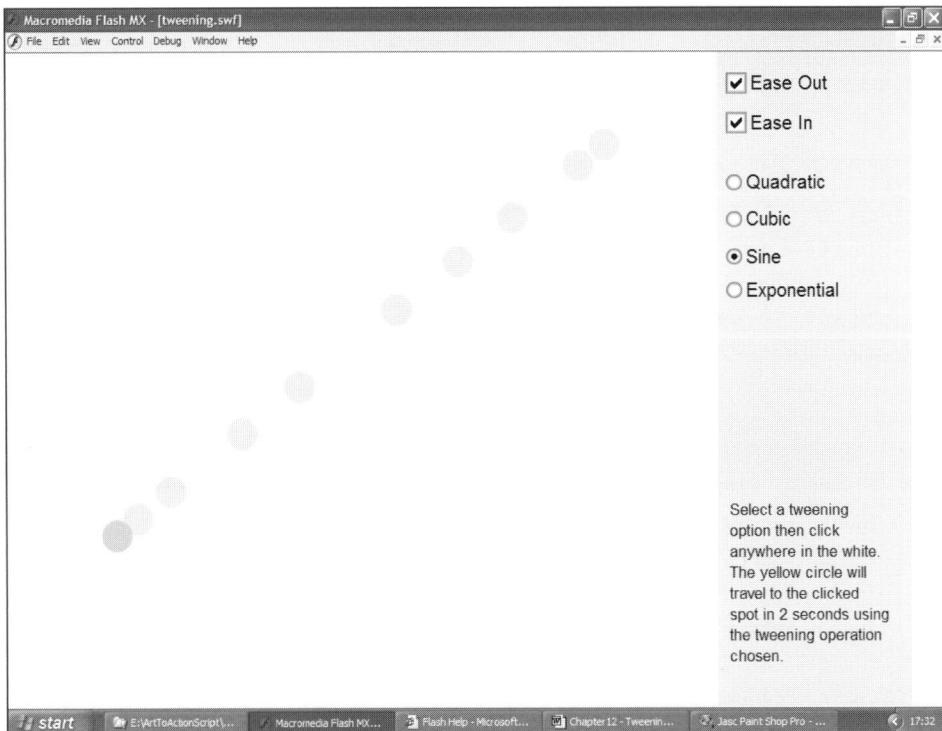

Figure B.8 *Using the tweening example*

Creating keyframes

So far the methods described will take a graphic element from one screen location to another. Suppose we want the element to move through several positions smoothly and with a curved motion. This is the principle behind computer animation programs. The interpolation through the key positions is handled in several different ways; one of the simplest yet controllable options is to use a variant on a hermite curve. To use such a curve we are going to need a structure that can contain all the information needed to manipulate each key position on the curve. Such a structure needs to contain values for

time, x, y, scale, rotation, tension, continuity and *bias*

The last three values allow you to control how the curves interpolate through the key positions; should the motion bunch up to a key, be very curved around the key or favour the start of a section rather than the tail. To store all this data we will create a *keyframe* class.

```
//Constructor for a keyframe object
function keyframe(i){
        //Member variables
        this.x = 0;
        this.y = 0;
        this.rotation = 0;
        this.scale = 100;
        this.ct = 0.0;
        this.bs = 0.0;
        this.tn = 0.0;
        this.millisecs = 0;
        this.linear = false;
        //Function pointers
        this.tween = tween_keyframe;
        this.dump = dump_keyframe;
}
```

Interpolating between keyframes using TCB curves

Suppose we have a series of keyframe values that must change over time smoothly. Figure B.9 indicates how the values change with respect to time. Notice that there is an abrupt change at K3. Here the tangent to the incoming curve does not match the tangent to the outgoing curve. Creating a smooth motion is in reality a curve fitting exercise. You are creating a curve that moves smoothly between certain defined positions.

The technique we will use is a piecewise fit. We will calculate the move between, for example, K1 and K2 using a cubic curve while ensuring that the tangent at K1 is also used when considering the section K0 to K1 and the tangent at K2 is used when interpolating between K2 and K3.

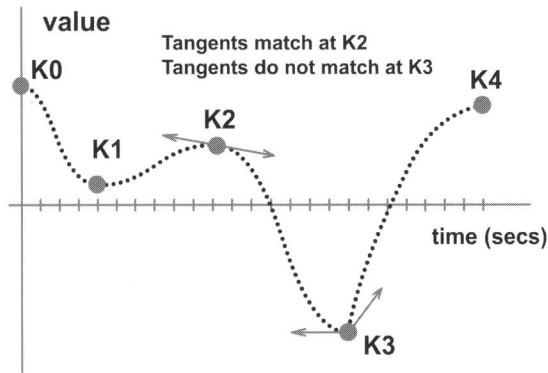

Figure B.9 *Piecewise curve fitting*

The curve we will use is

$$y = h_0{}^*K1 + h_1{}^*K2 + h_2{}^*T1 + h_3{}^*T2$$

where h_0 to h_3 are the hermite coefficients:

$$h_0 = 2t^3 - 3t^2 + 1$$
$$h_1 = 3t^2 - 2t^3$$
$$h_2 = t^3 - 2t^2 + t$$
$$h_3 = t^3 - t^2$$

and T1 and T2 are the smoothing parameters. If S1 and S2 are defined as:

$$S1 = (K2.time - K1.time)/(K2.time - K0.time)$$
$$S1 = (K2.time - K1.time)/(K3.time - K1.time)$$

then

$$T1 = S1{}^*((1 - K1.tn)(1 + K1.bs)(1 + K1.ct)(K1.value - K0.value)$$
$$+ (1 - K1.tn)(1 - K1.bs)(1 - K1.ct)(K2.value - K1.value))$$
$$T2 = S2{}^*((1 - K2.tn)(1 + K2.bs)(1 - K1.ct)(K2.value - K1.value)$$
$$+ (1 - K2.tn)(1 - K2.bs)(1 + K2.ct)(K3.value - K2.value))$$

If the curve section is between K0 and K1, then

$$T1 = 0.5{}^*(K2.value - K1.value){}^*((1 - K1.tn)(1 + K1.bs)(1 + K1.ct)$$
$$+ (1 - K1.tn)(1 - K1.bs)(1 - K1.ct))$$

and if the curve section is between the penultimate and the final keyframe then

$$T2 = 0.5^*(K2.\text{value} - K1.\text{value})^*((1 - K2.\text{tn})(1 + K2.\text{bs})(1 - K1.\text{ct})$$

$$+ (1 - K2.\text{tn})(1 - K2.\text{bs})(1 + K2.\text{ct}))$$

In the tweening function we first test to see if the time passed as a parameter is within range. If not then we set the motion to either the first or last keyframe. Then we look through the keyframe list to see which section to interpolate. If the current time is an exact match with a keyframe time then no interpolation is required and so the position is set directly and the function returns. If interpolation is required then we precalculate the value of tcb coefficients and store them in the variables $a - d$. These are used to derive the values of T1 and T2. A section of the curve can be set to be linear if required in which case the interpolation calculation is simplified to starting position plus the product of delta time and the offset value for the curve section. This arithmetic is applied to all the channels in the keyframe.

```
function tween_keyframe(name, channels, millisecs)
{
    if (millisecs<keys[0].millisecs){
        setDirect(name, 0);
        return;
    }
    if (millisecs>keys[keys.length-1].millisecs){
        setDirect(name, keys.length - 1);
        return;
    }

    //Must be within range
    var index = 0, i;

    for (i=0; i<keys.length; i++)
    if (millisecs>keys[i].millisecs) index = i;

    if (millisecs == keys[index].millisecs){
        setDirect(name, index);
        return;
    }

    //Interpolation required
    var t, tt, ttt, h1, h2, h3, h4, a, b, c, d;
    var secDur, s1, s2, dd0, ds1, result, p0, p1, p2, p3, d10;

    secDur = keys[index+1].millisecs - keys[index].millisecs;
    t = (millisecs - keys[index].millisecs)/secDur;

    //Hermite coefficients
    tt = t*t; ttt = t*tt;
```

```
    h1 = 2 * ttt - 3 * tt + 1;
    h2 = 3 * tt - 2 * ttt;
    h3 = ttt - 2*tt + t;
    h4 = ttt - tt;

    a = (1 - keys[index].tn)     * (1 + keys[index].ct) *
        (1   + keys[index].bs);
    b = (1.0 - keys[index].tn)   * (1.0 - keys[index].ct) *
        (1.0 - keys[index].bs);
    c = (1.0 - keys[index+1].tn) * (1.0 - keys[index+1].ct) *
        (1.0 + keys[index+1].bs);
    d = (1.0 - keys[key+1].tn)   * (1.0 + keys[key+1].ct) *
        (1.0 - keys[key+1].bs);
    if (index!=0)
      s1 = secDur/(keys[index+1].millisecs - keys[index-1].millisecs);
    if (index!=(keys.length - 2))
      s2 = secDur/(keys[index+2].millisecs - keys[index].millisecs);

    //Set the channel values
    for (i=0; i<channels; i++){
        p0 = GetKeyValue(i, index-1);
        p1 = GetKeyValue(i, index);
        p2 = GetKeyValue(i, index+1);
        p3 = GetKeyValue(i, index+2);
        if (!keys[index+1].linear){
            if (index==0){
                t1 = 0.5*(a + b)*(p2 - p1);
            }else{
                t1 = s1*(a*(p1-p0)) + b*(p2 - p1);
            }
            if (index==keys.length-2){
                t2 = 0.5*(c + d)*(p2 - p1);
            }else{
                t2 = s2*(c*(p2 - p1) + d*(p3 - p2));
            }
            result=h1*p1 + h2*p2 + h3*t1 + h4*t2;
        }else{
            result=p1 + t * (p2 - p1);
        }
        SetChannel(name, i, result);
    }
}

function GetKeyValue(channel, index){
    if (index<0 || index>=keys.length) return 0;
```

```
    switch (channel){
       case 0:
       return keys[index].x;
       case 1:
       return keys[index].y;
       case 2:
       return keys[index].rotation;
       case 3:
       return keys[index].scale;
    }

    return 0;
}

function SetChannel(name, channel, value){
    switch(channel){
       case 0:
       eval(name)._x = value;
       break;
       case 1:
       eval(name)._y = value;
       break;
       case 2:
       eval(name)._rotation = value;
       break;
       case 3:
       eval(name)._xscale = value;
       eval(name)._yscale = value;
       break;
    }
}
```

The TCB curves example

Figure B.10 shows 'Examples\AppendixB\tcbcurves.fla' in action. In the example you can move, scale or rotate the key positions using the mouse. For each key position you can set the time, tension, continuity and bias. The crosshairs give an indication of the curve used to move around the key positions, and as you can see there is a smooth motion throughout. The crosshairs bunch up when the section duration is long and appear widely spaced when the section duration is short. The crosshairs are positioned with a call to the function 'updateCrossHairs'. This function is called whenever the user adjusts the curve.

```
function updateCrossHairs(){
    var i, name, interval, time = keys[0].millisecs;
```

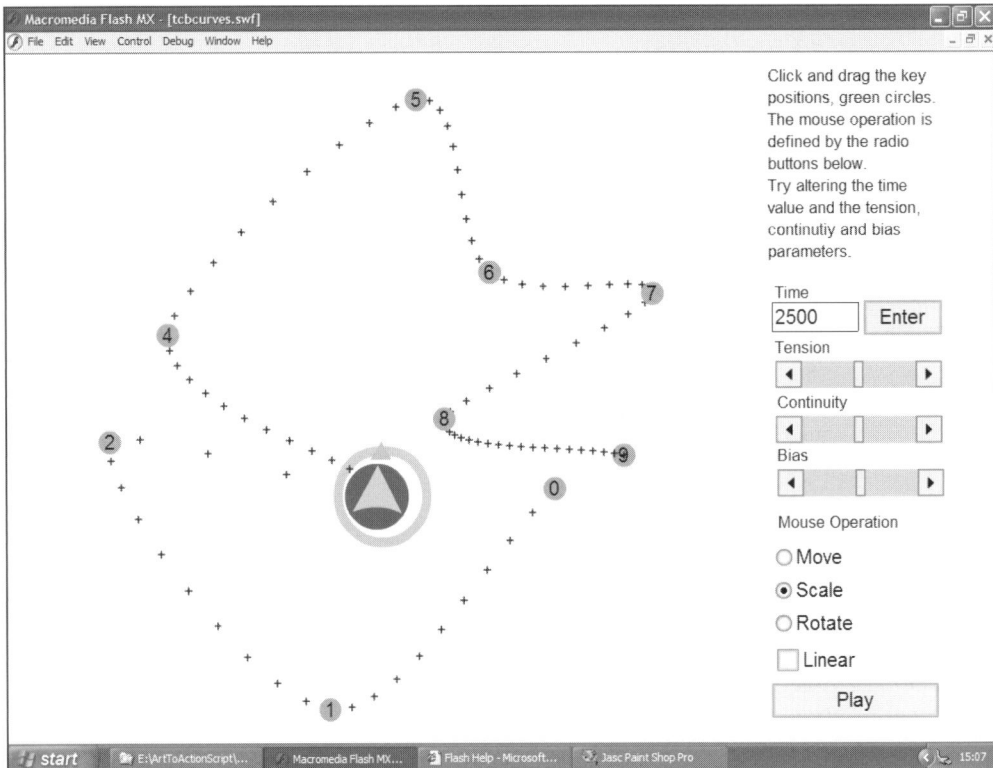

Figure B.10 *Using the TCB curves example*

```
interval = (keys[keys.length-1].millisecs
            - keys[0].millisecs)/100.0;
for (i=0; i<100; i++){
     name = "cross" + i;
     time += interval;
     tween_keyframe(name, 2, time);
}
}
```

Both http://www.robertpenner.com/ and http://www.gizma.com/easing/ provide more information on tweening from ActionScript.

Summary

Using ActionScript to tween your movie clips will give you a smoother movement and gives smaller file sizes. Although the maths can be intimidating at first, it well worth understanding enough to be able to cut and paste the code into your own games.

Bibliography

Art

The Illusion of Life, Frank Thomas and Ollie Johnston, ISBN 0-89659-232-4, Abbeville, 1981. Written by two of the nine old men of Disney, this book contains a wealth of information for anyone interested in animation.

The Animator's Survival Kit, Richard Williams, ISBN 0-57120-228-4, Faber and Faber, 2001. The best practical guide to creating great animation ever written, by one of the best in the business.

Code

Code Complete: A Practical Handbook of Software Construction, Steve C. McConnell, ISBN 1-55615-484-4, Microsoft Press, 1993. A modern-day classic on software engineering, *Code Complete* focuses on specific practices you can use to improve your code and your ability to debug it – and ultimately deliver better, more efficient programs in less time.

ActionScript for Flash MX, Colin Moock, ISBN 0-596-00396-X, O'Reilly, 2003. The definitive ActionScript guide.

Advanced

Programming Windows with MFC2, Jeff Prosise, ISBN 1-57231-685-0, Microsoft Press, 1999. The best MFC book available, if you want to get into writing native Windows code.

Programming Microsoft Visual InterDev 6.0, Evans, Miller and Spencer, ISBN 1-57231-814-7, Microsoft Press, 1999.

Mobile

Flash: the Future, Lentz, Turner and Chia et al., ISBN 1-886411-96-4, No Starch Press, 2002.

Web

www.macromedia.com/software/flash
Home page for Flash at Macromedia.

www.macromedia.com/devnet/devices
Home page for Flash use on mobile devices.

www.niklever.net/flash
Home page for the book; check it out for useful bug fixes and links.

www.catalystpics.co.uk
Home page of the author's company.

mohsye.com
After-hours site created by Catalyst staff, Christian Holland and Paul Barnes.

www.pocketpcdn.com
Great site for those involved in PocketPC development.

smartdevices.microsoftdev.com
The official Microsoft Smart Devices Developer Community.

www.asp.net
ASP.NET Web: the official Microsoft ASP.NET site: Home page.

www.4guysfromrolla.com
When you think ASP, think 4 guys from rolla.

www.actionscript.org
www.actionscript.com
Good resources for ActionScript code.

www.wpdfd.com/pixelfonts.htm
Useful source of Pixel fonts.

Index